COMPACT, CONTRACT, COVENANT:
ABORIGINAL TREATY-MAKING IN CANADA

One of Canada's longest unresolved issues is the historical and present-day failure of the country's governments to recognize treaties made between Aboriginal peoples and the Crown. *Compact, Contract, Covenant* is renowned historian of Native-newcomer relations J.R. Miller's exploration and explanation of more than four centuries of treating-making. The first historical account of treaty-making in Canada, Miller untangles the complicated threads of treaties, pacts, and arrangements with the Hudson's Bay Company and the Crown, as well as modern treaties, to provide a remarkably clear and comprehensive overview of this little-understood and vitally important relationship.

Covering everything from pre-contact Aboriginal treaties to contemporary agreements in Nunavut and recent treaties negotiated under the British Columbia Treaty Process, Miller emphasizes both Native and non-Native motivations in negotiating, the impact of treaties on the peoples involved, and the lessons that are relevant to Native-newcomer relations today. Accessible and informative, *Compact, Contract, Covenant* is a much-needed history of the evolution of treaty-making and will be required reading for decades to come.

J.R. MILLER is a professor and Canada Research Chair in the Department of History at the University of Saskatchewan.

COMPACT, CONTRACT, COVENANT

Aboriginal Treaty-Making in Canada

J.R. MILLER

UNIVERSITY OF TORONTO PRESS
Toronto Buffalo London

© University of Toronto Press Incorporated 2009
Toronto Buffalo London
www.utppublishing.com
Printed in Canada

ISBN 978-08020-9741-5 (cloth)
ISBN 978-08020-9515-2 (paper)

Printed on acid-free paper

Library and Archives Canada Cataloguing in Publication

Miller, J.R. (James Rodger), 1943–
Compact, contract, covenant : Aboriginal treaty-making in Canada /
J.R. Miller.

Includes bibliographical references and index.
ISBN 978-0-8020-9741-5 (bound)   ISBN 978-0-8020-9515-2 (pbk.)

1. Indians of North America – Canada – Treaties – History.
2. Native peoples – Canada – Treaties – History.
3. Indians of North America – Canada – Government relations.
4. Native peoples – Canada – Government relations.   I. Title.

E92.M544 2009   323.1197071'09   C2009-900519-0

University of Toronto Press acknowledges the financial assistance to its
publishing program of the Canada Council for the Arts and the
Ontario Arts Council.

University of Toronto Press acknowledges the financial support for its
publishing activities of the Government of Canada through the Book
Publishing Industry Development Program (BPIDP).

This book has been published with the help of a grant from the Canadian
Federation for the Humanities and Social Sciences, through the Aid to
Scholarly Publications Program, using funds provided by the Social Sciences
and Humanities Research Council of Canada.

To Andrew and Jennifer,
who know that they are treaty people

Contents

10 'We are all treaty people':
Conclusion　283

Maps

Preface and Acknowledgments

This volume is a historical examination of treaty-making by Aboriginal peoples and the Crown throughout post-contact Canadian history. While there are several studies that look at specific treaties, usually from a historical, but occasionally from a legal, perspective, there is none that surveys the entire field. That lack is unfortunate, because one of the important, if ill-understood, aspects of Canadian history is that treaty-making has evolved since the early seventeenth century. Natives and newcomers have moved from making agreements about trade to entering alliances of peace and friendship, and then proceeded to make treaties that focused upon ownership, control, and usage of territory. Finally, since 1973 the country has been engaged in developing new forms – the plural is chosen advisedly – for concluding agreements between indigenous and immigrant Canadians. The evolution of treaty-making – from commercial pacts to modern agreements – reflects the underlying Native-newcomer relationship. When that association was mutually beneficial, as it was especially in early commercial partnerships, the treaties were respectful of both parties and benefited all participants. When the relationship deteriorated, as it did when newcomers focused on settlement rather than trade, the treaties that resulted were much less advantageous to Aboriginal peoples. In short, treaty-making is an artifact and indicator of Native-newcomer relations in Canada.

Compact, Contract, Covenant is designed to be a historical survey that explores the motivations of the parties to treaty-making and the impact of treaties upon them. Except where necessary to explain later developments, it does not dwell on treaty implementation. Nor is it a legal history of Aboriginal treaties. If it is unavoidably an overview rather than an in-depth or exhaustive treatment, the justification must be that it is necessary and advisable to sketch the broad outlines of the narrative before more microscopic treatments are produced. Fortunately, there are a number of individual case studies available, and where that is so I have not attempted to redo that work. In selecting examples of individual treaties to illustrate my general argument about the evolution of treaty-making and in emphasizing one genre of treaty rather than another, I have used criteria that are in part Whiggish, to use a label from historiography. I have chosen to concentrate on those treaties that established a pattern, such as commercial compacts and the early Upper Canadian treaties, and those that have had a lingering effect down to the twenty-first century, such as the numbered treaties. As a result, this volume does not give equal weight to all types of treaty or even all regions where treaty-making occurred. The justification for such an approach must be that any other approach would have resulted in a project that I certainly could not have completed.

Relying on sound existing scholarship about treaties where it exists is merely one of the many ways in which I am indebted to other researchers and institutions. It is a pleasure to acknowledge the vast amount of help I have enjoyed from supportive institutions and generous colleagues. The Social Sciences and Humanities Research Council of Canada provided financial support for the research, as did my own institution. The University of Saskatchewan furnished facilities, a grant to make maps, and a valued atmosphere of collegiality from which I benefited. It was work with the Treaty Commissioner for Saskatchewan, the Hon. David R. Arnot, research I was invited to participate in by my good friends and colleagues Arthur J. Ray and Frank Tough, that first turned my attention to the study of treaty-making. The encouragement and example of both Dave Arnot and those colleagues have been enormously influential. I have also been the beneficiary of the Canada Research Chairs Program since 2001.

The cooperation and assistance that I have enjoyed from many archives and research libraries across the country, where highly skilled and dedicated professional staff have always been wonderfully helpful, was invaluable. Library and Archives Canada, Queen's University Archives, University of Western Ontario Regional Archives, the Archives of Ontario, the Toronto Reference Library, Provincial Archives of Manitoba, the Saskatchewan Archives Board, the Glenbow Museum and Archives, the University of Saskatchewan Special Collections, and the Public Record Office (Kew) all have staff who have greatly assisted my work on this project over the last five years.

Individual scholars, too, have lightened my research load. Fellow faculty, graduate students, and post-doctoral fellows have all responded generously and efficiently when I have asked them for help. I would like to thank Camie Augustus, Alain Beaulieu, Rebecca Brain, Alan Cairns, Christine Charmbury, Janet Chute, Paget Code, Luca Codignola, Peter Cook, Barry Cottam, Pat Deiter, Peter Dodson, Thomas Flanagan, Rob Flannigan, Hamar Foster, Sally Gibson, Maxime Gohier, Simonne Horwitz, Bonny Ibhawoh, Brendan Kelly, Whitney Lackenbauer, John Leslie, John S. Long, Jim Morrison, Kathryn Muller, Dianne Newell, Nicole O'Byrne, Stephen Patterson, Roberto Perin, Evelyn J. Peters, Myra Rutherdale, Brian Slattery, Christine Smillie, David Smith, Donald B. Smith, Lissa Wadewitz, Marley Waiser, Mark Walter, Angela Wanhalla, Richard White, and Ken Whiteway. Rebecca, Christine, and Paget were wonderful research assistants, demonstrating both imagination and endurance in responding to my many requests.

Several scholarly colleagues have been especially important in helping me bring this project to a conclusion. Arthur J. Ray, formerly of the University of British Columbia, has long been an inspiration for his seminal work on fur-trade relations. He has been a valuable collaborator since we worked together for the Office of the Treaty Commissioner. Recently I had the pleasure of working with John Borrows, an eminent scholar at the University of Victoria, as co-curator of an exhibit on the history of treaty-making for Library and Archives Canada. Saskatchewan colleagues, too, have been invaluable. Keith Carlson provided many suggestions, and saved me from several errors, especially in relation to Native-newcomer interactions in British Columbia. And Bill Waiser provided advice and read most of the work in draft form, taking time out from his busy schedule to help.

Brian and Mike of Articulate Eye Design in Saskatoon were both patient and creative in translating my thoughts – and sometimes my second thoughts – into the maps in the book.

I am appreciative of the many useful suggestions that three anonymous readers for University of Toronto Press and the Aid to Scholarly Publications Program provided. I am also grateful to my editors, Jill McConkey, with whom I started the project, and Len Husband, who ably took over when Jill left. I would also like to thank copy editor Ken Lewis for his careful attention to the manuscript.

Finally, during the early stages of my research, I benefited from the encouragement, advice, criticism, and suggestions of my late wife, Mary. For this project she was a source of ideas, an editor, and a critic – as she was for all my earlier work – until her untimely death. To our first-born son, Andrew, and his wife, Jennifer, this volume is dedicated. It is, I think, because we live in Saskatchewan that Mary, Andrew, Jen, and I are aware that 'we are all treaty people.'

While I have enjoyed the generosity of many family, friends, and colleagues in preparing this work, the errors that remain are exclusively my responsibility.

COMPACT, CONTRACT, COVENANT:
ABORIGINAL TREATY-MAKING IN CANADA

1

'There is no end to relationship among the indians':[1] Early Commercial Compacts

Treaties between the Crown and Aboriginal peoples are one of the paradoxes of Canadian history. Although they have been an important feature of the country since the earliest days of contact between Natives and newcomers, relatively few Canadians understand what they are or the role they have played in the country's past. Unfortunately, even fewer non-Native Canadians appreciate that treaties are a valuable part of the foundation of the Canadian state. Whereas treaties were once central issues in Canadian life and resonated with most Canadians for centuries, they have declined in visibility and shrunk in perceived importance. This development is all the stranger, given the lengthy history of Canadian treaty-making and the rich diversity in the types of treaties that Aboriginal peoples and Crown representatives have fashioned.

What is a treaty? A common dictionary explanation holds that a treaty is a 'formally concluded and ratified agreement between states,' 'the document embodying such an agreement,' 'an agreement between individuals or parties, esp. for the purchase of property.'[2] In other words, treaties are formalized records of negotiated agreements between parties, usually states, but sometimes people. As with most human creations that endure, their form also evolves over time. To understand the history of treaty-making by First Nations and the Crown in Canada, it is necessary to define 'nations' or governments broadly. On both the indigenous and the European sides of the encounter, the parties, espe-

cially in the earliest stages of relations, were not governments as
conventionally understood. In the case of First Nations, of course,
non-Native scholars generally classify them as non-state societies,
and consequently miss or misunderstand the way in which 'government' manifested itself in their communities.

Among the Europeans, too, the agencies that represented the
overseas state were sometimes non-governmental. From the seventeenth to the nineteenth century, a commercial monopolist
had usually been granted an exclusive licence to trade by its
monarch. That was the case with Canada. Early French initiatives
on the St Lawrence and in the Maritimes, and Britain's presence
in mainland North America, took the form of companies granted
a trade monopoly by their country's monarch. 'The Company of
Adventurers of England tradeing into Hudsons Bay,' more commonly known as the Hudson's Bay Company, represented
England in the North, while several companies, of which the
Company of One Hundred Associates was the most enduring,
flew the French flag on the St Lawrence. Both French monopo-
lists on the St Lawrence and Hudson's Bay men in the North
carried powers from their sponsoring sovereigns that went far
beyond simple commercial rights. Royal authority made them
quasi-governmental entities. For that reason the agreements they
forged with First Nations should be understood as treaties.

Commercial compacts created from the seventeenth century
onwards are only one example of the treaty-making tradition in
Canadian history. Alongside these ententes between European
fur traders and First Nations, systems of alliance developed in the
latter part of the seventeenth century and flourished in the eighteenth. The treaties of peace, friendship, and alliance within
these rival networks that were so prominent in Canadian history
from the late seventeenth century onward developed directly out
of the commercial relations between Native peoples and newcomers, and, like the earlier commercial compacts, manifested
many of the same characteristics.

Similarly, the third type of treaty between First Nations and
Euro-Canadians emerged directly, almost inevitably, from the
vicissitudes and pressures of Britain's alliance system in the latter

half of the eighteenth century. Territorial treaties were agreements governing non-Natives' access to and use of First Nations'
lands. They emerged in the 1760s and dominated relations
between indigenous and immigrant peoples in Canada until the
early 1920s. For half a century after 1923, the Canadian Crown
suspended making treaties about territory with First Nations for
a variety of reasons. When the practice resumed in the 1970s, it
took forms that differed somewhat from the earlier territorial
treaties. Canadians in the early twenty-first century are still
attempting to work out and achieve consensus on this latest way
of making formal agreements about territory between First
Nations, and now also Inuit, and the federal government.

To explore the long, complex, and fascinating story of the evolution of treaty-making in Canada from commercial compacts
through treaties of alliance to territorial treaties is the objective
of this work.

The commercial agreements that emerged in early New France
and then in the Hudson's Bay Company lands after 1670 were
built on a foundation of indigenous treaty-making. European
traders who came to the northern part of North America found
both pre-existing trade networks into which they had to fit themselves, and pre-contact treaty-making practices that they had to
learn and adopt. Although the many First Nations who occupied
the northeast woodlands and subarctic region north of it were
divided into hunting-gathering Algonkians and horticultural Iroquoians, all the indigenous societies of northeastern North
America were engaged in trade of one kind or another. And that
trade required them to establish amicable relations with Native
trade partners through formalized agreements. (See map 1.)

The reason for inter-tribal trade was simple: variations in
regional ecology meant that First Nations in one part of the
country could produce some commodities but not others. Crop-
growing Huron (Wendat) in what is now southwestern Ontario
might produce a surplus of corn and the Petun, the Huron's
neighbours, tobacco, but they had to trade with more northerly
groups for many products of the hunt. Algonkians on the north

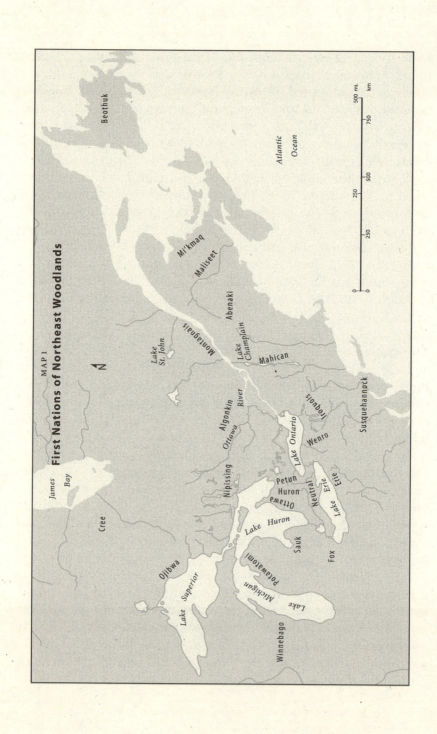

MAP 1

First Nations of Northeast Woodlands

shore of Lake Superior had access to copper, the only metal available to First Nations before the Europeans introduced iron, and that situational good fortune made them logical trade partners of less geographically favoured First Nations. Similarly, Atlantic peoples such as the Mi'kmaq had privileged access to maritime resources that provided them with parallel commercial advantages.[3] Regional ecological variation led to regional specialization of production by First Nations, and, inevitably, those conditions produced inter-tribal trade. Corn went north, tobacco went in all directions to fill the ceremonial pipes of First Nations in general, and copper transformed in a variety of ways was found far from the shores of Lake Superior. Trade among First Nations was an extensive, critically important reality long before Europeans turned up on the Atlantic shore.

For two First Nations to trade with each other, peaceful relations were required between them. Anyone from another group in Indian Country who was not recognized in some fashion as a friend had to be treated for reasons of safety as an enemy, actual or potential. To do otherwise was simply too risky in Aboriginal North America. Friendly relations were a prerequisite for trading safely. But how were such associations with strangers created?

The key to establishing and maintaining links was kinship. As tribal societies, pre-contact First Nations in northeastern North America organized themselves according to kin ties. Indeed, the concept of kinship was all-embracing and sometimes all-consuming among First Nations. As George Nelson, an exasperated non-Native fur trader, was later to put it, '... there is no end to relationship among the indians.' Kinship and sometimes also clan affiliations identified who a person was, who constituted his or her family, and, more important, who was obligated to show him or her friendship, hospitality, and support. If one did not know how another person was related in kinship terms, then it was impossible to know if that person was connected – a friendly person – or a potentially dangerous stranger. The notion of attempting to deal impersonally with unrelated people, whether in commerce or for any other purpose, was both alien and anathema to First Nations societies. One simply could not safely undertake commercial transactions impersonally with strangers. First Nations society was in a sense a gigantic extended family of kin-related people for the good and sufficient reason that it had to be in order to function effectively.

First Nations had a variety of mechanisms to establish kinship. Most obvious was the kinship that derived from one's birth family. In a matrilineal society such as was found among woodlands Iroquoians, for example, the kin links might run through the mother's lineage to her family, rather than through the father, or perhaps through both. Second was the kinship that came from marriage. Indeed, one of the primary purposes of the institution of marriage was to establish linkages between different kin networks with complementary interests and ambitions. This behaviour was not much different from past Europeans' practice of using marriages to develop or cement political, economic, or strategic linkages that would benefit them individually, as a family, or, indeed, as a monarchical dynasty. Finally, First Nations in North America often simply ascribed kinship – what anthropologists label 'fictive kinship' – to bring into the orbit of kin relationship strangers with whom association was considered desirable, but who were ineligible for the establishment of kin links through marriage or birth. The upshot of these strategies of kin creation was that First Nations societies were vast networks of linked people that functioned more harmoniously, effectively, and with greater comfort and security than would have been possible without the institution of kinship.

Indigenous societies made kin of strangers, and then maintained those links, through ceremonies. One of the clearest examples of making kin emerged from First Nations' rituals associated with incorporating prisoners of war into the victorious community. This practice was necessary because community losses of population in warfare could dangerously weaken the group. Accordingly, it was common in North America for victorious First Nations to 'adopt' captives rather than execute them. If an individual was to be incorporated into a different society, he or she would be formally welcomed, cleaned and groomed, given fresh clothing, and feasted by the captive's new 'family.' In the case of people from another First Nation, such as new trading partners, the community leadership would welcome the newcomers, smoke the ceremonial pipe with them, and provide a meal. In these instances, when the two parties got together again in future seasons, most likely to trade, the pattern of welcome, pipe, and feast would be repeated. The repetition of such protocol was effectively the renewal of the relationship that had been established earlier. Repetition of ceremony provided reassurance to both parties that amicable, peaceful relations still existed. In a world in which peace and trade were inseparable, such confirmations of continuing 'kinship' were essential for secure and productive relationships.

Examples of First Nations' practices in creating kinship among themselves were recorded in the early eighteenth century at Kahnawake, the Mohawk community on the south shore of the St Lawrence opposite Montreal. Kahnawake served as a home to Iroquois, most of them converts to Roman Catholicism, and as a base from which they often raided into the northerly Thirteen Colonies. Despite the fearsome reputation that Iroquois warriors have acquired in popular Canadian history, how the Mohawk of Kahnawake treated some of their captives when they got them back to the St Lawrence reveals a great deal about First Nations' practices in creating kin links. For example, a male prisoner might be adopted after a successful raid, even though some of his fellow warriors might have been tortured or killed on the trail back to Kahnawake or once the victors reached the settlement:

The moment that he enters the lodge to which he is given and where he is to be kept, his bonds are untied. The gloomy attire which makes him appear a victim destined for sacrifice is removed. He is washed with warm water to efface the colours with which his face was painted and he is dressed properly. Then he receives visits of relatives and friends of the family into which he is entering. A short time afterwards a feast is made for all the village to give him the name of the person whom he is resurrecting. The friends and allies of the dead man also give a feast to do him honour: and, from that moment, he enters upon all his rights.[4]

On another occasion a non-Native New Englander, taken in a raid, was adopted into a family at Kahnawake. According to James Smith's recollection of his treatment on returning to the Mohawk village, he was welcomed effusively by an interpreter:

> My son, you are now flesh of our flesh and bone of our bone. By the ceremony that was performed this day, every drop of white blood was washed out of your veins. You are taken into the Caughnawage [Kahnawake] nation and initiated into a war-like tribe. You are adopted into a great family and now received with great seriousness and solemnity in the room and place of a great man. After what has passed this day you are now one of us by an old strong law and custom. My son, you have now nothing to fear. We are now under the same obligations to love, support and defend you that we are to love and to defend one another. Therefore you are to consider yourself as one of our people.[5]

James Smith verified the accuracy of the interpreter's statement. He commented, '... from that day I never knew them to make any distinction between me and themselves in any respect whatsoever until I left them ... we all shared the same fate.'

Kinship, whether innate or created through marriage or adoption, was a vital social glue for First Nations in North America. In some northerly hunting-gathering societies, kin ties among a group of male hunters were the criterion by which the individual band was established. More widely, some sort of kin tie was essential to overcome fear of any stranger as a potential enemy, and to ensure peaceful dealings with the outsider. Within First Nations in northeastern North America, kinship, often bolstered by clan associations, facilitated the formation and peaceful maintenance of relatively large settled populations of horticulturalists such as the Five Nations Iroquois or the Huron. Manufactured kinship also made dealings with strangers from other communities possible. In other words, kinship of various types was vital to the successful functioning of First Nations in northeastern North America, where contact between European and indigenous societies first occurred.

Given the motives that drove the early interactions of Native and newcomer in the future Canada, it was hardly surprising that European visitors quickly had to learn to navigate the protocols, including those for making kin, of First Nations. The English, Basque, and French who came to the North Atlantic shores, and later penetrated major waterways such as the St Lawrence and the Hudson, were lured across the ocean for one or more of four goals: fish, fur, evangelization, and exploration. To pursue any one of these objectives, the Europeans were dependent on First Nations. Even fishing would have been extremely dangerous in the face of First Nations opposition, and certainly the other three activities required Native cooperation.

The fur trade, which emerged by the early seventeenth century as the main focus of Native-newcomer relations in the Maritimes, Labrador, and Quebec, was especially dependent on First Nations. In 1534 in the Bay of Chaleur, French navigator Jacques Cartier's ship encountered some First Nations who 'set up a great clamour and made frequent signs to us to come on shore, holding up to us some furs on sticks.' After some exchange, the Indians 'showed a marvelously great pleasure in possessing and obtaining these iron wares and other commodities, dancing and going through many ceremonies and throwing salt water over their heads with their hands.'[6] It quickly became apparent that First Nations were essential to the trade, especially if the European companies wanted to limit their expenses in North America. Not only did indigenous people have valuable knowledge about the animals to be hunted and how to survive in the forests of the Northeast, but they also 'processed' some of the furs, brought the pelts to trading locations, and in many instances provided sustenance to European traders during at least parts of the year. In the case of the Hudson's Bay Company, dependence on indigenous skills and labour was especially great. Both French and British traders looked to the Natives to procure the furs to trade. In addition, however, the HBC, particularly during the first century of its operations, confined its personnel to posts on the shore of Hudson Bay. Accordingly, the British relied on First Nations to bring furs to them at their posts. In

As wee have above directed you to endeavour to make such Contracts wth. the Indians in all places where you settle as may in
future times ascertain to us all liberty of trade & commerce and a
league of friendship & peaceable cohabitation, So wee have caused
Iron marks to be made of the figure of the Union Flagg, wth. wch.
Wee would have you to burn Tallys of wood wth. such ceremony as
they shall understand to be obligatory & sacred, The manner
whereof wee must leave to your prudence as you shall find the
modes & humours of the people you deal with, But when the
Impression is made, you are to write upon the Tally the name of
the Nation or person wth. whom the Contract is made and the date
thereof, and then deliver one part of the Stick to them, and reserve
the other.

'This,' the directors supposed, 'may be sutable to the capacities
of those barbarous people, and may much conduce to our quiet
& commerce, and secure us from forreign or domestick pre-
tenders.'[8]

The Company's policy-makers saw fit to repeat these instructions to the men in charge of other posts, such as John Bridgar,
two years later: 'There is another thing which we thinke of greate
Moment and therefore recommend to your particular care and
that is that you Endeavor to make such Contracts with the Natives
for the River in & above Port Nelson as may in future times ascertain to us a right & property therein and the Sole Liberty of trade
& Comerce there, and to make Leagues of friendship & peaceable Cohabitation with such Ceremonies as you shall finde tobee
most Sacred and Obligatory amongst them.'[9] The Company
repeated the same directions to Governor John Nixon: 'Wee have
formerly Given our Instructions, and Wee now earnestly press it
that you Endeavour to make such Contracts wth. the Natives for
there Rivers and land as may in future times ascertaine to us a
right and property therein, and the Sole liberty of Trade and
Comerce and to make as Leagues of Friendship and peaceable
Cohabitation with them, by such Seremonies as you shall finde to
bee most Sacred and obligatory to them.'[10]

Placing these instructions to establish 'a league of friendship &

peaceable cohabitation' alongside the Charter that purported to give the Hudson's Bay Company powers in Rupert's Land reveals a significant contrast. By the Charter the king claimed that he 'Doe give grant and confirm unto the said Governor and Company and theire successors the sole Trade and Commerce of all those Seas Streightes Bayes Lakes Rivers Creekes and Soundes in whatsoever Latitude they shall bee that lie within the entrance of the Streightes commonly called Hudsons Streightes together with all the Landes and Territoryes upon the Countryes coasts and confynes of the Seas Bayes Lakes Rivers Creeks and Soundes ...' The Company nonetheless directed its men in North America 'to endeavour to make such Contracts wth the Indians in all places where you settle as may in future times ascertain to us all liberty of trade & commerce and a league of friendship & peaceable cohabitation.' The Charter also declared the Company 'the true and absolute Lordes and Proprietors of the same territory lymittes and places aforesaid,' but the instructions from London to Hudson Bay repeatedly emphasized the necessity to secure agreement from the local First Nations before proceeding.[11]

The contrast between the rhetoric of the Charter and the language of instructions to Company servants signified the reality that, whatever King Charles II might say, the true proprietors of what he styled Rupert's Land were the First Nations who occupied the territory. On the ground, and in practical terms, all the grandiose Charter of 1670 conveyed to the gentlemen adventurers was an exclusive right to negotiate. In other words, the Company's charter rights amounted to the right to negotiate with the indigenous peoples for access in order to trade. Moreover, by acting on the gap between royal rhetoric and North American reality in the way they did, the directors of the Hudson's Bay Company effectively entered into binding commercial compacts – 'contracts' in the language of the Charter – with the leaders of local First Nations groups. In other words, the Company engaged in commercial treaty-making.

The practices that the Hudson's Bay Company developed to establish profitable trading relations with First Nations contained further revelations. It was not just that the directors in London instructed representatives such as Nixon and Bridgar to make commercial agreements but to do so by actions that 'By the Religion or Custome of their Country should be thought most sacred & obliging to them for the confirmation of such Agreements.' The men acting on behalf of the HBC on Hudson Bay were also to create physical confirmations of their pacts in a way that would be meaningful to the local First Nations, who were not, of course, literate in European languages. Instead of signed agreements, Bay men were to burn an insignia – 'the Union Flagg' – on two pieces of wood with 'such ceremony as they shall understand to be obligatory & sacred,' to give one of the inscribed tallies to the First Nation, and to 'reserve the other' for the Company. These measures were evidence that the Hudson's Bay Company was accommodating itself to indigenous protocols for making and commemorating agreements, as well as implicitly recognizing that First Nations controlled the territory in which the Europeans wished to operate.

Over time an elaborate trade ceremonial developed in Rupert's Land that embodied key elements of Aboriginal practice for maintaining fictive kinship relationships in trade. Most striking about the commercial etiquette that the Europeans learned to master was its formality. Trade, even within a commercial compact, was not a casual, purely businesslike transaction. Rather, trade was something that people in a close relationship engaged in only after important social observances occurred in a formal and ritualistic manner. As a First Nations party of traders got near a Hudson's Bay Company post in Rupert's Land, they made sure to stop short, and out of distance of the fort. One such stopping place near the mouth of the Rupert River on the east side of James Bay was called 'Dress-Up Creek.'[12] At such locations near the trading post, 'the women [would] go into the woods to get pine-brush for the bottom of the tents, while the Leaders smoke together and regulate the procession.' Leaders would collect an offering of one or two skins from each of the party, and they would prepare themselves to encounter the Europeans. If they were a large group, they would approach the post with their

1.1 The welcome at a trading post incorporated Aboriginal protocol.

canoes 'to the number of between ten and twenty in a line abreast of each other,' with 'a small St. George or Union Jack, hoisted on a stick placed in the stern of the vessel' containing the man designated as their leader, or trading captain. As they drew nearer, they would fire several muskets 'from the canoes to salute the Fort, and the compliment is returned by a round of twelve pounders.'[13]

The rituals became even more elaborate after the visiting trading party landed. While the 'women set about pitching the tents' and making camp, the leaders proceeded into the post to greet the Hudson's Bay Company officers:

The Governor being informed what Leaders are arrived, sends the Trader to introduce them singly, or by two or three together with their lieutenants, which are usually eldest sons or nighest relations. Chairs are placed in the room, and pipes with smoking materials produced on the table. The captains place themselves on each side of the Governor, but not a word proceeds from either party, until everyone has recruited his spirits with a full pipe. The silence is then broken by degrees by the most venerable Indian, his head bowed down and eyes immovably fixed on the floor or other object. He tells how many canoes he has brought, what kind of winter they have had, what natives he has seen, are coming, or stay behind, asks how the Englishmen do, and says he is glad to see them. After which the Governor bids him welcome, tells him he has good goods and plenty; and that he loves the Indians and will be kind to them. The pipe is by this time is [sic] renewed and the conversation becomes free, easy and general.[14]

When the preliminary conversation concluded, the first gift-giving took place as the post commander gave the trading captain and his principal men suits of clothing:

A coarse cloth coat, either red or blue, lined with baize with regimental cuffs and collar. The waistcoat and breeches are of baize; the suit ornamented with broad and narrow orris lace of different colours; a white or checked shirt; a pair of yarn stockings tied below the knee with worsted garters; a pair of English shoes. The hat is laced and ornamented with feathers of different colours. A worsted sash tied round the crown an end hanging out on each side down to the shoulders. A silk handkerchief is tucked by a corner into the loops behind; with these decorations it is put on the captain's head and completes his dress. The lieutenant is also presented with an inferior suit.[15]

The suits were the Hudson's Bay Company's way of recognizing the special roles of the men they termed trading captains. They were also intended as a means of ingratiating the Company with the Native leaders.

The stage was now set for another critical element in trade ceremonial: the giving of gifts to the whole party. In this particular instance, by the post commander's orders 'a basket of bread and prunes is brought and set before the captain, who takes care to fill his pockets with them before it goes out to be shared amongst his followers.' Two gallons of brandy, some tobacco, and pipes were supplied as well. The leaders who had been re-establishing the relationship ceremonially within the post now proceeded outside to the encampment that the Native visitors had set up:

> Everything being prepared he [the trading captain] is conducted to his tent with a procession. In the front are the spontoons [halberds] and ensigns, next the drummer beating a march, then several of the Factory servants bearing the bread, prunes, etc. Then comes the captain, walking quite erect and stately, smoking his pipe and conversing with the Governor and his officers; then follow the Second, and perhaps a friend or two who was permitted to come in with the Chief. The tent is all ready for their reception, and clean birch-rind or beaver coats are spread on the ground for the chief to sit on; and before him are deposited the prunes etc. The Chief then makes a speech to his followers, and then orders his lieutenant, or some respectable person, to distribute the presents, never performing this himself. I must take notice that the women and children are last served; the slaves get a little also.[16]

The visitors then spent some time enjoying the presents that the Hudson's Bay Company had provided.

Trade would commence on a subsequent day, and only after still more ceremony. The most important observance was the renewal of their association by smoking the calumet, or pipe, together:

> As the ceremony of smoking the calumet is necessary to establish a confidence, it is conducted with the greatest solemnity, and every person belonging to that gang is admitted on the occasion. The captain walks in with his calumet in his hand covered with a case, then comes the lieutenant and the wives of the captains with the present [of furs collected prior to the initial landing at the post], and afterwards all the other men with the women and their little ones. The Governor is genteely dressed after the English

1.2 Smoking the pipe was an important element of kin-making ritual.

fashion, and receives them with cordiality and good humour. The
captain covers the table with a new beaver coat, and on it lays the
calumet or pipe; he will also sometimes present the Governor with
a clear beaver toggy or banian to keep him warm in the winter.
The *Puc'ca'tin'ash'a'win* [gift of furs] is also presented. Then the
Governor sits down in an arm-chair, the captain and chief men on
either hand on chairs; the others sit round on the floor; the
women and children are placed behind; and a profound silence
ensues.

Then traders and visitors engaged in the all-important ritual.
'The calumet being lighted by the Governor, a servant holding
the bowl and applying the fire, it is pointed towards the east,

south, west, and north parts of the hemisphere, also to the zenith, and nadir. Every man takes a certain number of whiffs as fixed by the owner of the pipe, and thus it passes round the circle. When out, it is delivered again to the Governor who repeats the manoeuvres as when he lighted it; at which all the men pronounce the monosyllable Ho! which is expressive of thanks.'[17]

The pipe ceremony was profoundly important in First Nations society. 'In North America, the primary purpose of the tobacco smoke is as an offering to the spirits.' By smoking together, pointing the pipe to the four directions, and above and below, the participants in the ceremony were invoking the Great Spirit, communicating with 'all my relations,' human and non-human, or their kin, and renewing their own relationship. This use of tobacco 'allows for communication with the spirits.'[18] Among the Iroquois, tobacco 'induced a state of mind that opened one to supernatural ceremonial contexts, a religious act.' Tobacco smoke 'was a gift that pleased spirit beings as reciprocation for their blessings.'[19] Récollet missionary Father Christian Le Clerq observed, '... the Indians hold no assembly without the calumet in their mouth; and as fire is necessary to take tobacco, they almost always light one in every council, so that it is all the same with them "to light a council-fire," and "have a place to visit each other, and assemble as relatives and friends who wish to speak and decide on their affairs."'[20] Lest there be any doubt about the symbolic importance of the pipe in the fur trade, a Hudson's Bay Company observer noted, 'Each leader leaves his grand calumet at the fort he trades at unless he is affronted, and not designed to return next summer, which is sometimes the case ...'[21] If the First Nation trading captain left his pipe at the post when departing, he was signalling that the relationship would endure, and that he and his companions would return next trading season.

During the pre-trade ceremonies, the Europeans engaged in other practices learned from Aboriginal people. As a sign of respect for the visitors, the Company would share its medicines with those of the trading party who were 'doctors,' or medicine men and women. And after the trading of furs was almost completed, the post commander gave the trading captain another gift whose size was calculated according to the volume of business the captain had brought to the post:

> The traders have bargow [oatmeal porridge] made for them, and prunes are given them every day, and the leader gets a small bag of oatmeal and prunes at his going away, and if the person is a leader of fifteen or twenty canoes he dines every day with the Chief [principal trader] and officers, and receives the above present in full. But if otherwise several articles and indulgences are curtailed, and if he brings less than ten canoes, or any misfortune has befallen him, he is still looked on by the Chief in the former light as when he brought his former complement of canoes, which conduct in the Chief is a sure means of keeping up the Company's trade, and ingratiating himself into the natives' favour, who are a good natured people and very susceptible of wrongs done them.[22]

The trade ceremonies in which Hudson's Bay Company representatives engaged with First Nations were remarkable both for their extent and their alignment with First Nations' beliefs and practices. The whole string of events and practices – the fur-trade protocol – constituted the commercial compact. In other words, the relationship established in this way was the treaty.

Fur-trade kinship practices continued for some time in the western fur trade, whether the Europeans involved were Hudson's Bay Company men or not.[23] As a historian of the Hudson's Bay Company wrote in 1708, 'The Company, by their Governours and Agents, made such Compacts with the Captains or Kings of the Rivers and Territories where they had Settlements, for the Freedom of Trade there, exclusive of all others, that the *Indians* could not pretend they had encroach'd upon them. These Compacts were render'd as firm as the *Indians* could make them, by such Ceremonies as were most sacred and obligatory among them.'[24] Sixteen-year-old George Nelson, the fur trader from Lower Canada who complained that there was 'no end to relationship' among the Indians, found out first-hand on his initial journey west after being apprenticed to the XY or New

North West Company in 1802 that there was no end of customary practices, too. At the Grand Portage at the west end of Lake Superior, where fur brigades from the northwest rendezvoused with canoes from Montreal laden with trade goods for distant posts, he experienced another fur-trade custom, the *régale*. As Nelson put it, his companions 'feasted & got drunk upon the "régale" that was always given them when they arrived from, or departed for, their winter quarters.'[25]

More was in store for Nelson farther west. In the fall, 'the Indians took great pity upon me. One of them adopted me as his son, & told his own son, a lad of about my age, to consider me as his brother & to treat me so, and he did indeed the very few times we happened to meet after this.'[26] The next summer, another Indian named Le Commis decided it was time to make closer kin of Nelson. Through a companion-interpreter, Chaurette, Nelson tried to put Le Commis off. 'Chaurette told me that the old *fellow* wanted to give me his daughter ... I told Chaurette that it was impossible; that if my father was to know it he would be in the greatest rage with me; that beside I was yet only a boy'; and senior personnel in the fur trade company would take a dim view of such a step. Nelson held out initially, but with 'the men & every one else after me I at last was prevailed upon to take *her*. I did not much relish the thought.'[27] The *régale*, the adoption, and the country marriage to Le Commis's daughter that George Nelson experienced were all elements of Aboriginal kinship practices.

In addition to kinship links and securing permission from First Nations, fur-trade practices bequeathed another important institution to the general history of treaty-making in Canada: presents. Gift-giving was an important, expected part of fur-trade practice, whether it was a trading captain offering the furs of his followers to the post commander, or the Hudson's Bay Company post commander giving food, medicines, and liquor in return. Gifts were a symbol of goodwill towards another in Indian Country, and for that reason a powerful inducement to enter into a friendly relationship. According to Lumbee legal scholar Robert A. Williams, 'In Encounter era Woodlands Indian diplomacy, ritualized gift exchanges thus became peace treaties or at

least a part of the language used to communicate the message
that a relationship of law and peace was desired with a potential
treaty party.'[28] In some First Nation societies there was even a link
between gifts and kinship. 'In Ojibwa idiom, to "pity" another is
to adopt him and care for him as a parent or grandparent cares
for a child. To give someone a gift with no thought of an immediate return was to "pity" him and thus in a sense to adopt him.'[29]
'When groups of Ojibway hunters traveled into territory occupied by the Dakota, they might turn potential enemies into
friends by an exchange of goods as well as by a mutual smoking
of tobacco in a calumet.'[30] After Okeemakeequid, an Ojibwa
leader, exchanged clothing with a Dakota, the Dakota man called
the Ojibwa 'Brother.'[31]

The gifts that Europeans gave First Nations were important
both economically and symbolically. As an Onondaga warrior
told an English official early in the eighteenth century, trade was
what attracted some First Nations to visitors: '... antiently they
made use of [Stone Pots] Earthen Pots, Stone Knives & Hatchets
& Bows and Arrows, that after they had purchased from the
Christ[ns] Good Arms they conquered their enemies & rooted
them out so that where they then inhabited is now become a
Wilderness. Thus (they say) our first entering into a conven[t] with
you was Chiefly grounded upon Trade.'[32] Trade gave First
Nations in the northeastern woodlands access to iron and iron
products such as firearms, whose inaccuracy in the earliest years
of contact made them more useful for their psychological than
their ballistic effect. Sharp metal edges replaced the 'Stone
Knives' to which the Onondaga had referred. Metal axes were
much more efficient, both in war and the domestic sphere, than
stone hatchets. Metal arrow heads easily pierced wooden armour
that was impervious to most flint projectiles. Large metal pots,
meanwhile, could be suspended directly over a fire and replaced
smaller pottery vessels that did not travel well and required that
their liquids be warmed by immersing a succession of heated
stones in them. The introduction of hard metals in eastern
North America revolutionized domestic life, hunting, and military practices.

However important the gifts obtained in trade were in a practical sense, they were at least as significant symbolically. As the Hudson's Bay Company had quickly learned, regular meetings, rituals, and gift exchanges were essential to reassure the parties of the other group's continuing goodwill and interest. Unless elaborate protocol that included gifts were followed, how could First Nations be certain that the other group had not swerved from friendliness to enmity in the period between meetings? First Nations had a rich vocabulary to express the many positive things that gifts did to facilitate a relationship. Presents removed emotional obstacles to trade – whether losses the party had experienced by death or past conflict – and enabled the participants to see clearly. Gifts 'wiped away the tears.' They also 'unstopped the ears' so that the party that received them could hear what was said to them clearly and accurately. And presents could also 'clear the throat' so that the parties could communicate honestly and fully. As Father Le Clerq remarked, based on his experience of Montagnais who brought a suspect into Quebec to surrender him to authorities, 'In fact, by presents they wipe away tears, appease anger, arouse nations to war, conclude treaties of peace, deliver prisoners, raise the dead – in fact, nothing is said or answered but by presents; hence in harangues presents pass for words.'[33] A Jesuit missionary commenting on the Five Nations, the influential Iroquois confederacy south of Lake Ontario, made a similar observation: 'Presents among these peoples despatch all the affairs of the country ... They dry up tears; they appease anger; they open the doors of foreign countries; they deliver prisoners; they bring the dead back to life; one hardly ever speaks or answers except by presents. That is why, in the harangues, a present passes for a word.'[34] Conversely, a failure or refusal to offer presents when the relationship and the occasion required them could offend and alarm the other party, as well as disappoint.

The English in New York, like their countrymen on Hudson Bay and their French rivals on the St Lawrence, also had to learn the language and protocol of presents. Their dealings were mostly with the Five Nations of the Iroquois Confederacy, peoples who were adept at forest diplomacy. In 1684, for example, the

Seneca sealed an agreement about territory with gifts: 'in token thereof (according to the Indian Custom) they make presents thereupon.'[35] In 1715 an Onondaga chief told the English at the end of a speech, '... we expect you will now new steel our Hatchet (meaning give them some presents).'[36] If the receipt of presents was significant for those who received them, so was the Europeans' failure to give gifts on occasions that called for them. In 1717, a chief of one of the Five Nations reported an ominous rumour to the governor, then added, '... but as this Acc[t] did not come to them with any present according to the Indian Custom, they doubted the Truth of it.'[37]

Both France and England, the European powers that became influential in northeastern North America by the end of the seventeenth century, developed trade networks that depended on the commercial compacts they forged with First Nations. Although the Europeans did not realize it at first, their desire to explore and trade in the new continent drew them into the machinations of pre-existing alignments of First Nations. For example, Samuel de Champlain quickly became allied to the Montagnais in 1603. The explorer and cartographer, who knew that his ability to carry out his mission in New France depended on First Nations' forbearance and assistance, forged an agreement with Anadabijou, a Montagnais chief, who was engaged in a fierce rivalry with the Five Nations of the Iroquois Confederacy to the south. Champlain and his companions were warmly received and feasted in Anadabijou's lodge, and then subjected to a speech by a young Montagnais who had accompanied Champlain to France earlier:

Now when he had ended his oration, the said grand Sagamore Anadabijou, who had listened to him attentively, began to smoke tobacco, and to pass on his pipe to Monsieur du Pont-Gravé of St. Malo, and to me, and to certain other Sagamores who were near him. After smoking some time, he began to address the whole gathering, speaking with gravity, pausing sometimes a little, and then resuming his speech, saying to them, that in truth they ought to be very glad to have His Majesty for their great friend. They answered all with one voice, *Ho, ho, ho,* which is to say yes, yes.

The chief continued his speech: '... he said that he was well content that His said Majesty should people their country, and make war on their enemies, and that there was no nation in the world to which they wished more good than to the French. Finally, he gave them all to understand the advantage and profit they might receive from His said Majesty.' Champlain's pressing need for allies made it desirable to establish such a relationship. It would also be the case a few years later when he assisted the Huron against their Iroquois enemies on Lake Champlain. Anadabijou's interpretation of his exchanges with Champlain is revealed in the fact that the following morning he told his followers 'that they should break camp to go to Tadoussac, where their good friends were,' to trade.[38]

Just a few years later, in Acadia, the French established a similar relationship with a Mi'kmaq chief. In 1606 at Port Royal, Jean de Biencourt, sieur de Poutrincourt, and Chief Membertou exchanged gifts and speeches of friendship.[39] By creating reciprocal relations Poutrincourt, like Champlain north of the St Lawrence, was entering into a kinlike relationship that would pave the way for an enduring Mi'kmaq-French relationship for trade and diplomatic alliance.

South of the St Lawrence, in what would evolve into the northeastern United States, similar commercial pressures were at work. The Dutch, the first power to establish itself at New Amsterdam at the mouth of the Hudson River, entered into a pact with the Mohawk, easternmost of the Five Nations Iroquois, by formal agreement in 1645. Iroquois tradition claims that there was a commercial agreement between the Mohawk and Dutch in 1613. The more reliable date is probably 1645, three years after Arent van Curler set the stage for a treaty by an extended journey through Mohawk territory following all the elaborate protocol that relations required. At Fort Orange (later Albany), Governor Willem Kieft concluded a treaty between New Netherlands and the Mohawk Nation.[40] This pact initiated a long period of commercial relations for the Dutch in which van Curler was an essential go-between for Dutch and Mohawk. For the Europeans the motive was the same one that had moved the Hudson's Bay Company to engage in ceremonies with northern First Nations: to secure an agreement that would enable them to trade in the area controlled by the First Nation. To be able to locate and operate out of Fort Orange on the upper Hudson River, the Dutch merchants needed the permission of the Mohawk. From the Mohawk perspective, they established the pact with the Dutch to secure access to European goods.

When the English replaced the Dutch in what they named the colony of New York in 1664, the same commercial dynamics operated in precisely the same manner as before. The continuity of European practice underlined the importance of the First Nations in the commercial relationship. The English soon entered into agreements with the Mohawk that were replicas of the previous arrangements between the Mohawk and the Dutch. New Amsterdam became New York, and Albany replaced Fort Orange, but the lineaments of the trade, including commercial compacts between First Nation and Europeans, persisted.

While the Europeans did not at first understand that their agreements with the nearby First Nations drew them into relationships or networks that the First Nations had created long before Europeans arrived, they did comprehend the geographical imperatives that made commercial compacts necessary. From the Atlantic, access to the interior of the northerly portion of North America, where the best furs were to be found, was possible via three bodies of water: Hudson Bay, the St Lawrence River, and the Hudson River. The English would command the most northerly route, with one brief interruption in the late seventeenth century when the French temporarily evicted them from Hudson Bay. The French followed Basque and French fishing vessels and whaling boats into and up the St Lawrence, tentatively with Jacques Cartier's voyages between 1534 and 1542, and more permanently with the founding of Port Royal in Acadia and Champlain's explorations and establishment of an *habitation* at Quebec in the first decade of the seventeenth century. (The

French hold on the St Lawrence was suspended during 1629–32 when English adventurers operating with a royal commission captured the fledgling settlement at Quebec.) The English, of course, followed the Dutch up the Hudson River to the south.

Geography dictated that each of the water access routes would lead the respective European traders who probed them into more distant river networks, and along those interior rivers to a wide diversity of First Nation commercial partners. Hudson and James Bays were the outlet of a vast network that traversed what is now northern Quebec and Ontario, and north-central Manitoba, Saskatchewan, and Alberta, and that ultimately led by a strategically important portage in Saskatchewan to the Athabasca country, the Mackenzie River, and the Beaufort Sea. From the St Lawrence River, French fur traders and explorers were introduced by First Nation guides to a network of rivers that allowed them to range through most of northern Quebec via waterways that in some cases emptied into James Bay. To the west the French would learn to use the Ottawa River, which led northwestward to Lake Nipissing and the upper Great Lakes. Or they pushed up the St Lawrence, which took them to the lower Great Lakes and a series of access points leading to the upper Great Lakes and the North, as well as an inland empire south of the lower Great Lakes. (See map 2.)

Finally, the English soon found that commercial relations with the Mohawk, the 'Keepers of the Eastern Door' of the Iroquois League, facilitated communication with the Mohawk River, which ran from the west into the Hudson, and with the lower Great Lakes and the same internal river empire that the French could reach via the St Lawrence.[41] Iroquoia, the land of the Five Nations in the Finger Lakes region of New York, had the height of land running through it. What that topography meant was that from Iroquoia one could make one's way north to the lower Great Lakes, south by the Delaware River to an outlet on the Atlantic south of the Hudson, and also south via the Susquehanna River to the ocean outlet known as Chesapeake Bay. From Mohawk territory it was also a short portage into the Lake Champlain–Richelieu River route that took voyageurs into the centre

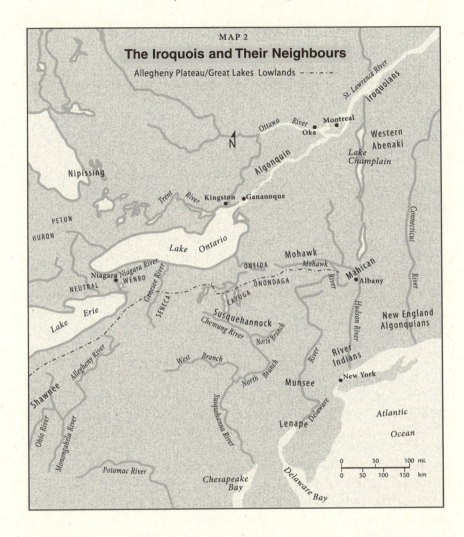

MAP 2
The Iroquois and Their Neighbours
Allegheny Plateau/Great Lakes Lowlands – – – – –

of France's St Lawrence colony. In other words, Iroquoia was at the heart of a vast water network.

Constellations of First Nations were oriented to each of the riverine routes into the interior of the northern part of North America. Hudson's Bay Company traders would encounter Innu and Montagnais in northern Quebec, and a variety of Algonkian and Dene peoples in the western and far northwestern reaches of

Rupert's Land. French traders operating out of the drainage system provided by the St Lawrence and its tributaries would find themselves dealing with Innu, Montagnais, and James Bay Cree to the north and northeast, several different Algonkian groups to the northwest, and Huron and a range of Algonkian groups to the west and southwest. Huronia, like Iroquoia, lay at the centre of a network of waterways that provided the Huron with access to northern, northwestern, southern, and southwestern First Nations and their trade goods. The English based in Albany soon learned that they had to exploit the fur-trade connections through the Mohawk, whose Iroquois name, Keepers of the Eastern Door, was not a collection of empty words. The Mohawk, like the Huron and Montagnais with the French, swiftly positioned themselves to act as commercial go-betweens with the Europeans and more inland First Nations who did not enjoy the immediacy of contact with the strangers that the geographically favoured nations did.[42]

Over the lengthy, sometimes troubled, history of the fur trade in the northeastern woodlands and the subarctic, there emerged a persistent pattern of interior nations trying to find a way around the indigenous intermediaries to trade directly with the Europeans. The intermediaries, in turn, worked determinedly to maintain their control of trade between newcomers and interior First Nations. Every link in the chains, or networks, of fur-trading partners – whether European and Mi'kmaq, Montagnais, Huron, or Mohawk, or Huron and Petun, or Mohawk and Susquehanna – was embodied in a commercial relationship formalized according to the Aboriginal protocol that the Hudson's Bay Company and Champlain had so quickly learned to adopt. If it was true, as George Nelson ruefully learned, that there was 'no end to relationship' among the Indians, it was equally the case that there was no end to the commercial compacts that competing fur-trade networks required to function effectively.

One final feature of the geographically based trading systems was vital: the further reaches of the networks overlapped. Whether it was Iroquois and Mi'kmaq competing in Acadia, or the Seneca – the Keepers of the Western Door in the Iroquois League

– in trade rivalry with any number of Algonkian First Nations to their west and southwest, those at the margins of the extensive networks found themselves in sharp competition and conflict with other First Nations. What this harsh reality meant in practice was that First Nations at the edges found themselves subject to competing pressures and dangers. The Seneca, for example, were located where New France's network of allies in the west and southwest overlapped with Albany's focused on the Mohawk and their Five Nations kin. They were the part of the Iroquois League that was least comfortable with a firm partnership with the English on the Hudson River. Unlike the Mohawk, Keepers of the Eastern Door, who were the principal beneficiaries of trade with the English and who had to worry only about infrequent raids from Canada that moved along the Richelieu River–Lake Champlain corridor, the Keepers of the Western Door had to deal with the most worrisome side effects of the Albany commercial partnership and the minimum of its benefits. These realities that flowed from the geographical underpinnings of the European–First Nation fur trade were the political consequences of commercial linkages. These political realities were a reminder that commerce and politics were inseparable in Aboriginal North America.

The fur trade, the second major industry of Canadian history after the fishery and one of the four motives Europeans had for approaching Canada from the Atlantic shore, brought First Nations of the northeastern woodlands and the subarctic, on the one hand, and European merchants, on the other, together for mutually beneficial commercial purposes. For the European newcomers, relatively few in number, unprepared for the North American woodlands, and heavily dependent on the First Nations for successful trade and even for survival, their commercial ambitions compelled them to adapt themselves to the First Nations who outnumbered them and exceeded them in locally relevant knowledge and economically essential skills. From the perspective of First Nations in the woodlands, the newcomers might have sophisticated trade goods that Natives wanted, but they were clearly the subordinate party in the relationship. Europeans had to fit themselves into a pre-existing Aboriginal trading system. Accordingly, it was the Europeans who adjusted to First Nations' protocols and standards, rather than the other way around, in the fur trade. Given the centrality and importance of kinship in the shaping of First Nations' social relations, the European fur traders had to enter into fictive kinship relationships that made meaningful and effective the commercial compacts. Moreover, since the various transportation systems on which the competing French and English relied to pursue the fur trade brought them into commercial partnership with different First Nations, European involvement in the fur trade meant their engagement with rival First Nation trading systems. In short, trade linkages led inexorably to political associations and enmities. Commercial compacts, an economic form of treaty, soon drew the parties in the northeastern woodlands into political alliances.

2

'Trade & Peace we take to be one thing':[1] Treaties of Peace, Friendship, and Alliance

As the Dutch, English, and French all found in their pursuit of North American furs, there was a close and indissoluble link between commerce and diplomacy among First Nations. A spokesman for one of the Iroquois nations expressed the connection clearly at a conference at Albany in 1735. On behalf of the Six Nations, he objected to a recently concluded agreement between New York and New France because the English, supposedly their allies, had agreed that the French might establish a post at Oswego, in territory the Six Nations considered theirs. 'Trade and Peace we take to be one thing,' he complained. For Iroquois leaders, an agreement to allow the French to trade in proximity to them was not just a commercial entente; inevitably it was a diplomatic pact because trade and peaceful relations were two sides of the same coin. As European fur traders had found in the seventeenth century, in order to pursue commercial objectives, they also had to perform diplomatic rituals of establishing and maintaining relationships with First Nations via fictive associations. The commerce-diplomacy link worked the other way, too. If the English were now contemplating opening up trade with the French in Iroquoia, they were *de facto* entering into a peace arrangement with them as well. From Europeans' perspective, peace and friendship treaties were the second stage of treaty-making, following commercial compacts and preceding treaties dealing with territory.

The diplomatic agreements between First Nations and Europeans were built on pre-contact foundations. Europeans inherited sets of relationships and rivalries among Aboriginal peoples into which the newcomers had to fit themselves. But, as in the case of commercial relations, the insertion of the Europeans, with their different interests and strengths, into pre-existing political systems complicated and modified indigenous alignments. The European powers sought First Nations as allies and comrades in arms by means of treaty relationships. And over time the alliances between First Nations of the northeast woodlands and the Dutch, English, and French increasingly involved warfare. The reason for the newcomers' aggressive pursuit of alliance, particularly from the late seventeenth century until about 1760, was that French and English were increasingly vying for control of North America. In the Maritime region that France called l'Acadie (Acadia), along the St Lawrence River and its principal tributaries, in the *pays d'en haut* (the upper country to the west), and in the region southwest of the lower Great Lakes, major European powers attempted to win First Nations' support and alliance in order to defeat their rivals and gain control of the territory and trade. By the 1750s it was obvious that the decades of on-and-off warfare were taking their toll of both Natives and newcomers. For First Nations, the cost of the recurrent wars was principally life and limb. For the Europeans, especially the British, the long period of territorial rivalry drove them towards modifying how they dealt with First Nations. Out of those policy preoccupations dramatically new forms of British–First Nations relationship consequently emerged in the period between 1755 and 1763. The era of peace and friendship treaties had major ramifications for both Natives and newcomers.

From the very first days of their presence in northeastern North America, Europeans encountered First Nations well versed in creating political agreements among themselves by means of kinship and ritual. In the East, the clearest examples of the phenomenon were the Huron Confederacy and the Iroquois League. The Huron Confederacy appears to have emerged sometime between the 1440s and 1550s or perhaps later, but the paucity of archaeological evidence makes it difficult to date by non-Aboriginal methods. For the Huron, who occupied a strategically important region southeast of Georgian Bay, such considerations were immaterial. (Their view was that the association formed about 1440.) What mattered to them was that initially two, and eventually four, tribal groupings came together into larger political communities. The level of political organization and commonality in these pre-contact systems was not great. The principal purpose of the confederacy that the Attignawantan and Attigneenongnahac nations established was the elimination of blood feuds that were the cause of most inter-tribal war between them. To that end, the new association established a confederacy council of headmen from the groups who convened regularly to resolve disputes, especially those that previously had sparked bloody retaliation. They also participated in feasts and discussions of common interest. The Confederacy does not appear, however, to have had any broader powers, such as common military action, whether defensive or offensive.[2] Indigenous societies placed a high premium on avoiding coercion of other members of their groups. This value limited the degree of political organization and the extent of coercive power within First Nations organizations in the pre-contact and early post-contact periods.

Evidence that kinship was a key element in the formation of larger political entities such as the Huron Confederacy was plentiful. As was common among all Iroquoian peoples, the Huron had elaborate kin linkages through the mother of the family. In addition to these kin ties, all Huron identified as members of a particular clan. There were eight clans – Turtle, Wolf, Bear, Beaver, Deer, Hawk, Porcupine, and Snake – and perhaps as many as fifty clan segments, or subdivisions of the clans. Clan structures were replicated in all four Huron nations, meaning that a member of the Attignawantan nation automatically had clansmen and -women in each of the other three nations of the Confederacy. Members of one's clan in another nation had obligations of hospitality, friendship, and protection that a visitor could invoke. Such ties not only eased the lot of Huron who visited another nation of the Confederacy for one reason or another, but also discouraged violence or even retribution against a visitor who was seen to have done something antisocial. Such a visitor's clansmen were obliged to intervene to protect the Huron outsider. If the Huron from another nation committed a major transgression, such as murder, some form of material compensation would be negotiated to dissuade the aggrieved kin of the victim from exacting retribution in the form of retaliatory violence against the nation of the Huron who had transgressed. For a major wrong, such as the murder of a prominent chief or a European missionary, many clan segments would contribute to the compensation for the aggrieved.[3]

The Huron Feast of the Dead was a mechanism of social integration on a large scale. Approximately every ten years, a major village would reinter the bones of those who had died in the previous decennial period. Remains that had been buried elsewhere would be repatriated to the village, and guests would be invited to attend the ceremony from communities with which the host village had good relations. The Feast as a whole took ten days, with eight of them devoted to the preparation of the bodies for reburial. On the ninth day, people would take the bones of their family members to a large, common burial pit, along with many new beaver pelts and presents. First, the bodies of the recently deceased would be installed on a bed of beaver pelts in the bottom of the pit. Then all would remain at the site overnight with the bones of the remaining deceased. At sunrise the skin bags that contained the bones would be emptied into the ossuary following the instructions of the Feast director. Other men in the pit would arrange the bones, ensuring that the remains of different people were mixed together. A quantity of presents would also be provided in the new grave. After the reburial was complete, the burial pit would be covered carefully, the presents that had not been interred would be distributed, and the crowd would disperse. The symbolism of the elaborate event was clear: by mingling the bones of their departed, the Huron reinforced the links between the living. Moreover, the sustained metaphor that was used to describe the stages of the Feast was 'the kettle,' evoking the symbolically powerful notion of all eating from a single kettle. Since their ancestors slept together in a common grave after the

Feast of the Dead, the living should strive to maintain good relations among themselves. The Feast of the Dead, in other words, was a potent symbol of Huron unity.[4]

Although the Five Nations of the Iroquois League did not observe the Feast of the Dead, there were strong similarities between their unifying mechanisms and those of the Huron. Indeed, their name for themselves, Haudenosaunee, People of the Longhouse, connoted a single community that lived together. According to their creation stories, the Great Spirit had placed them in Iroquoia, the region south of the lower Great Lakes stretching roughly from the Hudson River on the east to the Genesee River on the west. (See map 2.) They and all other humans lived on a land that rested on a turtle's back, yielding the Iroquois name Turtle Island for earth.

As with the genesis of the Huron Confederacy, dating the emergence of the Iroquois League is difficult. The Iroquois themselves said it formed thanks to the lessons, often termed the Great Law, taught by Deganawida and his spokesman Hiawatha about the middle of the fifteenth century. Over all there was a Grand Council composed of fifty sachems, most of whose preoccupations were with cultural matters. Given the First Nations' emphasis on consensus and group harmony, all decisions had to be unanimous. No unanimity, no decision.

A large portion of the Grand Council's work concerned the Iroquois rituals known as 'condolence' and 'requickening.' When groups which had a relationship got together after a period apart, each would 'condole' the losses the other had suffered. Presents were distributed to 'dry tears.' When a sachem died and was replaced, or when a prisoner was adopted, the person would be 'requickened,' signifying entry into a new office or family status. The condolence and requickening protocols were mechanisms for promoting inter-group harmony, and it was no accident that Iroquois treaty-making took the form of condoling and requickening the Five Nations' links with partners.

Like the Huron, Iroquois society also relied heavily on clans to establish and maintain social harmony. Among the Five Nations (Six Nations after the Tuscarora moved north and joined the

Confederacy in 1723), clan identities produced the same social effects as among the Huron. Members of a particular clan owed duties of friendship, hospitality, and protection to fellow clan members, no matter how distant they were geographically. Clans were particularly important in the key rituals of condolence and requickening. The role of clans also extended into the political realm – not that the dividing line between ritual and politics or the barrier separating politics and economics was distinct. It was here that the role of Iroquois women became especially visible. Clan mothers provided leadership to women in a clan segment among this matrilineal people, and clan mothers were charged with the duty of selecting the sachems who played roles as political representatives in the councils of the Iroquois. Like the Huron Confederacy, the Iroquois League had effective institutions and practices that acted as a social glue in the society.[5]

Many of the pre-contact social customs were carried over after contact with the Europeans and influenced treaty-making between newcomers and Natives. For example, the format of European-Iroquois negotiations followed the steps of the condoling-requickening ceremony, though Europeans did not realize it.[6] As well, diplomacy between Indians and Europeans was carried on in the indigenous language, even at Albany.[7] The names or titles that woodlands First Nations gave the leaders of the French and English in North America illustrated clearly the role of personality and personal links between individuals in political relations. At first the Huron and later all First Nations in the northeast woodlands called the French governor Onontio, or Great Mountain, a rendering of the name of the first French governor (1636–48), Charles Huault de Montmagny.[8] French governors came and went, but in council they were all addressed as Onontio by First Nations. Over time, however, treaty parleys between the French and their allies moved from a rhetoric of fraternity to a rhetoric of paternity. The transformation of the king from brother to father in speech-making reflected an important shift in the relationship.[9]

To the Iroquois the governor of the colony of New York, the officer with whom they dealt diplomatically, was always known as Corlaer. The origins of the title were similar to the French situation. The first Dutch representative to establish good relations with the Mohawk, the easternmost of the Five Nations, in the 1640s was Arent van Curler. Before long, van Curler became Corlaer, and when the Dutch were replaced by the English in the 1660s, the chief representative of the British newcomers inherited the title, Corlaer, that had originated with a Dutchman.[10] (The Iroquois were especially tenacious in their naming of prominent non-Natives whose activities affected them. The English translation of their name for the president of the United States is 'Town Destroyer' because the first American president, General George Washington, had played a destructive role in the Sullivan-Clinton military campaign that laid waste to towns in Iroquoia in 1775.)[11] Such labels for the leaders of the European groups illustrated both the power of personal relationships in Aboriginal societies and great continuity of practice.

An extremely important example of pre-contact First Nations practice that carried over into their relations with Europeans was wampum. Wampum took several forms: necklaces (or collars), strings, belts, or aprons, principally. Whatever the form, wampum in pre-contact times was constructed of two types of shells held together with a thread of deerskin. White shells were collected from maritime creatures known as periwinkles, while purple or black shells came from the quahog, a large hard-shell clam.[12] White wampum was associated with positive events, such as making peace, while purple or black was associated with death or war. According to the Iroquois founding legend, the wampum shells were words that relieved problems and helped to restore equanimity. Wampum 'carried an inherent spiritual power in addition to serving as mnemonic devices that recorded transactions.' Contact introduced glass beads, with which wampum could be made, but shell wampum remained the preferred form, especially for diplomacy.[13]

Whether pre- or post-contact, the uses of wampum were several and critical in conducting diplomacy. In many ways, wampum was

NICHOLAS VINCENT ISAWANHONHI,

PRINCIPAL CHRISTIAN CHIEF AND CAPTAIN OF THE HURON INDIANS ESTABLISHED AT LA JEUNE LORETTE NEAR QUEBEC — IN THE COSTUME OF HIS COUNTRY AS WHEN PRESENTED TO HIS MAJESTY GEORGE IV. ON THE 7TH OF APRIL 1825, WITH THREE OTHER CHIEFS — VIZ. ONE GIVEN BY GENERALS BROCK AND CARPENTER THE CHIEF BEARS IN HIS HAND THE WAMPUM OR COLLAR OF WHICH MENTION IS MADE, GIVEN BY HIS LATE MAJESTY, GEORGE III — THE GOLD MEDAL ON HIS NECK WAS THE GIFT OF HIS MAJESTY ON THE 18TH APRIL

They were accompanied and introduced into England on the 14th Dec. 1824 by Mr W Cooper who though an Englishman was always known to them as Chief Tsouhennahé

2.1 Reading wampum

like presents in general: it dried tears, opened ears, eased feelings of anxiety, and so on. It was routine practice in councils for Iroquois speakers, for example, to begin with expressions of condolence for losses their allies had suffered since their last meeting, followed by presentation of wampum to ease the pain. Wampum, however, had other specific functions in negotiations. It was a mnemonic, or memory-assisting device, a First Nations' archives in effect. Wampum belts recorded important discussions and agreements between nations, especially matters of peace and war. At subsequent councils, a First Nations speaker would remind the other party to the agreement by reading the wampum, that is, holding up the belt that commemorated the pact and going through the terms of the understanding between the parties that were recorded on the wampum 'document.'

Messages circulated to another nation that broached the possibility of their combining in war against others, or, conversely, overtures to make peace, had to be accompanied by wampum or they would not be accepted as credible and binding. In June 1714 Five Nations representatives met with Corlaer at Albany and agreed to defer a diplomatic mission to Canada until the New York governor had gone to Onondaga to speak with the sachems. 'This request the Sachems complied with & promised to send to morrow a Belt of Wampum to stop the s^d Deputation.'[14] In these circumstances, a belt that was accepted indicated a willingness to pursue the course proposed; a wampum declined signified rejection. At a memorable council with the Iroquois in 1694, French governor Frontenac was presented with wampum belts conveying three propositions for discussion. 'The Count kicked away these three propositions or Belts, and by this mark of contempt and haughtiness, indicated to the proudest nation throughout this New World his indifference for peace.'[15] In 1724 the Iroquois in council at Onondaga debated a proposal by Onontio that the Iroquois permit him to build two forts in their territory, one at Niagara and the other at Oswego. 'The said Belt was produced at Onondaga & the Govr of Canadas Proposal debated by the Assembly there ... But the s^d Assembly rejected the Belt & Proposal of the Govr of Canada, & it was resolved that the Belt should be returned him & a Message sent to him that he should not be admitted to build any Fort on their Land.'[16]

Conversely, any such message that was not accompanied by wampum was regarded as not serious. In 1738 when Laurence Claasse, an interpreter for the colony of New York, attempted to dissuade the Seneca from going to war against the Cherokee and Cattawba in the south, 'they made answer that he was certainly jesting with them for if Corlaer wanted them not to go he ought according to Custom to have sent a Belt of Wampum, but as Laur. Claasse spoke without one they should not lay aside their Expedition.'[17] The ways that First Nations diplomats used wampum were impressive both for their multiplicity and, sometimes, subtlety.

One of the striking features of post-contact diplomacy between indigenous leaders and European newcomers was the way in which the latter adapted to the use of wampum and sometimes became masters of it. Both French and British representatives, once tutored by Native allies, learned to appreciate and to practise the premium that First Nations placed on both diplomatic oratory and devices such as presents and wampum. North of the St Lawrence, a military man such as Louis Buade, Comte de Frontenac, governor of New France (1672–82 and 1689–98), took quickly to the methods of forest diplomacy and established his credentials with First Nations. His innate vanity, love of display and feasting, and bravura performances made him an effective diplomat.[18]

Very different in personality, not to mention the Crown that he served, William Johnson of New York from the 1750s till his death in 1774 was a master of diplomacy. From his manor and estates in the Mohawk Valley, Johnson used his trade among the Indians, and from 1755 his appointment as superintendent of the northern Indians, as instruments to expand his influence. Thanks in no small part to his marriage to Molly Brant, a Mohawk clan matron, he was adept at couching British policy in terms attractive to the Iroquois. Johnson was skilled in lavish oratory, gift-giving, and wampum deployment in both his commercial dealings and his diplomacy. Cadwallader Colden, lieutenant-governor of New York, reported that at a 1746 council 'Johnson was inde-

2.2 Sir William Johnson's seal combined indigenous and European elements.

fatigable among the Mohawks; he dressed himself after the Indian Manner, made frequent Dances, according to their Custom when they incite to War, and used all the means he could think of, at a considerable Expence ... in order to engage them heartily in War against Canada.'[19] The skills exercised by men such as Frontenac and Johnson in their dealings with First Nations illustrated that success in forest diplomacy required adaptation to Aboriginal rituals and behaviour.

The adaptability of men like William Johnson was simply one more example of the reality that European powers in North America, whatever their opinion of their lofty stature in Europe, had to fit themselves into First Nations' pre-existing alliances to succeed. France had always known the importance of establishing good relations with First Nations. King Henry's commission to the Sieur de Monts in 1603 instructed him to 'treat and contract to the same effect, peace, alliance and confederacy, good amitie, correspondence and communication with the said people & their Princes or others, having power or command over them.'[20]

Samuel de Champlain established a close alliance with the Huron that involved warfare. In the summer of 1609, after a visiting party of Huron entered into an agreement with Champlain at Quebec, Champlain accompanied his new allies south along the Richelieu River to Lake Champlain, where they encountered a party of Iroquois. The Huron-French party easily routed their opponents, owing to French use of muskets that threw the Iroquois into a panic. The incident cemented the alliance between the Huron and the French, a partnership that soon emerged as a lucrative commercial relationship that lasted until the Five Nations attacked and destroyed the villages of Huronia during 1649–50.[21] After the dispersal of the Huron, French trade relied especially upon the nations of northern Quebec, such as the Montagnais, and the several nations of the *pays d'en haut*, such as Algonkin, Ottawa, and others.

The English, France's principal trade and territorial rivals in the late seventeenth and eighteenth century, inherited the Dutch trade relationship that Arent van Curler had established with the Five Nations in the 1640s. The Iroquois were later to say that, when the Dutch arrived, they entered into an association with them that was symbolized by a rope they used to tie the Dutch vessel to the shore. In the case of the English, who moved into the relationship after 1664, the more enduring and valued nature of their alliance with the Five Nations was expressed in terms of an iron chain used to moor the English boat to the shore in Iroquoia. Over time, as in a 1748 council of Johnson and Iroquois, the English represented the link as 'a strong Silver Chain which would never break slip or Rust.' The silver chain between the English at Albany and the Iroquois at Onondaga would 'bind you and him [the king] forever in Brothership together,' and the mooring chain of silver signified the greater value of the link between Natives and the English.[22] Whereas earlier presents, including wampum, were used 'to remove the rust' that might have accumulated on the chain of friendship, from about the 1670s onward, the oratorical description was that presents and wampum 'burnished the silver' chain that bound Iroquois and English together.

The relations between French representatives and First Nations north of the St Lawrence also deepened and strengthened as the seventeenth century wore on. In fact, the first recorded peace treaty conference occurred on the St Lawrence in 1645, just two years after van Curler solidified relations between the Dutch and the Iroquois. There was a connection between the 1643 events in Fort Orange (future Albany) and at Trois-Rivières in 1645. The Iroquois approached the French for a pact because increased demand for beaver furs resulting from the 1643 agreement made them anxious for access to the rich hunting grounds north of Lake Ontario, in lands controlled by allies of the French.[23] Although the treaty talks at Trois-Rivières in 1645 produced a peace between Five Nations and the French and their allies that was short-lived, they were nonetheless important and revealing of First Nations diplomatic practices and European adaptability. The principal Iroquois spokesman on the occasion, Kiotseaeton (Le Crochet, Hook), arrived accompanied by two other Five Nations diplomats and a French hostage they had captured in war. Repatriation of prisoners was an extremely important part of the peace-making process for eastern woodlands First Nations, for whom the maintenance of their population numbers was a burning concern.

Naturally, Kiotseaeton, who was described as 'almost completely covered with Porcelain beads,' presented wampum to the French and launched into an elaborate speech. Before Governor Montmagny, he set up seventeen wampum necklaces and delivered an oration, accompanied by many gestures and re-enactment of some of his party's travails, to impress on his audience the courage they had displayed and the privations they had endured in travelling to the St Lawrence to meet with them. The first wampum marked his gratitude for a safe arrival, and the second, which he tied to the arm of the French hostage, conveyed 'my Nephew' back to the care of the French. 'The 4th present was to assure us that the thought of their people killed in war no longer affected them; that they cast their weapons under their feet.' 'The fifth was given to clear the river, and to drive away the enemy's canoes which might impede navigation.' He made use of a thousand gestures, 'as if he had collected the waves and had caused a calm, from Quebec to the Iroquois country.' He came to the most critical part of his proposal with the tenth wampum, which 'was given to bind us all very closely together. He took hold of a Frenchman, placed his arm within his, and with his other arm he clasped that of an Alguonquin [*sic*]. Having thus joined himself to them, "Here," he said, "is the knot that binds us inseparably; nothing can part us." This collar was extraordinarily beautiful. "Even if the lightning were to fall upon us, it could not separate us; for, if it cuts off the arm that holds you to us, we will at once seize each other by the other arm."' The eleventh wampum was also extremely important to the peace-making message: it accompanied an invitation to '"come and eat good meat with us. The road is cleared; there is no longer any danger."'[24] The symbolism of eating together – of all eating from the same bowl – was a powerful statement of peaceful relations between treaty and trade partners.

The degree to which the French had already adapted to First Nations practices by 1645 came out in Governor Montmagny's response to Kiotseaeton. Two days after the Iroquois' oration and performance, the governor 'replied to the presents of the Iroquois by fourteen gifts, all of which had their meanings and which carried their own messages,' to the great acclaim and satisfaction of the Iroquois negotiators. 'Thus was peace concluded with them, on condition that they should commit no act of hostility against the Hurons, or against the other Nations who are our allies, until the chiefs of those Nations who were not present had treated with them.'[25] The peace conference at Trois-Rivières in 1645 illustrated that the demands of the fur trade drew foes together, and that European political leaders, like European fur traders, quickly learned the ways of forest diplomacy.

Both France and England found themselves involved in more complex treaty systems in the last third of the seventeenth century. For New France, the single biggest influence on its diplomacy was the transfer of the colony from a commercial monopolist to royal control, in 1663. When New France became a royal colony it inherited the full range of French administrative institutions, as well as the aspirations and limitations of French diplomacy. In terms of the machinery of government, the key players for the next century were the intendant, generally speaking the official in charge of domestic and economic matters, and the governor, who acted as the Crown's representative in military and external affairs. French policy for Canada, the St Lawrence Valley colony, was known as the 'compact colony' strategy, meaning that under the direction of the great French minister Jean-Baptiste Colbert, Canada was to move away from its excessive reliance on the fur trade and develop a more diversified economy through subsidized immigration and state-sponsored industries. In reality, the pull of the fur trade proved irresistible, thereby limiting the success of Colbert's scheme. Moreover, the inclinations of the governor – especially Frontenac, who fought fiercely to profit from it personally – to pursue the fur trade because it helped to maintain fruitful alliances with the First Nations to the north and west often created friction between intendant and governor. Certainly, Onontio continued to play a major role on behalf of Louis XIV in diplomacy with First Nations in the late seventeenth century.

So far as Corlaer was concerned, there were similar opportunities, imperatives, tensions, and countervailing forces with which the officer charged with Indian diplomacy on behalf of England had to contend. When the English supplanted the Dutch at Albany in 1664, one of the first things their representative did was enter into a peace treaty with the Iroquois.[26] Moreover, successive governors – some with greater facility than others – learned to participate in the time-consuming process of condoling, requickening, present-giving, wampum distribution, and speechifying that was part and parcel of seventeenth-century diplomacy. Iroquois sachems must have tired of having to 'educate' yet another green Corlaer whenever the king in far-off London changed representatives.

Within the colony of New York, Corlaer's biggest problems were a board of Indian commissioners and the colonial legislature. The former were a group of colonists, located in Albany, who advised on Indian policy and often represented the Crown in dealings with First Nations in the absence of the governor. The problem with the commissioners was that a lot of them suffered acutely from conflict of interest. Since many commissioners were themselves merchants directly involved in the fur trade, they were often engaged in illicit trade with New France that supplied them with furs in exchange for English goods. The fact that goods could be smuggled into Montreal and furs back to Albany meant that Corlaer could not exploit First Nations' preference for English wares in order to advance New York's cause diplomatically. Albany's merchants often made diplomacy more difficult by charging high prices in trade with Iroquois allies. On occasion they were also accused, with cause, of using alcohol and violence to separate visiting Indians from their furs on terms highly advantageous to the merchant. Since First Nations took 'trade and peace to be one thing,' unfavourable terms of trade were interpreted as hostility. Honeyed words from Corlaer in council were often undone by the rapacity of Albany's merchants. From the governor's perspective, the problem with the legislative assembly was that it usually was loath to vote the money to conduct diplomacy as readily as Corlaer and his First Nations allies would like. Again, in council the governor could profess goodwill as fervently as he liked. But if his words were not accompanied by presents and goods to facilitate battling his allies' Indian foes, Corlaer's credibility would be jeopardized, and England's diplomatic well-being undercut.

The inconstancy of their European allies placed First Nations in both alliance systems in grave difficulty. Among the Five Nations by the mid-seventeenth century, pro-French, pro-English, and neutralist (or pro-balance) factions vied for influence in the councils that met at Onondaga. Indeed, the geographic location of Iroquoia allowed for, even encouraged, such diversity of strategic approaches. Following the Iroquois attacks upon and dispersal of the Mahican, Huron, Petun, Neutral, and others in the first half of the century, the pro-French faction had enjoyed ascendancy. The attraction of a peace with France increased. The king in Versailles had dispatched large numbers of French regular army troops to New France in 1663, and Onontio conducted a destructive military campaign in Iroquoia in 1666. A peace was fashioned in 1667, but it did not last long, given the demands of the fur trade and various Indian allies. If the short-lived peace did nothing else, it provided French Jesuit missionaries with an opportunity to proselytize in Iroquoia. As a leading authority on the Five Nations has noted, '... in the seventeenth century, nearly every Iroquois request for French missionaries occurred during peace negotiations.' The People of the Longhouse saw the Black Robes as personnel to be exchanged as a surety of maintaining peace. 'One party's missionary was the other's hostage.'[27]

By the 1670s and 1680s, the pro-English faction assumed the ascendancy in Iroquoia. In part the explanation lay in the influence of the Mohawk, always the most likely to emphasize the alliance with the newcomers on the Hudson River, who favoured closer ties with Albany. As well, the fact that English governors after the takeover from the Dutch attempted to impose greater order and decorum in the fur mart at Albany, thereby reducing somewhat the exactions that the Anglo-Dutch burghers made on visiting Indian fur providers, helped to improve the image of Corlaer's people. The English in these years also encouraged and assisted the expansion of Iroquois influence over neighbouring First Nations to the south and southwest. Gradually the Five Nations drew the Susquehannock and other First Nations into peaceful relations, and slowly an extended alliance network involving the English, Five Nations, and other First Nations took shape that has come to be known as the Covenant Chain. The Chain, a metaphor to describe the complex web of relations in which New York and the Five Nations were the key players, was an extraordinary creation that testified to the diplomatic skills of the Iroquois. This was the silver link that bound Corlaer and his allies together in opposition to the French and their Native partners in the *pays d'en haut* and in missionary settlements that gave succour to Christian converts from the Five Nations, the Abenaki of New Brunswick and New England, as well as the refugee Huron who had clustered near Quebec following the destruction of Huronia. The Covenant Chain was symbolized – memorialized, in fact – in an important wampum belt that showed First Nations at one end and Europeans at the other, linked in an alliance. The human figure at the left end was predominantly dark in colour, while that at the other end was mainly white.[28]

The Covenant Chain alliance and the wampum that represented it were different from the *gus wenta*, or Two Row Wampum, that has assumed epic proportions in some quarters. Thanks to an effective campaign by Six Nations leaders from the early 1870s onward, aided immeasurably by adoption of the *gus wenta* by the Royal Commission on Aboriginal Peoples in 1996, the Two Row Wampum is believed by many to embody an unchanging relationship between the Iroquois and their European partners, beginning with the Dutch and carrying on with the English and later Canadians. The belt, believed to represent twin sovereignties, is composed of two parallel lines of dark purple shells separated by a field of white shells. The two lines are said to symbolize two water craft, a canoe and a ship, that sail together peacefully and harmoniously without interfering with each other. This construct is held to represent the campaign by the Iroquois to maintain their sovereignty, first in alliance with the Dutch and English, and later within Canada. In fact, however, the Five Nations had entered into a close alliance with the English that was symbolized by the Covenant Chain, a wampum depicting linked – not separate – parties. While the Iroquois League always struggled to maintain the most autonomy possible within the alliance with Corlaer, there was never insistence on completely separate existence and operations by the Five Nations in these years. Mixing up the *gus wenta* and the Covenant Chain has led to considerable confusion about the nature of Haudenosaunee–European relations.[29]

A particularly clear example of how the Five Nations combined autonomy with their English alliance, and also of how Corlaer sometimes missed their subtlety, emerged at a council in Albany in the summer of 1684. Native representatives 'requested they might have the Duke of Yorks Arms to put up at each of their Castles as a mark of their Affection & Attachment,' to which Governor Dongan replied that 'I do give you the Great Duke of Yorks

Arms to put upon each of the Castles as a Sign that you are under this Government.' Two days later, spokesmen for the Onondaga and Cayuga announced, 'We have put all our Land & our Persons under the Protection of the Great Duke of York Bro^r to your Mighty Sachem [king].' However, the sachems also stressed that 'We desire you will let the Great Sachem over the Great Lake [King Charles] know, And also that we are a Free People & unite our Selves to the English, and it is therefore in our Power to dispose of our Land to whom we think proper, and We present you with a Bever.'[30] The Iroquois leaders in the 1684 talks were expressing their notion of close relationship and protection while maintaining their autonomy as 'a Free People' and their territorial rights. Given Governor Dongan's reply concerning the coats of arms, it is doubtful that the English understood the import of the speeches. (About the same time, Iroquois diplomats told French governor La Barre, 'We are born free, We neither depend on *Yonnodio* [Onontio] nor *Corlaer*. We may go where we please, and carry with us whom we please, and buy and sell what we please.')[31]

The expansion of the Covenant Chain alliance system in the late decades of the seventeenth century brought important changes to the Iroquois. Prior to this period, the Iroquois League, as noted, had been an association for principally ceremonial purposes. Indeed, its formal name among anthropologists is the Iroquois League of Peace. It was not dedicated to developing what Europeans would call a common foreign or military policy.[32] In the late seventeenth century, another organization, usually called the Iroquois Confederacy, began to emerge alongside – and in a few instances overlapping – the Iroquois League. The existence of the two bodies has often caused misunderstanding. The early Iroquois association was an informal, *ad hoc* network of military leaders who began to meet in an effort to coordinate their positions in dealing with the French and English. Since a few of these leaders who developed the later Confederacy were also sachems representing their peoples ceremonially in the League, there was some overlap between the two organizations.[33] The Iroquois never developed a coherent external policy towards Europeans, and they never had a collective agency that could have formulated and executed such a policy for the simple reason that the premium Iroquois culture placed on individual and local autonomy made such developments difficult. In an increasingly hostile northeastern North America, that quality was a source of Iroquois vulnerability.

Another complication for Iroquois diplomacy was the existence of a number of expatriate Five Nations communities within New France. These enclaves, sometimes called 'the Seven Nations of Canada' and *les domiciliés* (the domiciled people), were populated by groups of several First Nations who had relocated to the St Lawrence colony for refuge from hostile forces or because their conversion to Christianity made their home communities uncomfortable for them. Some of the Huron who had been dispersed by the Iroquois in 1649–50 had settled at Lorette, near Quebec City; Abenaki, displaced by warfare emanating from the New England colonies, had formed the settlements of Odanak (St Francis) and Bécancour. A mixed community of convert Christians had started out in a settlement known as La Montagne in what is now downtown Montreal, moved to the north side of Montreal Island late in the seventeenth century, and relocated finally to the eastern side of Lake of Two Mountains in the 1720s, under the guidance of Sulpician missionaries. Over time, this mixed community of Algonkin, Nipissing, and Mohawk Christians would become almost exclusively Mohawk as the Algonkian groups moved away from encroaching settlement. It would become known as Kanesatake, although non-Natives often referred to it by the name of a nearby town, Oka. On the south shore of the St Lawrence opposite Montreal, a Jesuit mission known first as Sault St Louis developed in the latter half of the seventeenth century. This Christian Mohawk mission and reserve was known as Kahnawake (At the Rapids), and would in turn produce a spin-off colony upriver on the St Lawrence known as Akwesasne (Where the Partridge Drums). The French usually referred to the younger community as St Regis.

These *domiciliés* Indians were a complication in the lives of the Five Nations south of the lower Great Lakes. For one thing, centres such as Kahnawake, Kanesatake, and later Akwesasne sometimes attracted converts out of Iroquoia, thereby weakening the Five Nations. During the period of heavy French missionary presence in Iroquoia in the 1670s, this was a particular danger. The existence of kin and people of their clan in French territory also worked against efforts by Corlaer to get his Five Nations allies – whom he sometimes mistakenly thought of as subjects – to participate in military expeditions against France's St Lawrence colony. The inability or unwillingness of New York's assembly to vote funds for Indian Affairs and the strong kin and clan ties between the villages of Iroquoia and Mohawk enclaves in New France help to explain why the much more numerous Anglo-Americans invaded New France so infrequently.

These considerations and complications arising from links to Mohawk in New France and Anglo-American colonists' equivocating about an aggressive policy were only part of the problems facing the Five Nations and the Covenant Chain by the 1690s. The Iroquois were increasingly uncomfortable with their strongly pro-English posture. The burdens of maintaining the extensive alliance system, especially in light of the parsimony and apparent irresolution of Corlaer's people, were exacerbated when New France became increasingly aggressive and expansionist in the last decades of the seventeenth century. New France's Governor Frontenac established the fort that bore his name at the eastern end of Lake Ontario in 1673, and in succeeding decades the French manoeuvred to establish themselves at places such as Oswego, Niagara, and Detroit. All these centres were in territory the Five Nations regarded as theirs, and, more important still, a foreign presence in these strategically important points threatened the Iroquois commercially and militarily. The most critical consideration for the clan matrons and other leaders of Iroquoia was the fact that increasing skirmishes were causing loss of life that weakened the Five Nations. It is estimated that Five Nations military strength was halved to 1,320 in the 1690s, while New France's population increased by 50 per cent.[34] The Treaty of

Ryswick, 1697, which brought temporary peace between France and England, made Corlaer unwilling to take overt action against New France, much to the frustration of his allies among the Five Nations.

Their growing sense of vulnerability moved some of the Five Nations to approach the French in search of a peace agreement.[35] In July 1700 a small party of Seneca and Onondaga visited Montreal to open up discussions about a possible treaty. Although Governor Callière was dissatisfied because the delegation represented only factions of the westernmost and central of the Five Nations, he agreed to continue talks at Onondaga the following month. At this meeting, the neutralist (or balance) faction pushed their Iroquois colleagues hard to open the path to peace. It was a good sign that leaders from the Seneca, Cayuga, Oneida, and even some Mohawk joined their Onondaga brethren at the conference. Efforts by New York to break the conference up were rebuffed, and the Iroquois leaders agreed to meet again in Montreal in September.

This next gathering included representatives of the Seneca, Cayuga, and Onondaga, as well as some leaders from French allied nations in the West and *domiciliés*. After three days of speeches and wampum exchanges, the parties agreed tentatively to a peace, the terms to be confirmed the next summer. Key provisions in the preliminary pact were that France's western allies were to be included in the peace between Onontio and the Five Nations, and that all the First Nations involved were to bring the prisoners they had collected in wars to Montreal in 1701 for repatriation. Essential for the Five Nations to 'sell' the plan to their colleagues was an agreement that the Iroquois would be able to trade at Fort Frontenac, a privilege which would greatly reduce their commercial dependence on Albany.

When peace-makers assembled at Montreal in the summer of 1701, their numbers were swelled beyond the groups who had been involved in the 1700 talks. Thirty-eight or thirty-nine First Nations that occupied territories stretching from Acadia on the east to the edge of the prairie on the west, most of them allies of the French, assembled. At least 1,300 First Nations delegates

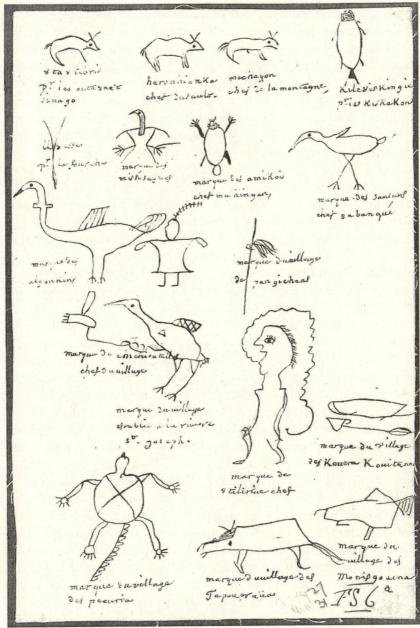

2.3 First Nations' totems on the Great Peace of 1701

more than doubled the town's population of 1,200, between July 21 and August 7. Governor Callière and his staff made elaborate preparations for the conclave, but other factors jeopardized prospects for success. For one thing, Montreal had recently been in the grip of illness, apparently a severe influenza, and all the visiting First Nations were uneasy about conditions. The talks were also threatened by a piece of diplomatic sharp practice that the Iroquois pulled: they brought to Montreal their French prisoners, but no Indian trophies from previous engagements with France's First Nations allies. This ploy angered France's western allies, especially Kondiaronk (Le Rat), a convert Huron from Michilimackinac with close commercial ties to the French who had laboured hard to persuade his western allies to journey to Montreal in search of peace. Though humiliated by the duplicity of the Iroquois concerning prisoners, Kondiaronk continued to advocate concluding a peace. Eventually, hard bargaining led to agreement that France's allies would hand their Iroquois prisoners over to the French governor, who would retain five of them until the Iroquois had delivered all the prisoners to Callière for repatriation to their home nations, and would hand the remainder over to the Iroquois right away. Although the sickness continued to cast a pall over the gathering – especially the death of Kondiaronk, who was respected by both the French and his First Nations allies – an important deal was eventually fashioned.

The terms of the Great Peace were critically important to both First Nations and Europeans. The return of prisoners met a profound desire among all the First Nation signatories to recover their kin. A term that specified that the Five Nations were to remain neutral in any future hostilities between English and French satisfied both Onontio and the Five Nations. The French view was that Callière had 'imposed' neutrality on the Iroquois, thereby robbing England of a potentially valuable ally in times of conflict. For the Five Nations, though, the neutrality provision satisfied the desires of the neutralist, or balance, faction within their villages. That point of view was growing stronger after six decades of destructive warfare and amidst a growing recognition by the Iroquois that Corlaer's people were frequently unreliable allies. For the Iroquois, the neutrality provision ensured their safety in the event of a showdown in North America between France and England. But what was probably more important – indeed, it was what made the Peace of 1701 the Great Peace – was the fact that France's western allies participated in the agreement to live together without hostilities. While this meant that the Iroquois had to share hunting grounds with France's western allies, it also ensured that the Five Nations could safely trade with the western nations. At Montreal in the summer of 1701, it seemed, the only loser was Corlaer and the English.

The Great Peace negotiated in Montreal was not, however, the only agreement the Iroquois concluded in 1701. At Albany that same year, Iroquois delegates pursued their balanced strategy and entered into what is sometimes labelled the Nanfan Treaty after the chief official, Lieutenant-Governor John Nanfan, who represented New York at the time. The Five Nations delegation in Montreal had been led by prominent francophiles who pursued a neutralist strategy; their chief representatives at Albany were anglophiles who also similarly sought balance in the Five Nations' external relations.[36] The Iroquois carefully avoided telling Nanfan of their commitment at Montreal to remain neutral, and reiterated the usual formulae of friendship towards New York. In addition, the Iroquois surprised the New Yorkers by offering to place under Crown oversight 'all that Land where the Bever hunting is' to the west and north of the Great Lakes 'wch we won by the Sword 80-years ago & pray that He (the King) may be our Protector & Defendor there; And desire that our Secretary may write an Instrument wch we will Sign & Seal that it may be carried by him to the King.'[37] Since the written version of this treaty exempts certain lands in what is now southern Ontario, the 'Nanfan Treaty' is often held to guarantee Iroquois hunting rights north of the Lakes today.

There are a number of problems with interpreting this concession as a binding treaty. For one thing, a leading expert on the Five Nations contends that the delegates at Albany did not mean to concede or alienate the lands, but merely made a gesture to ensure English protection of lands important to them.[38] An

essential part of the commitment was also the creation of a 'deed'
for the territory, but no such legal document was ever provided.
Third, the Five Nations did not possess the right to transfer these
lands to others because, despite their claim that 'we won [them]
by the Sword 80-years ago,' the territory was not under effective
Iroquois control. The Ojibwa had driven them out and forced a
peace on them during the last decades of the seventeenth
century.[39] What is particularly revealing about the Five Nations'
intentions in the Albany agreement and the true significance of
the 'concession' in 1701 is that for decades after the Albany pact,
Corlaer in council with the Iroquois repeatedly referred to a land
transfer, while the Iroquois negotiators ignored the reference. In
a council with the Mohawk, Cayuga, and Onondaga in May 1731,
for example, Governor Montgomerie 'renews the Cov^t with them'
and, among other topics, mentioned that 'you have put your
Lands under the protection of the King of Great Britain.' But the
sachems, while agreeing to 'renew the Cov^t Chain with this Gov^t
& all his Majesties Subjects in N. America' and responding to
several other topics in the governor's remarks, studiously avoided
any comment on their lands and British protection.[40] As a British
diplomat was to say ruefully many years later, '... tis true that when
a Nation find themselves pushed, their Alliances broken, and
themselves tired of a War, they are verry apt to say many civil
things, and make any Submissions which are not agreeable to
their intentions, but said merely to please those with whom they
transact Affairs as they know we cannot enforce the observance of
them.'[41]

Whatever the merits of the Albany agreement, there is little
doubt that the 1701 peace pacts were remarkable diplomatic
achievements. Although the French rejoiced that they had
'imposed' neutrality on the Five Nations, that status was also beneficial to the Haudenosaunee, both because of their internal
problems with differing factions and because of the costs of
involvement in wars between the English and French. The inclusion of several dozen First Nations allied to the French in a peace
pact between Onontio and the Iroquois was a major advance for
both New France and Iroquoia. As events were to unfold during

the first half of the eighteenth century, the Great Peace of 1701 was a vitally important achievement.

Strategic decisions in France and England ensured that the Great Peace provided merely a brief respite in North American hostilities. France, in particular under Louis XIV, embarked on an ambitious policy of expanding its grip on the interior of North America as part of its worldwide rivalry with Albion. Commencing in 1700, France ordered its representatives in the field to use the fur trade to strengthen its alliances with First Nations and thereby solidify the French presence in the West and down the Mississippi. Corlaer and other representatives of England understandably felt uneasy at the prospect of being hemmed in by a French–First Nations fence of trading posts, especially as the western alliances that New France enjoyed with First Nations stood as a barrier to westward expansion, which was increasingly favoured by New York, Pennsylvania, and Virginia as the eighteenth century went on. The balance between the two European powers was altered in 1713 by the Treaty of Utrecht, which concluded the War of the Spanish Succession in Europe. Two of Utrecht's terms had a direct impact on First Nations. First, the Treaty said that France recognized British suzerainty over the Iroquois, and that France conceded 'Acadia with its ancient limits' to the United Kingdom. (When England was united with Scotland in 1707, the United Kingdom, or Great Britain, was formed.) For the Iroquois, the part of Utrecht that purported to subordinate them to Britain was irrelevant: they simply ignored it. The Treaty's provisions concerning the Maritime region, however, would prove a major cause of diplomatic manoeuvring, including First Nations–European dealings, for fifty years. Utrecht is also historically significant because in the year following it, Great Britain began the practice of issuing medals to chiefs of First Nations with whom the Crown had good relations.[42]

Despite challenges from the Basques, Portuguese, and, later, New Englanders, the French had had things pretty much their own way in Acadia prior to the eighteenth century. The French had enjoyed generally good relations with the First Nations of the region, especially the Mi'kmaq, who dominated peninsular Nova Scotia and parts of northern New Brunswick because of their large numbers. The Maliseet of the St John River valley were comparatively minor players in this early period, while the Passamaquoddy of the more southerly coast and the Abenaki inland were more significant. French missionaries had established a beachhead for their country in the early seventeenth century when Membertou, the major Mi'kmaq leader, went through a ritual of adopting Christianity along with the rest of his large extended family. Also important to the positive relations between the Maritime First Nations and the French was the Europeans' reliance on the fishery and the fur trade, neither of which activity threatened the territorial interests of the Mi'kmaq. Some scholars have discerned in the 1610 conversion of Membertou the creation of a 'Mi'kmaq Concordat' with the Vatican, and sometimes point to a wampum that is said to commemorate the event.[43]

Indeed, relations between the indigenous population of the Maritimes and the Roman Catholic Church have always been close, even to the point that in the twentieth century some Mi'kmaq included Catholicism in their definition of what it meant to be Mi'kmaq. But no matter how close Mi'kmaq-Catholic relations historically were, they did not amount to a concordat, or treaty between the Vatican and a people. Whatever the Mi'kmaq thought of the Vatican and their relations with it, the Holy See did not regard the First Nation as the sort of organized society with which the papal state could or would have a formal relationship. Moreover, the Jesuit priests who early ministered to the Mi'kmaq did not have authorization to enter into a formal agreement such as a concordat. Finally, the wampum that is claimed to archive the agreement in fact was made in the early nineteenth century for First Nations people in Quebec.[44] Although relations between the Mi'kmaq and the Catholic Church were close, the link that joined them was not a concordat.

France would need its close relations with the Mi'kmaq in the years after the Treaty of Utrecht because Great Britain increasingly tried to assert the territorial claim that the treaty had given it over the Maritimes. Besides shoring up relations with the Mi'kmaq through French missionaries and present-giving, France in the 1720s moved aggressively to strengthen its position in the region by constructing a massive fortress known as Louis-bourg on the northeastern portion of Ile Royale, the island the English called Cape Breton. Louisbourg, whose defences were always more imposing than effective, served as the anchor for one corner of France's triangular trade with the Caribbean and Canada, as a base from which French warships could protect French interests, and as a rendezvous point at which to distribute presents to First Nations. Britain responded slowly at first, although it did take Louisbourg with New England's support during the War of the Austrian Succession, 1744–8. Its diplomats handed it back during peace talks, however. In the 1750s, Britain's efforts became more determined as it erected fortifications in the Isthmus of Chignecto, the neck of land between New Brunswick and Nova Scotia. It also founded Halifax in 1749 as a North Atlantic base to offset French power at Louisbourg. British offi-cers also tried repeatedly and unsuccessfully to get Acadians – the French, Roman Catholic population that was often intermarried with Mi'kmaq – to take an oath of allegiance to the British king.

As Britain and France manoeuvred in the Maritimes in search of strategic advantage in the period from Utrecht until the mid-1750s, their actions had a direct impact on the First Nations of the region. So far as France was concerned, in addition to con-structing and staffing Louisbourg, their principal efforts were encouraging French missionaries to keep the Mi'kmaq friendly to France and supplying presents with which to keep the chain of friendship burnished. In Britain's case, more dramatic efforts at establishing and maintaining formal relations with the First Nations were required. His Most Britannic Majesty lacked the ties of religion and commerce that His Most Catholic Majesty had enjoyed with First Nations for over a century. Moreover, the British presence in the region was more disruptive of First Nations' land use than was the French. The Acadians farmed on, and fished and traded from, land reclaimed and diked, not taken from the Natives. They left only a tiny 'footprint' on Mi'kmaq

decades after 1725–6. Behind the First Nations lurked the
French, whose missionaries quietly supported and encouraged
the Native opponents of the English with presents. The resumption of war between the European powers during 1744–8 naturally saw the low-grade conflict flare up anew. And once again
hostilities were followed in due course by a new peace treaty. The
Treaty of Halifax in 1752 made peace between the British, who
now were expanding their influence from their base in Halifax,
and some of the bands of Mi'kmaq that had been recently
arrayed against them. The pact restored peace and pledged the
First Nations signatories to 'use their utmost Endeavours to bring
in the other Indians to Renew and Ratify this peace ...' This pact
went further than the guarantee of gathering rights and peaceful
coexistence to offer assurances about trading rights:

> It is agreed that the said Tribe of Indians shall not be hindered
> from, but have free liberty of Hunting and Fishing as usual and
> that if they shall think a Truckhouse needful at the River Chibenac-
> cadie [Shubenacadie, in central Nova Scotia] or any other place of
> their resort, they shall have the same built and proper Merchan-
> dize, lodged therein, to be Exchanged for what the Indians shall
> have to dispose of and that in the mean time the said Indians shall
> have free liberty to bring for Sale to Halifax or any other Settle-
> ment within this Province, Skins, feathers, fowl, fish or any other
> thing they shall have to sell, where they shall have liberty to dispose
> thereof to the best advantage.[47]

Whereas the Treaty of Boston and Mascarene's Treaty (1725–6)
had recognized an unimpeded First Nations right to gather, the
1752 agreement enshrined a right to trade, including at govern-
ment-created and -subsidized truckhouses if they wished. Trade
and peace were still closely linked.

In the decade following the Treaty of 1752, events unfolded
unhappily for the Mi'kmaq and other First Nations of the Maritime region. The British increased their pressure on allies of the
French by renewing the demand that Acadians take the oath of
allegiance to the British king. The continuing Acadian refusal to

take the oath led British forces in 1755 to initiate the expulsion of the Acadians, the wholesale deportation of the people who were close to the Mi'kmaq of peninsular Nova Scotia. Three years later, the French fortress at Louisbourg fell again to the British, this time for good, and in the following two years, British victories at Quebec and Montreal sealed the fate of New France. The weakened state in which the Mi'kmaq found themselves after the defeat of their long-time ally and the removal of most of the missionaries who had been instruments of French policy, was also reflected in the treaties that a number of Mi'kmaq bands made with the British in 1760–1.

Where the Treaty of Boston had contained a full statement of continuing gathering rights, and the 1752 agreement had restored peace and articulated a broad right of trade, the post-hostilities treaties seemed to embody the weakened position in which the Mi'kmaq found themselves:

> And I do promise for myself and my tribe that we will not either directly or indirectly, assist any of the enemies of His most Sacred Majesty King George the third his Heirs or Successors, nor hold any manner of Commerce Taffick nor intercourse with them, but on the contrary will as much as may be in our power Discover and make known to His Majesty's Governor any ill designs which may be formed or contrived against His Majesty's Subjects.
>
> And I do further Engage that we will not Traffick, Barter, or Exchange any Commodities in any manner, but with such person or the Managers of such Truckhouses as shall be appointed or established by His Majesty's Governor at Fort Cumberland or elsewhere in Nova Scotia.[48]

Trade and peace were still tied together, but now in a way that suggested reduced Mi'kmaq autonomy.

The severity of the post-war treaty language was mitigated by continuing Mi'kmaq strength in many parts of the Maritime region and by strong oral tradition among the Mi'kmaq that their rights were more expansive than were recorded by the treaty documents British governors produced. In 1999 the Supreme Court of Canada in the *Marshall* decision found that these treaties represented a continuing Mi'kmaq right to gather to make a modest livelihood, thereby settling in effect the dissonance between oral tradition and European documents in favour of the former.[49]

In other theatres of the struggle that Europeans knew as the Seven Years' War and the Thirteen Colonists referred to, tellingly, as the French and Indian War, traditional alliances were also severely tested. In particular, France's allies of the far western posts, the Ohio and Illinois country, and the settlements of the *domiciliés* in the St Lawrence valley fought valiantly in the early part of the contest. British dominance of the sea lanes, however, forced France to abandon many of its more distant outposts and fall back on its Laurentian and Acadian bastions. When these, too, fell to the British, again owing more to sea power than mastery in land wars, groups such as the Ottawa, Algonquin, western Huron, *domiciliés*, and others found the venerable relationships they had established with His Most Christian Majesty through Onontio undercut. As the 1760s opened, First Nations from the Atlantic to the upper Great Lakes faced an uncertain future, both in terms of trade links and alliances.

3

'And whereas it is just and reasonable...':[1] The Royal Proclamation and the Upper Canadian Treaties

The Royal Proclamation of 1763 that mopped up some of the details left by the British victory in the Seven Years' War opened a new chapter in treaty-making between Aboriginal peoples and the British Crown. The Proclamation attempted to regulate relations between First Nations and settlers in the northeastern portion of North America, and set out conditions under which Indian lands could legally be acquired. The objective in both instances was to restore peaceful relations between First Nations in the interior of the continent and Great Britain. Its result, however, was to establish a long-lasting regime for negotiating land concessions that shaped the third phase of treaty-making with consequences still felt in Canada in the twenty-first century. The Royal Proclamation became the single most important document in the history of treaty-making in Canada. And no one was happier with the Proclamation's clauses dealing with Indians and their lands than Britain's superintendent of Indians in the Northern Department, Sir William Johnson.

For Johnson the summer of 1764 was an anxious, though hopeful, time, in contrast to the unrelieved stress and trouble of the previous years. Now that the Seven Years' War was over, he could look forward to getting back to reaping the profits of the Indian trade in the interior region south of the lower Great Lakes, on which he had originally made his fortune. There was more to the summer's events, however, than the prospects of renewed trade and profit. Sir William was a wealthy landowner and successful trader in the Mohawk Valley of New York as well as an Indian Affairs official. Since his appointment as superintendent in 1755, he had devoted his many talents to holding the Indians of the northern region, including several of the nations of the Iroquois Confederacy with whom he had close relations, to friendship and support of Britain. Simultaneously, as circumstances permitted, he had attempted to woo the western nations who were the long-standing trading partners and allies of the French and *Canadiens*. As 1764 approached, a major problem he faced was an Indian war of resistance that raged in the interior. In pursuit of good relations with the Indians, Johnson had long advocated centralization of British Indian policy, generous distribution of presents to potential and actual allies, and energetic measures to protect Indian lands from the encroachments of the rapacious agricultural settlement frontier of the Thirteen Colonies. Finally, many of the policies he favoured had been adopted in the autumn of 1763. (See map 3.)

The Royal Proclamation that was issued in London on 7 October 1763 dealt with many aspects of North American colonial policy, though arguably no part of it was more important than its terms concerning First Nations and their lands. The Proclamation made provisions for territories newly acquired by the Peace of Paris, such as the French colony of Canada on the St Lawrence, which Britain renamed Quebec. In addition to establishing boundaries and rules for new territories, however, the Proclamation took several measures to reassure Indians of Britain's good intentions towards them. (These positive steps were given greater urgency – though they were not inspired by[2] – the widespread Indian war that had broken out in the southern interior, in which a confederacy of Indian groups led by the Shawnee chief Pontiac captured all of Britain's interior posts and killed an estimated 2,000 civilians in reaction to the loss of their ally, France, and insensitive policies by British military administrators.) The 'Indian clauses' of the Proclamation were to have a profound impact on colonial developments, not least because of their formative influence on treaty-making policy.

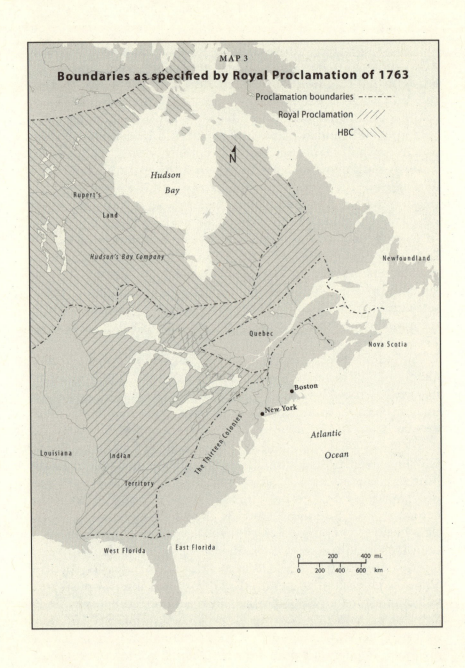

MAP 3

Boundaries as specified by Royal Proclamation of 1763

Proclamation boundaries –·–·–·–
Royal Proclamation /////
HBC \\\\\

N

Hudson
Bay

Rupert's

Land

Hudson's Bay Company

Newfoundland

Quebec

Nova Scotia

Boston

New York

Atlantic

Ocean

Louisiana

Indian

Territory

The Thirteen Colonies

West Florida   East Florida

| 0 | 200 | 400 mi. |
| 0 | 200 | 400 | 600 | km |

Reassuring First Nations about their lands was a key objective of the 'Indian clauses' of the Proclamation. 'And whereas it is just and reasonable and essential to Our Interest and the Security of Our Colonies, that the several Nations or Tribes of Indians, with whom We are connected and who live under Our Protection, should not be molested or disturbed in the Possession of such Parts of our Dominions and Territories as, not having been ceded to, or purchased by Us, are reserved to them, or any of them, as their Hunting Grounds' were the words with which the Proclamation introduced its final five paragraphs dealing with the Indians and their lands. To reassure First Nations and provide for 'the Security of Our Colonies,' the Proclamation forbade settlement by non-Natives on lands west of the Appalachian divide. This interior region had increasingly been a site of conflict before and during the Seven Years' War, as uneasy First Nations saw restive American settlers and traders begin to operate in the West. By striking a line along 'the heads or Sources of any of the Rivers which fall into the Atlantick Ocean from the West and North-West' and forbidding settlement inland of this new Proclamation Line, the new British policy sought to reassure interior First Nations that their lands were secure. In addition, access to this region to trade was conditional: a would-be trader had to obtain a licence from the governor of a colony before crossing the Proclamation Line to trade in Indian country. The Hudson's Bay Company territory known as Rupert's Land was explicitly excluded from the Proclamation's provisions.

Britain was aware that there were good reasons why First Nations should be concerned about their lands. The Proclamation noted that 'great Frauds and Abuses have been committed in the purchasing Lands of the Indians, to the great Prejudice of Our Interests, and the great Dissatisfaction of the said Indians,' and it proposed 'to prevent such Irregularities for the future.' The phrase 'great Frauds and Abuses' was an allusion to a favourite trick of colonial land companies and frontier entrepreneurs who by dubious means obtained a deed from some member or members of an Indian community – perhaps by the use of inducements such as bribery and alcohol – and then claimed the document was sufficient title to the lands. Needless to say, such trickery had caused anger, and sometimes violence, against non-Natives in Indian country. To counter frauds and abuses over Indian territory, the Proclamation laid down rigid requirements governing acquisition of Indian lands. First, 'no private Person' was allowed 'to make any Purchase from the said Indians of any Lands reserved to the said Indians, within those Parts of Our Colonies where We have thought proper to allow Settlement.' In the event that a First Nation chose to dispose of some of its lands, they 'shall be purchased only for Us, in Our Name, at some public Meeting or Assembly of the said Indians to be held for that Purpose by the Governor or Commander in Chief of Our Colonies respectively within which they shall lie.'[3]

Collectively, the 'Indian clauses' of the Royal Proclamation of 1763 were intended to reassure both Britain's Indian allies and the former allies of France who resided in what Europeans now considered British territory that their territorial rights would be respected. At the time this policy initiative – a measure that had been developing for at least a decade – was a pacific gesture aimed at First Nations. Historically it has become even more important as the foundation of Britain's treaty-making policy in Canada. The limitation that only the Crown or its representative could treat with First Nations for land, that negotiations about acquiring Indian lands must take place publicly, and that other members of the First Natio 1 community should be aware of what was being considered would evolve over time into the protocol that was generally followed by the British and later Canadian governments in negotiating with First Nations for land. The Royal Proclamation, as a result, became a vitally important document in the history of treaty-making.

For administrators of Indian policy such as Sir William Johnson, the Royal Proclamation was a godsend. It responded to legitimate grievances among First Nations that had jeopardized relations for many years, and it laid down rules that, if followed consistently, would avoid trouble in future. On a personal level, Johnson acted in concert with the new policy by securing a grant of land from the Mohawk in 1769 to legitimize his occupation of

S.ʳ William Johnson Baᵗ.

Major General of the English Forces in North America.

3.1 Sir William Johnson, forest diplomat

the extensive territory in the Mohawk Valley on which Johnson
Hall and his many other buildings stood.[4] The Indian superintendent realized that the new policy, though promising for the
future, did not remove all major irritants. 'This Proclamation,'
he wrote, 'does not relieve their present greiviances [sic] which
are many, being calculated only to prevent the like hereafter.'
Nonetheless, when he used the Proclamation with the Six
Nations in a conference during the winter of 1763–4, it was effective in persuading the Iroquois that British intentions towards
them were positive. At that meeting, he argued successfully that
the Proclamation demonstrated the king's 'gracious & favorable
disposition to do them Justice,' and in future he proposed to
'communicate the same to all the rest of the Indians.'[5] He saw to
it that the Proclamation's terms were made known widely to First
Nations, and he began to organize a vast conference with First
Nation leaders the next summer at Niagara.[6] At such a conference, he advised Britain's acting commander-in-chief, General
Thomas Gage, 'we should tye them down ... according to their
own forms of which they take the most notice, for Example by
Exchanging a very large belt with some remarkable & intelligible
figures thereon.' What he had in mind was 'a Treaty of Offensive
& Defensive Alliance' that would, among many things, 'assure
them of A Free fair & open Trade, at the principal Posts, & a free
intercourse, & passage into our Country, That we will make no
Settlements or Encroachments contrary to Treaty, or without
their permission.'[7]

Johnson carried out his plan at Niagara in the summer of 1764.
A vast assemblage of more than 2,000 leaders from twenty-four
First Nations scattered across most of eastern North America
gathered to treat with the king's Indian superintendent. Several
outstanding issues with a number of nations, especially with First
Nations who had been close allies of the French, were resolved,
and all those represented at the Niagara Conference were admitted to the Covenant Chain of friendship and alliance. At the
climax of the conference, Sir William presented the Indians with
'a large Belt with a Figure representing Niagara's large House,
and Fort, with two Men holding it fast on each side, and a Road

through it.' To 'the Western Nations,' in particular, he said, 'I desire you will take fast Hold of the same, and never let it slip, to which end I desire that after you have shewn this Belt to all Nations you will fix one end of it with the Chipaweighs at St. Mary's [Sault Ste Marie] whilst the other end remains at my House.'[8] In effect, the British were trying to assume the place of the French in that alliance with western Indian nations. Another interesting example of continuity was the use of wampum. Using these indigenous devices to record the important pact for First Nations was an example of the bicultural practice that by now was common in eighteenth-century treaty-making. The protocols involved were ones of which the Indian superintendent was a master. So far as Johnson was concerned, this agreement concluded at Niagara was intended to be the 'Treaty of Offensive & Defensive Alliance' he hoped would 'tye' First Nations to Britain with bonds of friendship and mutual support.

The Royal Proclamation did not lead to a total abandonment of the practice of concluding treaties of peace and friendship. Indeed, the anxious last months of the Seven Years' War had provided both an opportunity and a need for some of the *domiciliés*, or First Nations in the St Lawrence valley who had been allied with the French, to enter into agreements guaranteeing amicable relations in future. As early as the autumn of 1759, William Johnson had approached the mostly Onondaga population at Oswegatchie, near present-day Ogdensburg, New York, to drop their support of the French. For the British, neutralizing this group was important because they were located on the St Lawrence River, a transportation route vital to imperial plans to complete the conquest of Canada in 1760. Not only did the British diplomatic overture persuade the Iroquois at Onondaga, but representatives of Kanesatake and Kahnawake also entered into an agreement to cease supporting the French and to live in harmony with the British henceforth. On the other hand, a similar diplomatic overture to the Abenaki *domiciliés* at Odanak in French territory resulted in the British emissaries being taken prisoner by Indians, who obviously were not interested in normalizing relations with His Britannic Majesty.[9]

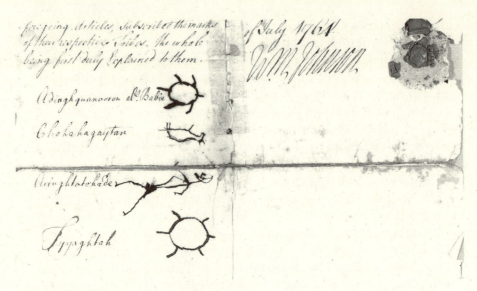

3.2 Signature panel of treaty with a former French ally, 1764

As the fighting in the St Lawrence valley had drawn to a conclusion with the capitulation of Montreal in 1760, more hastily
negotiated pacts of friendship were agreed to by erstwhile Indian
allies of the French and the victorious British. The most significant of these treaties of peace and friendship was what became
known as the Murray Treaty of 1760. In the early autumn, as
General James Murray advanced towards Montreal from Quebec,
he was approached by a delegation of *domiciliés* Huron seeking
peace. The swiftly negotiated agreement that ensued was
recorded in a document guaranteeing safe passage that Murray
gave to the Huron of Lorette. Not only did this document assure
the Huron safe passage through British-controlled territory, it
also said that 'they are received on the same terms with the Canadians, being allowed the free Exercise of their Religion, their
Customs and liberty of trading with the English Garrisons.'[10]
Here, again, Britain was stepping into the role previously played
by the French, continuing respect for indigenous practices and
trade ties. Though little remarked at the time, the Murray Treaty

flared into prominence and notoriety in 1990. The Supreme
Court of Canada in a decision known as *Sioui* upheld the right of
the Huron band at Lorette to enter a provincial park and cut
saplings for ceremonial use in spite of a provincial legal prohibition on such actions. Arguing that the 1760 document was a
treaty protected by the Canadian constitution, the high court
held that it superseded provincial law. The ruling was controversial, being scorned particularly by Quebec nationalists. On the
other hand, other scholars have argued vigorously that it was a
genuine treaty. They point out that the Murray Treaty conformed
to a long-standing British policy of concluding peace treaties with
First Nations, and it referred explicitly to the Huron as 'allies'
('sujets et alliés'), in contrast to references to the *Canadiens* only
as subjects ('sujets'). The formulation 'sujets et alliés,' they point
out, was standard language in other contemporary treaties with
First Nations.[11]

Peace pacts such as the Murray Treaty aside, the protocol for
acquiring First Nations land that the Royal Proclamation out-
lined came at a propitious moment. British authorities in the
eastern part of North America would soon find it necessary to
make a series of Indian treaties whose purpose was the acquisition of First Nations' lands. Indeed, Sir William Johnson had
found himself initiating such a process even before the grand
gathering at Niagara in July and August 1764. During the early
stages of Pontiac's war of resistance, the British had learned
painfully how tenuous their communication links to the inflamed
interior were. In the summer of 1763, the Seneca had attacked a
military expedition bound inland to supply Britain's posts. The
loss of goods and more than seventy men a short distance down-
stream from the falls underlined the critical and vulnerable
nature of the vital portage at Niagara. Dealing with the Seneca,
especially during Pontiac's War, was ticklish. As 'the keepers of
the western door,' the Seneca were forced to try to maintain good
relations with the pro-French Indian nations beyond their lands.
Taking advantage of the fact that the Seneca were short of food
in the spring of 1764, Johnson met them at Niagara and negotiated a treaty that contained many concessions, including their

agreement to 'cede to His Maj[es]ty and his successors for ever' a strip of land four miles (approx. 6.4 km) on either side of the Niagara River. The procedure of negotiating in open council for land followed the letter of the six-month-old Royal Proclamation of 1763; the coercion involved in the process and the punitive nature of the terms did not, however, conform to the spirit of the policy.[12]

The treaty process pioneered at Niagara to obtain Seneca lands for the Crown was merely a preliminary to several phases of territorial treaty-making in what became Upper Canada between the Proclamation and the middle of the nineteenth century. Two forces drove this long process of dispossessing the indigenous occupiers of their lands by treaty: American pressure and immigration to British North America. The American colonists regarded the western lands beyond the Proclamation Line as their undeniable birthright, and they would not be thwarted for long in their desire to move westward in search of lands for agricultural expansion and trade. An augury of the future – Proclamation or not – had come in 1768, when Sir William Johnson persuaded the Indians to accept the Treaty of Fort Stanwix. This agreement effectively moved the boundary of territory open to settlement further west in New York and Pennsylvania, appeasing somewhat the land hunger of the colonists. For their part, the Six Nations accepted the new line, believing – vainly it proved – that it was permanent.[13] But the successful revolt of the Thirteen Colonies against British rule in the War of the American Revolution, 1775–83, freed them from the restraint of British policy. In the decade after the Revolution, the United States had to contend with sporadic resistance, often encouraged by the British, from western Indian nations. An American military victory over western Indians at the Battle of Fallen Timbers in 1794 effectively put an end to First Nations resistance as well.

Indian nations tried repeatedly to hold their lands – by Pontiac's War in the 1760s, by allying themselves with the British during the Revolutionary War, and ultimately by siding with the British and Upper Canadians in the War of 1812. In all these cases, they were fighting against the movement of the agricultural frontier westward. Pontiac's call to arms in the 1760s had captured the antipathy of the interior Indians to expansive American agriculture: 'And as for these English, – these dogs dressed in red, – who have come to rob you of your hunting grounds, and drive away the game, – you must lift the hatchet against them. Wipe them from the face of the earth, and thus you will win my favour back again, and once more be happy and prosperous.'[14] Though both sides, American and British, frequently accused the other of 'using' Indians in war against each other, the truth of the matter was that First Nations chose the side with which they would fight, or in some cases chose not to fight at all, based on their calculations of what was in their own interest. The tragedy of the situation was that, although most Indians fought against the expansionist Americans on many occasions between 1763 and 1814, they lost every time. The triumph of the westward-moving agrarian frontier displaced First Nations by force south of the lower Great Lakes, and in many cases they sought new homes north of the Lakes, in territory the British considered theirs, in British North America.

For their own reasons, the British encouraged and sometimes supported the First Nations' resistance in the interior. It suited British interests to retard American expansion, and planners in London even dreamed fondly at times of helping to create an Indian territory south of the lower Great Lakes that would act as a buffer between the United States and British territory to the north. Even following the Battle of Fallen Timbers, Britain quietly encouraged continuing resistance, although now the American victory over the Indians and the negotiation of the Jay Treaty in 1794 that normalized relations between themselves and the Americans required them to be more circumspect in their support of the Indian opponents of the expansionist republic. Great Britain and its Indian Department in North America pursued this slippery policy down to the eve of the War of 1812, quietly encouraging First Nations to resist but not taking overt action that would violate their treaty with the Americans. Unfortunately for the interior Indians, U.S. power and ambition were simply too great. Repeatedly they had to give ground before the victorious American farmers.

From a British perspective, First Nations refugees moving away from the advancing American farm frontier were merely the first of several groups of migrants who would populate Upper Canada. They, along with later non-Native immigrants from Great Britain, created a dramatic need for access to lands nominally under the control of the Mississauga, an Anicinabe people. Britain was motivated to negotiate territorial treaties, in part, because of the necessity created by the Royal Proclamation of 1763, in part, because of a guilty conscience, and, in part, because it recognized that negotiation was the prudent approach to take in dealing with First Nations north of the lower Great Lakes.

After the American Revolution, the Battle of Fallen Timbers, when British officers shut the gates of Fort Miami in the face of Indian warriors fleeing General 'Mad Anthony' Wayne, and the War of 1812, Britain found that the anger of its Indian allies threatened them directly. Following the Treaty of Versailles of 1783, by which Britain blithely surrendered Indian lands to the Americans as part of the peace, they were upbraided by angry Indian leaders. One chief told a British official, 'They were allies of the King, not subjects; and would not submit to such treatment ... If England had done so it was an act of cruelty and injustice and capable only of *Christians*.'[15] After the disgraceful affair at Fort Miami in 1794, Joseph Brant, a major Mohawk leader, bitterly observed 'this is the second time the poor Indians have been left in the lurch.'[16]

By the 1780s, with the horror of Pontiac's War a fresh memory, Britain knew only too well what angry and disappointed First Nations who were disillusioned with their treatment by Europeans might do. A shamefaced British Indian Department consequently negotiated for new lands on which to settle their angry allies, and turned to the Mississauga for access to their lands, first in the immediate aftermath of the end of the Revolutionary War. In light of the twenty-first-century argument by Mohawk in Ontario that a clause in the Albany agreement (or Nanfan

Treaty) of 1701 gave them a territorial interest north of the lower Great Lakes, one aspect of Mississauga-Crown negotiations in the 1780s and 1790s is striking. If the Albany agreement had protected Iroquois territorial rights north of the lower Lakes, it was to be expected that officials would involve Iroquois leaders in negotiations with the Anicinabe. But Britain never considered involving the Six Nations in these talks. Joseph Brant, it is true, contended that discussions with the Mississauga were unnecessary because the Mohawk were the true owners of the lands on the upper St Lawrence.[17] Neither British officials nor the Mississauga said or did anything that indicated they thought any group but the Anicinabe had a claim to the lands to which Britain hoped to move displaced Loyalists and First Nations allies. On at least one occasion in 1783, 'three Onandaga Chiefs lately from Montreal were present [at negotiations between the Mississauga and the Crown] and approved much of what the Missasaugas had done.'[18]

In 1783–4, as the Revolutionary War was ending and the flow of Loyalists across the border increasing, Britain initiated a series of territorial treaties north of the lower Great Lakes and St Lawrence River. The prime consideration was obtaining lawful access to lands on which to settle recent allies of the war against the American rebels. The primary zones for expected Loyalist settlement were the regions from the eastern part of Lake Ontario to the Ottawa River, the Niagara Peninsula, and adjacent lands north of the eastern part of Lake Erie. (See map 4.) Of particular concern to British officials such as General Frederick Haldimand was making provision for Iroquois who had fought with them. Initially, it was expected that some of the allied Haudenosaunee would be settled along the St Lawrence across from established mission sites such as Oswegatchie and Akwesasne. The Indians in the easternmost part of the territory, however, surprised British officials by indicating that they would not object to sharing the district with non-Native comrades. As a result, the most easterly townships of what would become Upper Canada were dominated numerically by non-Natives. Another

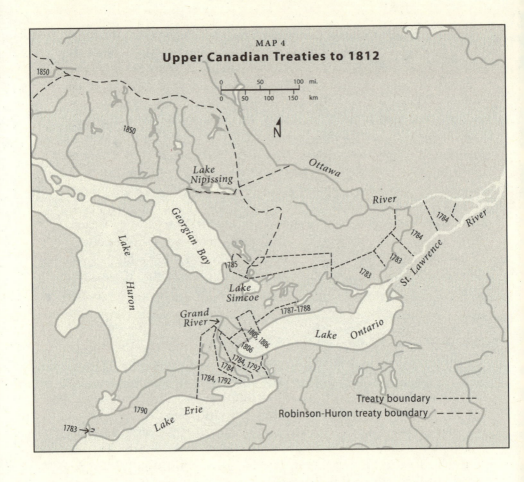

part of the initial plan had been to settle the Mohawk led by Captain Joseph Brant and Captain John Deserontyon together in a large tract in the Bay of Quinte area on eastern Lake Ontario. However, plans soon changed, with Deserontyon and his followers going to Tyendinaga, near present-day Belleville, and Brant's community being granted a large concession along the Grand River, which flowed into Lake Erie. Non-Native refugees were settled principally along the St Lawrence at or near sites that developed as Cornwall, Brockville, and Kingston (formerly Cataraqui or Fort Frontenac).

If the motivation of the United Kingdom in initiating the territorial treaties in 1783–4 is straightforward, the reasons why the Mississauga acceded to British overtures and entered into a series of treaties are comparatively obscure. No doubt one consideration was that the numbers of proposed settlers did not seem a threat: the future Upper Canada was so huge that the roughly 6,000 incoming Loyalists could easily be accommodated. From the Aboriginal perspective, Loyalist settlers were not menacing in another sense. Those who had opposed the formation of the new American republic would undoubtedly bring their hostility to the victorious Americans with them. If First Nations continued to fear the land hunger and expansionism of the new American republic, augmenting the population in British territory north of the lakes with sturdy pro-British settlers would be attractive. The mostly Onondaga population at Oswegatchie, near present-day Johnstown in eastern Ontario, for example, agreed in 1784 to make '"the Front of the Water [the St Lawrence]"' available in order to '"give lands to the troops."'[19] And the Crown negotiator of an important 1783 agreement along the St Lawrence River reported that the 'Missassagues appear much satisfyed [sic] with the white people incoming to live among them.'[20] Finally, entering into treaty represented a way for the Mississauga to get access to a large amount of British goods.

Whatever the precise motives of the parties to these early territorial treaties, the contents of the agreements were clear and simple. The area covered by the 1783–4 treaties with the Mississauga stretched from the last French seigneury just west of where the Ottawa River joined the St Lawrence to what is now Prince Edward County, near the Bay of Quinte on Lake Ontario. Another large block of land included the Niagara Peninsula stretching far to the northwest and on the west to a north-south boundary that met the shore of Lake Erie west of Long Point.

A number of distinctive features characterized these treaties in the future Upper Canada. British negotiators continued the use of Aboriginal protocol that had been such a prominent feature of both commercial agreements and treaties of peace and friendship earlier. Captain Crawford, for example, reported from the St Lawrence in 1783 that after negotiating with the Mississauga, 'a large one [wampum belt] was Delivered to the other Chiefs concerned in the Sale, with the usual ceremonys [*sic*] to be kept in the nation [as] a memorial to their Children that they may know what their Fathers had done at this Time.'[21] Britain also stepped up the presentation of medals in association with these territorial treaties. Medal-giving, initiated in 1714 following the Treaty of Utrecht, had another period of popularity, as Britain issued medals to chiefs following Pontiac's War and again to those who had been allied with them after the Revolutionary War. The practice carried over to the territorial treaties that soon followed peace in the 1780s. Medals bearing a likeness of George III were numerous during the period of the early territorial treaties.[22]

The early Upper Canadian treaties also had distinctive geographic features. They all fronted on major waterways – the St Lawrence, Lake Ontario, the Niagara River, or Lake Erie – for the simple reason that rivers and lakes were the highways on which people travelled in these regions. The depth of the treaties back from the water varied considerably. One memorable 1783 agreement, known as the Crawford Purchase, referred to lands 'extending from the Lake Back as far as a man can Travel in a Day.'[23] (Such a descriptor was not unique: the Indians referred to a 1787 treaty west of the Bay of Quinte area as the 'Gunshot Treaty' because it covered land stretching back from Lake Ontario as far as the report of a firearm could be heard on a clear day.)[24] Eventually the northern boundary of the Crawford Purchase was struck two or three townships inland.[25] Since a township was nine miles (14 km) in length from south to north and there were no roads to speak of in Upper Canada at this time, this represented quite a day's travel for a person. The 1784 treaty that embraced the Niagara Peninsula and lands north of the eastern part of Lake Erie comprised a vast area of fertile, though largely wooded, lands that amounted to more than 1,000,000 hectares (2,471,054 acres).

In return for such large areas covered by the Crawford Purchase and the other 1783–4 agreements, the Mississauga received a specified quantity of goods. The chiefs who dealt with Captain Crawford in the Bay of Quinte 'Demanded ... that all the Familys [*sic*] Belonging to them shall be clothed and that those that have not Fusees [*sic*; i.e., firearms] shall Recive [*sic*] new ones, Some powder and Ball for their winter's hunting as much coarse Red Cloth as will make about a Dozen Coats and as many Laced[?] hats. This I have promised them ...'[26] Presumably, the hats and coats were for the leaders of the Indians, such gifts being traditional markers of headship. The 1784 treaty in the Niagara–Lake Erie region cost the British Crown £1,180 in goods. These payments in kind, which were found in all the early Upper Canadian treaties, were one-time concessions only.

Securing the early treaties in 1783–4 facilitated the settlement of non-Native Loyalists and conciliated Native allies at the same time. Loyalist towns were established at such places as New Johnstown (Cornwall), Brockville, and Newark (now Niagara-on-the-Lake). The largely Onondaga population of Oswegatchie agreed to the settlement of Loyalist veterans on the waterfront. Equally important, the agreement eased relations with resident First Nations, who might have been expected to be uneasy in the aftermath of American military victory and British diplomatic betrayal. In this respect, the early treaties facilitated good relations between Natives and newcomers in Upper Canada. The treaties also smoothed the way for resettlement of First Nations who had fought with the Crown against the rebellious Americans. Tyendinaga was established near present-day Belleville for Captain John Deserontyon and his followers. In the vast treaty area that included the Niagara Peninsula and territory north of Lake Erie, Governor Haldimand made a grant of lands stretching back ten miles (16 km) on both sides of the Grand River from its source to its outlet on Lake Erie for Captain Joseph Brant and his approximately 2,000 Six Nations followers. Although both Tyendinaga and Six Nations would be whittled down in area in the early nineteenth century in response to non-Native settlement and desire for reserve lands, these remain important, though shrunken, centres of First Nations presence and influence in Ontario in the twenty-first century.

The 1783–4 flurry of treaty-making by no means concluded the process of obtaining access to First Nations land in the region north of the St Lawrence River and the lower Great Lakes. A number of treaties were made in the 1780s, not all of them following procedures that met the requirements of the Royal Proclamation of 1763. In particular, several of the agreements reached in the 1780s were flawed by the Crown negotiators' failure to document precisely what had been agreed upon.[27] In 1785 a John Collins apparently secured a two-mile (3 km) strip along a traditional path from the Narrows of Lake Simcoe (present-day Orillia) to Matchedash Bay near Georgian Bay. Collins's account of the negotiations is incomplete, the area covered is vague, and specific compensation was apparently not included.[28] The region in question was embraced by another treaty properly made by a Crown representative in 1815. Treaty 13, made in 1787 at the Carrying Place on the Bay of Quinte, left blanks where descriptions of territory should have appeared.[29] A set of transactions in 1787 and 1788 supposedly secured access to an extensive area along the north shore of Lake Ontario from the Bay of Quinte to what is now Toronto, and from the lake approximately fifteen or sixteen miles (24 or 25 km) inland for the Crown.[30] Unfortunately, the document recording the agreement did not contain a description of the area, a deficiency that the lieutenant-governor of Upper Canada, John Graves Simcoe, pointed out in 1794. Since the Mississauga of the region did not seem perturbed about the situation, officialdom left matters alone. The legal deficiency would be corrected more than a century later in what are known as the Williams Treaties (1923).

In 1794, Governor General Dorchester attempted to regularize procedures and ensure that transactions were carried out more carefully in future. He issued instructions that henceforth territorial treaties were to be negotiated only by senior representatives of the Crown and only 'in public Council with great Solemnity and Ceremony according to the Antient Usages and Customs of the Indians, the Principal Chiefs and leading Men of the Nation or Nations to whom the lands belong being first assembled.' Moreover, the Crown representative 'will employ for the purpose such Interpreters as best understand the Language of the Nation or Nations treated with,' and a copy of treaty 'is to be delivered to the Indians, who by that means will always be able to ascertain what they have sold and future Uneasiness and Discontents be thereby avoided.'[31] Thereafter, treaty-making practice in Upper Canada improved, although adherence to Royal Proclamation procedures was never perfect.

The intense treaty-making activity in the region was attributable to a steady trickle of non-Native settlement, largely from the United States, which would increase in the 1790s. Britain recognized that population growth west of the Ottawa River was creating a society there that was different in religion and language from that to the east, and established the region as the colony of Upper Canada by the Constitutional Act in 1791. The provision came none too soon because international events in the 1790s were going to have an impact on groups who would want to move into Upper Canada. In 1794, by the Jay Treaty, Great Britain normalized relations with the United States that had been strained by British retention of a series of posts south of the lower Great Lakes. London had excused itself for the violation of the Treaty of Versailles by claiming that it was retaining the posts because the Americans were not honouring claims of Loyalists, as had also been required by the peace of 1783. In reality, Britain stayed at posts such as Oswego, Niagara, and Detroit largely to keep Indian allies from erupting in another version of Pontiac's War. As the years passed, Whitehall also flirted with the notion of encouraging the emergence of an Indian buffer state south of the Great Lakes that would keep the Americans in check and insulate British North America to some extent. Such a strategy would work only as long as Britain's First Nations allies in the south were a credible military force, but the American victory over them at the Battle of Fallen Timbers in 1794 made it clear that Indian resistance in this portion of the new republic had been crushed forever. Britain's response was to enter into the Jay Treaty, by which it agreed finally to vacate the western posts.

This diplomatic concession set off a chain reaction among First Nations allies of Britain in affected regions, and then in Upper

Canada. The Onondaga at Oswegatchie on the south shore of the
upper St Lawrence, for example, soon found themselves dispossessed by the Americans once the British military presence was
withdrawn from nearby Fort Oswego. Similarly, in the part of the
United States west of Lake Erie and Lake St Clair, many non-
Native settlers had stayed in American territory because of the
British military presence at Detroit. There was also intermittent
movement of settlers into the southwestern peninsula of Upper
Canada in the early years, some of it resulting in the occupation
of First Nations territory where no treaty was yet in force. Indeed,
Britain made treaty provisions in this territory early on by concluding a small treaty in 1783 across the Detroit River in British
territory, and then securing a large strip along the shore of Lake
Erie from the Detroit River to the site west of Long Point where
the Niagara area treaty ended. Such provisions, though provident, would prove inadequate to deal with the consequences of
the Jay Treaty in the Fort Detroit area.

Roughly 3,000 Indian allies wanted to move out of American
territory after the withdrawal of British troops from Detroit. They
were settled in an area east of Lake St Clair by a treaty in 1796 for
£800 worth of goods. In the same year, an agreement for a tract
near the forks of the Thames River, where a small number of non-
Natives had already located without benefit of treaty, was confirmed between the Mississauga and the Crown for £1,200 in
goods. Lieutenant-Governor Simcoe wanted these lands to relocate Upper Canada's capital from Niagara-on-the-Lake, which he
believed was vulnerable to American attack, inland to the forks of
the Thames River. The townsite of London was established, but
the capital never moved there.

The final disruption caused to First Nations by the Jay Treaty
occurred in the relatively remote region where Lake Huron,
Lake Michigan, and Lake Superior were linked by water routes.
The strategically important point in this region was Fort Michilimackinac, which commanded transportation routes to the west
and northwest. The British had negotiated a treaty for the island
of Michilimackinac with the Ojibwa in 1781 for a large quantity
of goods, but this base, too, now lay within American territory.

After conclusion of the Jay Treaty, Britain recognized that it had to make alternative arrangements for a gathering point at which to distribute presents and negotiate arrangements with its Indian allies. In 1798, two years after Britain moved its garrison from Michilimackinac to St Joseph Island in western Lake Huron, the Crown and local Anicinabe agreed to a treaty 'selling and disposing' of St Joseph Island to George III, 'our Great Father,' for 'twelve hundred pounds Quebec currency value in goods estimated according to the Montreal price delivered to us.' The agreement was signed by Alexander McKee, deputy superintendent general of Indian affairs, for the Crown, while seven Anicinabe chiefs drew their totems on the document for the local population.[32]

(The following year, a similar transaction took place between western Ojibwa at Thunder Bay and representatives of the Montreal-based fur-trading company. The leaders stated that 'in consideration of the good Will, Love and affection which we and the whole of our Tribe bear unto Simon Mactavish, Joseph Frobisher, John Gregory, William McGillivary and Alexander Mackenzie' and 'Three Pounds current money,' and 'also for divers other good causes and valuable considerations,' they gave the Nor'westers 'a tract of land' running five miles (8 km) along Thunder Bay on either side of the mouth of the Kaministiquia River and stretching twelve miles (19 km) back from the lake.[33] However, since the Montreal-based traders, unlike the leaders of the Hudson's Bay Company, did not represent the Crown, this agreement was not, strictly speaking, a treaty. All the same, it was significant that even within the fur-trade relationship, non-Natives had begun to seek formal agreements to give them control of Aboriginal land.)

Additional territorial treaties were negotiated in the late 1790s and early nineteenth century to make provision for principally non-Native settlers in Upper Canada. From Britain's perspective, while making lands attractive to immigrants to Upper Canada was important, the continuing numerical strength and strategic importance of First Nations to the United Kingdom meant the

interests of the indigenous peoples had to be taken into account.
Upper Canadian settlement was changing, as could be seen in
two developments. First, the areas of treaty negotiation in 1805
and 1806 covered parts of the lakefront further west than the
Loyalist territory from the Bay of Quinte to the province's eastern
border. Treaties in those years dealt with First Nations' territorial
rights from Toronto to Burlington Bay, known at the time as
Head of the Lake. The other sign that settlement was proceeding
apace was that Crown negotiators began to encounter more
Native resistance and greater demands during negotiations. In
1794 some Indians along the Thames got into a dispute with
provincial surveyor Augustus Jones, denying Jones's assertion
that their lands had been surrendered by another chief. A short
time later, they said to two other Indians 'that the English were
nearly as bad as the Americans in taking away their lands, and in
consequence of which they would take cattle where they could
find them, in lieu of Deer.' In the end, Jones had been able to
smooth things over with this group.[34]

A few years later, the Mississauga of Rice Lake and the Credit
River complained to Peter Russell, the provincial administrator
who succeeded John Graves Simcoe, that settlers were infring-
ing on their fisheries. After an investigation, Russell issued a
'Proclamation to Protect the Fishing Places and Burying
Grounds of the Mississagas' that began, 'Whereas, many heavy
and grievous complaints have of late been made by the Mississaga Indians, of depredations committed by some of His
Majesty's subjects and others upon their fisheries and burial
places, and of other annoyances suffered by them by uncivil
treatment, in violation of the friendship existing between His
Majesty and the Mississaga Indians.' The Crown committed
itself to investigate such complaints in future and to act 'with
the utmost severity' against settlers found to be intruding on
indigenous rights.[35]

Not all First Nations in Upper Canada resisted treaty-making,
but even those who entered negotiations now tended to be more
demanding than earlier groups had been. The Mississauga did
not request concessions for the 1805 treaty in the Toronto area,

because their collective memory was that they had agreed in 1787 to allow non-Natives to settle there. They were much more concerned, though, about a treaty covering the lakefront from Toronto to the west end of Lake Ontario. By the time the question of treating for this land arose in the late 1790s, they were upset with settler encroachments on Mississauga land and fishing places. They were also angered by the murder, which went unpunished, of one of their chiefs by a non-Native man.[36] When treaty talks for the Head of the Lake Treaty did occur in the first decade of the nineteenth century, the Mississauga had a series of requirements, most notably retention of sites for their fishery at the mouths of a number of rivers and streams that flowed into Lake Ontario. They were no longer willing to accept bland assurances of future cooperation, because they had already found that settlers in some parts of the colony had insisted on exclusive use of the lakeshore, forcing the Mississauga to stop using important waterfront property. After stiff negotiations, a deal was worked out for the land from Toronto to Burlington Bay in return for £1,000 worth of goods and reservation of lands at five fishing sites.[37]

An 1811 set of treaty negotiations at Port Hope, on the shore of Lake Ontario east of York (Toronto), illustrated how the conditions in which the Upper Canadian treaties were negotiated were shifting. There was continuity in the rhetoric employed by Crown negotiator James Givins: 'Children – I am happy to see you, and I return thanks to the Great Spirit, that has been pleased to enable us to meet at this place in good health. Children – I am sent by Your Father the Governor to make an agreement with you for the purchase of a small piece of land, the plan of which I now lay before you ... Children – As your women and children must be hungry, I have brought some of Your Great Father's Bread and milk, and some ammunition for your young men, which I will give you before we hear this.' The speech-making and present-giving continued the use of traditional protocol, although now with an implied acknowledgment that conditions were worsening for the Mississauga: 'your women and children must be hungry.'[38]

The reaction of the Mississauga also revealed how the context of treaty-making was changing. When the Indian spokesman responded, he complained about 'white people' who 'come and settle in our Islands.' Nonetheless, he indicated that they agreed to the requested cession of land but added: 'Father – We wish to reserve these Islands for our corn[?] fields[?] and we wish you would now give us a writing to show these people that they might be sent off.' He also complained that the 'white people ... cut great quantities of timber ... without our consent. We therefore request that you will take charity upon us, and assist us in turning the white people away.' The Mississauga on this occasion also asked that their compensation include axes and spears, as well as 'a blacksmith to repair and make them for us.'[39] These and other negotiations indicated that by the early nineteenth century in Upper Canada, settler pressure on First Nations lands and resources was beginning to be a problem, and that the First Nations were beginning to resist that pressure in a variety of ways.

The first phase of Upper Canadian treaty-making drew to a close by the end of the first decade of the nineteenth century, a generation after the influx of the Loyalists and more than forty years since promulgation of the Royal Proclamation of 1763. In those four decades, a great deal had been accomplished, and many elements of what would become the Canadian treaty-making tradition had been put in place. By the outbreak of the War of 1812, twelve treaties had given the Crown access to all the land along 'the front,' the most accessible lands along the rivers and lakes that constituted Upper Canada's southern boundary. A thirteenth agreement dealt with St Joseph's Island in the far northwest. These treaties covering vast amounts of territory had been concluded without bloodshed, while adhering, generally speaking, to the protocol for negotiating treaties that had been set out in the Royal Proclamation. In the rush to make agreements in the 1780s, a number of treaties had been made – or at least recorded – so sloppily that their validity was questionable. Indeed, the treaty that dealt with the lakefront from the Bay of Quinte west to Toronto would have to be redone in the twentieth century. The Crown's most senior representatives had responded to early treaty-making deficiencies in 1794 by issuing instructions for treaty negotiations that in part recapitulated the requirements of the Royal Proclamation, and in 1797 by issuing a proclamation intended to protect Mississauga fisheries from settlers' intrusions. It would remain to be seen if those orders would continue to be followed.

One of the most remarkable features of Upper Canadian treaty-making was how cooperative First Nations were for at least the first few decades. Their behaviour suggests that they did not initially see the relatively few newcomers who were seeking land through treaty as a threat, while the treaties' promise to deliver material goods was obviously attractive. But by the early years of the nineteenth century, conditions had begun to change, as the pressure of settlement started to impinge seriously on First Nations. The events preceding the negotiation of the Head of the Lake Treaty in 1805–6 and the request from a band in 1811 for 'a writing to show these people,' settlers who took their resources without consent, 'that they might be sent off,' suggest that as time went on settlers were increasingly encroaching on Aboriginal lands. First Nations became distressingly aware that settlers' promises, even those made through the Crown, were unreliable, and that their relationship with the newcomers was deteriorating. In the first phase of treaty-making down to the War of 1812, a major factor underlying the relatively harmonious relations in Upper Canada was the continuing numerical strength and utility of First Nations. In the earliest years of settlement, indigenous people were often useful to the struggling newcomers as sources of information, advice, food, and sometimes labour in making farms.

The first stage of Upper Canadian treaty-making was a transitional phase between the earlier commercial-military period and the looming era of settler dominance. Elements of the old, positive relationship were still present in the Aboriginal protocol that

4

'From our lands we receive scarcely anything':[1] The Upper Canadian Treaties, 1818–1862

As had been the case in the 1780s, the second stage of treaty-making was precipitated by the conclusion of a war. The War of 1812 between Great Britain and the United States was in some ways a replay of the War of the American Revolution. In 1812 the Americans tested the definition of an international boundary that had been negotiated in 1783, but which Britain had not recognized very faithfully in the following decade. From the viewpoint of the First Nations, the War of 1812 was a final opportunity to ally themselves with the British against the Americans in an effort to stem the advancing tide of American western expansion and protect their lands. In 1812 a coalition of interior nations below the Great Lakes, under the leadership of the Shawnee military leader Tecumseh and his brother, The Prophet, joined with First Nations from the Michigan-Wisconsin region and sedentary groups such as the Six Nations and *domiciliés* from Lower Canada to fight alongside British regulars and colonial militias. Their support was critical in 1812–13, a time when Britain had few troops in the colonies and settler loyalties in some districts of Upper Canada were uncertain. British victories such as the fall of Michilimackinac, the surrender of Detroit, and the clashes at Queenston and Beaver Dams owed a great deal to First Nations' military efforts. The death of Tecumseh in the Battle of the Thames in 1813 discouraged the Indians, however, and their military contribution declined. In 1814, when the Treaty of Ghent was signed, Britain's Indian Department in

Canada found itself obligated to make some provision for First Nations allies from south of the border who might want to relocate to British territory.

Within a few years, the demographic situation in Upper Canada would be affected drastically by international developments. First, in 1817, Britain and the United States signed the Rush-Bagot Convention, which demilitarized the Great Lakes. This pact reflected an acceptance of the boundary settlement of 1783, reinforced by the Treaty of Ghent in 1814. For the British, Rush-Bagot both reflected and in turn strengthened a decision by imperial planners to de-emphasize Britain's military alliance with First Nations in what was now American territory. These developments paved the way for normalizing relations between the two countries, and thereby facilitated emigration from Great Britain to British North America. As it happened, once the Napoleonic Wars were over, Britain began exporting large numbers of emigrants. The strategic reasons for keeping a large population at home no longer prevailed now that a major war with France was over, and changes in the economy began to undermine the livelihoods of some industrial and agricultural workers. Both labourers and farm owners in the agricultural sector would be even more adversely affected by changes in the 1840s. In that decade, the Irish potato famine and changes to United Kingdom trade laws dealt both the potato farmers of Ireland and grain producers of England devastating blows.

These strategic, economic, and political factors combined to propel large numbers of Britons to emigrate to British North America (BNA) between 1815 and 1850. The demographic change was reflected in population figures for BNA, in general, and Upper Canada, in particular. On the eve of the War of 1812, the limited immigration of that era, in combination with First Nations' losses to disease, had already reduced the Aboriginal people of Upper Canada to 10 per cent of the colonial population. Between 1821 and 1851, British North America's population increased from 750,000 to 2.3 million; Upper Canada's soared from 95,000 at the end of the War of 1812 to 952,000 in 1851. All those immigrants needed land. As Deputy Superintendent of

Indian Affairs William Claus put it to Ojibwa chiefs at Port Hope in November 1818, 'You must perceive the number of your Great Fathers [*sic*] children about here have no home, & out of pity for them, he wishes to acquire Land to give to them.'[2] These Upper Canadian demographic changes would be accelerated from mid-century on as the introduction of railways led to more rapid and extensive spread of settler population.

In seven treaties between 1815 and 1827, the Crown secured access for non-Natives to almost all of the remaining arable land in southern Ontario. The post-war treaties covered a broad swath between the northern limits of the earlier treaties and the Canadian Shield. Parts of the territory covered by these treaties intruded into Shield country. (See map 5.) In some cases, such as the 1819 treaty in eastern Ontario, a major preoccupation was getting access to territory for a strategically important transportation corridor. Following the War of 1812, military planners worried about the vulnerability of the St Lawrence River route to American attacks. The British response was to build the hugely expensive Rideau Canal system from Ottawa (then Bytown) to Kingston, allowing supplies to reach the Upper Canadian capital in relative safety. The strategically inspired 1819 treaty was the exception to the rule. The other six post-war treaties were negotiated principally to secure land for disgruntled allies who had fought with Britain in the struggle against the Americans, and then for the stream of British immigration that entered Upper Canada.

The earliest treaties concluded after the War of 1812 demonstrated both continuity with past practice and innovation. The old protocol of commercial dealing and treaty-making persisted, particularly in negotiations conducted for the Crown by officers who had been influenced by the William Johnson tradition of forest diplomacy. So, for example, in the 1818 session that William Claus, son of Johnson's son-in-law, had with Yellow Head and a group of Mississauga, talk began only 'after the usual ceremonies.' And at the end of the negotiating session, Claus assured the chiefs that the 'words which have passed between us I trust

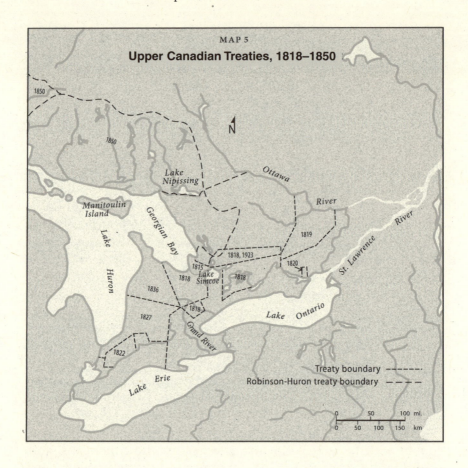

MAP 5

Upper Canadian Treaties, 1818–1850

will be sacred. It is done in the presence of the Supreme Being, who sees & hears everything.'[3] Similarly, ten days later at the River Credit west of York (Toronto), parleys between William Claus and the chiefs commenced in a familiar, formal style: Claus, 'having saluted the Chief and Indians in the usual manner, addressed them as follows. My children, I am come here by the desire of your Great Father, to speak to you on the subject of the remainder of your Country.' And Claus concluded discussions on that occasion by distributing goods, which he described as 'the Presents which your Great Father annually sends out for the comfort of his Indian children.'[4] Again, at Port Hope in November 1818, 'after the usual ceremonies,' William Claus addressed the chiefs: 'I salute you in behalf of your Great Father & condole with you for the loss you have met with since I last met you.'[5] Employing the rhetoric of family and relationship, invoking the deity, and distributing gifts from the Crown were all reassuring indications that familiar practices were being continued.

On the other hand, the post–War of 1812 agreements' provision for compensating the First Nations who signed them signalled a new departure in treaty-making. Before 1812, the Crown had provided a single payment, expressed in pounds but paid in goods. So, for example, the Head of the Lake Treaty, 1805–6, had promised the Mississauga 'one thousand pounds Province currency, in goods at the Montreal price ...'[6] Two minor treaties concluded in 1815 and 1816 maintained the practice of one-time payments. However, when treaty-making resumed in earnest in 1818, the Crown persuaded First Nations negotiators to shift from one-time disbursements to annual payments, or annuities. For example, the treaty made at Smith's Creek (Port Hope) on Lake Ontario in October 1818 promised that 'a yearly sum of seven hundred and forty pounds Province currency in goods at the Montreal prices to be well and truly paid yearly, and every year ...' Later this commitment was spelled out: 'Every man, woman and child to receive to the amount of ten dollars in goods at the Montreal prices, so long as such man, woman or child shall live, but such annuity to cease and be discontinued to be paid in right of any individual who may have died between the respective periods of payment ...'[7] Claus explained to another group that their Great Father 'does not mean to do as formerly, to pay you at once, but as long as any of you remain on the Earth to give you Cloathing [sic] in payment every year, besides the presents he now gives you.'[8] (In the British North American colonies in this period, monetary amounts were expressed in pounds sterling or dollars. In the 1850s the central BNA colony, Canada, adopted the dollar exclusively.) During negotiations in 1818 at Amherstburg, the chiefs of the region reiterated what the Crown's representative had told them: 'The payment for our lands is to be separate and distinct from the presents our Great Father the King gives us yearly for our loyalty and past service.'[9]

Later still, the Crown's obligation for annuities was capped. An agreement in 1822 stipulated that the Crown would pay 'unto each man, woman and child of the said Mississauga Nation of Indians who at the time of entering the said agreement inhabited and claimed the said tract of land, and to their descendants and posterity forever, an annuity of two pounds and ten shillings of lawful money of Upper Canada, in goods and merchandise at the Montreal price, provided always that the number of persons entitled to receive the same shall in no case exceed two hundred and fifty-seven persons, that being the number of persons claiming and inhabiting the said tract ...'[10] The shift from one-time, upfront payments to commitment to annuities represented a substantial change in treaty policy for the Crown.

The shift to annuities was attractive to government and acceptable to the First Nations of Upper Canada. So far as the Indian Department and its imperial masters were concerned, using annuities would avoid large initial outlays. Moreover, the plan was to raise the funds that would be needed to pay the continuing annuities from revenues generated by the settlers who would settle on and develop these lands for farms or town lots. Much of the newly acquired Indian lands would be sold at auction, with purchasers expected to make a down payment at once, and then to pay at least the annual interest on mortgages on their lots. Settlers' annual payments on their land purchases were expected to generate a revenue stream to furnish annuities to the First Nations.[11] As well, the growth of the colony's population and economy would increase state revenues, providing additional funds to pay annuities should the other plan not realize all the revenue needed. Accordingly, the overall effect of the change in treaty payments would be to shift the cost of treaty-making from the imperial government to the colonists.

Of course, these were not the arguments used to get First Nations agreement to the use of annuities. Rather, Crown negotiators stressed that annuities would be a means of ensuring long-term financial security, for they would represent a reliable annual income source. For example, when Deputy Superintendent General of Indian Affairs William Claus met some Mississauga at the River Credit in the autumn of 1818, he noted regretfully that they looked 'poor & miserable.' He suggested that their lands were useless to them – 'laying [*sic*] dead,' he observed – and said that in a treaty the king would take that useless land off their hands and 'give you goods yearly to cover your Women & children, besides those which he now gives you.'[12] It is also possible that annuities were attractive to the Aboriginal treaty-makers because they resembled the annual presents that they were accustomed to receive from the Crown, presents that were highly appreciated as symbols of renewal of the close ties between the monarch and the Indians. Although Claus in 1818 distinguished between annuities for treaty and the annual presents 'which he now gives you,' the manner in which that treaty was negotiated tended to blend the two forms of gift. At the River Credit in 1818, it was only after the Mississauga agreed to surrender land that Claus issued instructions to distribute the annual presents. Over time, especially when the giving of presents was phased out in the later 1850s, treaty annuities would become the major symbol of annual renewal of the link between Crown and First Nations.

Certainly there was evidence that some Mississauga groups in Upper Canada were beginning to feel so hard pressed by settlement that they were desperate for aid. At Port Hope in November 1818, Buckquaquet of the Rice Lake Mississauga responded to William Claus's request for land in return for annuities by saying that he hardly had a choice: 'From our lands we receive scarcely anything and if your words are true we will get more by parting with them than by keeping them. Our hunting is destroyed and we must throw ourselves on the compassion of our Great Father the King.' The chief contended that 'if it was not for our Brethren the farmers about the Country we should near starve for our hunting is destroyed':

Father. We hope that we shall not be prevented from the right of Fishing, the use of the Waters, & Hunting where we can find game. We hope that the Whites who are to come among us will not treat us ill, some of young [*sic*] men are giddy, but we hope they will not hurt them.

Father. The young men, I hope you will not think it hard at their requesting, that the Islands may be left for them that when we try to scratch the Earth, as our Brethren the Farmers do, & put any thing in that it may come up to help our Women & Children.[13]

The eminent chief Yellow Head also told Claus on another occasion, 'I am an object of compassion.'[14] As settlers interfered with the Mississauga's fishing sites and cut down the forests that provided a home for the game that the Natives hunted, the Indians' material conditions began to deteriorate severely. In such a situation of increasing deprivation, the regular support that annuities represented looked attractive.

There was also a shift in tone to treaty-making after the War of 1812: Crown behaviour became more legalistic. In the versions of treaties recorded by government prior to 1812, the document had varied between a standard agreement among parties and an indenture, or purely legal document. After treaty-making resumed in 1815, the pacts that were fashioned were more likely to be recorded by government as 'indentures' than as agreements.[15] More disturbing was the beginning of divergence between oral and written accounts of treaty undertakings that became obvious after the War of 1812.

Two examples, both dating from 1818, reveal the problem. During talks at Amherstburg on 16 October 1818, the Ojibwa chiefs indicated they were 'willing to sell our lands but we wish to make the following reserves':

1st Four miles square at some distances below the River St. Clair
2nd One mile in front by four deep bordering on said river and adjoining to the Shawnee [?] Reserve
3rd Two miles at Kettle Point Lake Huron
4th Two miles square at the River au Sable
5th Two miles square at Bear's Creek. Also a reserve for Tomago and his band up the Thames which he will point out when he arrives.[16]

The First Nations leaders obviously wished to protect access points for their fishery by keeping those economically important sites out of the treaty concession. Unfortunately, however, the Indian Department's version of what was agreed at Amherstburg on 16 October 1818 made no reference to the request to retain these tracts as unsurrendered Aboriginal land. The recollection of a number of chiefs years later was that they had decided 'to Reserve a part of the mainland the Points and mouths of the Rivers and Islands. And this is what the Governor said. Your great father is very glad. And I thank you very much. And I promise that these Islands, points, mouths of rivers, and part of the mainland shall be reserved for your hunting fishing purposes, and that the supplies of clothing, blankets etc from the Govmt shall never stop, and that this promise shall be good as long as the Sun lasts, and rivers flow and as long as grass grows.'[17] Similar disputes would develop over contrasting accounts – oral from First Nations, and written from government – over agreements made concerning Rice Lake and at York Garrison in the same period.[18] Such differences would be the source of disputes and claims in subsequent periods.

The changes in Crown treaty-making behaviour after the War of 1812 are explained largely by the evolving relationship between the Crown and First Nations in Upper Canada. The reason that the imperial government sought to shift the cost of treaty compensation from the treasury in London to the colonists, as well as the rationale for eliminating presents, was that military dependence on First Nations was diminishing rapidly after the War of 1812. In large part, this change in governmental attitude was occurring because the military usefulness of Indians was declining precipitously at the time. Following the Treaty of Ghent, and more especially after the Rush-Bagot Convention of 1817, there was a growing realization among government planners that it was increasingly unlikely that they and their commanders in the field would have to call upon First Nations for military support. In fact, Britain transferred jurisdiction over Indian affairs, which in 1816 had been moved from civil to military officers, back to civil over-

sight in 1830. The more remote the chance of renewed war with
the United States appeared, the less interested in maintaining
good relations with the First Nations through presents and other
means the British were. The consequence of this change in governmental attitude was a less accommodating approach to treaty-
making.

Not surprisingly, this declining regard for erstwhile Aboriginal
allies was aggravated by the changing population balance in the
colonies. As British immigration to Upper Canada, in particular,
increased after 1820, the less imposing, both numerically and
strategically, the First Nations appeared. In other words, the fear
of Aboriginal strength that had earlier underlain Indian policy
disappeared. Simultaneously, among the settler population itself,
regard for Indian peoples was in rapid decline from the 1820s
onward. Now that Aboriginal people were not obviously useful to
the non-Native population as military allies or trading partners,
they increasingly took on the role of obstacles to settler ambitions
for economic development. In particular, a continuing migratory
First Nations population that moved about the country to harvest
the resources of the land at various points during the cycle of the
seasons was not compatible with the emergence of a sedentary
agricultural-commercial society. Put most simply, migratory
hunter-gatherers and fields with crops could not coexist very
easily. Cutting down the pine forests to 'make farms' threatened
the habitat on which Natives depended for game, fowl, and fish.
On the other hand, the establishment of farms and towns often
threatened fishing sites – as the Mississauga of the Head of the
Lake region had complained in the 1790s – and freedom to move
about on familiar paths. From the settler perspective, Indians
were ceasing to be desirable partners and assuming the role of
barriers to the winning of wealth. Such changes in the economic
and social relations of the Aboriginal population and the rapidly
growing immigrant society did not augur well for Native-newcomer relations, in general, nor for treaty-making, in particular.

During the second major phase of treaty-making in Upper
Canada after 1818, First Nations demonstrated in treaty negotiations that they understood and were concerned about the

changes going on all around them. One sign was that occasionally First Nations began to mention a desire for guarantees about continuing rights to hunt and fish.[19] Another indication that First Nations were feeling hard pressed by settlement was that in some negotiations they asked that the creation of reserves be included in the treaty. There were a few reserves in Upper Canada already, but reserve creation was not a regular part of treaty-making. From the mid-1820s onward there were signs that First Nations' anxieties were making them eager to have provision for a refuge from the pressure of European settlers included in their agreements with the Crown.[20] Finally, a sign of decreasing confidence in Crown negotiators on the part of First Nations leaders was that both the Wyandot of Amherstburg and the Mississauga of Rice Lake requested written documents that confirmed their ownership of their reserves.[21] Evidence of declining confidence in the Crown's agents and of increasing concern about their long-term future were auguries of what lay ahead in Native-newcomer relations in Upper Canada. As recently as 1822, the legislature of Upper Canada had continued the policy articulated in 1797 by Peter Russell when he issued a proclamation to protect Mississauga fisheries from settlers. The 1822 Act for the Preservation of Salmon contained an important proviso: '... nothing in this act contained shall extend, or be construed to extend, to prevent the Indians fishing as heretofore when and where they please.'[22] Frequent petitions from First Nations about infringement of their rights indicated poor enforcement against colonists.

The experience of the River Credit Mississauga suggested the regulations were not effective at all. This group of Anicinabe had settled down on a reserve created by the Crown and tried to develop a sedentary farming economy. They also inclined increasingly towards Methodism, thanks to the teachings and example of young Peter Jones (Kahkewaquonaby), one of the band. In 1825, Kahkewaquonaby was one of three leaders who signed a petition to the lieutenant-governor asking for protection of their fishery from white intruders, but they failed to get it. Four years later, led by Peter Jones, who had recently been elected chief of the band, they petitioned the provincial Assembly for relief from non-Native intruders who 'burn and destroy our fences ... watch the salmon and take them as fast as they come up,' and 'swear & get drunk and give a very bad example to our young people.' They 'often in the dark ... set gill nets in the River and stop all the fish. By these means we are very much injured & our children are deprived of bread.' The Legislative Assembly responded by passing 'An act the better to protect the Credit River Mississauga's fishing and hunting rights' within their reserve. The statute referred explicitly to their petition and duplicated much of the language that it had used to describe the problems non-Natives were causing. It provided for jail terms of one to three years for violators, and authorized the band to confiscate the equipment of convicted offenders.[23] Nonetheless, pressure from settlers continued to be a problem.

During the 1830s the consequences of this new and more troubled relationship between indigenous and immigrant peoples in Upper Canada worked themselves out most noticeably in the policy that government fashioned and tried to apply to First Nations. One sign of the changing times was a dramatic transformation of the personnel of the Indian Department. From its inception in 1755 until the 1820s, the Department was staffed with men whose familiarity with First Nations derived either from relations with them in the fur trade or diplomacy and military association with them, or both. Typical were officials such as the 'founding father' of Indian Affairs, Sir William Johnson, whose fur-trade links gave him the connections and knowledge to conduct diplomacy with First Nations very effectively until his death in 1774. He was followed in leading roles in the Indian Department by figures such as his nephew Guy Johnson, Daniel Claus, son-in-law of Sir William Johnson, and Claus's son William, who negotiated several of the post–War of 1812 treaties in Upper Canada. All these figures were experienced forest diplomats who learned much of what they knew initially from serving with Indians as allies. These officials had come to value and respect Indians through their diplomatic and military dealings with

them, and some of that regard carried over into their administration of Indian affairs. Their era came to an end, symbolically,
when Britain shifted responsibility from military authorities to
civil administrators in 1830. From the 1830s on, the Indian
Department steadily became more influenced by products of the
settler society who had never learned to appreciate First Nations'
commercial, diplomatic, and military skills, and who consequently had less consideration for them than their bureaucratic
forebears.

The transition from a military to a civilian spirit in Indian
affairs coincided with a shift in Indian policy in British North
America from an emphasis on trade, diplomacy, and alliance, to
a focus on what became known in the 1830s as a 'civilization
policy.' The motivation behind this move towards a new policy
was summarized in an observation of Britain's secretary of state
for war and the colonies: 'It appears to me that the course which
has hitherto been taken in dealing with these people, has had reference to the advantages which might be derived from their
friendship in times of war, rather than to any settled purpose of
gradually reclaiming them from a state of barbarism, and of
introducing amongst them the industrious and peaceful habits of
civilized life.'[24] In Upper Canada in the 1830s, the new policy
meant de-emphasizing such things as giving presents, and con-
centrating on encouraging First Nations to adopt sedentary
habits, learn to maintain themselves by farming, become Christian, and expose their children to Euro-Canadian schooling. In
the 1840s the policy would be modified to encourage First
Nations to send their children to 'manual labour schools,' a
species of residential school. In short, the new policy was frankly
assimilationist in purpose: it sought to 'reclaim them from a state
of barbarism, and ... introduce[e] amongst them the industrious
and peaceful habits of civilized life.' The ultimate aim of the new
policy was to make First Nations economically self-sufficient, an
evolution that would allow Great Britain to eliminate the presents
it gave them each year. The first attempt at implementing this
policy in the Coldwater-Narrows region during 1830–6 proved a
colossal failure. Agriculture and reserve life did not succeed, and

Christian proselytization and educational efforts were weakened
by denominational competition among missionaries, on the one
hand, and the persistence of Aboriginal beliefs and practices
among many First Nations, on the other.

In fact, it was an attempt to abandon the new 'civilization policy'
that led to the next major event in Upper Canadian treaty-
making. A new lieutenant-governor, Sir Francis Bond Head,
arrived in Upper Canada in January 1836, by which time the
failure of the reserve-creation experiment had become indisputable. Head believed that in any conflict between indigenous
people and European newcomers, the former would inevitably
succumb to the power and drive of the latter. 'Whenever and
wherever the two races come into contact with each other, it is
sure to prove fatal to the red man,' he wrote. Well-intentioned
'civilization' policies could never succeed in the long run. All
they did while they were in force was vex and oppress people who
would be happier pursuing a hunter-gatherer existence. His view
was:

> 1st. That an attempt to make farmers of the red men has been, gen-
> erally speaking, a complete failure.
> 2nd. That congregating them for the purpose of civilization has
> implanted many more vices than it has eradicated; and conse-
> quently
> 3rd. That the greatest kindness we can perform towards these intel-
> ligent, simple-minded people, is to remove and fortify them as
> much as possible from all communication with the whites.[25]

Obviously, the best policy 'is to induce them, as I have done, to
retreat before what they may justly term the accursed progress of
civilization.'[26] Clearly, the new lieutenant-governor's views on
Indian affairs were directly opposed to the new 'civilization
policy.'

Head pursued the implementation of his alternative to 'civilization' at the annual meeting of First Nations at Manitowaning
on Manitoulin Island in the summer of 1836. Although the

purpose of this gathering, which attracted Indians from all over Upper Canada and the upper Great Lakes, was the Crown's annual distribution of presents, the lieutenant-governor turned it into a treaty-making session. He addressed representatives of the Odawa and Ojibwa, who owned the Manitoulin islands chain:

> My Children
>
> Seventy snow seasons have now passed away since we met in Council at the crooked place (Niagara), at which time and place your Great Father, the King, and the Indians of North America tied their hands together by the wampum of friendship.
>
> Since that period various circumstances have occurred to separate from your Great Father many of his red children, and as an unavoidable increase of white population, as well as the progress of cultivation, have had the natural effect of impoverishing your hunting grounds it has become necessary that new arrangements should be entered into for the purpose of protecting you from the encroachments of the whites.

Regrettably, the Crown was finding it 'has now great difficulty in securing it [hunting land] for you from the whites, who are hunting to cultivate it.' 'Under these circumstances, I have been obliged to consider what is best to be done for the red children of the forest, and I now tell you my thoughts.' He asked those who were proprietors of Manitoulin Island to surrender it to the Crown on the understanding that it would be available as a place of refuge to all First Nations who wished to withdraw from cultivable areas and 'to be totally separated from the whites.' Head's use of wampum on this occasion was interesting, given that his object was to dispossess the First Nations in the interest of settler society.[27]

Head then turned to the Saugeen Indians, who inhabited the Bruce Peninsula, and proposed that they give up their lands in favour of moving to Manitoulin Island. This Saugeen land, totalling some 1.5 million acres (600,000 hectares), was the last large piece of arable land south of the Precambrian Shield in Upper Canada. While the Saugeen appeared desirous of complying with the Crown representative's wishes, their leaders initially opposed a surrender that involved relocating to Manitoulin Island. After protracted and difficult negotiations, Head modified his position: they could, if they preferred, move northward on the Bruce Peninsula and occupy the Shield lands north of Owen Sound, 'upon which proper houses shall be built for you, and proper assistance given to enable you to become civilized and to cultivate land, which your Great Father engages for ever to protect for you from the encroachments of whites.' (Having threatened the Ojibwa and Odawa of Manitoulin with the colonial government's inability to prevent settler intrusions into their territory, the lieutenant-governor promised the Ojibwa of the Bruce Peninsula that the Crown would 'for ever' protect them 'from the encroachments of whites.') Head proposed that after entering treaty, the Saugeen 'should repair either to this island [Manitoulin] or to that part of your territory which lies on the north of Owen Sound.'[28] Reluctantly, four of the Saugeen men who were present signed to cede their lands to the Crown. Since the Saugeen had earlier agreed that no land surrender would be valid unless its signatories included their General Council and hereditary chief, the legitimacy of their action, taken under great pressure from the Crown, was questionable.[29] Nonetheless, Saugeen opposition did not matter, because the transaction went through, and in 1854 they were even dispossessed of much of the land north of Owen Sound that they had been promised was theirs 'for ever.'[30]

Although the agreements that Head negotiated soon encountered opposition, the resistance did not deter the lieutenant-governor from pursuing acquisition of other First Nations' lands in 1836. He also persuaded the occupants of a large portion of Huron lands, those on the Moravian reserve, and the leaders of the failed experiment in 'civilization' west of Orillia to give up the lands that had been set aside for them. Fierce opposition to Head's rejection of the 'civilization policy' soon erupted both in the colony and in Britain. Within Upper Canada the principal opponents of abandoning the creation of agricultural reserves and the promotion of schooling and Christianity were the Methodists, who were the most active and successful missionaries among the Indians in the colony. In the United Kingdom, the Society of Friends, or Quakers, and a newly formed philanthropic organization, the Aborigines Protection Society, protested loudly to the government at Head's radical departure in Indian policy. Both metropolitan and colonial protesters objected that jettison-ing the 'civilization policy' amounted to the 'abandonment' of the Indians, who were in many cases suffering badly as a result of their collision with British immigrant society. Because of the strong political pressure, British officials fairly quickly an-nounced that Head's policy of promoting relocation to remote hunting-gathering locations would not be pursued. The various surrenders that Head had taken at Manitowaning and elsewhere in the colony in 1836, however, were not reversed. Now almost all of southern Ontario was covered by some sort of treaty.

Abortive as it was, Head's initiative revealed the forces that shaped and reshaped Indian policy, including treaties. For one thing, Head, although he did not refer to it, was pursuing a course of action that was directly parallel to what U.S. president Andrew Jackson was doing south of the border. In the United States after 1830, the federal government aggressively followed a relocation policy that compelled the movement of almost all Indians in the East to lands west of the Mississippi River in what is often termed the 'trail of tears.' Though inspired by different assumptions and ideological goals, Head's policy, had he been allowed to follow through with it, would have had similarly destructive effects. The other controversial aspect of Head's ini-tiative, one unnoticed at the time, was that the treaties concluded at Manitowaning violated both the requirements of the Royal Proclamation of 1763 and the rules laid down by Lord Dor-chester in 1794. The Proclamation had said plainly that surrend-ers of lands under First Nations' control were to be taken only at 'a meeting called for the purpose.' The assembly at Manitowan-ing was not convened as a treaty-making session.

Upper Canada was spared both the misguided policies of a Francis Bond Head and more treaties for over a decade after 1836. This is hardly surprising, because by that time the Crown had acquired access to all the arable land in Upper Canada south of the rocks and forests of the Shield. When treaty-making did resume in 1850, the activity in fact focused on those more northerly lands where, not agriculture, but mining, for which minerals were needed, was the mainstay of the economy. What drew settler society's attention northward to lands on Lake Huron were the riches to be found – minerals, in other words – in Shield country. The development of mining activities in the upper Michigan peninsula had excited prospectors with thoughts that similar deposits might be found north of the St Mary River, the international boundary. By the 1840s, prospectors and mining interests were focusing on the north shore of Lake Huron as a region of considerable base mineral potential. In the mid-1840s the Province of Canada, the political unit formed by the union of Lower and Upper Canada in 1840–1, authorized mining licences in the region. Very quickly 'location tickets,' licences to prospect and mine, were issued to a number of prospectors and mining companies. No one, apparently, had yet twigged to the requirements of the Royal Proclamation of 1763, or to the fact that colonial actions to this point had paid them no mind. Significantly, the governor general, Lord Elgin, disapproved of the colonists' presumption and haste, taking the position that Canada should treat with the Indians of the region on behalf of the Crown before authorizing mining activity there. (See map 6.)

If colonists had largely forgotten the dictates of the Royal Proclamation and Lord Dorchester's regulations of 1794, the First Nations of the Lake Huron district quickly reminded them. When miners began operating in the Sault Ste Marie area as early as 1846, Chief Shinguakonse of Garden River, near Sault Ste Marie, sent a petition to the governor general to protest the intrusion and indicate that he expected royalties from any mines that might be developed. 'I want always to live and plant at Garden River and as my people are poor to derive a share of what is found on my lands,' he said.[31] Shinguakonse and other leaders in the region were aware that American prospectors had overrun Michigan's northern peninsula and extracted wealth without providing much benefit to local Native Americans.[32] Shinguakonse

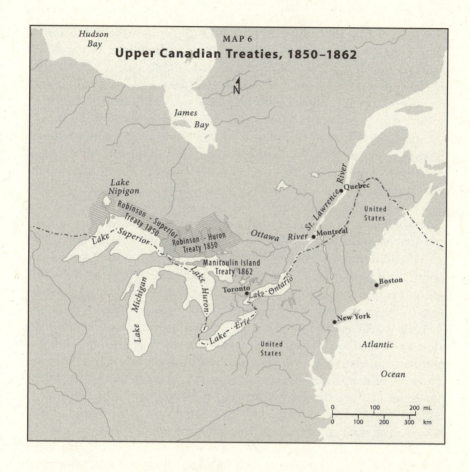

and the other Ojibwa chiefs of the region were motivated to protest by two concerns. They objected to non-Native mining companies taking riches out of territories they considered theirs, and they were uneasy about their communities' economic future. because game was becoming depleted in the region. Shinguakonse felt the problems particularly acutely. His own community at Garden River had begun to experiment with farming as early as the mid-seventeenth century, after the Iroquois dispersed the Huron to the south of their region, and one of the mining companies had received a 'location ticket' that included the land where his village was established. 'One ground of complaint on the part of this [Garden River] band deserves consideration, it is that the Government has sold as a mining location, the tract of land at Garden River, on which their Village is built, and they have cultivated the soil to some extent for many years, and although this has been several times represented to the Government, no relief has yet been afforded.'[33] Garden River Ojibwa seemed likely to feel the direct impact of mining. Shinguakonse hoped to issue leases to mining companies himself, deriving a continuing stream of revenue for the Garden River Ojibwa by that means.[34]

The colonial government's response to these local appeals for consideration turned a difficult situation into a crisis. The province made a half-hearted inquiry into the claims in 1847, when the commissioner of Crown lands reviewed and dismissed them, much to the disappointment of the governor general, who thought they should be dealt with. Shinguakonse made two futile trips to Montreal to place his people's concerns before the governor general. In 1848 a single government representative, T.G. Anderson, a veteran of the Indian Department, went north to inquire, but nothing came of that investigation either. More serious attention was paid to the problem on Lake Huron the following year. Canada sent Anderson and Alexander Vidal, a provincial land surveyor from Sarnia, who was put in charge of the mission in spite of Anderson's seniority, to discuss the issues associated with mining with the First Nations of the north shore of Lake Huron and Lake Superior. The mission did not go well. Vidal and Shinguakonse had had a run-in in 1846. The First Nations were irritated that Vidal and Anderson had come to inquire, not negotiate, as was shown by the fact that they did not bring funds to compensate the First Nations. Moreover, the commissioners' journey to the upper Great Lakes took place in the late autumn, at a time when many of the inland bands had returned to their traditional hunting territories far away. To make things worse, some leaders who had come to meet with the government representatives fled back to their homes when a cholera scare briefly flared up at Bruce Mines on Lake Superior.[35]

Finally, the commissioners got into an altercation with Shinguakonse. He and other chiefs from Lake Huron had agreed that Allan Macdonell, a mining developer who was close to the Garden River chief, would speak for them. Vidal and Anderson refused to deal with Macdonell, arguing that they were instructed to talk with the Indians about their grievances. The upshot was that negotiations at Sault Ste Marie broke up, and the commissioners formed a poor opinion of Shinguakonse and Macdonell. In spite of the dispute, Vidal and Anderson endorsed the claim of the Garden River Ojibwa. 'The claim of the present occupants' of Garden River 'derived from their forefathers, who have from time immemorial hunted upon it, is unquestionably as good as that of any of the tribes who have received compensation for the cession of their rights in other parts of Province; and therefore entitles them to similar remuneration.'[36] All the same, according to the Rev. Gustavus Anderson, missionary at Garden River and son of T.G. Anderson, 'because there is no prospect of anything being done this year they [the Indians] are enraged.'[37]

It was interesting that one of the issues that First Nations leaders like Shinguakonse and Peau de Chat of the Thunder Bay region on Lake Superior raised was their desire that the Métis in the community also receive the benefits of any treaty that was made.[38] According to two Métis informants, Alexis and Joshua Biron of Sault Ste Marie, Shinguakonse had attempted to recruit Métis to join his band 'several years before the Robinson Treaty was made,' promising them a share in 'the presents that his band was then getting. That some day he might sell his land, and that if so, his claim should be our claim, and then we half-breeds would have a right to a share of what he, the Chief, might get for it.'[39] First Nations and Métis raised the stakes in the dispute about access to Native lands in November 1849. Not long after Vidal and Anderson's fruitless mission, a party of First Nations and Métis travelled 200 miles (320 km) north from Sault Ste Marie to Mica Bay on Lake Superior and forced the representatives of the Quebec Mining Company to hand over control of their operations. This incident led the government to send a military force to the area and to arrest Shinguakonse and Chief Nebe-

nagoching of Sault Ste Marie, as well as two Métis leaders. It was
interesting that the governor general, Lord Elgin, thought colonial politicians were remiss in not dealing with the northern
Indians' claims before events degenerated into confrontation. 'I
cannot but think,' he wrote to the Colonial Office, 'that it is
much to be regretted that steps were not taken to investigate
thoroughly and extinguish all Indian claims before licenses of
exploration or grants of land were conceded by the Government
in this Territory. This omission is the pretext for the present dis-
turbances and renders the Indians much more difficult to treat
with.'[40]

Governor General Elgin got his way belatedly in 1850 when the
Province of Canada dispatched William B. Robinson, the first
treaty commissioner to be appointed from outside the Indian
Department. Robinson, a son of Loyalist stock and well-connected
to the colony's ruling Family Compact, had begun his working life
in the fur trade, but later shifted to politics and business affairs
related to the projects promoted by his Compact friends.[41] That
the colonial government chose to appoint a career politician close
to the Tory party rather than sending an experienced Indian
Department official such as T.G. Anderson north to negotiate was
a striking development. Robinson's task was eased somewhat by
the fact that the Crown had pardoned Chiefs Shinguakonse and
Nebenagoching, as well as the Métis leaders who had been
arrested during the Mica Bay incident in 1849. In spite of this conciliatory gesture, as well as a reconnoitering trip by Robinson to
the Sault in the spring and Governor General Elgin's personal
visit to Sault Ste Marie in late August 1850, negotiations were protracted and difficult.

Although commissioners Vidal and Anderson had reported in
1849 that the First Nations leaders in the region did not understand the value of their lands, Robinson's experience a year later
showed that that judgment was faulty. When Vidal and Anderson
had asked Chief Joseph Peau de Chat of Fort William what compensation he sought, the chief responded, 'If I knew how long
the world would last I could answer, but now I can not.' Presumably, Chief Peau de Chat meant that he could not respond

because he could not say how long his community would need the payments.[42] In 1850, Commissioner Robinson discovered that chiefs' demands, especially those of Shinguakonse, were well beyond what the government had anticipated. What Vidal, Anderson, and Robinson did not appreciate was that the chiefs around Sault Ste Marie and Lake Superior were aware – some of their communities were beneficiaries – of treaties on the American side that were more generous than the terms the Canadian government was offering.

For a time, the demands of Shinguakonse and some others threatened to frustrate the talks. Not only was Shinguakonse asking for thirty dollars per person as an annuity, he and other chiefs also requested that the Métis receive treaty benefits as well. Robinson argued, as Vidal and Anderson had the previous year, that the lands north of Lake Huron and Lake Superior were inferior in value to those further south in the arable region. He 'explained to the chiefs in council' that the lands covered by the southern treaties 'were of good quality and sold readily at prices which enabled the Government to be more liberal. [They] were also occupied by the whites in such a manner as to preclude the possibility of the Indian hunting over or having access to them.' The lands in the north, on the other hand, 'are notoriously barren and sterile, and will in all probability never be settled except in a few localities by mining companies.' The chiefs, knowing the eagerness of miners for access, were not impressed by such arguments.[43]

Commissioner Robinson, however, knew that chiefs from Lake Superior were less concerned about some of the details, presumably because their communities were being less adversely affected than those on Lake Huron by the increasing presence of Europeans. Robinson wrote out two copies of a treaty, had it translated and explained by an interpreter, and got it signed by Peau de Chat and other chiefs from Lake Superior. Then – this was on a Saturday – he indicated to Shinguakonse and the rest that he would prepare a similar treaty and offer it to them at their next meeting. When they convened following a day off for Sabbath observances, Robinson presented and had translated a treaty with

terms similar to the pact that the Lake Superior chiefs had
signed. Shinguakonse continued to balk at the terms, arguing for
'ten dollars a head by way of annuity,' and 'securing to some sixty
half-breeds a free grant of one hundred acres of land each.'
However, when other leaders made it clear that they were ready
to sign, Shinguakonse and Nebenagoching capitulated and were
the first to sign. Robinson, according to his own account, left a
copy of both treaties with the respective groups.[44]

During negotiation of the Robinson Treaties, the First Nations'
principal preoccupations were initial payment, annuities,
reserves, recognition of their hunting and fishing rights, and provision of land grants to area Métis. The effort to provide land to
the Métis failed, but they were allowed to decide themselves
whether they wished to be regarded as Indians and included in
treaty, or not. The Superior bands and Huron bands were each to
receive £2,000 as initial compensation; the Superior bands would
get an annuity of £500, and the Huron £600. Since there were
1,240 Indians in the Lake Superior bands and 1,422 in the Lake
Huron bands, these sums represented approximately $6.40 and
$1.60 per person for the Superior bands, and $5.60 and $1.70 for
the Huron bands. (A pound of provincial currency was worth
approximately four dollars.)

Commissioner Robinson's revealing comments about what he
agreed to on reserves and hunting rights were striking. For one
thing, he said that he had 'succeeded in obtaining the surrender
of all the lands in question, with the Exception of some small
reservations made by the Indians,' indicating that the First
Nations of the upper Great Lakes had retained the reserve lands
under Aboriginal title. Moreover, 'in allowing the Indians to
retain reservations of land for their own use I was governed by
the fact that they in most cases asked for such tracts as they had
heretofore been in the habit of using for purposes of residence
and cultivation,' he wrote, 'and by securing these to them and the
right of hunting and fishing over the ceded territory, they cannot
say that the Government takes from [them] their usual means of
subsistence and therefore have no claims for support, which they
no doubt would have preferred had this not been done.'[45]

Robinson also explained that he had included a feature unique to treaty-making to that point: an escalator. 'I inserted a clause securing to them certain prospective advantages should the lands in question prove sufficiently productive at any future period to enable the Government without loss to increase the annuity.' In the government's printed version of the treaties, the escalator read: '... in case the territory hereby ceded by the parties of the second part shall at any future period produce an amount which will enable the Government of this Province without incurring loss to increase the annuity hereby secured to them, then, and in that case, the same shall be augmented from time to time, provided that the amount paid to each individual shall not exceed the sum of one pound provincial currency in any one year, or such further sum as Her Majesty may be graciously pleased to order.' There were further provisos: if the number of Indians in future was less than two-thirds of their 1850 complement, not only would they not receive the escalated annuity, but 'the annuity shall be diminished in proportion to their actual numbers.'[46] After considerable argument over interpretation of the escalator clause, annuities were raised finally in 1875 to four dollars per person.[47]

The Robinson Huron and Superior Treaties of 1850 were enormously significant, both at the time and later. The background to their negotiation revealed that the more a settler society developed and controlled Indian affairs, the less it seemed to remember traditional Crown obligations to First Nations. Shinguakonse mournfully described the deterioration: 'When your white children came into this country, they did not come shouting the war cry and seeking to wrest this land from us.' In response, the Anicinabe welcomed them. 'Time wore on and you have become a great people, whilst we have melted away like snow beneath an April sun; our strength is wasted, our countless warriors dead, our forest laid low, you have hunted us from every place as with a wand, you have swept away all our pleasant land ...'[48] The terms of the Robinson Treaties were also extremely important: this was the first of the Upper Canadian treaties to deal with very large areas of territory, to include reserves as part of the treaty, and to recognize continuing Aboriginal hunting and fishing rights. These characteristics, plus the inclusion of annuities, would be essential elements of treaty-making in western Canada after 1867.

There were other ways in which the Robinson Treaties set a pattern for the future. For one thing, a major reason that chiefs such as Shinguakonse were so eager to secure recognition of their rights and regular payments in the form of annuities was that they were anxious about their people's continuing economic security. Heavy hunting and fur trading had somewhat depleted game resources in the region by the early nineteenth century, and many First Nation bands, particularly around Sault Ste Marie, had adjusted by developing some farming, fishing, gathering maple sugar, and hunting. The intrusion of mining ventures threatened the future viability of their mixed economy, inducing them to pursue other means of assured economic support through treaty.[49] The Robinson Treaties foreshadowed future dealings in another way. Commissioner Robinson had hardly finished his talks at Sault Ste Marie when he encountered other Ojibwa chiefs who claimed that some of their lands fell within the treaty zone. When he landed at Penetanguishene, Robinson was met by Chiefs Yellowhead, Snake, and Aisance, all southern Ojibwa, who told him that some of the Robinson Huron Treaty area near the Severn River was part of their traditional territory.[50] Such overlapping or competing claims would become very familiar to Crown representatives in the future.

Pre-Confederation Upper Canadian treaty-making came to a conclusion in 1862 with the Manitoulin Island Treaty. The colonial government, which had gained control of Indian affairs from Great Britain in 1860, took the position in dealings with the local Ojibwa, Odawa, and Potawatomi that the 1836 cession of lands had been rendered void by First Nations' failure to relocate to Manitoulin Island in the numbers that had been expected, or at least hoped. Not only had other bands not moved north to the island chain, but the efforts to inculcate agriculture and Western ways among those who were there were not very successful. Crown officials argued that if the land was taken into treaty and

Indians assigned specific areas as reserves, 'the conditions of the Indians as well as the settlement and improvement of the country' would be ameliorated.[51] Significantly, the colonial government appointed the commissioner of Crown lands and superintendent general of Indian affairs, William McDougall, to negotiate. McDougall, of Loyalist stock, trained in the law, and experienced in progressive journalism and politics, followed expansionist policies that included opening up new farmlands and building a colonization road to remote Parry Sound. 'McDougall also presided over the repossession of Indian reserves on Manitoulin Island, on the pretext that, since these lands had not been put to agricultural use, they obstructed further settlement.'[52]

McDougall had to overcome serious obstacles to negotiate a new Manitoulin Island Treaty. Behind the pretext that non-migration by First Nations north to Manitoulin necessitated a new treaty lurked the now familiar menace of increasing non-Native pressure on and desire for First Nations territory. In the case of Manitoulin Island, the attraction lay especially in the rich fisheries adjacent to the islands. In a misguided action that paralleled the background to the Robinson Treaties, the Province of Canada had issued fishing leases to a number of non-Native commercial fishing companies. First Nations on Manitoulin Island had responded by harassing the fishers that the commercial companies sent into their waters.[53] It was hardly surprising, then, that when the Indian Department approached local bands in the early 1860s about a treaty, the officials faced considerable resistance. Many of the First Nations there were hesitant to enter treaty, but those who lived on the east side of Manitoulin Island in and near Wikwemikong were adamantly opposed. Wikwemikong had been the site of Jesuit missions to the Indians since the 1840s and stood in marked contrast to the west side, with the village of Manitowaning at its centre, where governmental and Anglican influence was strong.

First Nations' opposition on Manitoulin Island emerged in October 1861 at a conference that the local superintendent and a commissioner held at Manitowaning.[54] When officials broached

4.1 Present-giving at Wikwemikong

the subject of a treaty, the Odawa chief Edowishcosh responded on behalf of 'my brother Chief and Warriors, women and Children': 'The Great Spirit gave our forefathers land to live upon and our forefathers wished us to keep it. The land upon which we now are is our own, and we intend to keep it. The whites should not come and take our land from us; they ought to have stayed on the other side of the salt water to work the land there. The Great Spirit would be angry with us, if we parted with our land, and we don't want to make Him angry.' Repeated entreaties would not budge Edowishcosh and other leaders. 'We have the laws God has established. I wish you would take back your proposition and your Surveyor with you.' An unnamed warrior revealed how personal the matter was to them: 'This island, of which I speak, I consider my body; I don't want one of my legs or arms to be taken from me.'[55]

With considerable difficulty, William McDougall managed to get an agreement in 1862. His success resulted from the influence of a respected pro-treaty Odawa chief, Jean-Baptiste Assiginack, a long-time advocate of Indian-settler cooperation,[56] and from use of a familiar tactic of Indian Department officials: splitting the First Nations. At first the Indian leaders uniformly rejected the Crown's offer, but McDougall, noting that those from the west side seemed more amenable to settling than those from Wikwemikong, announced that he was ready to treat with any groups who were prepared to conclude an agreement with him.[57] In this way, he succeeded in getting most groups to sign the treaty, although the Wikwemikong area bands still held aloof. Reserves amounting to 100 acres (40 hectares) for each head of family, 50 acres for each single adult, and 50 acres per orphan member of the band, chosen by the individuals so 'that the lots selected shall be contiguous or adjacent to each other, so that Indian settlements on the island may be as compact as possible,' were promised. The bands would receive revenue from interest on sale of their former lands, but as soon as 100,000 acres (40,000 hectares) of public land were sold, the expenses of the local superintendent and his office would come from the proceeds of land sales. Signatory Indians were guaranteed fishing rights, although there was no explicit mention of hunting and gathering rights. The holdouts on the east side of Manitoulin Island were promised the right to adhere to the treaty on the same terms whenever they wished to do so.[58] It turns out that they never have wanted to enter treaty.

The Upper Canadian treaties negotiated in the half-century after the War of 1812 reflected the shifting nature of Native-newcomer relations in British North America. Most noticeably after 1840, the personnel that government sent to negotiate with First Nations were representative of the new settler society, rather than the earlier military-diplomatic tradition. Shunting aside the old-timer T.G. Anderson in favour of W.B. Robinson to achieve what became the Robinson Treaties was one sign of the accelerating change. Another was the role and behaviour of William McDougall on Manitoulin Island in 1862. Settler society was firmly in command, especially after Britain transferred jurisdiction over Indian affairs to the colonies in 1860. The changed environment was reflected in a tendency on the part of government to view the treaties as simply contracts that recorded the exchange of land for compensation. Another reflection of change was the diminished use of traditional Aboriginal protocol. Presents were distributed in treaty-making at the Sault in 1850, but there was little other evidence of the old ways. (Robinson was instructed by government not to distribute gifts. He nonetheless issued presents at Garden River during his exploratory trip north in the spring of 1850, and might have provisioned the chiefs at Garden River in September.)[59]

Another indicator was colonial fisheries law. In contrast to Peter Russell's proclamation of 1797, the 1822 Upper Canadian statute that exempted First Nations' fisheries from the provisions of fisheries legislation, and the 1829 measure to protect the River Credit Mississauga's rights, a new fisheries Act in 1857 did not. Significantly, this more threatening statute became law the same day as another measure that provided for removing Indian status from First Nations adult males, the Gradual Civilization Act.[60] On the other hand, the eloquence of Edowishcosh and the unnamed warrior at Manitowaning in 1861 revealed a First Nations relationship to the land that suggested that the Aboriginal view of these treaties was not simply contractual and had not changed under settler pressure. The increasing importance First Nations negotiators attached to the creation of reserves reflected their growing concern. Truly, treaty-making in Upper Canada before Confederation left a decidedly mixed legacy.

5

'When they once come settlers will follow':[1] Prelude to the Western Treaties

William McDougall and the Clear Grit political faction were important in bringing about constitutional change that compelled Canada to negotiate treaties in the West. Grit radicalism on political and ecclesiastical questions contributed substantially to the forces that made the Province of Canada so unworkable that its leaders sought a way out of their constitutional impasse in a general union of British North America (BNA). Given the state of imperial relations in the middle decades of nineteenth century, a BNA union would lead to the acquisition of the Hudson's Bay Company lands by the newly formed state. And that step – the annexation of Rupert's Land to the fledgling Dominion of Canada – would bring Canada's political leaders face to face with the necessity to establish a political relationship with the Aboriginal peoples of western Canada. In other words, given the circumstances prevailing in the 1860s, Clear Grit radicalism of the sort William McDougall espoused led by a circuitous path to treaty-making in the Hudson's Bay Company lands.

As important as the Hudson's Bay Company (HBC) was in Rupert's Land, it was only one of several groups with which Canada had to deal. The HBC had established a long-standing and generally fruitful relationship with both First Nations and the Métis, the mixed-blood offspring of the fur trade, by the nineteenth century. Although on paper the Hudson's Bay Company was the monopoly trader, landlord, and political overseer, in reality it had to accommodate the needs, demands, and protocols of the First Nations who were essential to the trade. In any event, by the eve of Canadian Confederation, the HBC was experiencing a corporate transformation that would revolutionize its role in western Canada. Those changes would diminish the HBC's traditional hostility towards settlement, and make it a willing partner with Canada in negotiating treaties that would pave the way for settlement of the Plains.

The other major actors in the West – the First Nations and the Métis – were not likely to cheer the onset of agricultural migration from Canada as the Hudson's Bay Company did. Both First Nations and Métis had participated successfully in the European fur trade that the HBC, and later the North West Company, brought to the West. However, unlike the HBC, these two groups were not able to respond as readily to change in the nineteenth century. Queen Victoria's era, in fact, would prove a most trying time for both, as shrinking food resources on the Plains brought about a series of wars between First Nations, and between some First Nations and the Red River Métis, whose underlying cause was competition for resources. Since the era of the 'Buffalo Wars' coincided with a time of epidemic disease on the Plains, First Nations were in a weakened and anxious state there by the end of the 1860s. While the Métis were not as severely affected by the epidemics, they, too, were buffeted by the decline of the buffalo. Soon, the Métis in Red River found themselves challenged by the advances of a clumsy and insensitive Dominion of Canada, rude overtures that led to armed resistance in the winter of 1869–70. The Resistance, and the hardships occasioned by declining food resources, inter-tribal warfare, and epidemic disease, made the Métis and western First Nations both respond anxiously when Canada initiated treaty-making in the early 1870s.

If Canada was represented by William McDougall, both Indians and Métis in the West could be forgiven for viewing the new country with a jaundiced eye. It was McDougall, of course, who as superintendent general of Indian affairs in the Province of Canada had worked to dispossess First Nations on Manitoulin Island of lands. However, there was more to McDougall's political pedigree than his role in Indian affairs. He had entered political journalism in the late 1840s and then the Canadian legislature in 1858 as a proponent of radical political ideas, the wide-ranging platform of the reformist movement known as the Clear Grits.[2] (The name came from Grits' assertion that they wanted no political triflers in their ranks; they wanted men – only men could vote, of course – who were 'grit clear through.') They stood for radical reform of Canadian politics, by means such as voting by ballot (rather than open voting) and elective institutions throughout the colony's legislative apparatus. Many Grits were admirers of American political practices, and a minority of them was annexationist. What was most unsettling about the Clear Grit platform for the Canadian political state, however, was its support of voluntarism. Voluntarism, sometimes known to its opponents as 'ecclesiastical free trade,' was a belief that religious institutions should be supported solely by the contributions of their adherents, not the state. Such voluntarist ideas set the Grits apart from Roman Catholics, who favoured cooperation between state and church, Anglicans, who regarded themselves as the Established Church in Upper Canada, and the branch of Presbyterianism known as the Church of Scotland Presbyterians. (The other, voluntarist wing was the Free Kirk Presbyterians.)

Victorian Canadians – especially, it seemed, in the central colony known as the Province of Canada from 1841 to 1867 – could and did obsess about such religio-political questions. However, what turned Clear Grit attacks on state-supported denominational schools and the Clergy Reserves, the one-seventh of Crown lands set aside for support of 'a Protestant clergy' in the former Upper Canada, into destabilizing political issues was the way in which the colony was organized. The Province of Canada had been set up following the report of Lord Durham into the reasons for the rebellions of 1837–8 in Lower and Upper Canada. Durham found that the cause of the more serious Lower Canadian insurrection was the antagonistic nationalisms of French and English, and he advocated the assimilation of the French Canadians as the solution to that part of the problem. To bring about assimilation, Durham proposed uniting

Lower Canada and Upper Canada into a single colony, and giving equal legislative representation to the two sections in spite of Lower Canada's larger population. These recommendations were implemented: the Province of Canada came into being in 1841 with an equal number of seats for the representatives from each section, now known officially as Canada East and Canada West, though still referred to by most by their old labels of Lower Canada and Upper Canada. The French-Canadian population east of the Ottawa River seethed.

Roman Catholic French Canadians got over the insult in fairly short order. In less than a decade, the political movement that had supported the rebellion of 1837–8, the Patriotes, evolved into a new group called Les Bleus (literally, The Blues), who were known for their moderation, relative conservatism, and support of Montreal-based commercial, financial, and transportation interests. By the late 1840s, they settled into a Reform coalition with the descendants of the old Upper Canadian Reform Party, who for their part were feeling hard pressed by radical Clear Grittism. In the 1850s, this coalition of the centre-left would dissolve and be replaced by a coalition of the centre-right composed of Bleus, Upper Canadian Tories, and a new moderate Conservative wing from Upper Canada that soon looked to John A. Macdonald, a Kingston lawyer, for leadership. By means of forming and then evolving dominant coalitions, the principal political party of Canada East ensured that it maintained a grip on political power. Through Les Bleus, French Canadians tamed the Union that was designed for their assimilation, and used its legislature to protect their cherished institutions such as language and religion. Since Canada West's population outnumbered Canada East's by the 1850s, the constitutional provision for equal sectional representation now advantaged the French Canadians.

The formation of a powerful centre-right coalition provoked a realignment of progressive forces, and eventually two equally balanced political parties emerged in Canada. One set of issues that divided Conservatives and Reformers in the 1850s were the church-state questions, such as government support of denominational schools, usually Catholic and Protestant schools in

Canada East, and the Clergy Reserves in Canada West. One symptom of the impasse over church-state issues was the inability of Canada West to abolish the Clergy Reserves until 1854, principally because Canada East legislators opposed the step as an attack on religion. Denominational or separate schools were another grievance to Canada West voluntarists, who preferred the supposedly non-denominational Common Schools in their section. In fact, by the early 1860s, Canada West found that separate school rights in that section of the Province were expanded for Catholics by the votes of Canada East legislators. Given the sensitivity of issues of religion, schooling, and church rights, protracted disputation over the voluntarist demands of Reformers exacerbated relations between Canada West and Canada East. Now it was the turn of the English Protestant majority of Canada West to seethe.

The tensions that arose in church-state matters in the 1850s were aggravated by a parallel set of economic issues that had a similarly polarizing effect. Canada East, with Montreal at its economic centre, favoured a series of measures to support trade, banking, and transportation interests that were rooted mainly in Montreal. These issues included incidental tariff protection in the late 1850s to support fledgling industry, support for the Bank of Montreal against the criticism of Canada West Reformers, and lavish financial contributions to railway construction, especially the Grand Trunk Railway, which was intended to run from Montreal to Chicago. The population west of the Ottawa River, and more especially from Belleville west to Windsor, was not opposed to economic development. However, most of the Canada West economy revolved around primary production, wheat and timber, in particular, which could not benefit from tariff protection. Canada West business leaders also resented being held in economic thrall to Montreal-based transportation and a Montreal bank. Producers in the central and western sections of Canada West always had the option of shipping goods through Toronto and the Niagara peninsula to the Erie Canal or American railway lines that ran from upper New York State to the port of New York. Moreover, Canada West entrepreneurs had railway dreams of their own. They hoped to build a rail network that would attract the trade of southwestern and northern regions, including that of the western Plains someday, to Toronto, whence it might be directed down the St Lawrence route to tidewater or via the American system to New York. These economic issues tended to reinforce the sectional tensions that developed initially over matters such as schools and Clergy Reserves.

Given the Province of Canada's constitution, these two constellations of issues pitting Reformers against Conservatives evolved into a condition of political stasis. Because of the sensitive nature of the issues, voters in each section increasingly rallied behind one or the other of the major parties. By the early 1860s, the centre-right coalition known as the Liberal-Conservative Party represented the rural interests of Canada East, the economic ambitions of Montreal, and a small group of conservatively inclined politicians from Canada West. The Reformers were the political vehicle of Canada West's resentments and political aspirations, led by George Brown of the Toronto *Globe* and working in an uneasy alliance with a small band of Canada East radicals known usually as Les Rouges (literally, The Reds). The problem was that each section of the Province had equal representation in the Legislative Assembly, the elected lower chamber in which most of the political action occurred. If each section had equal legislative representation, and each section was represented solidly in the Legislative Assembly by one political party, then it followed that the two large parties were of roughly equal strength. That, by and large, was the situation in the Assembly from the late 1850s on. The result was that both Conservative and Reform governments were unstable, lasting in office a short time, unable to pass controversial legislation, and falling when they ventured a courageous measure or lost a few adherents. Sectional political equality and ensuing governmental instability was a condition that politicians and political observers by the 1860s called political deadlock.

As Goldwin Smith, a political sage in late-nineteenth-century Toronto, put it, '... whoever may lay claim to the parentage of

Confederation – and upon this momentous question there has been much controversy – its real parent was Deadlock.'[3] From 1858 until 1864, the political leaders in Canada's Assembly canvassed solutions to the problem of deadlock. Finally, Reformers and Conservatives reached a consensus that a solution should be sought in a general federal union of Britain's North American colonies.[4] Between 1864 and 1867, meetings in Charlottetown, PEI, and Quebec City hammered out the terms of union, and in 1867 the union to be known as the Dominion of Canada was created by the British North America Act. This legislation joined Nova Scotia, New Brunswick, and the Province of Canada in a federal union with a central parliament and four provinces: Nova Scotia, New Brunswick, Quebec, and Ontario. Upper and Lower Canada, Canada West and East, had freed themselves from the vexations of union by submerging themselves in a broader union. Two of the terms on which Confederation was created were of particular relevance to western treaty-making. One clause provided for the entry of new territories 'on Address from the Houses of the Parliament of Canada, and from the Houses of the respective Legislatures of the Colonies,' and specifically listed 'Rupert's Land, the North-western Territory, and British Columbia' as candidates for inclusion. As well, the British North America Act assigned jurisdiction over 'Indians, and Lands reserved for the Indians,' to the Parliament of Canada.[5] The largest province, Ontario, regarded the acquisition of the Hudson's Bay Company lands as a pressing national necessity.

As the new Dominion turned to the acquisition and integration of Rupert's Land, it faced a number of obstacles. One important one was that central Canadians' enthusiasm for the Northwest greatly exceeded their knowledge of it. Since large blocks of unalienated Crown land were no longer available in southern Ontario by the mid-1850s, Ontario expansionists looked to the Hudson's Bay Company lands as the next frontier on which to settle farmers' sons and families, and from which transportation and commercial interests in Toronto hoped to extract riches. However, neither the missionaries nor the Hudson's Bay Company, who constituted the non-Native presence in the West, encouraged agricultural migration with rosy reports about the suitability of Rupert's Land for farming. That image was somewhat altered by two investigations – a Canadian one led by Henry Youle Hind in 1857–8, and the other under John Palliser, sponsored by the British government, 1857–9 – that reported in positive terms on the agricultural potential of the West. Hind's report was uncritically positive, Palliser more discerning. Although Palliser concluded there was a 'fertile belt' suitable for cattle and crops through what today is central Manitoba, Saskatchewan, and Alberta, he also reported that there was a large semi-arid prairie region south of that green belt.

Ontario's aspirations to take over Rupert's Land took human form in the 1860s, when a trickle of young settlers began to make their way to Red River. By the late years of the 1860s, this group, known unaffectionately to the local population as 'the Canadian party,' had established a beachhead for Ontario expansion to the Plains. Unfortunately, their presumptuous ways, including their loudly proclaimed assumption that the West and all in it would inevitably be remade in Ontario's image, made them intensely unpopular with at least part of the population of Red River. To many Red River people, if the Canadian party represented what the Dominion had to offer them, then they wanted no part of Canada. These feelings of local pique were especially strong among Aboriginal peoples because many of the bumptious Canadians held the racist views that were common to their time.

If Canadians' ignorance of the West in general was substantial, what they did not know about the Aboriginal peoples of the West was enormous. Roman Catholic missionary publications had portrayed the West as a land filled with dangerous Indians, the better to encourage generous support of missionaries from Quebec who laboured at St Boniface in Red River, and from 1846 in Ile à la Crosse in what would later be Saskatchewan.[6] The Hudson's Bay Company, which as a fur-trading enterprise had everything to gain by keeping agriculturalists out of the region, did nothing to dispel the West's forbidding image. Central Canadians knew generally that there were both Indians and mixed-blood people, Métis, in the region, but beyond such rudimentary knowledge they had little appreciation of the diversity, numbers, and attitudes of western Aboriginal peoples. The government of Canada at least knew that if it was going to make overtures to these peoples, it would have to rely on the Hudson's Bay Company for logistical support, information, and help bridging the language barrier. The old Province of Canada had found out how useful the HBC was when commissioners Vidal, Anderson, and Robinson made their sorties to the upper Great Lakes between 1848 and 1850. Explorers Hind and Palliser similarly discovered that their expeditions would have been impossible without HBC help. For a Euro-Canadian to do anything in Rupert's Land, the cooperation of the Hudson's Bay Company was indispensable.

On the eve of western treaty-making, the Hudson's Bay Company was changing in ways that would make the Gentleman Adventurers eager partners of the Canadian government. Although the HBC had traditionally been passively hostile to missionaries and agricultural settlement, in the nineteenth century it had had to moderate its attitudes towards these outriders of European civilization. Indeed, one of their number had been the first promoter of Prairie agricultural settlement and the architect of the first Plains treaty with First Nations. Lord Selkirk, a Scottish noble with a keen interest in colonizing British North America with surplus agriculturalists from Scotland, had taken leadership of the HBC and established the Selkirk Settlement near the confluence of the Red and Assiniboine Rivers with the arrival of colonists in 1812.

The presence of sponsored agricultural settlement angered both the local Saulteaux First Nations population and Métis, many of whom were associated with the North West Company, the HBC rival that traded out of Montreal. For example, Grandes Oreilles, a major chief among the Saulteaux, railed against the people he called 'the Landworkers,' 'these makers of gardens.' He asked rhetorically, 'Who gave them our lands?' and threatened to stand with the Nor'Westers if conflict developed with the new settlers.[7] The response from the Métis was more than rhetorical. Their resistance to settlement at Red River came to a head

in 1816 in a clash at Seven Oaks with the forces of Governor
Semple that resulted in the death of twenty-one settlers and one
Métis. The following year, Selkirk's representative negotiated a
treaty with local Saulteaux and Cree for peaceful access to a strip
two miles (3 km) back from the Red and Assiniboine Rivers in
return for two hundred pounds of tobacco annually to the Saulteaux and Cree. The treaty, or 'indenture' as Selkirk's man styled
it, covered a tract back from the rivers that on the Red stretched
from the confluence with the Assiniboine southward to Red Lake
River (now Grand Forks, North Dakota), and westward along the
Assiniboine from the confluence to Musk Rat River. When First
Nations signatories asked how far two miles was, they were told
that 'it was the greatest distance, at which a horse on the level
prairie could be seen, or daylight seen under his belly between
his legs.'[8]

The attitude of the directors of the Hudson's Bay Company to
agricultural settlement in Rupert's Land changed only slowly.
The Selkirk Treaty of 1817 was followed by the Company's facili-
tation of the arrival of an Anglican missionary in 1820. Permitting
the Rev. John West to set up a mission in Red River was a concession because the leadership of the HBC regarded missionaries as
a force likely to 'spoil' Indians for participation in the fur trade.
The directors agreed to West's entry as a concession to the
humanitarian side of British imperialism that was growing in
influence in Great Britain. By the 1850s the Company found itself
under attack by the twin forces of Canadian expansionists and
British humanitarians, both of whom alleged that the HBC delib-
erately thwarted development to retain the West as its fur-trading
preserve. The critics had a field day at the hearings of the British
parliamentary committee on renewal of the Hudson's Bay
Company licence in 1857. While the HBC's authority to trade was
renewed, it was becoming obvious that the writing was on the wall
for the Company's monopoly control of its fur-trading empire.

In the 1860s the Hudson's Bay Company began to shift its policies in response to the new forces that it now faced. One of those
threatening innovations was American competition from the
south, which began in earnest in the 1840s with an expanded

buffalo robe trade, and took on a more menacing form with tech-
nological innovations that the Americans introduced. The
coming of rail service to the American West in the 1860s would
lead the HBC to reorient its transportation system. Instead of
relying on ocean transport to ports on Hudson Bay and canoe
brigades to carry trade goods to inland posts and furs out to tidewater, the Company would use American lines, river boats, and
lake steamers for transport to and from Norway House, the
inland entrepot a bit north of the head of Lake Winnipeg that
served as the HBC distribution point for inland posts.[9] This
change in transport orientation would mean that many First
Nations men who previously had relied on the Company for seasonal employment in canoe brigades would find that income disappearing.

More dramatic was the HBC's reorientation away from fur
commerce. In 1863 control of the Hudson's Bay Company fell
into the hands of entrepreneurs who were as interested in land
development as they were in furs.[10] The new leadership would
orient the HBC towards settling farmers in the southern portion
of Rupert's Land and the promotion of telegraph and railway
construction across the Prairies to the Pacific. They were interested in land development and mining. The Company was now
controlled by directors whose aim was 'to realise the values of the
southern parts of Rupert's Land rather than to manage a trade to
the north.'[11] What these changes meant for Canada's ambition to
control the Northwest and the consequent necessity to make
treaties with First Nations was that the Hudson's Bay Company in
the West would be as important an agent for getting treaties as it
had been at Sault Ste Marie in 1850, but now the Company would
not see treaties and settlers as a threat to its core business.

The impact of changes emanating from southern Ontario and
HBC headquarters in London fell on a varied group of First
Nations in the West. The Indians of Rupert's Land could be
divided into two major categories: woodlands nations and Plains
peoples. While there certainly were similarities between these two
Aboriginal cultures, there were also important distinctions. From

the Lake of the Woods area on the east to the Rocky Mountains on the west, the group of woodlands peoples who inhabited the boreal forest included Saulteaux (Western Ojibwa), Woodland Cree, Woodland Assiniboine, and Dene. (With the exception of the Saulteaux, who were found in the southeastern portion of this large area, these First Nations are often classified by anthropologists as Subarctic.) Their societies were characterized by small concentrations of population and seasonal migration to pursue the resources of the rivers, lakes, and forests of their homelands. Social organization focused on the families of male hunters, often relatives, who travelled and worked together to gather freshwater fish of various species, moose, woodland caribou, hare, beaver, and muskrat. The necessity for wide-ranging movement to harvest a large number of resources ensured that the bands of the woodlands First Nations tended to be small. The resources of the land usually would not support large concentrations of hunter-gatherers.

The Plains nations who lived in the prairie region south of the forest were equally numerous. From east to west, they included Saulteaux near Red River, Assiniboine (a Siouan people), Plains Cree, and the Blackfoot Confederacy (Siksika, or Blackfoot proper; Kainai, or Blood; and Piikuni, or Peigan). These groups sometimes cooperated with the Tsuu T'ina (Sarcee), an Athapaskan people, and the Stoney, a Siouan nation in the foothills. While the Plains peoples relied on fishing at some seasons, as well as small game, what distinguished them most from woodlands First Nations was their dependence on the bison. In fact, these shaggy animals were a central prop of Plains culture, and, along with the horses that came from the Spanish in the south and the firearms that came from the British in the north in the early eighteenth century, constituted the foundations of the Plains way of life. Plains peoples were equestrian hunters, traders, and warriors whose entire existence depended on the bison. The buffalo provided meat, of course, but also hides that were used for everything from tipi coverings to the drive belts of factory machines in the East. The bison head and horns figured in Plains religious observances such as the Sun Dance, the stomach was a storage

5.1 Plains First Nations hunting bison on horseback

vessel, and dried manure even served as fuel. When outsiders, such as land-hungry Ontarians, thought of the First Nations of the West, they envisaged mounted hunters in galloping pursuit of thundering bison herds.

In addition to the woodland and Plains First Nations, the West was also peopled by Métis, the mixed-blood population that was one of the most important products of the fur trade. The male European fur traders who spent long periods in the western interior had often formed relationships with indigenous women, even though the Hudson's Bay Company officially forbade such unions. The North West Company, on the other hand, had no policy against 'country marriages.' By the nineteenth century, particularly in the Red River area, it was possible to distinguish between two subgroups, those who were fathered by English-speaking men, Scottish or English, and those whose European parentage was French-Canadian. When the missionaries began their work in Red River, Norway House, west-central Saskatchewan, the North Saskatchewan River near Fort Edmonton, and southern Alberta, religious difference also figured in the distinctive characteristics of the two subgroups.

Anglophone Métis, who were usually known as halfbreeds or countryborn, were usually Anglican or Presbyterian in faith and English in speech. The francophone Métis, known usually as Métis though sometimes as *bois-brûlés* (literally burntwood people), were Roman Catholic and French-speaking. Both groups were also likely to speak an indigenous Métis tongue, which the French speakers called *michif* and the anglophones *bungee*. Too much should not be made of these ethnic and religious differences because, in spite of occasional religious tensions, the two branches of the larger Métis family cooperated and lived harmoniously.

Certainly both groups of the Métis had played a similar role in the fur trade. They served as the collectors of furs, boatmen, hunters for the posts, and, later, as gatherers of provisions for the Hudson's Bay Company. Beginning in the early nineteenth century, Métis of both religious persuasions had begun to establish winter homes in the Red River District, along the Red and Assiniboine Rivers, and also a bit further west of Red River in a district known as the White Horse Plain. In their respective Catholic and Protestant parishes, they formed the beginnings of a permanent population, along with Selkirk's largely Scottish settlers and a number of fur-trade managerial personnel, often with First Nations or Métis wives and families, who began to use Red River as a retirement colony. In the hinterland regions, communities usually did not distinguish between who was First Nation and who Métis. Such distinctions apparently mattered only to Europeans.

For its first 150 years, the fur trade that produced the Métis and heavily involved the First Nations of the West was one dominated by its Aboriginal participants. Whether the non-Native trade partner was the Hudson's Bay Company or, from the 1780s onward, also the North West Company, the outsiders were dependent on the Natives. The economics of the fur trade only made sense if the companies had to support and pay just a small number of representatives in fur-trade country. Such requirements ensured that the Aboriginal participants would provide by far the largest share of the labour that kept the trade going. So

Native peoples gathered the furs and transported them to trading posts, for the first century on Hudson Bay, but from 1774 onward at inland posts as well. These arrangements made the European and Canadian traders dependent in many ways on their Native partners, although at some seasons Native traders short of food might need the resources of the post, such as oatmeal. Western Natives always looked to the European traders for tea, tobacco, firearms and ammunition, specialized services such as musket repair, and alcohol. The dynamics of the relationship changed after the first century, first when the incursions of the Nor'West-ers introduced competition that sometimes benefited the First Nations, and again after the amalgamation of the HBC and North West Company as a new Hudson's Bay Company in 1821 removed the advantages that competition had conferred on First Nations and noticeably diminished the employment prospects of young Métis males. Although the fur trade was less Native-domi-nated after 1821, throughout its existence it remained a com-merce that depended for success on Aboriginal participants.

Aboriginal protocol emerged during the first century of fur commerce, persisted through the competitive fur-trade era, and would influence relations as late as the treaty-making era. In addi-tion to the initial negotiations by which newcomers secured entrance and permission to operate in First Nations territory, each new season fur traders renewed their relationship by means of a series of ceremonies that were rooted in Aboriginal custom. On the approach of a brigade of Indian canoes bringing pelts to the post, the chief trader would order that the cannon be fired as a salute to the arriving party. Next, the chief trader or another senior officer would proceed to where the party had landed and welcome them officially. Then, the chief trader would entertain the visitors in the post at a highly ritualized meeting. The Indians' trading captain and the post's senior official would smoke the pipe, exchange greetings again, inquire as to how the respective parties had fared since their last meeting, and express sympathies for untoward developments such as major illness and death that the other group had suffered. The officer would provide food to the visitors, and the two parties would exchange presents. The Indians would give the chief trader a collection of skins gathered from their party, and the officer later would provide clothing. If the company supplied alcohol to the Indians, they would take it to their encampment to consume it communally, along with any remaining food. Only after such welcoming ceremonies did trading actually start, usually beginning on the next day. In Rupert's Land, as throughout North America, 'exchange between North American Indian groups was a political as well as an economic activity. Indians would not trade with groups with whom they were not formally at peace. Therefore, prior to the commencement of trade, ceremonies were held to conclude or renew alliances.'[12]

Observance of First Nations protocol persisted through the nineteenth century. According to Canon Edward Ahenakew, an Anglican Cree clergyman and historian, Plains Cree chief Thunderchild noted that the Hudson's Bay Company 'gave one boat load of goods for the use of the Saskatchewan River' to Indians at Fort Carlton before establishing themselves in that location for trade.[13] Archdeacon Abraham Cowley of the Anglican Church Missionary Society observed in the spring of 1852 at Fort Pelly, in southern Rupert's Land, that an approaching Cree trading party stopped at the home of Native catechist Charles Pratt, 'as I believe is their custom, to dress & prepare to appear at the Ft.' Then, when 'painted &c to their satisfaction they left Pratt's on their way to the Ft. firing salutes at intervals as they advanced.' When they reached the trading post

in due marching order [they] were met & welcomed by Mr. Buchanan. In the same stately order they proceeded through the yard & into the room where I was sitting. The Chief walked first, an old Ojibwa followed & after him all the rest in single file & very stately. This seemed remarkable as I had never seen anything like it among Indians before; there was a dignity in their deportment which was quite imposing. The room had been previously prepared for their reception & they took their seats in the same dignified manner in which they had hitherto conducted themselves. Tobacco was on the table & the Interpreter filled & handed a pipe to the Chief, who having smoked a little while passed it on to the next. Meanwhile the Interpreter filled another pipe for him which he used as before. Mr. Buchanan now made a speech which was interpreted by Mr. McKay on the state of the trade & its prospects & on the duties of the chief &c after which the Chief replied. One glass of rum was then passed out to each & they left the room to go and trade the articles which they had brought for barter.[14]

Similar ceremonial was observed in the 1850s at Fort Edmonton, as well. Henry Moberly noted that 'the chiefs were met at the main gate by the officer in charge. As the hands of the head chief and the Hudson's Bay Company official joined, the flag of the old organization rose to the peak of the mast in the square and the cannon in one of the bastions boomed.' Inside, after the pipe and some liquor had been shared, 'the head chief then rose and made his talk asking the master to pity and favour them proclaiming that they had done their best and would try to do better in the future.' The trading post factor reciprocated with a genial speech.[15]

This continuity in Europeans' recognition of First Nations protocol was a vital formative influence on the western First Nations who would enter treaty negotiations in the 1870s. They were accustomed to dealing with European and Euro-Canadian fur traders who respected their culture, operated according to the precepts of Indian Country, and followed their rituals. Western First Nations would, not surprisingly, approach government treaty commissioners who were accompanied by prominent Hudson's Bay Company officers in the 1870s with the expectation that they were dealing with the same kind of people who held similar attitudes.

The Métis, especially around Red River, experienced no such continuity in their relations with either the Hudson's Bay Company or the new Dominion of Canada. After the disruption occasioned by the coming of the Selkirk settlers in the second decade of the nineteenth century, the amalgamation of 1821 dealt them more blows. The cost-cutting undertaken by the

Company's governor, Sir George Simpson, fell with particular severity on the traders' mixed-blood offspring. Increasingly, young Métis found their career prospects in the Company limited, as those in charge of the HBC apparently operated in a racially discriminatory way in selecting men for promotion. By the middle of the nineteenth century, even the most talented and energetic Métis could realistically expect to advance no higher than command of an individual post.[16] This discrimination was exacerbated by two other factors. European traders showed a preference for mixed-blood women over First Nations women as spouses, and from the 1820s onward the most highly placed Bay officers, such as Simpson himself, chose Caucasian women as wives.[17] These forms of discrimination occurred at the same time as rabble-rousing Protestant clergy introduced severe denominational tensions into Red River by depicting francophone, Catholic Métis negatively.[18]

In addition to diminished career prospects and worsening cultural strife, Red River Métis faced increasing economic problems in the decades after 1821. A major problem was the growing pressure on the bison resource that resulted from a heavy reliance on the provisioning trade by both Plains First Nations and Métis, as well as increasing pressure on the southern plains from hunters. Besides cutting down the size of the herds, these pressures accounted for conflict between Red River Métis and some First Nations, as well eventually as the inter-tribal battles known as the 'Buffalo Wars' between Blackfoot and Plains Cree, in particular.[19] When the bison-hunting parties ranged out from Red River further each season in search of their prey, they began to run into parties of Dakota who defended their hunting territories militarily. While these martial encounters gave the Red River Métis some of their most glorious community memories, they also were a reminder that the shrinking bison resource threatened them with economic hardship.

By the later 1860s, both First Nations and Métis in Red River and its hinterland were beginning to feel pinched by changes brought on by an advancing tide of non-Native settlement and development. In the environs of Lower Fort Garry, near the fork of the Red and Assiniboine Rivers, the unsettling harbinger of change was the Canadian party, with its airy assumption that the inevitable fate of Rupert's Land was annexation to Canada and submission to the economic ambitions of Ontario. East of Fort Garry, in the treed and lake-dotted area known as the North West Angle, the incursions of Canada were a provocation to the Cree and Saulteaux of the region, too. It had been a dream of ambitious Canadians to create easier access to Rupert's Land by building a road along what was known as the Dawson Route, a land version of the water links from Thunder Bay, the head of the Great Lakes, to the prairies and Fort Garry. Simon Dawson, an Ontarian who gave his name to the route, had warned as early as 1858 that the sensibilities and interests of Natives in the region had to be accommodated to avoid trouble.[20] A manifestation of government interest in both the Dawson Route and westward expansion was Canada's support of a crew to hack out a road from St Boniface to the North West Angle of the Lake of the Woods in 1868.

Canada sent road builders west because the new country planned to move swiftly to acquire territorial rights to Rupert's Land from the Hudson's Bay Company and incorporate the vast western territory into the new federation. Acquisition of the West had for many years been a major plank in the program of Upper Canadian Reformers. For them, Confederation was attractive for both the separation and the extension it would bring about: separation from the French Roman Catholics of Canada East, and extension of Ontario farmers and Ontario interests west to HBC lands. The first post-Confederation cabinet headed by Sir John A. Macdonald moved relatively quickly, considering the other challenges it faced, to open negotiations with the Hudson's Bay Company and the United Kingdom to secure Rupert's Land for Canada. Bargaining between the Company and Canada did not go well at first, principally because Ottawa initially was not willing to pay anything for the land. However, Canada was able to get British influence to work for it with the Company, and in due course a bargain was struck whereby the HBC would surrender its rights and claims in Rupert's Land to the United Kingdom for transmission to the Dominion on 1 December 1869 in return for £300,000, land around the posts to a maximum of 50,000 acres (20,000 hectares), and one-twentieth of the arable lands in the 'fertile belt' where settlement was expected to take place.

Conspicuous by their absence from these deliberations were the people whose land it was, the First Nations and Métis. It had been generally understood for several decades in Ontario that negotiation for access with First Nations would take place. That was well-established precedent in Ontario by 1867, and early post-Confederation federal cabinets were dominated by Ontarians. However, no consideration apparently had been given to the Métis of the region. The Red River Métis, led by men from the French-speaking, Roman Catholic portion of the community, would soon make those opinions clear. Rumours had swirled around Red River about the discussions among Canada, Britain, and the HBC, and when Canadian surveyors began laying out their lines in the narrow Métis lots stretching back from the Red River in the autumn of 1869, a party of men led by Louis Riel, Junior, stepped in, halted the proceedings, and ordered the surveyors away.

Riel was the right man in the right spot in 1869. He had been born in 1844 in St Vital Parish, the son of Louis Riel, a local leader, and Julie Lagimodière.[21] A bright child, he had been singled out by the local Catholic clergy for further education, perhaps preparatory to a vocation as a priest, and sent to Montreal to study in 1858. In the early 1860s, Riel imbibed the potent ideologies of Catholic ultramontanism and French-Canadian nationalism along with his studies. He dropped out of college and began to read law with Rodolphe Laflamme, a Rouge firebrand newspaperman and Quebec politician. The 1864 death of his father left him disconsolate and guilty about not being with his mother and siblings in Red River at a difficult time. He also fell in love with a young Québécoise, but found his suit rejected, apparently, at least in part, because her parents did not approve of a racially mixed marriage. A failure in schooling and love, buffeted emotionally by family loss and racial discrimination, Louis Riel made his way back to Red River in July 1869. A bright, well-educated man from a prominent family, he soon emerged as the real leader of what quickly became the Red River Resistance to Canada's assertion of control over Rupert's Land.

Although the Resistance was a success for Riel and the Métis, it led to events with lamentable consequences. At the outset, Canada fumbled badly. William McDougall, the negotiator of the 1862 Manitoulin Island Treaty, went west as lieutenant-governor of Manitoba and the North-Western Territory via the United States, armed with his commission and instructions to govern the western territory with an appointed council.[22] That the new government was not going to have a locally elected assembly, as well as the fact that its vice-regal head had a reputation as a rabid Clear Grit and his instructions said nothing about the property, educational, and religious rights of local inhabitants, merely confirmed the worst fears of the parishes along the Red and Assiniboine Rivers. Métis horsemen blockaded the road north along the Red River from American territory and deterred the would-be governor from entering Rupert's Land. When Canada learned of the opposition to McDougall, it cabled the British government that Canada would not accept the 1 December transfer of title because Rupert's Land was not in a peaceful state, and then Ottawa sent word to its lieutenant-governor cooling his heels in Pembina not to enter Rupert's Land and proclaim Canadian control. McDougall, however, ignored his instructions. He slipped over the border in the dead of night on 30 November, and read to the prairie wilderness the proclamation of the transfer of Rupert's Land to Canada and his own appointment as its lieutenant-governor.

Riel, backed by Métis, walked a dangerous tightrope for the next six months as he tried to compel Canada to come to terms with his community. Serious tensions arose along ethnic lines among the Métis, especially after Riel moved quickly to create a Provisional Government.[23] Riel's followers attacked an armed force of the Canadian party, seized supplies, and imprisoned the armed Canadians. Riel was able to maintain his Provisional Government in force thanks in no small part to the unwavering support he had from Métis boatmen who were back in the colony because of their seasonal unemployment in winter. Eventually, Riel and the Provisional Government appointed three delegates to travel to Ottawa in early 1870 to negotiate terms for entry of the territory into Canada. Matters might have proceeded harmoniously and productively, save for two things. First, Riel and the Provisional Government unwisely shot a young Canadian prisoner, Thomas Scott, to death for 'insubordination and striking his guards.' Second, the entire Resistance, especially the shooting of Scott, enraged those parts of Ontario opinion where expansionist fervour was strongest.

When they looked west, Ontarians saw Catholic priests in Red River and French-Canadian politicians in Quebec conniving to prevent the entry of the West on terms Ontario approved.[24] When the Provisional Government's emissaries negotiated the entry of the Red River district as a new province of Manitoba, with a bicameral (two-house) legislature, official recognition of both French and English languages, and constitutional guarantees of denominational schools, Ontarians were furious. What was being set up on the Plains was not the first of several provinces created in Ontario's image, but a miniature Quebec. In spite of the fact that the union terms were acceptable to both the government and the people of Red River, Ontario anger pushed the government into sending an unnecessary military force to Lower Fort Garry in 1870. Riel fled from the oncoming troops, many of whom were Ontarians with vengeance on their minds.

Although the Red River Resistance ended unfortunately, it did produce some results that were important to the future of both Métis and First Nations in the West. In the legislated version of the negotiated terms of union, the Manitoba Act passed by the Canadian Parliament in 1870, there were guarantees of the existing property rights of Red River property holders that would shelter Métis control of the river lots that they held only by customary title. Furthermore, the founding Act authorized setting aside 1.4 million acres (560,000 hectares) of public land for future land grants to 'the children of the half-breed heads of families residing in the Province at the time of the said transfer to Canada.' As important as the clause itself was the language that was employed both in the statute and in the government's parliamentary defence of the legislation to justify it. The Manitoba Act said, 'And whereas, it is expedient, towards the extinguishment of the Indian Title to the lands in the Province, to appropriate a portion of such ungranted lands ...'[25] In the House of Commons, Prime Minister Macdonald defended the provisions by saying that the 1.4 million acres were 'a reservation for the purpose of extinguishing the Indian title ...'[26] Such statutory and parliamentary language acknowledged that Aboriginal title existed in the West. And, if the Métis of Red River had to be compensated for their share of Aboriginal title by the provisions of the Manitoba Act, did it not follow logically that Canada would have to negotiate its way into the West with First Nations, too?

In addition to the language in the Manitoba Act that protected Métis and First Nations territorial rights, the agreement among the Hudson's Bay Company, Britain, and Canada for the transfer of Rupert's Land from the HBC to Canada included a clause that obligated the Dominion to negotiate with First Nations. The Imperial Order in Council that proclaimed the transfer said: 'Any claims of Indians to compensation for lands required for purposes of settlement shall be disposed of by the Canadian Government in communication with the Imperial Government; and the Company shall be relieved of all responsibility in respect of them.'[27] If the precedent of Upper Canadian treaty-making, the Manitoba Act's language justifying the 1.4-million-acre land grant to the Métis, and the salutary lesson Canada had learned at Red River about the consequences of ignoring the local inhabitants had not inclined Ottawa towards quick negotiations with western First Nations, the language of the transfer agreement would have.

Reinforcing the obligations that flowed from the Manitoba Act and the Rupert's Land agreement were threats of resistance from First Nations along the access route to Red River. The activities of Canadian road builders and the government's announcement that a military force would be making its way west to Red River in 1870 caused great unrest among the Saulteaux groups in the woodlands in and adjacent to the North West Angle. Simon J.

Dawson had been warning Ottawa politicians for a decade of the importance of the land route to Red River, as well as the necessity to stay on good terms with the First Nations whose territory it was. When Canada sent an emissary, Wemyss S. Simpson, to the region in June 1870, he learned that the local 'people if illused or pro-voked would become a most serious bar to the settlement of the Northwest and could prevent any but strongly armed parties from going through their lands.' On the other hand, local leaders seemed conciliatory. Simpson reported the head chief of the 1,500 Indians he held council with near Fort Frances as saying, 'I do not intend to try and stop the soldiers from passing through my lands on their way to Red River but I expect a present & if Mr. Dawson is to make roads through our country I expect to be paid for the right of way. They Surveyors [illegible words] & we know that when they once come settlers will follow.'[28] The Dominion made haste to send provisions into the district to assist the Indians, and no doubt accelerated planning for making treaties with the First Nations of Fort Frances, the North West Angle, and vast portions of Rupert's Land.

Canada moved more circumspectly in bringing British Colum-bia into Confederation in 1871, but the expansion to the Pacific merely raised additional treaty-related challenges. British Colum-bia was an essential element of any transcontinental state, making it, despite of its sparse non-Native population and limited eco-nomic attractions for easterners, a vital partner in Confederation. Little noticed at the time was the fact that colonial BC's history of relations with First Nations had been dramatically different from that of the eastern part of the country. Although mainland British Columbia and Vancouver Island had also participated in the fur trade, ensuring that commercial interactions dominated Native-newcomer relations from the 1770s until almost the middle of the nineteenth century, other elements of the relationship found in eastern Canadian history were absent. For one thing, there was no era in which military relations had necessitated forging treaties of peace and friendship such as had dominated in the East. Nor was there any Royal Proclamation tradition in British Columbia for the simple reason that that declaration was never intended to apply to the lower mainland, let alone Vancouver Island.

Even British Columbia's limited experience with territorial treaties was sharply different from that of the rest of the country. Between 1850 and 1854, James Douglas, former Hudson's Bay Company man and governor of the Vancouver Island colony, had responded to the beginnings of settlement at a number of points on the island by negotiating treaties with the local Coast Salish and Kwagiult groups. When he consulted Britain's Colonial Office, officials provided him, not with any of the Upper Canadian treaties that had by then been negotiated, but with a sample of land agreements that the New Zealand Company had made with Maori for land in the South Pacific. Douglas also asked the chiefs whether they would prefer one-time payments or annuities, and was told that the former were more to their taste. Accordingly, when he negotiated fourteen such agreements in limited locales around Victoria, Nanaimo, and Fort Rupert at the northern tip of the Island, these Douglas Treaties were for very small tracts of land and were in return for payments of goods that the governor obtained from the Hudson's Bay Company stores. Even this limited experiment in Pacific treaty-making soon ceased when the colony acquired an elected assembly whose members were unwilling to provide the resources for more treaties. The assemblymen took the position that funding territorial treaties was the imperial government's responsibility, whereas London thought that those who benefited from such agreements, the colonists, should pay for them. As a result of this difference of opinion, treaty-making came to a halt on Vancouver Island.[29]

Prior to the last years of the nineteenth century, the only other form of treaty that was made in what became the Province of British Columbia in 1871 were the commercial-territorial agreements that semi-organized groups of gold miners made with Coast Salish groups along the Fraser River during the gold rush there in the later 1850s. Were these truly treaties as the term is used here? While they were not made by the British Crown or Hudson's Bay Company personnel, they were negotiated by groups who had organized themselves – sometimes as militias – into the only form of non-Native government that existed in the near-vacuum created by miners rushing in and First Nations resisting them. In any event, these pacts were agreements to permit the prospectors and miners to exploit the mineral potential of the valley under agreed-upon conditions. Even the term 'agreement' strains the language, because some of these pacts were concluded under duress. Belligerent miner militia groups made it clear by their behaviour and words that the alternative to Natives' agreeing to permit their economic activities was extreme violence.[30] Thus, when British Columbia entered Confederation, it did so with a distinctive history of Native-newcomer relations and, by standards that prevailed in the rest of the country, an unusual tradition of making treaties.

The terms on which British Columbia became a province dramatically affected future Native-newcomer relations, including treaty-making, in the province. The terms of union contained clauses that bore directly on these two policy areas. 'The charge of the Indians, and the trusteeship and management of the lands reserved for their use and benefit, shall be assumed by the Dominion Government, and a policy as liberal as that hitherto pursued by the British Columbia Government shall be continued by the Dominion Government after the Union,' was the article regulating jurisdiction over First Nations. This clause would constitute the basis for a marathon battle between the federal and BC governments over Indian affairs, especially the vexed question of reserve lands, for more than half a century. The article of the union agreement concerning a transcontinental railway at least appeared to be more straightforward: Canada promised 'to secure the commencement' of such a line 'within two years from the date of the Union' and 'to secure the completion of such railway within ten years from the date of the Union.'[31] Although the railway commitment caused relations between Victoria and Ottawa more intense grief than the article on jurisdiction over Indian affairs in the short term, both would prove extremely contentious. More to the point, the undertaking to construct a transcontinental rail line with what in hindsight can only be called breakneck speed ensured that the federal government would find the pressures on it to negotiate treaties with First Nations on the Plains greatly increased.

In 1870, Canada and its newly acquired West were poised uncertainly on the brink of an era of negotiation to legitimize and facilitate settlement of the Prairies. A potent symbol of the changing times were the new Dominion's plans for railway construction across the West. There was great uneasiness among Native peoples in the region about their future with Canada. Inter-tribal wars and epidemic disease had taken their toll among First Nations. The shrinkage of the bison resource, on which all western Aboriginal peoples relied, was a cause for worry about the sustainability of their way of life in future. To that anxiety was added the prospect of the entry of large numbers of agricultural settlers, an influx that Canada fervently hoped would bring the fulfilment of eastern dreams for the success of Confederation. Christian missionaries and Hudson's Bay Company men, the Europeans with whom western First Nations were used to dealing, had told western Natives these changes were coming. On the other hand, Canada had obligations towards the people of the West that somewhat offset the worries westerners had to face. Having made dozens of treaties in Ontario in the past, having agreed to settle Native claims in the transfer of Rupert's Land to the Dominion, having negotiated the terms of entry with the Métis after the Red River Resistance, and having acknowledged the existence of 'Indian title' in the federal Parliament, Canada could hardly avoid negotiating treaties with the First Nations of western Canada.

6

'I think that the Queen Mother has offered us a new way':[1] The Southern Numbered Treaties, 1871–1877

On a fine Sunday afternoon in October 1874, an imposing Plains Cree man and a Métis man rode up to the cabin of John Hines, a young missionary, at Whitefish Lake, in the Saskatchewan country. The tall man, Chief Ahtahkakoop, had a lot on his mind. For over a decade, he had watched and worried about the changes that were occurring in his territory. It had been obvious for some time that the bison on whom his people depended were declining in numbers and accessibility. The band's recent autumn hunt, during which they had had to range out much farther to the south than usual to locate their prey, was a reminder of the problem. 'I never had to go so far before to seek buffalo, and then we only saw a few,' he said. 'When I think of the large herds of buffalo and other animals that used to roam about our country, and compare the state of things then with what they are now, my mind gets troubled.' Concerns about food security had led him to experiment with keeping gardens ten years earlier; he had found that it was not easy to pursue the bison and maintain crops at the same time. Ahtahkakoop had also been troubled by the inter-tribal wars, especially with the Blackfoot, that had been destructive until just a few years ago, and the succession of epidemics that had afflicted the Plains through the late 1860s and early 1870s. Just this year, several more novelties had arrived: the Rev. John Hines, a steamboat on the North Saskatchewan River, and a party of mounted policemen who travelled through on their way to Fort Edmonton.[2]

6.1 Ahtahkakoop (left front) and Mistawasis (right front) were major influences at treaty talks at Fort Carlton in August 1876. The other figures are Chief Osoup (back), Peter Hourie, interpreter, and Flying in a Circle (front centre).

Ahtahkakoop knew what he wanted from the missionary. He sought help mastering horticulture so that his people would have another source of food. 'I have seen this calamity coming upon us for years past, but some will not believe it even now, and I have had a longing desire to settle down and get my living like the white man, but I have had no one to teach me.' He also wanted schooling for the younger generation. For Hines, Ahtahkakoop's interests appeared to be a gift from heaven. He had been looking for a site at which to carry out the mission for which his sponsor, the Church Missionary Society, had sent him to North America. The missionary

> ... told him my object in leaving the country across the great water, where the great Queen lived, and coming many miles to see his country was that the praying masters over there had heard from one of their Bishops that the Indians in the Saskatchewan country were likely, in the course of a few years, to come face to face with starvation, owing, as he had just said, to the disappearance of the wild animals, and this same Bishop had asked the praying masters to send some one who would live with these Indians and teach them, not only how to cultivate the ground and raise food from it, but also teach them to raise cattle which would to a certain extent take the place of the buffalo, and also teach the Indians how to make grease from the milk of the cow.

If the missionary provided these useful lessons, 'he could have a school and teach the children to read and understand the white man's language, and so prepare them for the change that was coming; and he could also teach the old people about "Keche Munnato" (the Great God) from His own great Book.' Ahtahkakoop and Hines agreed that the Englishman could instruct Ahtahkakoop's people in farming, Christianity, and secular learning.[3] Although Ahtahkakoop was unusually far-sighted, his concerns were widely shared by Plains First Nations.

More typical of the response of western First Nations to the incursions of newcomers in the few years after Confederation were the

actions of groups that threatened to resist the newcomers. As well
as the Saulteaux near Fort Frances who told Wemyss Simpson
they expected remuneration for use of their land, First Nations
from present-day Manitoba to the foothills of the Rockies made
it clear to the Canadian government that failure to negotiate with
them prior to the entry of settlers would lead to difficulties. Near
Portage la Prairie, Saulteaux bands objected in 1870 about settlers cutting wood and asked for a treaty, and, when Canada did
not respond, in 1871 Chief Yellow Quill's band nailed a warning
to a church door that settlers were not to cut any more firewood:
'When we speak first we speak softly; but when we speak again we
will speak louder. We hardly need say that this alludes to an
attempt that has been made to claim and occupy lands that do
not yet belong to them, for they know that we have not yet
received anything for our lands, therefore they still belong to
us.'[4] In present-day central Saskatchewan, Plains Cree ordered a
telegraph-construction gang and a party from the Geological
Survey of Canada out of the country in 1875. In the same year,
the Blackfoot in southern Alberta sent a message to the lieutenant-governor of the North-Western Territory expressing their
expectation that the Crown would deal with them in advance of
settlement. Among other things, the Blackfoot said that 'we pray
for an Indian Commissioner to visit us at the Hand Hills, Red
Deer River, this year and let us know the time that he will visit
us, so that we could hold a Council with him, for putting a stop
to the invasion of our Country, till our Treaty be made with the
Government.'[5]

The message that these First Nations sent was unmistakable. By
actions, gestures, and words, they made it clear that the territories in which they resided were theirs, and that the Crown had to
take action to secure their agreement before strangers could use
their resources. At the same time, most of the First Nations who
asserted their rights in these ways also said that they bore no ill
will to the government or the people who wanted to enter their
territory. They did, though, express frustration at the dilatory way
the Crown approached the task. The Indians who warned settlers
in southern Manitoba in 1871 did so only after the treaty com-

mission that they had expected did not materialize. The 1875 Blackfoot petition to Lieutenant-Governor Alexander Morris pointedly reminded the official that in 1871 his predecessor, Adams Archibald, had seemed 'to promise us that the Government, or the white man, would not take the Indian lands without a Council of Her Majesty's Indian Commissioner and the respective Chiefs of the Nations.' Nonetheless, in the intervening years, 'the white men have already taken the best locations and built houses in any place they pleased in our "hunting grounds,"' while the Métis 'and the Cree Indians in large Camps are hunting Buffalo, both Summer and Winter, in the very centre of our lands.'

The feelings that motivated western First Nations to broach treaty-making with the Crown were encapsulated in an 1871 petition from Cree chiefs along the North Saskatchewan. Sweet Grass, the most eminent of the group, addressed the lieutenant-governor:

> Great Father, – I shake hands with you, and bid you welcome. We heard our lands were sold and we did not like it; we don't want to sell our lands; it is our property, and no one has a right to sell them.
>
> Our country is getting ruined of fur-bearing animals, hitherto our sole support, and now we are poor and want help – we want you to pity us. We want cattle, tools, agricultural implements, and assistance in everything when we come to settle – our country is no longer able to support us.
>
> Make provision for us against years of starvation. We have had great starvation the past winter, and the small-pox took away many of our people, the old, young, and children.
>
> We want you to stop the Americans from coming to trade on our lands, and giving firewater, ammunition and arms to our enemies the Blackfeet.
>
> We made a peace this winter with the Blackfeet. Our young men are foolish, it may not last long.
>
> We invite you to come and see us and to speak with us. If you can't come yourself, send some one in your place.

Further reassurance came from another petitioner, Kihewin (The Eagle), who said, 'Let us be friendly. We never shed any white man's blood, and have always been friendly with the whites, and want workmen, carpenters and farmers to assist us when we settle. I want all my brother, Sweet Grass, asks.'[6]

The pacific, if at times exasperated, response of western First Nations to Canada's bumptious and insensitive approach to developing Rupert's Land was attributable both to the past they had experienced and the future they anticipated. Until the 1820s, the only Europeans with whom Aboriginal people in the West had dealt were Hudson's Bay Company officials, who, for their part, had adjusted their methods to accommodate indigenous values and practices. After 1820 a few Christian missionaries entered the region from the United Kingdom and eastern Canada, and it was only in the 1850s that a trickle of settlers began to arrive. Natives knew 'government' only in the form of a boundary commission that had traversed the plains to stake the 'medicine line,' the international border, in the early 1870s, and the mounted police who had begun to make their presence felt only in 1874. There was no tradition of defensive warfare against the invaders such as had become common south of the forty-ninth parallel, and at least one western First Nation, the Dakota in Manitoba and Saskatchewan, counted alliance with Great Britain against the Americans in the War of 1812 part of their heritage. Encouraged by Hudson's Bay personnel and missionaries, Plains First Nations were prepared to meet with the representatives of the queen. Collectively, they had begun to worry, as Ahtahkakoop, Sweet Grass, and Kihewin made clear, about the future. They knew of the American Buffalo Lodge Treaty of 1855, which promised various forms of assistance. Might the queen and her government, whatever that was, be a means of coping with their well-founded anxieties?

For its part, the government of the young Dominion of Canada was committed to negotiating western treaties, however incompetently it appeared to be going about the task. The threats of resistance and encouragement to negotiate that officials received from a number of western First Nations strengthened the lesson that Red River Métis had administered about the preferability of negotiating to fighting. If Canada's political leaders looked forward, they could also see that their plans for the West required peaceful relations that could best be secured through treaties. As Ontario expansionists never tired of emphasizing, the success of the new Dominion was dependent on the successful development – by which they meant moulding in the image of southern Ontario – of the Prairies. Attracting farmers to the Plains was essential if the region was to mature and play a role in the nation's future. Obviously, settling the West would be difficult, perhaps impossible, if newcomers could not settle in peace. The military option that the United States was pursuing from 1871 onward to pacify its West was simply not available to Canada. For one thing, the Dominion could not afford it. At a time when the entire annual budget of the federal government was $19 million, the Americans were expending $20 million annually on their western Indian wars.

The final reason that treaties were the only thinkable approach to integrating Rupert's Land into the new Dominion was the transcontinental railway. Could Canada build a line to the Pacific Ocean, as Ottawa was committed to do, through a Prairie region beset by Indian wars? The Conservative governments headed by Sir John A. Macdonald until 1873 recognized that, as the prime minister was later to phrase it, the Dominion would be 'little more than a "geographical expression"'[7] until its far-flung regions were knitted together with bands of steel. Acquisition of the West required agricultural settlement, which necessitated a railway to bring farmers and their goods into the region and their produce out to tidewater. Constructing a railway through the West made peaceful relations with the First Nations indispensable, and good relations were not likely, as a variety of First Nations had made clear, without treaties.

Once the federal government began to respond, it found it needed several different instruments to achieve its objective. One was individuals, such as Member of Parliament Simon Dawson, who already had ties to the regions where treaties were to be made. Dawson also encouraged the government to use locals such as Wemyss Simpson and Nicholas de Chastelain, the men who met with the Saulteaux near Fort Frances in 1870 to reassure them that the passage of troops through their lands posed no threat. A second important group, men who turned out to be principal government treaty commissioners for the seven numbered treaties negotiated in the 1870s, were the lieutenant-governors of Manitoba and the North-Western Territory. Adams G. Archibald, a Nova Scotian, proved a pacifying force in Manitoba following the Resistance of 1869–70 and the disruptive behaviour of some of the military expedition that Canada sent west in the summer of 1870. Alexander Morris, a Conservative lawyer, served as lieutenant-governor after Archibald and negotiated Treaties 3, 4, 5, and 6 (1873–6). Morris's Conservative ties did not lead to his replacement immediately once a Reform (Liberal) government took office in Ottawa in 1874. The costly concessions that Plains Cree negotiators extracted to agree to Treaty 6 in central Saskatchewan and Alberta in 1876, however, contributed to his replacement as lieutenant-governor and principal negotiator by David Laird, a Prince Edward Island politician of impeccable Grit credentials. Laird headed negotiations for Treaty 7 with the Blackfoot in 1877.

The successive lieutenant-governors who led the government's negotiating teams exploited the symbolism of their office. Although they all were appointed by and answerable to the federal government, they portrayed themselves as representatives of Queen Victoria and insisted throughout that the treaties were being made with the Crown. The preamble to the government version of Treaty 1 (1871), for example, said that it was between 'Her Most Gracious Majesty the Queen of Great Britain and Ireland' and the Saulteaux of a portion of Manitoba, mentioned 'Her Most Gracious Majesty' four times in its first paragraph, and concluded this portion of the agreement by stating that its aim was to ensure that Saulteaux negotiators 'may know and be assured of what allowance they are to count upon and receive from Her Majesty's bounty and benevolence.'[8] Alexander Morris showed the greatest awareness of the

6.2 Alexander Morris, government negotiator of Treaties 3, 4, 5, and 6

6.3 Mounted police encampment at Blackfoot Crossing, 1877

potency of the Crown. In 1873, he advocated a combined mili-
tary-police force outfitted in red serge because '50 men in red
coats are better than 100 in other colours.'[9] As lieutenant-governor, he regularly associated his office with the monarchy, and
as a treaty commissioner he frequently linked his mission to
Queen Victoria. 'I wish you to understand we do not come here
as traders, but as representing the Crown, and to do what is just
and right,' he told the Saulteaux.[10] As Morris implied, the
Crown was perceived as a symbol of power and compassion, an
identity of some significance when dealing with First Nations
who knew what 'the long knives,' American cavalry, were doing
to their southern kin. Police serge was visible at the negotiation
of Treaties 6 and more especially 7, where Lt-Col. James F.
McLeod was a government representative and NWMP camped
near the negotiation site.[11]

Although Christian missionaries were not numerous in the Canadian West in 1870, the Canadian government used them intensively – and in a variety of ways – in making treaties. The principal groups were the Roman Catholics, Methodists, and Anglicans, the latter represented by the agents of the Church Missionary Society (CMS). Missionaries were enthusiastic promoters of treaty. First, their contact with Plains First Nations made them anxious about the sustainability of Plains society as the bison declined and settler invasion loomed. Moreover, persuading Indians to enter treaty and adopt sedentary agriculture on reserves was attractive to these men, who tended to view a settled way of life as a marker of 'civilization.' Even before Canada began to make treaties west of Manitoba, it used Methodist John McDougall in 1874 as an emissary to Plains nations to reassure them about the peaceful intentions of the mounted police who were on their way west, and later, following the Cree disruption of the Geological Survey party, Canada dispatched his father, Rev. George McDougall, to distribute presents and assure First Nations in the westerly portion of what would be Treaty 6 that commissioners would be coming next year.[12] During treaty negotiations, church people played a variety of roles. Native catechist Charles Pratt of the CMS and Anglican archdeacon John McKay were interpreters at Treaties 4 and 6 respectively, as was Methodist John McDougall at Treaty 7 in 1877. A number of them were official witnesses of treaty signings: Abraham Cowley of the CMS at Treaty 1; Methodists Egerton Ryerson Young, John H. Ruttan, and O. German at Treaty 5; Catholic bishop Vital Grandin and Oblate Father Constantine Scollen, as well as John McDougall, at the Fort Pitt signing of Treaty 6; and Scollen and McDougall again at Treaty 7.[13]

Missionaries and Christian observances were prominent during treaty negotiations. For example, government representatives often invoked the name of their God in the talks, as Alexander Morris did at Fort Carlton in August 1876: 'I will trust that we may come together hand to hand and heart to heart again. I trust that God will bless this bright day for our good, and give our Chiefs and Councillors wisdom so that you will accept the words of your Governor.' The Cree would have understood when, the following day, the Cree Anglican priest John McKay conducted 'divine service' for the Euro-Canadians in English, and then, on request, 'preach[ed] in their own tongue to a congregation of two hundred adult Crees.' Another government commissioner, William J. Christie of the Hudson's Bay Company, even referred to one of the numbered treaties as 'a covenant' between First Nations in northwestern Ontario and the Crown.[14]

William Christie, the HBC man who had forwarded the comments of Sweet Grass and the other chiefs in 1871, symbolized the HBC's contributions to treaty-making in the 1870s. Given the Company's close ties to First Nations and its desire to see the West peopled with farmers so that it could sell its extensive holdings in the fertile regions, the eagerness of the HBC to facilitate Canada's project was hardly surprising. It was Hudson's Bay carts and boats that moved treaty parties between negotiation sites, and HBC posts such as Fort Qu'Appelle, Fort Carlton, and Fort Pitt that served as venues for the talks. As Treaty Commissioner Wemyss Simpson observed about negotiating Treaties 1 and 2, 'In a country where transport and all other business facilities are necessarily so scarce, the services rendered to the Government by the officers in charge of the several Hudson's Bay Posts has [sic] been most opportune and valuable.'[15] Government representatives frequently found their accommodations in Company facilities, where they were briefed on indigenous matters. Indeed, Saulteaux in the Qu'Appelle district in 1874 objected to holding the treaty talks on HBC property because of their continuing resentment about the 1869–70 transfer of Rupert's Land to Canada, and Beardy of the Willow Cree chose not to meet at Fort Carlton in 1876, necessitating a separate meeting with them to get agreement. (In 1877, the Blackfoot also declined to meet the treaty commissioners at Fort MacLeod, home of the NWMP.) The HBC and its personnel were intimately engaged in the Plains treaty talks from 1871 to 1877.

Métis were the final important players in the treaty talks. Even before Canada initiated treaty negotiations, it found itself making use of mixed-blood emissaries to promote good relations with

First Nations. Nicholas de Chastelain accompanied Wemyss Simpson to Fort Frances in 1870, and James McKay followed up on that mission by travelling to the district and arranging for employment of Indians to relieve their economic distress. Although there were a number of men of mixed Native-European ancestry who participated as pre-negotiation emissaries, interpreters, or even treaty commissioners, probably the most important of them were James McKay and Peter Erasmus.[16] McKay was a former HBC man who had emerged as a successful Red River businessman prior to 1870, and would go on to be a respected member of the first Manitoba Council. A man in whom both First Nations and Métis of Red River had confidence, he frequently served as a sounding board for Native frustrations and a tactful advocate of Canada's cause in negotiations. In situations such as the North West Angle in 1873 and Fort Qu'Appelle in 1874, where there was considerable unease on the Native side, he was a persuasive champion for Canada. Less interventionist, but still highly influential as an interpreter at Treaty 6, was Peter Erasmus, a mixed-blood trader who had sufficient credibility with First Nations that Plains Cree chiefs Ahtahkakoop and Mistawasis hired him to be their independent interpreter at Fort Carlton. When neither of the government interpreters, James McKay and Rev. John McKay, could translate to the satisfaction of the Indians, Morris also retained Erasmus – he apparently was paid both by the chiefs and the government – as official interpreter as well. In Treaty 7, mixed-blood men Jerry Potts and 'Jimmy Jock' Bird provided similar translation services. Although the motivation of Métis who acted on behalf of Canada in the talks is not completely clear, it appears that they had taken the measure of the change going on in the prairie West and concluded that, given their mercantile backgrounds, the best bet for their future lay with Canada.[17]

Although the Stone Fort Treaty was the first pact to be negotiated in 1871, the government had not intended it to be the initial treaty. At first, Ottawa had focused on getting formal agreement covering the strategically and economically important region of northwest Ontario that included the Dawson Route, but negotiating difficulties with the mainly Ojibwa Indians there prevented a meeting of minds for several summers. Consequently, commissioner Wemyss Simpson, with James McKay and Adams Archibald, lieutenant-governor of Manitoba and the North-Western Territory, as witnesses, met a large group of Indians – perhaps as many as 1,000 – at Lower Fort Garry, the major Hudson's Bay Company establishment a short distance north of Winnipeg. There were difficulties with the First Nations in the Treaty 1 region. For one thing, their concern about the arrival of troops in the summer of 1870 and the imminence of settler immigration had caused them to petition the lieutenant-governor urgently in 1870 asking for a meeting. They were not pleased that Archibald put them off until 1871. When the meeting actually occurred late in August 1871, some of the chiefs were also angry because four Swampy Cree had been imprisoned for breach of contract for boatmen services with the HBC. Once Archibald established that granting the chiefs' request to free the men would be regarded, not as a matter of right but as an act of grace and favour by the Crown, he ordered the men released and treaty negotiations proceeded.[18]

All the same, getting an agreement in 1871 took nine days of sometimes difficult discussions. One consideration was having the bands confirm that the men who spoke for them were in fact their desired representatives. Officials required them to do this because the bands were insisting that the Selkirk Treaty of 1817 was null, necessitating these talks. As Governor Archibald put it, 'Some of the Indians now deny' that those who signed the Selkirk agreement 'ever were Chiefs or had authority to sign the treaty.'

Another reason for the protracted talks, in the words of Wemyss Simpson, was that the Indians made 'demands of such an exorbitant nature, that much time was spent in reducing their terms to a basis upon which an arrangement could be made.' That was simply the commissioner's way of saying that the First Nations' representatives pressed hard for the resources that they believed would enable them to make a successful transition to drastically changed circumstances. In their minds, one of the key resources was reserve land, which they demanded in very large quantities. The government men claimed that the Indians were asking for two-thirds of the Province of Manitoba. Chiefs also pressed hard for assurances of assistance in making a transition to agriculture. Farming was something that the band of Peguis, a Saulteaux group who had assisted the Selkirk settlers earlier, had been experimenting with in their parish on the lower Red River. The difficulty for Commissioner Simpson was that he did not have authority from the federal government to promise the sorts of assistance – a plough and harrow for each family that settled on a reserve, 'a cow and a male and female of the smaller kinds of animals bred upon a farm,' and 'a bull for ... each reserve'[19] – they sought. The upshot was that Canada's representatives promised agricultural assistance orally, but did not include it in the written treaty that was signed on 3 August 1871.

The treaty, oral and written, reflected both First Nations' and government's concerns and objectives. Certainly, First Nations regarded oral promises as every bit as much a part of a treaty as commitments in writing. Treaty 1 promised the Indians a reserve whose area would be calculated by a formula of 160 acres (64 hectares) for each family of five, an initial payment of $3 per person and an annuity to be paid in goods, and the orally promised farming assistance. The written text silently passed over a lengthy, sometimes acerbic, argument over the extent of reserve lands. The treaty also asserted that 'Her Majesty agrees to maintain a school on each reserve hereby made, whenever the Indians of the reserve should desire it,' and promised to prohibit the sale of alcohol on the reserves. During Governor Archibald's opening statement, the Crown also assured the First Nations that 'when you have made your treaty you will still be free to hunt over much of the land included in the treaty. Much of it is rocky and unfit for cultivation, much of it that is wooded is beyond the places where the whiteman will require to go, at all events for some time to come.'[20] The promise about hunting, however, was not part of the government text. Nor was a promise of a uniform for each chief and two councillors, and a buggy for each of the chiefs save one.[21] In return, the First Nations, in the language of the government version, agreed to 'cede, release, surrender, and yield up to Her Majesty the Queen' a substantial portion of southeastern and south-central Manitoba stretching up to the lower reaches of Lake Winnipeg and Lake Manitoba. (See map 7.) Less tangible elements of the proceedings included the traditional speech by the queen's representative and reciprocal responses, and generous presents of food that kept the Indians fed for the duration of the negotiations.

The aftermath of Treaty 1 talks left many issues unresolved. Commissioner Simpson found considerable opposition to accepting treaty on the Treaty 1 terms when he visited bands in the Pembina area. On the other hand, the bands that gathered later in August 1871 at Manitoba Post, another HBC location, on Lake Manitoba, proved amenable to accepting the terms of Treaty 1. Treaty 2, or the Manitoba Post Treaty, covered a tract of land in central, west-central, and southwestern Manitoba extending into present-day southeastern Saskatchewan. More serious was the opposition that developed among some of the Treaty 1 bands when it became clear in 1871 and 1872 that the government did not intend to honour Treaty 1's oral promises concerning agricultural assistance. The federal government proved dilatory and ineffective in responding to these protests, and it was not until a new lieutenant-governor, Alexander Morris, arrived in 1872 and learned that three of the Treaty 1 bands had refused to take their 1872 annuities in protest that there was action. Once it became clear that Crown negotiators at the Stone Fort in 1871 had made verbal promises that were not reflected in the published text, the government moved to correct the situation. Even so, Ottawa would not acknowledge that it had breached its obligations. As 'there seems to have been some misunderstanding,' it wrote in 1875, 'the Government out of good feeling to the Indians and as a matter of benevolence' increased the annuity in both Treaty 1 and Treaty 2 from $3 to $5, augmented the annuity to the chief and two councillors per band, furnished the promised agricultural implements and stock, and sent silver medals to the chiefs.[22]

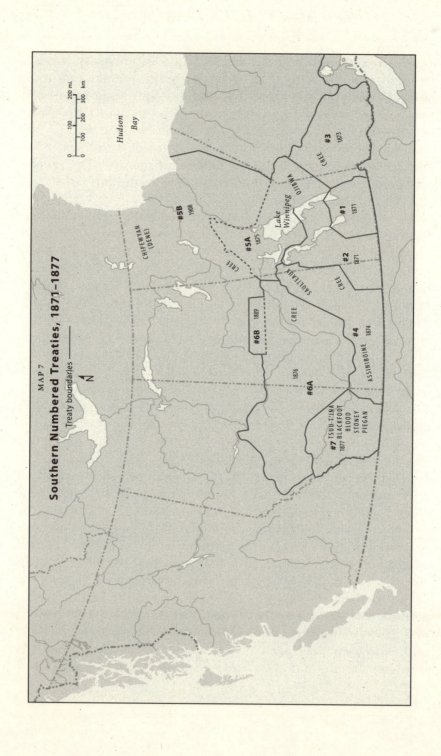

MAP 7

Southern Numbered Treaties, 1871–1877

Treaty boundaries

N

Hudson
Bay

200 mi.
300 km
100   200
100   200
0   0

CHIPEWYAN
(DENE)

#5B
1908

CREE

#5A
1875

#3
1873

CREE

OJIBWA

#1
1871

Lake
Winnipeg

#2
1871

SAULTEAUX

CREE

CREE

#6B
1889

#4
1874

ASSINIBOINE

#6A
1876

#7 TSUU-T'INA
1877 BLACKFOOT
      BLOOD
      STONEY
      PIEGAN

The inauspicious introduction of treaty-making in Manitoba was merely a prelude to equally difficult negotiations in northwestern Ontario. Efforts there between 1870 and 1872 had proved unavailing, as a combination of government thrift and the indigenous population's well-developed sense of property rights proved insurmountable. These convictions were eloquently expressed by Chief Mawedopenais, who on the third day of meetings in 1873 said, 'This is what we think, that the Great Spirit has planted us on this ground where we are, as you were where you came from. We think where we are is our property.' And later, as the debate grew hotter, the chief added, '*The sound of the rustling of the gold is under my feet where I stand;* we have a rich country; it is the Great Spirit who gave us this; where we stand upon is the Indians' property.'[23]

What permitted an agreement in 1873 was a change in the federal government's approach to negotiations, the contributions of a new chief negotiator, and the critical intervention of Métis intermediaries. The new commissioner was Alexander Morris, an able lawyer with scholarly inclinations and good connections with the Conservative party. He had studied law with one prime minister, John A. Macdonald, and articled with another, Sir John Abbott, as well as served as a Conservative member of parliament and cabinet minister prior to his appointment as chief justice of Manitoba in 1872. Morris would not only craft federal treaty tactics, he would record them for posterity. He was an Ontario expansionist who advocated the acquisition and integration of the Hudson's Bay Company lands, but he was an unusual one: as early as 1858, he had said that Canada should incorporate the West while keeping 'a proper sense of the responsibilities to be assumed in regard to the well-being of the native and other habitants, and the due development of the resources of the territory.'[24]

Besides a volume on treaty negotiations, Morris's major contributions were a heavy emphasis on the monarchy in negotiations and the exploitation of divisions within First Nations' ranks. At the talks in 1873, he detected a split when the chief from Lac Seul, to the north, indicated he was willing to settle while leaders of bands in more southerly locations persisted with demands the commissioner was not willing to meet. When Morris responded, 'I have learned that you are not all of one mind,' and threatened to conclude the talks, others suggested they might fall into line and agree to terms. Even then unanimity probably would not have been achieved had not three Métis – James McKay, Pierre Léveillée, and Charles Nolin – held 'a very lengthy and exhaustive discussion' with the Indians. Only then was agreement achieved. As a Saulteaux chief said, 'I wish you to understand you owe the treaty much to the Half-Breeds.' In fact, the Saulteaux tried unsuccessfully to convince Morris to include the Métis – 'those that have been born of our women of Indian blood' – in Treaty 3.[25] Morris contended that the more southerly holdouts had been so independent because their location made it possible for them to get casual or seasonal employment, but equally important was the fact that the northerly bands, whose seasonal work was disappearing because of HBC changes to its transportation system, were justifiably uneasy about their economic future.[26]

Morris also succeeded because the Dominion finally yielded on some of the treaty terms. On the size of reserves, a sticking point in Treaty 1 talks, even though the territory embraced by the North West Angle Treaty was far less suited to agriculture than that covered by the two earlier treaties, the Crown agreed to reserves four times greater in size – 640 acres (256 hectares) per family of five – than those in Manitoba. In Treaty 3, unlike Treaties 1 and 2, the location of the proposed reserve was not specified; Crown officials were to pick 'convenient and advantageous locations' for bands after consulting them. Moreover, Canada now was willing to make explicit in the written treaty what had been recorded only in oral exchanges at the Stone Fort: a Crown guarantee of continuing hunting and gathering rights. Treaty 3 First Nations 'shall have the right to pursue their avocations of hunting and fishing throughout the tract surrendered ..., subject to such regulations as may from time to time be made by her Government of her Dominion of Canada, and saving and excepting such tracts as may from time to time be required or taken up for settlement, mining, lumbering' or infrastructure created by the Dominion. Each man, woman, and child was to receive twelve dollars initially, and an annuity of five (rather than three) dollars. The treaty promised implements and livestock 'for the encouragement of the practice of agriculture among the Indians,' as well as a commitment of $1,500 per year for ammunition and twine. Pledges to maintain a school and to bar alcohol from the reserves were repeated.[27] While the government's motives for loosening the purse strings with Treaty 3 are not clear, the difficulties officials were having with bands in Treaty 1 and Treaty 2 over the unfulfilled oral promises were likely a factor.

Treaty 3 also was noteworthy for its protocol and rhetoric. The two earlier Manitoba treaties had been notable for the absence of recorded ritual. The treaty commissioners noted a large flag flying at the centre of the Indians' encampment at the Stone Fort, and a local newspaper reported that Miskookenew (Henry Prince) 'made a speech in which he expressed strong attachment to the British flag.' That, presents in the form of food, the chiefs' uniforms and medals, and the fact that the proceedings began with the commissioner's presentation and then recessed so that the Indians could consider their response, were the only ritualistic elements that Morris reported.[28] At Treaty 3, perhaps because Morris kept the record, more evidence of traditional protocol was noted. After the commissioner arrived at the North West Angle, 'the Indians, who were already there, came up to the house I occupied, in procession, headed by braves bearing a banner and a Union Jack, and accompanied by others beating drums. They asked leave to perform a dance in my honor, after which they presented to me the pipe of peace. They were then supplied with provisions and returned to the camp.' Mawedopenais raised the issue of commemorative medals, sneering that the medals given to Treaty 1 and 2 chiefs were not of silver, and therefore unworthy 'of the high position our Mother the Queen occupies.'[29]

Chief Mawedopenais also figured in some of the rhetoric that evoked traditions of Aboriginal kin-making protocol during the closing phase of the talks:

Now you see me stand before you all: what has been done here today has been done openly before the Great Spirit and before the
nation, and I hope I may never hear any one say that this treaty has
been done secretly: and now in closing this Council, I take off my
glove, and in giving you my hand I deliver over my birth-right and
lands: and in taking your hand I hold fast all the promises you have
made, and I hope they will last as long as the sun rises and the
water flows, as you have said.

Morris replied, 'I accept your hand and with it the lands, and will
keep all my promises in the firm belief that the treaty now to be
signed will bind the red man and the white together as friends for
ever.' Then 'a large amount of presents, consisting of pork, flour,
clothing, blankets, twine, powder and shot, etc., were distributed
to the several bands represented on the ground.'[30] Treaty 3 talks,
begun amid difficulty, ended well, and on a note that connected
them to indigenous practices for preserving kinship.

Commissioner Morris must have felt like Sisyphus, the figure in
mythology who interminably rolled a stone up a hill only to see it
tumble back down every time, when he negotiated the Qu'Appelle Treaty the following year. In addition to the limitations
imposed by his instructions from Ottawa, Morris in 1874 also had
to contend with unrest concerning the unfulfilled Treaty 1 and
Treaty 2 promises stirred up by envoys from bands in those areas,
anti-treaty agitation by some unnamed Métis, and, most of all,
enormous resistance because of the 1869–70 Rupert's Land transfer among the Saulteaux bands that met him at Fort Qu'Appelle.
The principal obstacle, which delayed substantive talks for over
four days, was First Nations' anger over the fact that the Hudson's
Bay Company had been compensated for transferring territory to
Canada that the Indians considered theirs. The Gambler said
flatly, 'The Company have stolen our land,' and, when Morris
demanded to know what the HBC had stolen, replied: 'The
earth, trees, grass, stones, all that which I see with my eyes.'
Another spokesman demanded the £300,000 the HBC had
received for Rupert's Land: 'We want that money.'[31] Over this
issue, a dispute that provided further proof of the First Nations'

sense of proprietorship, the Saulteaux raised a series of objections, including the fact that talks were being held on Bay property and that the commissioners were staying at the post. They declined to negotiate on substantive matters for five days. The opposition weakened only after Alexander Morris made it clear that he would not, or could not, compensate them, and some of the Cree present showed impatience with the continuing roadblock. Even at that, First Nations at Fort Qu'Appelle did not offer Morris a pipe ceremony, a slight presumably motivated by lingering unhappiness over the Rupert's Land transfer compensation.

So far as the main talks were concerned, they differed more in tone than in substance from those of 1873. One noticeable difference was Morris's strong emphasis on assisting First Nations' adjustment to agriculture. For example:

> What the Queen and her Councillors would like is this, she would like you to learn something of the cunning of the white man. When fish are scarce and the buffalo are not plentiful she would like to help you to put something in the land; she would like that you should have some money every year to buy things that you need. If any of you would settle down on the land, she would give you cattle to help you; she would like you to have some seed to plant. She would like to give you every year, for twenty years, some powder, shot, and twine to make nets of ... We are ready to promise to give $1,000 every year, for twenty years, to buy powder and shot and twine, by the end of which time I hope you will have your little farms.[32]

Now that the talks had shifted to the Plains and involved Plains Cree and Saulteaux, the issue of maintaining livelihood was addressed more explicitly. The written treaty promised reserves of 640 acres per family of five, farming implements, livestock to help with the transition, and carpentry and other tools that suggested a sedentary existence. '[A]ll the aforesaid articles to be given once for all, for the encouragement of the practice of agriculture among the Indians.' And yet it was clear that the transition was to be gradual and voluntary, for Treaty 4 also contained

a promise of continuing hunting and gathering rights, and a
commitment to provide ammunition and twine with which to
exercise them. Similarly, Treaty 4 contained a promise of schools
on the reserves once the Indians asked for them: 'Whenever you
go to a Reserve, the Queen will be ready to give you a school and
a schoolmaster.'[33]

Treaty 4 – or, at least, the government version – was also the
first in which the Crown inserted a 'blanket extinguishment'
clause. Earlier, as in Treaty 3, for example, the written version
had said that the First Nations agreed to 'cede, release, surrender, and yield up to the Government of the Dominion of Canada,
for Her Majesty the Queen and her successors forever, all their
rights, titles and privileges whatsoever to the lands included
within the following limits ...' Treaty 3 then delineated the area in
question. The Qu'Appelle Treaty the next year similarly defined
the Treaty 4 area that it asserted the First Nations agreed to 'cede,
release, surrender and yield up to the Government ...,' but then
added: 'Also all their rights, titles and privileges whatsoever to all
other lands wheresoever situated within Her Majesty's North-
West Territories, or any of them, to have and to hold the same to
Her Majesty the Queen and her successors forever.'[34] Given the
First Nations' careful protecting of their lands and their obvious
concern about their livelihood, it is doubtful the oral version of
the agreement had such a sweeping provision.

In Treaty 4, as with Treaty 3, the Métis were also a factor. Apparently some Métis used their influence against making treaty with
the Crown because of dissatisfaction, and one Saulteaux chief
treated Morris's failure to shake hands with a Métis as pretext for
taking offence early on, when debate still revolved around the
Rupert's Land transfer. At Qu'Appelle, First Nations leaders
again asked for inclusion of their mixed-blood kin, and the commissioners put them off with vague assurances that the monarch
would take care of Métis interests. While there is no evidence
from 1874 that influential Métis such as James McKay had to
intervene to prevent the talks from breaking down, the interests
of the Métis and the close association between them and First
Nations were again evident.

Treaty 4 is also noteworthy as the first numbered treaty that was followed soon after by a series of adhesions to its terms by groups of First Nations who had not been present at Fort Qu'Appelle in 1874. In 1875 a number of chiefs whose bands were established in the Treaty 4 area signed on, as did three bands to the south-east that were actually located in the area covered by Treaty 2. In all these, and other, cases of adhesions, the late joiners had to accept the treaty as already negotiated. Over time, the number of adhesions increased as conditions worsened and bands became more eager for the assistance treaty represented. In the case of Treaty 4, these inducements were the same as Treaty 3: an initial payment of twelve dollars and an annuity for the rank and file; for each chief 'twenty-five dollars in cash, a coat, and a Queen's silver medal' right away and twenty-five dollars each year; and for each of up to four councillors in each band 'fifteen dollars in cash, and a coat' now and an annuity of fifteen dollars.[35]

The negotiation of Treaty 5 with more northerly bands revealed the range of government motives in making the western treaties. As historical geographer Frank Tough has noted, Treaty 5 in central Manitoba 'was as much about water as it was about land.'[36] That statement was true for both the First Nations who initiated the treaty-making process by petitioning, and the federal government that sent commissioners north to deal with them and other groups in 1875. As 'the Christian Indians of Rossville and Nelson River' petitioned in 1874, 'the Tripping to York Factory which has been carried on by the Honourable Hudson's Bay Company for very many years, will cease after this summer and by this means nearly two hundred of our people are thrown out of employment, and we have no way of our own, in this country, to procure the clothing and food which was thus earned by us.'[37] This band wished to relocate to agricultural lands west of Lake Winnipeg. From the government's perspective, a treaty covering the northerly portion of the Manitoba lakes and key waterways would guarantee peaceful access to critically important transportation routes, including the Saskatchewan River, which cut through the so-called 'fertile belt' that was expected to be a route for immigration and settlement.

Both continuity and change were discernible in Treaty 5 talks. Morris was once more the principal Crown commissioner, and James McKay accompanied him. This time, however, the official party also contained two women, Christine Morris and Elizabeth Young, wife of Methodist cleric Egerton Ryerson Young, a witness to the signing at Norway House. The First Nations involved were concentrated near Norway House and at Berens River on Lake Winnipeg, and at Grand Rapids, just to the west of Lake Winnipeg. Although the personnel involved in Treaty 5 were similar in part to those who participated in the North West Angle Treaty two years earlier, one of the striking features of Treaty 5 was its reversion to an earlier, less generous formula for reserves. Perhaps because the landscape embraced by Treaty 5 was not suitable for agriculture, the allotment of reserve land was only 160 acres per family of five. Why lands equally inhospitable to agriculture in northwestern Ontario were handed out at a rate four times that in Treaty 5 was not obvious, unless the explanation was that the Saulteaux and Woods Cree of Treaty 3 were harder bargainers. The initial per capita payment in Treaty 5 was also reduced from twelve to five dollars. As matters transpired in 1875, Morris and McKay did encounter some resistance concerning reserves, but it was not long-lasting.

By 1875, the team of Morris and McKay, who had been negotiating treaties for two years, had begun to shift tactics. According to Morris's own account of the talks for Treaty 5, there was much less reliance on rhetoric involving the Crown and the queen's bounty and benevolence. One major innovation was the deliberate separation of the main territorial issue from discussions about reserves. The Crown's representatives insisted on settling the main treaty, which they took to be agreement on the Indians' part to cede territory, before dealing with the more specific question of reserves. Once control of the whole territory was settled to their satisfaction, Morris found it easier to resist requests about reserves. Thus, for example, the commissioners were able to prevail over the Swampy Cree at Grand Rapids as to the location of the future reserve: the Indians wanted the reserve to be on both sides of the waterway, but the government was opposed to their controlling a vital water passage. The Crown won out, in part because it promised to provide $500 to move the band holdings from the north to the south shore.

On the other hand, First Nations maintained continuity with fur-trade practice and Aboriginal protocol by firing salutes for the government treaty party at Berens River, Norway House, and Wapang Point. Commissioners made presentations of uniforms and medals, too. Oral tradition at Berens River recorded that the commissioners also promised continuing hunting and gathering rights: 'When we made this Treaty, it was given us to understand that although we sold the Government these lands, yet we might still hunt in the woods as before and the fish and the waters should be ours as it was in our Grandfathers' time.' The government version of Treaty 5 was similar to Treaty 4 and Treaty 3, recognizing a continuing right subject to regulation by government and by settlement or economic activity. Government commissioners continued to rely on facilities provided by the Hudson's Bay Company, in 1875 travelling on the HBC's *Colville* at no charge.[38]

As had been the case with Treaty 4, the Lake Winnipeg Treaty of 1875 also required follow-up in the form of adhesions signed the following year by a number of bands. Morris and McKay's 1875 voyage had been hurried because it occurred in October, quite late in the season. The next year, two commissioners took adhesions from five bands on Lake Winnipeg, as well as three bands from The Pas and the Cumberland regions of the lower Saskatchewan River. Commissioner Thomas Howard reported resistance from these groups, who had heard of the superior terms obtained by Plains Cree at Treaty 6 negotiations less than two months earlier.[39] Agreement was achieved by granting their request 'to give them reserves where they desired.' As had been the case with bands adhering to Treaty 4 earlier, those who joined Treaty 5 in 1876 were presented with the terms of Treaty 5 on a take-it-or-leave-it basis.

Cree who negotiated Treaty 6 at Fort Carlton and Fort Pitt in 1876 obtained improved terms thanks to their leaders' resourcefulness and tenacity. By then conditions had changed in two

6.4 Treaty 6 site, Fort Carlton, August 1876

crucial ways. The decline of the bison herds was becoming unmistakable, and fear of their eventual disappearance was great. Second, by now western First Nations had had enough experience with government negotiators to become cautious. Ahtahkakoop and Mistawasis, two influential Plains Cree chiefs in the Fort Carlton area, prepared for talks with the Crown's representatives in 1876 by hiring their own interpreter. Peter Erasmus would report how concern about food security in future and the skill of Ahtahkakoop and Mistawasis combined to carry the day in favour of entering treaty over the opposition of a handful of younger chiefs, such as Poundmaker, Young Chipewyan, and The Badger.

In a private caucus of leaders held following Commissioner Morris's opening statement, the two older Cree chiefs laid out their case for treaty. Mistawasis addressed the treaty opponents directly: 'I speak directly to Poundmaker and The Badger and those others who object to signing this treaty. Have you anything better to offer our people?' He said that he thought 'that the

Great White Queen Mother has offered us a way of life when the buffalo are no more. Gone they will be before many snows have come to cover our heads or graves if such should be.' Mistawasis explained that the queen, besides offering them another 'way of life,' would provide protection from the wicked men who sold 'white man's firewater,' and would 'stop the senseless wars among our people, against the Blackfoot, Peigans, and Bloods.' He reminded his audience that 'the great Indian nations in the Long Knives' country who have been fighting since the memory of their oldest men' were helpless against 'the Long Knives.' Neither could they withstand the impending arrival of immigrants. Ahtahkakoop carried on, arguing that they could not 'stop the power of the white man from spreading over the land like the grasshoppers that cloud the sky and then fall to consume every blade of grass and every leaf on the trees in their path,' and urging his listeners to choose 'the right path now while we yet have a choice.' They should go where 'the Queen Mother has offered us a new way,' take up agriculture or ranching, and enjoy the benefits of an arrangement with the Great White Queen Mother and her people. They would enter into a relationship with the Queen's people: 'I for one will take the hand that is offered,' Mistawasis said; 'I will accept the Queen's hand for my people,' agreed Ahtahkakoop.[40]

The allusions by the two respected Plains leaders to entering into a relationship with the queen and her people were an example of the rhetoric and practice of kinship that marked treaty talks at Fort Carlton. After Morris and his party had arrived, they heard firearms from the Indian encampment and then half an hour later a large party approached in formation singing and beating drums, led by some twenty warriors on horseback who performed equestrian manoeuvres. When they got close to Morris's tent, they stopped, and a pipe ceremony was carried out. Strike Him on the Back advanced with 'a large and gorgeously adorned pipe stem,' raised the pipe to the heavens, then pointed it to each of the cardinal directions, and presented it to Morris.[41] These ceremonies had important purposes in Plains Cree culture. They re-enacted the Aboriginal protocol that had been

6.5 Generic 1870s treaty medal. The symbolism included kinship (shaking hands), peace (buried hatchet), and eternity (sun and flowing river).

incorporated into fur-trade practice as early as the seventeenth century. In effect, the ceremonies drew the Euro-Canadians representing the government into a circle of kinship. Participation in the pipe ceremony also bound the participants to speak truth-

fully. Finally, the ceremony invoked the Great Spirit and effectively made it party to the proceedings. The terms that were then
negotiated thus became a covenant – an agreement that involved
First Nations, the Crown, and the deity. Although the Euro-Canadians did not understand the full significance of what transpired,
Morris at least knew that the pipe ceremony, the absence of
which he had lamented in 1874, was extremely important.

Treaty 6 contained two unique clauses. The arrangements for
initial payments and annuities, reserve allocation and start-up
equipment and livestock, and uniforms and medals for chiefs and
councillors were the same as those in Treaty 4. However, the 1876
treaty responded to the worsening conditions on the Prairies with
clauses dealing with famine and health care. Because Plains Cree
leaders were conscious of the dwindling bison stocks, as
Ahtahkakoop had remarked to John Hines in 1874, at Fort
Carlton they pressed hard for assistance in times of severe hardship. Morris acknowledged that 'the Indians were apprehensive
of their future' because they saw the bison disappearing 'and
were anxious and distressed,' but the commissioners tried to
avoid making such a promise, which exceeded their mandate,
saying that 'we could not assume the charge of their every-day
life.' The Cree objected 'that they did not wish to be fed every
day, but to be helped when they commenced to settle because of
their ignorance how to commence, and also in case of general
famine.' Ahtahkakoop also explained that 'they wanted food in
the spring when they commenced to farm, and proportionate
help as they advanced in civilization.' Morris appeared to
concede, agreeing 'that in the event of a *National* [Morris's
emphasis] famine or *pestilence* such aid as the Crown saw fit would
be extended to them.' The Indians' concern about disease, an
obvious consequence of the smallpox scourge that had recently
ravaged their camps, was also met in a fashion with a clause that
promised 'that a medicine chest shall be kept at the house of
each Indian Agent for the use and benefit of the Indians, at the
discretion of such Agent.'[42]

Treaty 6, like Treaty 5, was made in stages in several locations.
Following agreement at Fort Carlton in late August, the commis-

sioners stopped on their journey to Fort Pitt to offer the treaty to Chief Beardy and the Willow Cree. These Indians had declined to go to Fort Carlton for talks, but they remained interested in entering into treaty, presumably because of the same concerns that had motivated Ahtahkakoop and Mistawasis. Talks in September 1876 at Fort Pitt, another Bay post, went well with some groups but not with others. Some bands were absent from the talks. The Saulteaux of the Jackfish Lake area had chosen to pursue bison rather than travel west to Fort Pitt, and Mistahimusqua (Big Bear) arrived from his hunt only after the main talks were concluded. Sweet Grass, the venerable Cree chief and Christian convert who had been one of the petitioners in 1871, proved quickly amenable to accepting treaty on the terms to which Ahtahkakoop and Mistawasis had already agreed. Once more Commissioner Alexander Morris offered them 'the cunning of the white man,' assistance with an economic transition, and the continued enjoyment of 'their hunting and fishing as before.' Sweet Grass said, 'I have pity on all those who have to live by the buffalo. If I am spared until this time next year I want this my brother to commence to act for me, thinking thereby that the buffalo may be protected. It is for that reason I give you my hand. If spared, I shall commence at once to clear a small piece of land for myself, and others of my kinsmen will do the same. We will commence hand in hand to protect the buffalo.' According to Morris, the other Indians 'assented to' Sweet Grass's remarks 'by loud ejaculations.' Agreement was quickly reached. Officials presented 'the Chiefs' medals, flags and uniforms,' and made 'the payments and distribute[d] the presents.'[43]

Mistahimusqua was another matter entirely. His suspicions had been aroused when he was not summoned to the talks as Sweet Grass and some others had been, and he felt at a loss to agree to the terms already negotiated because most of his followers were not present. He could not assent, although he assured Morris, 'I am not an undutiful child, I do not throw back your hand; but as my people are not here, I do not sign.' He also expressed a desire that action be taken to conserve the bison, and asked that the officials 'will save me from what I most dread, that is: the rope to be about my neck.' Big Bear apparently meant that he had no wish to surrender his freedom – to have the halter round his neck – but he was misunderstood as meaning that he feared hanging. This sentiment, not surprisingly, put Morris off, and his disapproval of Mistahimusqua was not lessened by the chief's refusal to agree to treaty terms. The fact that Big Bear, like Sweet Grass, had used the language of kin relationships – not an undutiful child, my brother – was forgotten, and Mistahimusqua was identified in official minds as a troublemaker.[44]

Treaty 6 was not well received by the federal government. The Reform (Liberal) administration of Alexander Mackenzie that had replaced Macdonald's Conservatives in 1873–4 emphasized frugality, in part for ideological reasons and in part because they found themselves hobbled by stagnant government revenues during an economic slowdown. The potential cost of having to provision the Indians of Treaty 6 in the event of a collapse of the Plains economy alarmed them. Those concerns probably were a factor in the decision to replace Alexander Morris with a reliable Grit, David Laird, but the fact that Morris wanted to return to Ontario was also significant. The other major change that occurred during the Mackenzie regime was the adoption of the Indian Act, the consolidation of existing legislation affecting Indians that treated First Nations as wards, or legal dependants. Morris did not see fit to mention it in August and September 1876 when he was assuring the adherents to Treaty 6 that it would not infringe on their autonomy. How would Laird deal with it in 1877?

When First Nations of southern Alberta assembled in September 1877, the meeting was viewed differently by the two parties. David Laird and NWMP Lt-Col. James McLeod, the Crown commissioners, held to the usual governmental view that they were there to take a surrender of Aboriginal lands from the Blackfoot, but the indigenous population regarded the gathering as a response to their petition and protest of 1875–6. Moreover, a deeply entrenched oral tradition among the Blackfoot since treaty days holds that the talks at Blackfoot Crossing concerned a treaty of peace and friendship, a pact that did not involve any surrender of land or sovereignty. The government version of the agreement, of course, emphasized the land-transfer aspects and stated baldly that the First Nations involved were subjects of Queen Victoria.[45] Had there been a systematic discussion of the Indian Act at Blackfoot Crossing, those differences might have surfaced, but Laird's only mention of the statute referred to protecting reserves from trespass.[46] Perhaps agreement could not have been secured had the different assumptions and approaches of the two parties been explored, but sliding over them at Blackfoot Crossing merely postponed the day of reckoning.

Treaty 7 had both similarities to and differences from the southern Prairie treaties, 4 and 6, that preceded it. Because the Blackfoot had close ties to kin south of the nearby international border, they were strongly influenced by American treaties. A distinctive feature of the proceedings was the prominence of the mounted police. Lt-Col. McLeod, who had become a confidant and friend of the highly respected chief Crowfoot, was a commissioner, and the treaty grounds at Blackfoot Crossing had a large police encampment from Fort MacLeod. The police had won friends through their contribution to driving out the whiskey peddlers, and helping ensure that trouble did not break out between different groups, including the refugee Lakota who had come into the Cypress Hills area after their victory over the U.S. Army, and First Nations normally resident north of the medicine line. Crowfoot attributed his readiness to agree mainly to the police: 'The advice given me and my people has proved to be very good. If the Police had not come to the country, where would we be all now? Bad men and whiskey were killing us so fast that very few, indeed, of us would have been left to-day. The Police have protected us as the feathers of the bird protect it from the frosts of winter. I wish them all good, and trust that all our hearts will increase in goodness from this time forward. I am satisfied. I will sign the treaty.'[47] While missionaries like the Methodist John McDougall and Oblate Constantine Scollen, both of whom were strong treaty advocates, were present at Blackfoot Crossing, it appears that the queen's red-coated soldiers were more influential.

Treaty 7 accorded the Blackfoot signatories the usual initial sum and annuities of twelve and five dollars, and reserves of one square mile per family of five, but Treaty 7 explicitly recognized the different environment of the region by containing an extensive clause that covered 'cattle for raising stock' that any signatory band could apply for. Spokesmen from the Blackfoot Confederacy made it very clear that they, too, were concerned about food security, but Laird brushed the issue aside with a bland assurance that 'the local government,' that is, the territorial council, had recently passed an ordinance 'to protect the buffalo' that would discourage groups such as the Métis encroaching on Blackfoot lands 'in the close season.' Treaty 7 did not contain the famine relief and medicine chest clauses that had distinguished Treaty 6 from the others, though not because the Blackfoot were any less concerned about these matters than their neighbours. Rather, it appears that in 1877, Crown commissioners stuck more closely to their mandate and refused to budge. A combination of Indian desire to obtain the security of a treaty relationship in threatening times, and confidence of a senior leader such as Crowfoot in the assurances provided by the mounted police, appears to have carried the day in 1877.[48]

There were several other differences, or variations, in the Blackfoot agreement. One was that signatory chiefs were promised 'a Winchester rifle,' as well as 'a suitable medal and flag' right away. A second was the schooling clause: instead of promising a 'school on reserve,' Treaty 7 said: 'Her Majesty agrees to pay the salary of such teachers to instruct the children of said Indians as to her Government of Canada may seem advisable, when said Indians are settled on their reserves and shall desire teachers.' The difference between promising reserve schools and agreeing only to pay teachers potentially had major consequences. A final difference in 1877 was the presence of a Plains Cree band, led by Bob Tail, that was there to adhere to Treaty 6 because they had not been at the 1876 talks. Large numbers of Blackfoot and a Cree band in the same vicinity caused some unease among officials, but no untoward events occurred.[49]

The numbered treaties of the 1870s constitute an important milestone in the evolution of treaty-making in Canadian history. In many important ways, they reverted to elements that had figured in the earlier negotiations in the northeast, but begun to fade in eastern Canada by the time of Confederation. The first seven numbered treaties also serve as reminders of the growing strength and rapacity of settler society, its self-absorbed qualities, and its limited concern for the interests and institutions of other societies. Events in the West during 1871–7 reveal important processes in transition.

The re-emergence of Aboriginal protocol and kinship preoccupations in treaty-making demonstrates that fur-trade practices had remained central in Rupert's Land, even if they had been overtaken by other ways of relating in Maritime and central British North America. The recurrent references to 'my brother,' to child-parent relationships, and to the Crown as the Great White Queen Mother, as well as the use of pipe ceremonies and equestrian demonstrations were consistent with fur-trade practices. First Nations were making kin of the Canadians with ceremonies.[50] Crown representatives in the 1870s understood the significance of the terminology and ritual they encountered only imperfectly. The language of family relations, including childhood, stemmed from a society in which youth was a time of autonomy during which children could count on protection and assistance from adult family members. It was not, as it was in Euro-Canadian society, a time of dependence and submission, a time to be 'seen but not heard.' It was noteworthy that Crown commissioners who used the language of childhood usually coupled it with statements about Native submission to governmental authority, while First Nations spokesmen never linked the two. Similarly, an astute representative such as Alexander Morris knew that the pipe ceremony was significant, even if there is no evidence that he and his colleagues appreciated its spiritual aspects.

More than other commissioners, Morris was adept at using symbolism and rhetoric effectively. He played heavily on the image of the Crown, as a source of 'bounty and benevolence' and

protective custodianship that contrasted with the ways of the
'Long Knives' and their government. The issuing of treaty uniforms and medals also was a resort to older traditions of alliance
that the Canadian government quickly learned to use. The creation of the North West Mounted Police enabled commissioners
to provide a visible reminder of the monarchical link, especially
at Blackfoot Crossing.

Morris was also skilled at exploiting differences between different elements among the First Nations that came to negotiate.
Tensions arose between different ethnicities, such as the differences of opinion between Saulteaux and Cree at both Treaty 3
and 4 sessions. There were also generational variations in
outlook, as the stand taken by the elderly chiefs Ahtahkakoop
and Mistawasis against The Badger, Poundmaker, and Young
Chipewyan at Treaty 6 talks at Fort Carlton showed. Finally,
there is reason to suspect varied attitudes towards treaties and
the government between First Nations leaders who had become
Christians and those who had not. At Fort Pitt in 1876, Sweet
Grass, the Christian, was an ardent pro-treaty spokesman, while
Mistahimusqua, a follower of strictly Aboriginal spirituality, was
a skeptic. The missionary allies of the Crown had particular
influence on First Nations leaders who considered themselves
Christian.

The Bible and the schoolroom were also important indicators
of the trend of events in treaty negotiations in the 1870s. Missionaries were useful in promoting the treaty-making agenda, as
clergy urged their First Nations congregations to enter into
treaty both because of their own identification with Canada and
because of concern for Natives' future welfare. Reverend John
Hines, the Church Missionary Society representative who
worked with Ahtahkakoop, was a good symbol of this. Schooling, a favourite missionary activity, was also an important gauge.
It was clear in treaty negotiations that First Nations were interested in gaining access to 'the cunning of the white man' for
their young. It was equally obvious that over time the government tried to whittle down its commitment in education. The
shift in Treaty 7 from promising 'schools on reserves' to simply

7

'An empire in itself':[1] The Northern Numbered Treaties, 1899–1921

The post-treaty experience of the Plains people with the first seven numbered treaties was so negative that it blighted their existence and made negotiations more difficult for Canada when it returned to making treaties a generation later. The fundamental problem in the post-treaty relationship in the southern portion of Rupert's Land was that the federal government forgot its treaty obligations to First Nations once its objective of securing peaceful access to the territory was secured and the ability of western First Nations to force it to live up to its commitments waned. The federal government adopted the paternalistic approach of the recent Indian Act as the basis of its approach to western Indians, rather than the kin-like relationship of equals that First Nations believed was embodied in the treaties. The result of the changed circumstances was that the post-treaty relationship soured, western First Nations suffered grievously, and government provoked suspicion and reluctance among other First Nations with whom it would find itself in treaty talks before the end of the nineteenth century. Canada's failure to honour its treaty commitments after 1877 seriously harmed its southern partners in the short term, and sowed suspicion among potential northern treaty partners in the future.

The work of surveyors who laid out the reserves promised in the numbered treaties symbolized the problems of treaty implementation. Surveyors had long been regarded askance by Aboriginal peoples, who rightly saw them as harbingers of settler society. Anicinabe at the North West Angle had warned the government not to send surveyors or settlers to their region prior to treaty-making, and the first step the Red River Métis took in 1869 to resist the assertion of Dominon authority was to halt the work of surveyors. The experience of Ahtahkakoop, the pro-treaty Plains Cree chief in Treaty 6, epitomized many of the problems. It was August 1878 before a surveyor turned up at Sandy Lake to lay out the band's reserve. There were more problems to come. Although the government text of Treaty 6 said plainly that surveyors were 'to determine and set apart the reserves for each band, found to be most suitable for them,' Ahtahkakoop could not get the government surveyor to survey his reserve as the chief wished. Even after Ahtahkakoop appealed to government officials at the annual gathering to pay treaty annuities and got, he thought, their support, the surveyor still did not run the lines of the reserve's boundaries as the chief wanted. Such experiences, unfortunately, were all too common in the post-treaty period, as surveyors and other government representatives frequently did not understand what was desired or simply chose to disregard the wishes of First Nations leaders. Little wonder that surveyors were despised by many Plains groups. One seasoned surveyor who did a lot of work for the government on the prairies recalled, 'Plains Indians, in certain areas, expressed some disapproval of the white man's entry into their land.' They 'would sometimes express their resentment by defecating upon the top of every available [survey] stake ...'[2]

Government failure to assist Plains First Nations with a transition to sedentary agriculture, as the treaties envisaged, caused enormous hardship in the West. By 1879 the vast herds of bison on which Plains peoples had relied were effectively gone from the prairies north of the international border. The drastic change meant that Plains societies lacked replacement materials for housing, in the form of tipis, as well as for food, clothing, some domestic implements, fuel in some situations, and even the bison skull that was part of Plains summer spiritual ceremonies. Provident leaders such as Ahtahkakoop expected treaties would be the means to learn the skills that would provide an alternative way of supporting their communities, though few truly believed the bison would vanish completely, and none anticipated that the disappearance would take place so quickly. Soon many Plains groups were destitute and facing possible starvation. In 1879, Edgar Dewdney, a senior government official, reported that the Blackfoot, who called bison 'real meat' in their language, 'have been selling their Horses for a mere song, eating gophers, mice, Badgers & for the first time have hunted the Antelope & nearly killed them all off ... Strong young men were now so weak that some of them could hardly walk. Others who last winter were fat & hearty are mere skin & bone.'[3]

In the face of this crisis, the federal government's dilatory implementation of treaty undertakings to create food-producing reserves was devastating. Besides taking years to establish the reserves, Ottawa was slow to provide both the means to pursue agriculture and emergency aid. The experience of bands in Treaty 1 and Treaty 2 that had petitioned, and in some cases refused annuities, to compel the government to honour the so-called 'outside promises' of livestock and farming implements was matched by other First Nations further west that had to wait for ploughs, seed, and instruction in farming. Equipment and seed were slow to arrive, and when farm instructors were finally sent, some of them turned out to be friends of the government with little knowledge of how to overcome the challenges of dryland farming in high latitudes. To compound the problem, the early 1880s were years of meagre precipitation, and some winters, such as that of 1884–5, were especially severe. It was extremely difficult for non-Native farmers to harvest a crop, and, in fact, it would not be until the later 1890s and early twentieth century, when a combination of American immigrants with plains farming experience and a number of relatively wet years made the prairies bloom, that agriculture succeeded. For bands struggling to eke out a living by pursuing a way of life unfamiliar to them in climatically difficult times, further damage was done when the federal government supplied inadequate and defective food rations to help them stave off starvation.[4] Federal government neglect caused enormous problems.

The explanation for Ottawa's insensitive treatment of hard-pressed Plains people went beyond the inability of a remote and lightly populated region to get its needs understood in the far-off capital. In the latter part of the 1870s, the government of Canada began to reformulate the basis of its policies towards First Nations. Principal in this realignment was the passage by Parliament in the spring of 1876 of the Indian Act, a compendium of all legislation dealing with First Nations. The hard centre of the Act was casting the relationship of government and Indians as that between trustee and ward. Under the Indian Act, First Nations people were legally children, and their legal parent, the federal government, had the right and responsibility to make decisions on their behalf. The trustee-ward, adult-child relationship embodied in the Indian Act was the antithesis of the kin relationship – brother to brother and sister to sister under their mutual parent, the Great White Queen Mother – that both sides had talked about during treaty negotiations. The federal government pushed this evolution to its perversely logical end in 1880 with the creation of the Department of Indian Affairs (DIA). Ottawa had transformed First Nations into administered peoples with the Indian Act; it equipped itself with the machinery to administer them in the Department of Indian Affairs.

A series of policies developed in the 1880s revealed the impact of Ottawa's changed attitude towards western First Nations. For example, federal officials reneged on treaty commitments to permit bands to select reserves where they wished in order to deny them access to the Cypress Hills, the food resource–rich region that straddled southwest Saskatchewan and southeast Alberta. The DIA went so far as to close Fort Walsh, the mounted police post in the region, so that want would drive chiefs out of the Hills to locations such as the Qu'Appelle Valley and the North Saskatchewan River district near Battleford. Government also refused bands' requests to locate their reserves close to one another, frustrating chiefs' aim of establishing large Indian territories by this means. Indian Commissioner Edgar Dewdney, the

Indian commissioner for the West and a close confidant of Prime Minister John A. Macdonald, instituted in the early 1880s a 'no work, no rations' policy to increase the compulsion on bands to act as the government wished. In 1883, Ottawa cut allocations for food relief and agricultural assistance, and initiated a new industrial-school policy that would force some bands to send their children to distant residential schools rather than the 'schools on reserve' that the treaties had promised. And under Dewdney's guidance, Indian Affairs adopted a policy of 'sheer compulsion' to force the impoverished and hungry Plains bands to adhere to government requirements. All these steps were breaches either of the government text of treaties or the kin relationship that First Nations thought the treaties had created.[5]

The striking change in governmental attitudes towards western First Nations, perplexing as it must have been to the Natives, was relatively easily explained. In part, the shift was the consequence of Ottawa's having achieved its goal of securing peaceful access to western resources. In addition, the collapse of the bison economy had largely destroyed the military capability of Plains First Nations. They were weakened, often horseless, and without the means to buy ammunition. Ottawa had feared the power of the Plains Cree and the Blackfoot on the eve of treaty-making, but on the morrow its attitude turned to pity, then contempt, and ultimately impatience. In the altered circumstances of a post-bison West, government officials and politicians focused on the language of their own treaty texts, with their descriptions of alienating Indian lands and subordinating First Nations to the authority of the queen's government, and completely forgot the rhetoric of treaty talks that had emphasized the creation of a new relationship between Natives and non-Natives to share use of the land and its resources. For First Nations, everything that was *said* in negotiations was part of the treaty, not just what government scribes chose to *write* down. Western Indian leaders fully appreciated the dramatic changes that had occurred in the Plains ecology, but they were unaware of the policy consequences they had had in far-off Ottawa. Even if they had known of the negative transformation of their links to Victoria's Euro-Canadian chil-

dren, they would have found the change difficult to understand
and impossible to accept.

The response of Plains First Nations to the government's provo-
cations was remarkably pacific. A historian of the mounted police
points out that prior to the North West Rebellion of 1885, the
federal force did not fire a shot in anger at Native people in the
West, and it is a remarkable fact that between 1876 and the outbreak of insurrection in the spring of 1885, settlers in the North
West Territories were five times as likely as First Nations people to
be charged with a criminal offence.[6] If the hard-pressed First
Nations did not respond with violence to the treatment they
received, they were not passive. They protested and petitioned,
most notably and pointedly in 1881, when the governor general,
Lord Lorne, toured the Prairies. The Marquis of Lorne was of
special interest to western Indians because his marriage to the
Princess Louise made him a son-in-law of Queen Victoria. At
meetings at Fort Qu'Appelle and Battleford, aggrieved First
Nations leaders first greeted Lorne as kin – one addressed him as
'brother' – before explaining that the government's administration of the treaties prevented them from maintaining themselves
and asking for a 'reformation' of the agreement to provide them
with subsistence.[7] The avenue of formal protest reached a pinna-
cle in August 1884 when a delegation of Treaty 6 chiefs met with
Indian Agent J. Ansdell Macrae to complain of being deluded by
Ottawa's 'sweet promises' in the treaties and to demand assistance. Even then, however, they told Agent Macrae that they
would give the Department until 'next summer' to respond positively. They said that they were not threatening violence: 'a sug-
gestion of the idea of war was repudiated,' Macrae reported.[8]
   Beyond protest and petition, western chiefs resorted to political and diplomatic action to resist the government's abrogation
of treaty commitments. In particular, Mistahimusqua (Big Bear)
in the north and Piapot in the south worked to organize a united
diplomatic front of First Nations that could put political pressure
on Ottawa to live up to its commitments. By means of personal
diplomacy and thirst dances, these leaders made considerable

progress towards forming common cause by the summer of 1884, and in 1885 there was a meeting scheduled with leaders of the Blackfoot Confederacy to explore the possibility of a broader diplomatic alliance. Although the manoeuvres of Big Bear were viewed with suspicion and hostility by government officials, the intention of the chiefs was non-military. Having chosen the path of peaceful coexistence and sharing when they decided to enter into treaties, Plains leaders were committed to non-violent measures to achieve their objective of getting the treaties properly implemented. Unfortunately, the outbreak of a Métis rebellion in the Saskatchewan country in March 1885 provided the government with a pretext and opportunity to crack down on First Nations leadership. In the aftermath of Riel's rebellion, Canada successfully prosecuted a number of innocent Plains leaders, including Big Bear and Poundmaker, effectively decapitating the leadership of their diplomatic movement, and imposed a series of draconian measures to control Plains people. Most egregious of the official responses was the pass system, by which government required reserve residents to obtain a pass signed by the agent or farming instructor before leaving the reserve. The policy, which had no legislative basis, was a plain violation of treaty promises about mobility.[9]

Canada's other major Native policy development in the immediate post-treaty era was the creation of scrip for Métis. A type of promissory note for land, scrip had been used in Manitoba as part of the flawed program to administer the 1.4 million acres promised to people of mixed ancestry in that province. Although this first attempt was problematic, in large part because the promissory paper was negotiable and land speculators quickly acquired a large portion of it at prices well below its market value, the federal government returned to its use with the Saskatchewan Métis. Part of Ottawa's response to the growing unrest in the Saskatchewan district in 1884–5 was the creation early in 1885 of the Half-Breeds Claim Commission to investigate and settle land claims from Métis settlers. Although the North West Rebellion delayed the work of this body, the Commission did eventually complete its work, issuing scrip to claimants it judged to have valid claims. With all its flaws, in the 1880s Métis scrip became an established part of federal government policy that incidentally responded to the repeated requests from First Nations that provision be made for their mixed-blood relatives. Such petitions had surfaced in negotiations for the Robinson Treaties of 1850 and the numbered treaties of the 1870s, especially Treaties 3 and 4. While the government had no desire to swell the numbers of western Natives included in treaty because of the ongoing financial obligations that annuities for them would have involved, scrip seemed acceptable. As far as the federal government was concerned, scrip extinguished Métis Aboriginal title as effectively as treaties did First Nations' title, and scrip had the advantage of involving a one-time outlay with no continuing financial liability. Moreover, it was popular with bankers and land speculators, some of whom counted politicians among their friends. Dispensing scrip became federal policy, closely associated with treaty-making.[10]

It was a measure of the economic straits in which many First Nations found themselves from the 1880s on that, in spite of the harsh manner in which Indian Affairs dealt with those Indians with whom Canada had established a treaty relationship, many northerly groups sought entry to treaty. The decline in fur markets, thanks in part to settlement and southern economic activity that was beginning to penetrate the northern boreal forest and in part to decreased international prices for pelts, fell especially hard on northern First Nations. Because the Hudson's Bay Company was experiencing competition both from another company, Révillon Frères, and independent traders, the HBC was reluctant to advance the credit to Aboriginal traders that it had in the past for fear the recipients would take their furs elsewhere. In some cases, particularly northern British Columbia and northern Ontario, the expansion of southern resource companies and, in the case of Ontario, the creation of new rail infrastructure meant greater disruption of trap lines, fishing grounds, and forest resources by outside users. In northern Ontario, too, devel-

7.1 Scrip certificate.

oping use of Shield country for recreational purposes proved a two-edged sword: increased seasonal employment opportunities as guides and other support staff; and interference with seasonal harvesting rounds. As was always the case where newcomers and Natives began to interact, the encounter caused economic difficulties for the indigenous hunter-gatherers. Hard-pressed First Nations now knew that the treaties that their counterparts to the south had entered into, whatever the shortcomings of their implementation, provided cash income in the form of annuities and sometimes assistance with hunting and other supplies as well. Some northern First Nations responded by seeking, cautiously, to enter a treaty with Canada themselves. (See map 8.)

First Nations' petitions for treaty came from a wide range of areas over a lengthy period. For example, in Lesser Slave Lake, in what would become part of Treaty 8, Dene in 1890 met and asked a trader to write Edgar Dewdney about their situation. 'The fur in

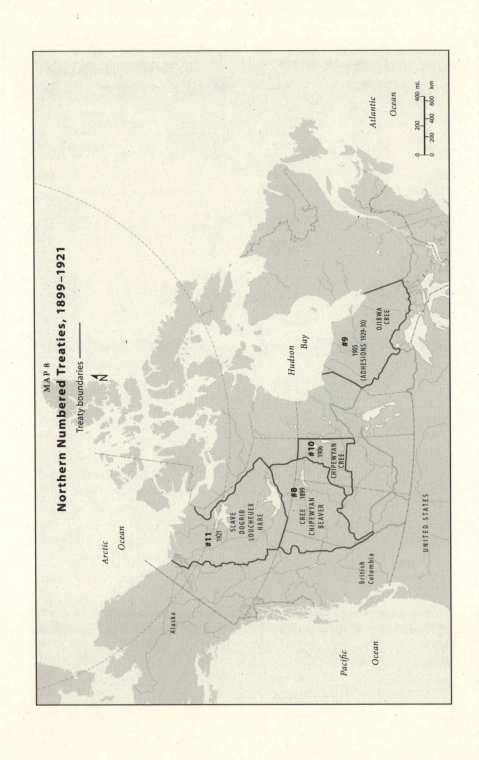

MAP 8

Northern Numbered Treaties, 1899–1921

Treaty boundaries ——

N

the country is getting scarcer each year and the Indians poorer,'
they complained. 'Those in Peace River are starving every winter,
and need assistance very much. The traders and missionaries
assist them as much as they can, but they cannot afford to do it
all the time. The government should begin to do something.'
Specifically, the trader said, a number of First Nations in the district were 'anxious to have the treaty.'[11] In 1899, DIA officials J.A.
Macrae and D.C. Scott met with Indians north of Lake Superior.
The Indians, who 'had come from considerable distance,' were
eager to know what the government proposed to do about
making treaty with them. Macrae reported 'that they heard that
railroads were projected through their country, and that already
miners, prospectors, and surveyors were beginning to pass
through it [in] such largely increased numbers that the game was
disturbed, interference with their means of livelihood had commenced, and their rights were being trespassed upon.' The officials assured them that all would be well: '... when the Government permitted projects to proceed which might affect their
interests it would certainly not fail to properly consider their
claims.'[12]

Back in the West, First Nations around Ile à la Crosse, the venerable fur-trade post and mission located where the Methye
Portage permitted transfer from the river systems that ran to
James Bay to waterways that emptied in the Arctic Ocean, even
earlier had petitioned through the Roman Catholic bishop for a
treaty. Lawrence Vankoughnet, the deputy minister of Indian
affairs, noted in 1883 that he had been informed 'from several
quarters while in the North West that very much uneasiness exists
among the Indians in the unceded part of the Territories at
parties making explorations into their country in connection
with railroads, &c., without any Treaty being made with them.'
The official had been credibly informed that 'they are most
anxious to enter into Treaty relations with the Government and
that it is in the interest of humanity very desirable that the Government, should render them assistance, as their condition at
many points is very wretched.'[13] Further north, in future Treaty
11 territory, deteriorating economic conditions were similar.
When mounted police sergeant Richard Field's 1909 patrol

reached Fort Providence, the mountie learned that 'great scarcity of fur is reported also, game and fish were also stated to be very scarce. The Indians were in a very destitute condition, this state being made worse by the traders having closed down upon them, giving no credit whatever because of no fur.' Like other First Nations, these Dene thought that a treaty relationship would provide relief from their economic problems: 'The Indians spoke to me regarding treaty, wondering when they would be taken into treaty. I think the time has now arrived when something will have to be done as they are in a deplorable condition.'[14]

To all such entreaties and suggestions, the federal government had the same answer: no. From the early 1880s, the federal government declined to enter into treaties with hard-pressed northern Indians and suggested that responsibility for providing them with relief still lay with the Hudson's Bay Company. The government position was articulated baldly by Indian Commissioner David Laird in 1904, in response to renewed entreaties on behalf of the Ile à la Crosse Indians. 'There was no particular necessity that the treaty should extend to that region. It was not a territory through which a railway was likely soon to run, nor was it frequented by miners, lumbermen, fishermen, or other whites making use of the resources of its soil or waters, in which case, in my opinion, the Indians and Halfbreeds are better left to their hunting and fishing as a means of making a livelihood ... The matter, I suggest, may very well stand over for the present.' When the provinces of Alberta and Saskatchewan were created, 'if it is found that any Province or organized territory with representation, extends over a considerable tract of country in which the aboriginal title has not been relinquished, then in such case, or from the entrance of a railway, the discovery of mines, or other cause to bring an inrush of whites, a Treaty should be made without delay.'[15] In other words, until non-Natives became interested in First Nations' lands where treaties did not exist, the government would not, no matter the conditions of the Indians there, make treaty. Ottawa also maintained, in clear contravention of the terms of the 1869–70 transfer of Rupert's Land, that the HBC was still obligated to provision destitute Natives in regions beyond treaty limits.

The exception to the rule of not making treaty that demonstrated the force of the federal government's policy was the Montreal Lake adhesion of 1889. This large (11,066 sq mi; 28,661 sq km) adhesion to Treaty 6 (Fort Carlton), which involved the Montreal Lake and Lac la Ronge bands of Woods Cree, differed from the adhesions made earlier, such as those to Treaty 4 concluded in 1875, or the adhesion of the Willow Cree to Treaty 6 in 1876. Those agreements had involved a First Nations group joining an existing treaty without altering its territorial boundaries. Such adhesions are often referred to as internal adhesions, in contrast to external adhesions such as the Montreal Lake adhesion that involved the addition of territory as well as population to an existing treaty.[16] The 1889 Montreal Lake adhesion was an external or territorial adhesion, adding the land between the northern boundary of Treaty 6 and the Churchill River watershed. (See map 7.)

Otherwise, the motivations underlying the Montreal Lake adhesion were the same as those that would characterize later treaties negotiated in more northerly regions. In 1887 the two Woods Cree bands got an Anglican missionary, John Sinclair, to write on their behalf to the newly elected Conservative Member of Parliament for the area. They stressed that 'they were loyal during the rebellion and therefore think they have a claim on the good offices of the Gov. on which they depend for a living,' and complained that 'the fur-hunting is getting scarce.' Since these bands had seasonal associations with a band that had signed Treaty 6, they knew about annuities and recognized the potential for these annual payments to ease the hardship they were experiencing. So far as the government was concerned, while there was no immediate need for the territory the bands occupied, Ottawa was aware that the district held prime timberlands that would soon attract harvesters' attention. 'The section of country above described was included in the said timber and land district, and complications were not unlikely to occur, owing to the Indians not having surrendered the same.'[17]

Negotiation of the adhesion in February 1889 demonstrated that the act of adhering to an existing treaty was not always simply a matter of rubber-stamping the existing document. Commissioners Lt-Col. A.G. Irvine and Roger Goulet met with the bands accompanied by Anglican archdeacon John Mackay. The Indians greeted the commissioners' party ceremonially with a rifle salute and individual salutations, and then Mackay, who was well known to the Anglican bands because of his service as a missionary among them for fourteen years, spent a day explaining the terms of Treaty 6. The next day, a Sunday, was as usual marked by Christian services in Cree conducted by Mackay both morning and afternoon.

During the actual negotiations on Monday, the chiefs of the two bands requested alterations to the existing treaty. They explained that, while they were interested in some farming – provision of seed potatoes and agricultural instruction being the items they emphasized – they did not desire other related items, such as cattle and a plough for every three families. Rather, they specified three light ploughs that could be transported in canoes, and requested that those items they did not take be converted into additional ammunition and twine. Specifically, they did not want wagons because they relied on canoes in summer and dogs in winter. Most important, they demanded that they receive arrears of annuities dating back to 1876, and they requested that in future annuities be paid in September, not the depths of winter. Commissioner Irvine agreed to most of their requests, though not retroactive annuities, and, after concluding the adhesion, paid them and furnished medals and flags to the leaders. Commissioner Goulet, an experienced scrip commissioner, issued scrip to eligible Métis. Although Commissioner Irvine used the language of land cession and total alienation to describe the discussions, oral history of the talks from the Woods Cree uniformly insists that talks concerned only land, not waterways and resources. As Angus Merasty of the Peter Ballantyne Cree Nation put it, 'In the signing of the treaties the Indians just gave up their land, land exclusively. Only land. Not their natural resources.'[18]

Both treaty-making with First Nations and issuing scrip would soon be prominent features of negotiations when the economic ambitions of non-Natives focused on the North. In 1890, shortly after the deputy minister of Indian affairs recommended not responding to the petition from Lesser Slave Lake area Indians for treaty, the discovery of large quantities of petroleum in the Athabaska and Mackenzie River Districts began to change official minds. Deputy Minister Lawrence Vankoughnet pointed out to the federal cabinet that these findings, the potential to extract sulphur and salt, and the possibility that railways might have to be built to these resources 'appear to render it advisable that a treaty or treaties, should be made with the Indians who claim those regions as their hunting grounds, with a view to the extinguishment of the Indian title in such portions of the same as it may be considered in the interest of the public to open up for settlement.' The federal executive went as far as recommending a treaty to cover the critical northern areas east of the province of British Columbia.[19]

When it came to Indian affairs, the Pacific province was a problem as far as Ottawa was concerned. The two governments had been locked in a quarrel since the mid-1870s over the allocation of reserve lands in BC, the federal government favouring larger reserves than the province. At the heart of the dispute was the reality that BC, unlike Canada, did not recognize Aboriginal title. And the fact that British Columbia, unlike Rupert's Land, had jurisdiction over its 'crown lands and natural resources' under the 1867 constitution meant that provincial views mattered. Northern experts argued against omitting British Columbia, pointing out that some of the First Nations with whom the government wanted to make a treaty in the Peace River region were closely related to others across the provincial boundary. It would not do to enter treaty with some, but not all, of them. As it turned out, the 1891 proposal for a new treaty in the region east of northern BC went nowhere. While the reasons are not clear, probably the turmoil that beset the Conservative party after Macdonald's 1891 death contributed to federal inaction.

When treaty-making returned to the federal agenda in the later 1890s, all the conditions had changed. The hesitancy and bumbling of the former Conservative governments were gone, replaced by the confidence of a majority Liberal government. The Liberals of Sir Wilfrid Laurier benefited from a dramatic turnaround in the economy, as a decade and a half of expansion and heavy immigration displaced the stagnation of the Tory years that had seen western development slowed. The new federal government had an aggressive minister of the interior, Clifford Sifton from Manitoba, who favoured entrepreneurs and had little time for First Nations and Métis. The other major difference was that British Columbia was now a key part of any treaty-making plans. The discovery of gold in the Klondike made northern BC the second most popular route for southern prospectors headed for the Yukon, the White Pass from Alaska into southern Yukon being the first choice. In light of these changes, bureaucrats revived plans to make a northern treaty that included northeastern British Columbia.

What had not changed were the views of the First Nations in the proposed treaty area. Most Indians in the North were still adversely affected by the decline in fur prices that made them look to treaty annuities as a potential source of sustenance. Nor had their views that outsiders had no right to use the resources of their territory in the absence of treaty faded. These forces among First Nations manifested themselves most noticeably in northern British Columbia, where Indians confronted Klondike-bound southerners who blundered through their lands. Prospectors, a species never renowned for its esteem for indigenous peoples, disregarded protocols about land use, First Nations' traps and other equipment, and even domestic animals. A particularly nasty dispute erupted in the Fort St John area in 1897, when prospectors killed two stallions that belonged to the local chief, Montaignee. When the chief learned what had happened, he dispatched search parties to locate the transgressors. He threatened to shoot all the travellers' horses, as well as the prospector responsible for the deaths of his own stock. This particular set-to apparently 'was settled,' according to a mounted policeman, but

7.2 Treaty 8: 'an empire in itself'

it was ominous of future trouble. For their part, the outsiders held mining licences from the provincial government that they thought gave them permission to be on Aboriginal land and use its resources. They looked to government to protect what they believed to be their 'rights.'

The situation had great potential for open conflict, a development that filled the federal government with dread because it would attract adverse international attention. By late 1897 the mounted police were urging Sifton to make a treaty before an expected surge of trekkers moved north. The Indians, a policeman wrote, 'will be more easily dealt with now than they would be when their country is overrun with prospectors and valuable mines be discovered. They would then place a higher value on their rights than they would before these discoveries are made.'[20] As with the southern treaties in the 1870s, the threat of First Nations resistance belatedly motivated the government to act.

The Laurier government faced a significant problem when it began dusting off the plans to make a treaty that had been formulated in the early 1890s. Then the proposal had been to make a treaty east of BC, but the tense situation in the northern part of that province now made it essential that any new treaty include at least a portion of the westernmost province. However, British Columbia's relations with the federal government over Indian policy were dreadful, and Victoria was unlikely to recognize the existence of Aboriginal title by participating in treaty-making. Federal bureaucrats' solution to this dilemma was simple. Ottawa gave written notice to BC in December 1898 that it intended to make a new treaty the next year that would take in 100,00 square miles (160,900 sq km) of northeastern BC because 'it will neither be politic nor practicable to exclude from the treaty Indians' who were kinfolk of First Nations in the Athabaska District and 'will look for the same treatment as is given to the Indians whose habitat is in that district.' The provincial government received this missive, but Victoria apparently turned a blind eye to federal intentions.[21]

The problems associated with negotiating Treaty 8 in 1899 did not end when British Columbia chose to avoid a confrontation. Federal planners had only an imprecise notion of the topography of the region, and even less understanding of the difficulties of conducting negotiations with many different First Nations over a vast region in the relatively short season when travel was possible. The treaty region that Ottawa eventually prescribed ended up leaving some of the BC bands that it wanted to cover out of the agreement, with considerable litigation difficulties resulting in the late twentieth century. Moreover, the treaty party of J.A.J. McKenna, David Laird, and J.H. Ross got started so late in the season that they reached only a minority of the bands intended. After the initial session at Lesser Slave Lake, the party split in two, with Laird heading northeast to the Lake Athabaska area, and the other two moving northwest towards Fort St John, BC, even though they knew they would not make that destination in time Ironically, in 1899 the treaty commissioners never made contact with the British Columbia bands whose confrontations with prospectors had been one of the primary factors behind the government's decision to seek a treaty. Still, Ross and McKenna thought that the very fact they had tried to reach the centre of tension would impress First Nations there favourably. Finally, in their haste the commissioners simply assumed that the agreement they reached with only a few bands in 1899 somehow bound all First Nations who resided in the extensive Treaty 8 region. Because of ignorance and haste, the government of Canada made a hash of its first attempt at negotiating Treaty 8.

In addition to logistical and climatic problems, the Crown negotiators in 1899 faced tough bargainers on the other side of the table. Presumably because they had learned about government efforts to restrict mobility of Indians on southern reserves, northern chiefs were apprehensive that entering treaty might mean interference with their seasonal gathering practices. Crown commissioners had to reassure them on this point, pointing to a treaty clause that provided ammunition and twine to show that the government could hardly be seeking to interfere with their hunting and fishing if it was going to furnish the means of doing so. As the commissioners recalled, '... over and above the provision, we had to solemnly assure them that only such laws as to hunting and fishing as were in the interest of the Indians and were found necessary in order to protect the fish and fur-bearing animals would be made, and that they would be as free to hunt and fish after the treaty as they would be if they never entered into it.' The Crown promise was quite sweeping: 'We assured them that the treaty would not lead to any forced interference with their mode of life, that it did not open the way to the imposition of any tax, and that there was no fear of enforced military service.' As a Treaty 8 Elder, August Lidguerre, put it, 'The animals, the wildlife is here for us; the Creator put it here for us. No government can own that.'[22] One interesting innovation in

Treaty 8 was that the government offered the land that was provided to bands – the now standard one square mile (259 hectares) per family of five – in a communal reserve or individual
plots, as the Indian signatories should choose.[23]

The slapdash treaty-making of 1899 left matters so unsatisfactory that Canada sent another commissioner in 1900 to try to get
adhesions to Treaty 8 from other groups. Starting several weeks
earlier than his predecessors, long-time Indian Affairs employee
J.A. Macrae acted as sole commissioner. He managed to reach
agreement with Dene (Beaver) Indians at Fort St John, proceeded to Lesser Slave Lake, where he secured the adhesions of
several Woods Cree chiefs, and then made two more successful
stops at Vermillion and Fort Resolution, in Dene territory. At Vermillion five Slave chiefs adhered, while at Fort Resolution chiefs
from the Dog Ribs, Yellow Knives, Chipewyan, and Slave Indians
were brought into treaty. In all cases, these groups were expected
to accept the agreement negotiated with some difficulty the previous year at Lesser Slave Lake. Even when these First Nations
were counted in after the expedition of 1900, there remained a
number of groups, both in British Columbia and more easterly
territories, who were left out of the process. One of the groups,
the Lubicon Lake Cree in northern Alberta, would became
embroiled in litigation in the late twentieth century.[24]

Treaty 8 negotiations were also remarkable for the scrip
process that accompanied talks with First Nations. So far as government commissioners were concerned, Natives who were
'living an Indian life' could enter treaty or opt for Métis scrip for
either 240 acres of Crown land or $240 in lieu of land. Adminis-
tering scrip had severe problems. A major one was that a recipi-
ent of land scrip who wished to convert the government's
promise into a land grant had to 'locate' the scrip by travelling to
a Dominion land office to register it and select a tract of surveyed
land. Unfortunately, the nearest land office where this could be
done was hundreds of kilometres to the south. There was an
alternative. Scrip buyers, often representing banks, followed the
treaty commissioners and offered cash at a discounted rate in
exchange for scrip signed over to them. As the doctor who

accompanied Commissioner Macrae in 1900 explained, 'The larger part of the cash value of scrip issued last year was $60 to $70 a scrip. If a man had say 6 in the family, this would give him a lump sum of say $400, a sum of money very tempting to the breed [*sic*].'[25] Four hundred dollars in cash at a time when many working-class Canadians did not earn that much in a year, and $400 cash available without travelling hundreds of kilometres, was irresistible to many Métis. The result of these circumstances was that the land that scrip was supposed to represent rarely ended up in Métis hands, and they did not assemble a land base of any sort.[26]

Although Treaty 9 was negotiated far from the Northwest and under dramatically different conditions, in many ways it resembled Treaty 8. Treaty 9 was a northern Ontario treaty designed to deal with First Nations lands north of the height of land, the northern boundary of the Robinson Treaties, and the Albany River. In this region, too, First Nations made overtures for entering treaty long before the government was amenable to the idea, and here as well the Crown's attitude shifted once considerations of resource wealth and infrastructure in which southerners were interested took centre stage. One thing that was different with Treaty 9 was that the government made no effort to deal with Métis people's share of Aboriginal title through scrip.

The Cree and Ojibwa peoples in the 90,000 square miles (582,000 sq km) petitioned for treaty for familiar reasons. Underlying the many petitions that the federal government received from the 1880s onward were problems in the fur trade, the staple industry on which northern Ontario Native peoples relied. The lengthy period of depressed fur prices that had triggered requests for treaties from the Woods Cree of the Montreal Lake adhesion in 1889 to the Woods Cree and Dene of Treaty 8 had a similarly destructive effect in northern Ontario. In addition to low prices at the trading posts, northern Ontario fur gatherers also had to contend with non-Native trappers who did not follow the conservationist practices that indigenous people employed to ensure that the fur resource would last for future generations.

Rather, fur trappers from 'outside' tended to 'strip mine' a region of all the furs they could gather, and then move on to other areas. As early as 1884, Sahquakegick (also known as Chief Louis Espagnol) wrote from Pagomasing to Ottawa: 'All my old Indians who used to hunt near here are in great need. The trappers have stolen all our beaver, so there is nothing left for them to hunt and they are too old to go anywhere else ... they all join me in asking you to help us.'[27]

The fur depletion problem in northern Ontario was exacerbated by other non-Native intrusions. Gold, silver, and valuable base metals were plentiful in the Precambrian Shield that dominated the future Treaty 9 area, and by the later nineteenth century prospectors were avidly pursuing them. First Nations soon came to regard those hunting for minerals as posing as big a threat as those who denuded a region of furs. In northwestern Ontario, for example, a Geological Survey of Canada geologist in 1904 encountered a chief near Osnaburgh House who warned the young man 'that he did not like white men coming into his country. He knew from Indians who lived nearer the railroad that everywhere the white man went he took anything of value in the country and left the Indian to starve.' Having failed to dissuade the geologist from proceeding further north, the chief said he would meet the outsider on his way back 'to search my canoe, open my bags and boxes to see if I had any gold or silver. He wasn't going to allow any of these metals to leave the country, his idea being that if I found any gold, his country would soon be overrun by white men and the Indian brought to starvation.' The geologist conceded that he 'couldn't argue with the old man on this point because I knew that was exactly what would happen.'[28]

By the early twentieth century, the depredations of non-Natives were facilitated by the arrival of railways that made the territory easier to transit. Thanks to the economic boom that occurred during the Laurier years (1896–1911) and the pro-business attitudes of governments in Ottawa and Toronto, more northerly territory was being invaded by federally and provincially sponsored railways. Laurier's government promoted the construction of a new transcontinental railway, which was designed to cross more northerly portions of Shield country than the Canadian Pacific had reached in the interest of expanding economic development. In addition, a private firm, the Grand Trunk Pacific, proposed its own line to the western ocean in this period. And the government of Ontario in the early years of the twentieth century set about facilitating development of forestry and mineral resources in the provincial north with the Temiskaming and Northern Ontario Railway, which would find its terminus on James Bay. Ottawa became aware of these problems from a variety of sources, including its officials such as J.A. Macrae and D.C. Scott.[29]

When these developments turned the federal government towards action, Indian Affairs officials faced a problem with the Province of Ontario. Relations between Ottawa and Toronto had been bad from Confederation until the 1890s, as the two governments battled in the courts over the location of Ontario's western boundary. Toronto argued that the proper border lay well west of Lake of the Woods, while Ottawa favoured a more easterly location because Sir John A. Macdonald feared that a greatly expanded Ontario would become dangerously powerful. The dispute eventually ended up in the courts, with the Judicial Committee of the Privy Council ruling in favour of the province in 1884. Feelings ran so high over the boundary dispute that it took another decade for Ontario and Canada to iron out the details of implementing the decision, including aspects such as the status of reserve lands in Treaty 3. In 1894 an intergovernmental agreement settling these issues said in part that in future treaties in Ontario, the national government 'shall be deemed to require the concurrence of the government of Ontario.'[30] Reluctantly, federal officials began negotiations with their counterparts about a new treaty in 1904. When Ontario appeared to drag its feet, Ottawa renewed its proposal, now arguing that it was important to 'conclud[e] the treaty before the Indians come into closer contact with white people, as they are apt to be easily influenced to make extravagant demands.' By the time agreement was finalized in early 1905, Queen's Park in Toronto had extracted major concessions from Ottawa.[31] Ontario would name one of the three commissioners, no sites at which hydroelectric power greater than 500 horsepower could be developed would be included in any reserves, and Ottawa would pay all three commissioners.

The difficult and protracted negotiations between Parliament Hill and Queen's Park were a contrast to the relatively harmonious talks that led to the conclusion of Treaty 9 in 1905 and 1906. In both years, the federal party consisted of D.C. Scott and Samuel Stewart, Ottawa-based Indian Affairs men, while D.G. MacMartin, a miner, represented Ontario. (The commissioners were accompanied, as in the second year of Treaty 8 talks, by a medical doctor.) The treaty parties were escorted by two strapping young constables of the Dominion Police Force, who reportedly impressed the Indians. At the various stops over the two summers, the commissioners explained the terms of the proposed treaty, responded to questions, took signatures, assigned reserves, and provided amenities to the Indians. Indeed, a regular pattern of ritual was observed, with the Natives greeting the arriving and saluting the departing commissioners with fusillades of gunfire, and the commissioners giving speeches that introduced them as representatives of the king, providing a feast after treaty signing and annuities payment, and furnishing each community that signed with a twelve-foot (3.7 m) Union Jack flag.

From the First Nations side there was little resistance over the two summers. At two locations, bands had to be reassured that entering treaty would not infringe their mobility or hunting and fishing rights. At Lac Seul, for example, 'Missabay, the recognized chief of the band, then spoke, expressing the fear of the Indians that if they signed the treaty, they would be compelled to reside upon the reserve to be set apart for them, and would be deprived of the fishing and hunting privileges which they now enjoy.' As at Treaty 8 in 1899, the commissioners were reassuring: 'On being informed that their fears in regard to both these matters were groundless, as their present manner of making their livelihood would in no way be interfered with, the Indians talked the matter over among themselves,' and, after reflection, the following day agreed to sign 'as they believed that nothing but good was

7.3 '... we made a short stop to put up our flags, in order to make a good appearance coming into the post just across the lake' (Samuel Stewart's journal, 8 Aug. 1906).

intended.' The written version of the treaty was more restrained on continuing hunting and fishing rights than the oral promises had been.[32] At another treaty site in 1905, Chief Moonias was initially suspicious about, as he put it, getting a number of benefits for nothing. 'If I buy as small an article as a needle I have to pay for same, [but] you come here offering money we have not asked for. I do not understand.' According to Commissioner Mac-Martin, 'after an explanation he along with the others signified his assent and the Treaty was signed.'[33]

The benefits were principally a twelve-dollar initial payment and an annuity of four dollars, sums that the federal government had assured a reluctant province in 1904–5 were about the same as remuneration provided more than half a century earlier in the Robinson Treaties. When it came to locating reserves, the com-

7.4 All Treaty 9 negotiations ended with a 'feast.'

missioners were particularly ungenerous. Requests for long sections of river shoreline were rebuffed, and, of course, no band that wanted a reserve where the waterways held potential for hydroelectric power generation had its request granted.[34] Nonetheless, at the feasts that Canada gave at the end of treaty-making, the speeches of First Nations leaders were amazingly positive. To quote one emphatic example, Chief Missabay at Osnaburgh House said, 'The money they would receive would be of great benefit to them and the Indians were all very thankful for the advantages they would receive from the treaty.' He also lectured his young male followers 'to listen well to what the white men had to say and to follow their advice.'[35] Whether Treaty 9 chiefs were thoroughly assured by the oral promises they received, or just terribly anxious for the cash payments that would help with the problems of want that their bands faced, is not clear.

Treaty 10 generally conformed to the other northern numbered treaties negotiated from 1899 on, although it did have some distinctive features. This agreement covered 84,942 square miles (220,000 sq km) in northern Saskatchewan east of Treaty 8 and north of the limits of Treaty 6 and the Montreal Lake adhesion of 1889. This was a region of Woods Cree and Dene bands that had been interested since the early 1880s in gaining access to the treaty relationship that would provide some financial assistance through annuities. Like other groups in regions that the federal government labelled 'out of treaty,' their overtures had been spurned until early in the twentieth century. Official attitudes began to change because of increasing concern about Métis demands and the creation of the provinces of Alberta and Saskatchewan in 1905.[36]

The Métis had long been an issue associated with treaty-making, even though the Crown had steadfastly refused to include them collectively in the treaties. They certainly had played a role in the background to the Robinson Treaties of 1850, and chiefs such as Shinguakonse had asked for their inclusion in the treaty they helped to secure. Similarly, in 1873 at Treaty 3, the

7.5 Chief Missabay, Osnaburgh House, Treaty 9

North West Angle Treaty, it was widely recognized that, as the chief of the Fort Frances band told Commissioner Morris, after years of difficult negotiations 'you owe the treaty much to the Half-breeds.' Canada's refusal to include them as a group led to Métis disgruntlement that sometimes complicated later treaty talks. Their efforts to stir up opposition among the Saulteaux complicated negotiations at Fort Qu'Appelle in 1874. Even more noticeable was the negative role of Métis, at least as reported by the mounted police, in the background to Treaty 8 in the Lesser Slave Lake region in the late 1890s. According to policemen stationed in the area in 1897, they were 'very cooly [*sic*] received by Half-breeds & Indians.'[37] At the making of Treaty 8 the following year, Métis were given the option, if they 'lived an Indian life,' of entering treaty or taking scrip. Métis requests for compensation continued after the turn of the century, as officials reported demands from the Ile à la Crosse area for scrip.[38] Since Indians and Métis further west had been accommodated by the Treaty 8 and scrip commissions of 1899–1900, other Natives, some of whom were kinfolk, further east were unhappy about not being provided for. In fact, Chief William Apesis of the English River band said to Commissioner McKenna at Ile à la Crosse in 1906, '... it wasn't us who called you, it was the Metis.'[39]

The final impetus to make Treaty 10 came in 1905, with the creation of Saskatchewan. Northwestern Saskatchewan was the only portion of the new province not covered by treaty. Unlike the eastern provinces and BC, but in the tradition created with Manitoba in 1870, the new provinces did not gain control of the Crown lands and natural resources within their boundary. The continuing federal role in administering public lands and responsibility created by the Canada Act 1867 (British North America Act) for 'Indians and lands reserved for the Indians' meant that Ottawa had a stake in relations with the indigenous population. From an administrative point of view, it made sense to complete treaty coverage of the new provinces with a treaty with Woods Cree and Dene.

Canada sent treaty and scrip commissions to northwestern Saskatchewan relatively late in the season in 1906. Both the treaty negotiations and scrip commission were assigned to the veteran J.A.J. McKenna. The party met with leaders of two First Nations at Ile à la Crosse late in August, and with the Canoe Lake band at Canoe Lake several weeks later. Because of the late start, Commissioner McKenna was not inclined to tarry too long negotiating or even answering questions, but the insistence of the First Nations at his first stop forced him to slow down. Chief Apesis and his headman flatly refused McKenna's proposal to agree in principle to the treaty on the understanding that details would be negotiated later. They told the commissioner, 'If you are in a hurry, then just go, if you are in such a rush. What you are in a rush for, go and do that first.'[40] They forced a somewhat more considered approach. All the same, the late start meant that the treaty and scrip commissioners did not get to Stanley Mission on

the Churchill River in 1906. The following year, Thomas Borthwick, agent at Mistawasis Reserve, near Duck Lake, Saskatchewan,
completed the task with talks at Lac du Brochet with both Woods
Cree and Dene leaders. In both years, the talks were facilitated by
Roman Catholic priests who urged their adherents to take treaty,
and, again, the commissioner relied on the HBC for transportation and other assistance.

The principal issues in the Treaty 10 talks were the now familiar ones of maintaining autonomy and the continuing right to
hunt and fish, although some other matters appeared as well. As
had been evident in the Treaty 8 and Treaty 9 talks, First Nations
were greatly concerned about securing health care. A doctor
accompanied the Treaty 10 commission in both years, and in
1906 McKenna responded to chiefs' requests for medicine and a
resident doctor with a promise 'that medicines would be placed
at different points in the charge of persons to be selected by the
Government, and would be distributed to those of the Indians
who might require them.'[41] Requests that the government
respect the religious affiliations of the bands when providing
schools elicited ready agreement from the commissioner, who no
doubt recognized that denominational schooling was the preferred DIA practice. The other new request that arose from First
Nations in Treaty 10 talks was for arrears of annuities dating back
to the signing of Treaty 6 in 1876. Chief Apesis broke the news to
McKenna at Ile à La Crosse: 'I see, however, you handed out
money to other areas. It's been quite long since then and you
went around us. Since the day you started handing out money,
how many years now? I like you to give us all what you have given
since that day.'[42] McKenna rejected the demand, supposedly
because it was unprecedented. First Nations leaders also asked
for help for their elderly indigent, to which the commissioner
responded that he would convey their information to the government and try to arrange for some assistance to be provided.

The most pressing concern of Treaty 10 bands, as had also
been the case earlier, was the linked matters of autonomy and
livelihood. Simply put, First Nations leaders sought assurance
that taking treaty would not mean subjection to rules and regu-

lations that would interfere with their mobility, particularly move-ment to harvest the resources of the country. Commissioner McKenna reported that 'I guaranteed that the treaty would not lead to any forced interference with their mode of life. I explained to them that whether treaty was made or not, they were subject to the law, bound to obey it and liable to punishment for any infringement thereof.'[43] Treaty 10 Elders remembered the exchange about autonomy and hunting differently. Elder Eugene Sylvestre explained that 'there was supposed to be no impedi-ments to our way of life, nothing was supposed to be closed from us. It was like that, you can hunt, you can fish, and you can trap and that's how it was.' And Elder Frank McIntyre recalled that 'the Indian commissioner said, "If you take this money, this treaty money, your way of life will not be subjected to anything. You can kill game anywhere so you can feed your people. We will not even speak on it, there will be no policy made on it."'[44] However, the written, or government, version of Treaty 10 had the usual wording: First Nations 'shall have the right to pursue their usual vocations of hunting, trapping and fishing throughout the terri-tory surrendered as heretofore described, subject to such regula-tions as may from time to time be made by the government of the country ...' In later years, of course, Treaty 10 bands were sub-jected to fish and game laws, resulting in the plethora of litigation that seemed to be the lot of First Nations in twentieth-century Canada.

As the mixed messages about hunting and gathering rights indicate, the results of Treaty 10 generally conformed to what other groups, including those of the boreal forest after 1899, had experienced. In return for familiar terms such as an initial payment of twelve dollars and annuities, uniforms and additional payments for chief and headmen, and land allocations – once more offered as either collective reserve or in severalty – First Nations joined the treaty in northern Saskatchewan in 1906–7. The haste with which the commission operated, especially under McKenna in 1906, in combination with the view of at least some of the First Nations chiefs that it was the Métis, not they, who were pushing for an agreement, resulted in some pointed questions and protracted talks that the commissioner later smoothed over in his official report. McKenna never indicated to Ottawa that the leaders at Ile à la Crosse essentially threatened to terminate proceedings if he did not slow down and deal with their concerns. Given the discrepancy between the commissioner's and Elders' accounts on this point, there is good reason to doubt the reliability of the official version of limited undertakings on continuing harvesting rights. Even though the government instructed Commissioner Borthwick not to make 'outside promises' in 1907, it seems likely that his predecessor had already made some.

Treaty 11, the last of the modern numbered treaties, was remarkably similar in its dynamics to the other three northern agreements. As in the other northern treaty regions, the Dene of what would become Treaty 11 had responded to hardship brought on by the decline of the fur trade by making overtures for treaty that they thought might provide assistance. Like other northern First Nations who had been requesting treaties since at least 1883, the Dene in the extensive area – Treaty 11 would embrace 372,000 square miles (963,480 sq km) – east of Yukon Territory were ignored by the federal government. As long as they were occupying lands that had not attracted the attention of southern economic interests, Ottawa was content to leave them as 'out of treaty Indians,' expecting that any needed assistance would be supplied by the Hudson's Bay Company. What changed the situation was the discovery of oil at Norman Wells, NWT, in 1920. With striking, even unseemly, haste, the federal government commissioned a treaty party under H.A. Conroy, former Indian inspector in Treaty 8, to make an agreement in 1921. Conroy's mandate was to make treaty in an enormous region north of Treaty 8, east of the Yukon Territory border, south of the Arctic Ocean, and west of an uneven line that formed the treaty's easternmost boundary. Canada might drag its feet in initiating northern treaties, but, once it put its mind to doing so, it did it with a vengeance.

Conroy headed a treaty party composed of the usual elements. In addition to the commissioner, there were Royal Canadian

Mounted Police personnel and a doctor. Moreover, the 1921 commission relied as usual on the services and facilities of the Hudson's Bay Company, and also benefited from the pro-treaty influence of Roman Catholic missionaries who had been stationed in the North for some time. Once more, Canada's treaty commissioner followed the practice of 'negotiating' terms with the first group it encountered, in this case at Fort Providence, and then taking what Commissioner Conroy styled 'adhesions' from other bands at Fort Simpson, Fort Wrigley, Fort Norman, Fort Good Hope, Arctic Red River, Fort McPherson, and Fort Rae. The implication of the practice, of course, was that all but the initial band at Fort Providence had no say in establishing the treaty terms.[45] The treaty terms, as approved by the federal cabinet, included remuneration for chiefs and headmen, annuities of five dollars for all, reserves calculated on the basis of one square mile (259 hectares) per family of five, a commitment 'to pay the salaries of teachers to instruct the children,' tools once a reserve was selected, and agricultural assistance 'in the event of any of the Indians aforesaid being desirous of following agricultural pursuits,' and 'a silver medal, a suitable flag and a copy of this Treaty' for each chief as well as the familiar triennial uniform for chiefs and councillors.

Treaty 11 also resembled the other northern numbered treaties in its ambivalent handling of Dene autonomy and livelihood. Conroy recorded that at Fort Providence,

> ... as in all the other posts where the treaty was signed, the questions asked and the difficulties encountered were much the same. The Indians seemed afraid, for one thing, that their liberty to hunt, trap and fish would be taken away or curtailed, but were assured by me that this would not be the case, and the Government will expect them to support themselves in their own way, and, in fact, that more twine for nets and more ammunition were given under this treaty than under any of the preceding ones; this went a long way to calm their fears. I also pointed out that any game laws made were to their advantage, and whether they took treaty or not, they were subject to the laws of the Dominion.[46]

The government-approved version of the treaty contained the usual recognition 'that they shall have the right to pursue their usual vocations of hunting, trapping and fishing throughout the tract surrendered ..., subject to such regulations as may from time to time be made by the Government of the Country ...'

As had been noticeable with the previous three northern treaty negotiations, the oral traditions of the Dene nations involved in Treaty 11 concerning livelihood and autonomy differed dramatically from the official account. Elders from Fort Providence who were interviewed in the late 1960s and early 1970s were unanimous that their leaders agreed to the treaty in 1921 only after firm assurances from Commissioner Conroy that there would be no interference with their ways of living and maintaining themselves:

> *Victor Lafferty:* When Conroy asked [Chief Paul Lefoin] if he wanted to take Treaty, 'Well,' Lefoin says, 'well, if we do, what I say about my country? This is my country,' he says, 'I'd like to hunt all over as far as I can go, there's forts all around us. Fort Rae, Simpson, Liard, Upper Hay, in fact nearly everywhere I go down, that's my country.' He says, 'If you don't stop us from hunting ... We want to hunt just the same as before, the way we are making a living. Hunt big game, and fur and fish, birds, everything and we don't want you to put us on a reserve.' He says, 'I'm an Indian. I don't read, I don't write, but still, I know what you've done outside [in the Prairie provinces]. You put the Crees on the reserves and the country's so small it didn't last long, they didn't have nothing to hunt. And we don't want to be like that here. Do all that,' Lefoin says, 'then I'll take Treaty.'
>
> *William Squirrel:* There was nothing said about setting lands aside for the Indians. You could live and do your things anywhere you felt like it ...
>
> *Jean Marie Sabourin:* The only thing talked about was hunting rights ... 'You will not take away our hunting rights,' that is what the chief said ... The hunting, fishing, and migratory rights were the topic discussion [*sic*] ... The Commissioner said, 'Your hunting rights will not be taken away from you ...'[47]

Oral history accounts of negotiations in other centres are unanimous in backing up the view of Fort Providence Elders that the Crown promised their lifeways and economic pursuits would not be interfered with if they took treaty. Like other First Nations, they entered treaty on that understanding, only to be bitterly disappointed later.

The northern numbered treaties, covering a vast 'empire in itself,' contained common features that provide a good reading of the state of Native-newcomer relations in Canada by the twentieth century. The government of Canada consistently acted in the interests of non-Native economic concerns. It ignored early requests from First Nations for treaties to evade financial responsibility for relieving them when hardships inflicted by southern development undercut their livelihood, and initiated treaty talks when northern lands became valuable to southerners. During negotiations, treaty commissioners, who usually had been instructed to avoid making 'outside promises,' gave chiefs ringing assurances of non-interference with indigenous ways of life, but the government's written version of the treaties always contained qualifying clauses that severely limited those undertakings. Treaty negotiations also revealed that the Crown continued to rely on useful auxiliaries such as the Hudson's Bay Company, Christian missionaries, and the mounted police to bolster its case. And northern treaty deliberations also indicated that the attachment to Aboriginal protocols that had been prominent in most of the southern numbered treaty negotiations was declining. The most persistent element of the elaborate old ceremonies was the feast provided after talks were concluded and agreement reached. In the North, it was clear that in gaining an 'empire,' Canada was ever more clearly acting like an oppressive colonizer.

8

'Get rid of the Indian problem':[1] The Hiatus in Treaty-Making, 1923–1975

Duncan Campbell Scott, deputy superintendent general of Indian affairs from 1913 to 1932, was a man on a mission in the spring of 1920. The career civil servant who had been a commissioner for the Crown in Treaty 9 had stored up many frustrations with Canada's Indian policy over his long career in Indian Affairs as a bookkeeper and later superintendent of education. Were it not a libel on accountants, Scott's attitude towards administering policy might be described as that of someone with the soul of a bookkeeper. Ironically, the man who was now the most prominent bureaucrat in Indian Affairs was well known and respected as a poet. First Nations might have been forgiven for not knowing that important cultural fact, for Scott's behaviour towards them always seemed to be determined by prosaic considerations of economy. Indians were too demanding in treaty negotiations, too uncooperative about sending their children to residential schools, too obdurate about not adopting the DIA's preferred model of band governance, the elective system. To Scott it was obvious that, if First Nations would not voluntarily do what Indian Affairs knew to be best for them, then compulsion would have to be applied.

The matter of enfranchisement, the topic that preoccupied Deputy Minister Scott that spring, was a typical source of his frustration. Since 1857 governments had tried to get First Nations males to renounce their Indian status and become citizens. However, enfranchisement, even aided by the Department's aggressively assimilative educational program, was a failure. The compulsory enfranchisement bill that Scott went to the special parliamentary committee to promote in 1920 would empower government to strip Indian males the Department thought were ready for full citizenship of their Indian status whether the men wanted to be citizens or not. Scott made his reasons clear: 'I want to get rid of the Indian problem. I do not think as a matter of fact, that this country ought to continuously protect a class of people who are able to stand alone. That is my whole point. Our objective is to continue until there is not a single Indian in Canada that has not been absorbed into the body politic, and there is no Indian question, and no Indian Department and that is the whole object of this Bill.' Scott might also have added: 'no need for treaties, either.'

Scott's attitude before the parliamentary committee exemplified one of the factors – government opposition – that were responsible for bringing treaty-making to a halt soon after the negotiation of Treaty 11. Canada also proved unwilling to enter into more agreements because non-Native economic interests, traditionally the major spark plug behind treaty initiative, were busy for some time digesting the enormous empire that had been acquired between 1871 and 1921. In addition, the Great Depression of the 1930s halted most economic activity in Canada, acting as a damper on the push to acquire more Native lands. Government attitudes were important, too. In common with many in North America, federal government planners believed that First Nations were dwindling noticeably in numbers because of disease, assimilation, and enfranchisement. The suppressed hostility expressed in D.C. Scott's utterance to the parliamentary committee, especially when combined with government parsimony in Indian policy, was another argument against more treaties. The combined force of those factors would effectively end treaty-making for half a century.

The suspension of agreement-making after 1921 was not absolute. Exceptions to the rule were an Ontario treaty and some major external adhesions. The Williams Treaties of 1923 with certain Ojibwa and Mississauga bands were intended to repair deficiencies in the early Upper Canadian treaties. The agreement that Commissioner John Collins had made in the late eighteenth century for a tract from the Narrows of Lake Simcoe to Matchedash Bay near Georgian Bay, land essential for the ancient route from the Ottawa River to Toronto, was soon found by imperial officials to be defective because it did not document the area to be covered. Similarly, Upper Canadian Treaty 13 of 1787, made at the Bay of Quinte, also failed to spell out the tract's boundaries. It was to prevent the creation of more of these sorts of problem that the governor, Lord Dorchester, issued regulations in 1794 that largely reiterated the land-surrender requirements of the Royal Proclamation of 1763.

Officials contemplated measures to repair the omissions, but nothing effective was done. Administrator Peter Russell, successor to Lieutenant-Governor John Graves Simcoe, tried a cute ploy in 1798. He invited Mississauga chiefs to make a land cession 'lest the King's subjects should by mistake at any time encroach upon the Indian Territory and give offence.' Chief Yellowhead reassured the official – after a fashion: 'Father, If you white people forget your transactions with us, we do not. The Land you have just now shewn to us belongs to you; We have nothing to do with it; We have sold it to our Great Father the King, and was [sic] well paid for it. Therefore make your mind easy. There may be some of our young people who do not think so; They may tell your people that that Land is ours, but you must not open your ears to them, but take them by the arm and put them out of your houses, for as long as you will listen, you will be plagued by them.'[2] Since First Nations were not inclined to make an issue of shortcomings in early Upper Canadian treaty-making, officials let the matter rest.

However, Yellowhead proved a reliable prophet. According to an inquiry held in 1923, claims for territory in due course emanated from Ojibwa bands near Lake Huron and Lake Simcoe, as well as from the Mississauga of Mud, Rice, and Scugog Lakes and were 'before the [Indian Affairs] Department for many years.'[3] In addition to these unsatisfied First Nations claims, there was continuing uneasiness among at least some Euro-Canadians about security of title in regions where territorial treaties had not been properly made. The three-man inquiry that Ottawa commissioned in 1923 held extensive hearings among affected bands, collecting evidence at Georgina Island, Christian Island, Rama, Scugog, Hiawatha, Curve Lake, and Alderville. The result was a stunning report in which Commissioner Sinclair concluded unequivocally that 'the claim to the whole territory as hunting grounds is asserted by the declarations of 27 Indians in terms so positive and explicit as to render it extremely difficult to disregard the evidence. The Indian title to these lands has never been extinguished and I am of the opinion that some arrangement should be made for quieting the title by the payment to the claimants of compensation in the same way that the Crown has dealt with other Indians whose title has been extinguished by Treaty.'[4] In accordance with a prior agreement between Canada and Ontario, the commissioner now moved to make a treaty with the claimant groups.

The two Williams Treaties that were concluded between 31 October and 21 November 1923 contained a familiar package of treaty elements. In exchange for renunciation of any and all claims, including the disputed tracts that amounted to 21,100 square miles (54,649 sq km), the signatory bands would receive a one-time per capita payment of twenty-five dollars, and a further $233,375 'for the said tribe by His Majesty's Department of Indian Affairs under and pursuant to the provisions of the Indian Act.' In all, the compensation for a vast tract of valuable land along Lake Ontario east of Toronto and lying between the Ottawa River and Georgian Bay was, the Department estimated, $250,000. (See map 9.) Next to the meagre compensation, three other items were significant: the agreements did not include the guarantees of hunting and fishing that had become standard features of territorial treaties; there was no evidence in the deliberations of traditional relationship-renewing protocol; and there were no real negotiations involved. The Williams Treaties were put to the various bands in a take-it-or-leave-it form.

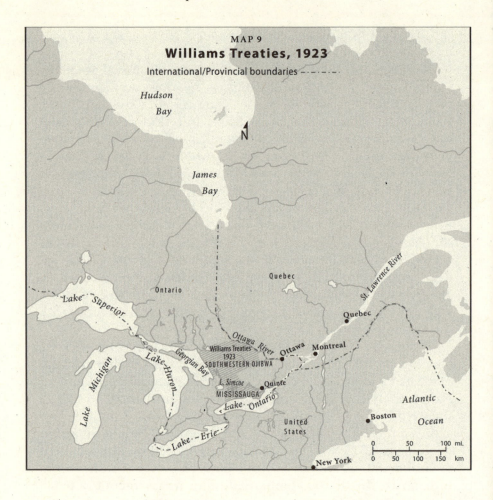

MAP 9
Williams Treaties, 1923
International/Provincial boundaries — - — - — -

Hudson
Bay

James
Bay

N

Quebec

St. Lawrence River

Lake Superior

Ontario

Quebec

Williams Treaties
1923
SOUTHWESTERN OJIBWA

Ottawa River

Ottawa

Montreal

Lake Michigan

Lake Huron

Georgian Bay

L. Simcoe

Quinte

MISSISSAUGA

Lake Ontario

Atlantic

Lake Erie

United
States

Ocean

Boston

New York

| 0 | 50 | 100 mi. |
| 0 | 50 | 100 | 150 | km |

The absence of negotiations notable in the Williams Treaties also typified the other exception to the rule of no treaty-making after the conclusion of Treaty 11 in 1921. The major northern adhesions to Treaty 5 and Treaty 9 were similarly concluded without meaningful negotiation. In the case of northern Manitoba, for example, where adhesions to Treaty 5 occurred in 1908, 1909, and 1910, the familiar pattern of First Nations initiative and government indifference prevailed for many years. For a long period after Treaty 5 was signed in 1875, First Nations beyond its northern boundary expressed a desire to be taken into treaty in order to acquire income from annuities that would ease the problems brought on by the decline of the fur trade. Like northern Ontario First Nations, in the early years of the twentieth century these Manitoba bands also became concerned about the likely impact of a railway to Hudson Bay – long anticipated, energetically lobbied for by a variety of western interests, and now, apparently, likely to be constructed – on their already diminished ability to maintain themselves by traditional hunting-gathering. In some locales in the region, there were also concerns about the activities of non-Native commercial fishers, whose methods caused severe problems to the more conservation-minded First Nations gatherers.[5] As usual, the federal government rejected these requests for more than three decades after Treaty 5 was signed.

The Department of Indian Affairs was pushed into action by the possibility of First Nations' resistance to non-Native activity and the imminence of railway construction. A missionary to the Split Lake band, who were not in Treaty 5 though their lands were close to it, raised possibly contentious issues when he argued that commercial fishers had no business taking sturgeon in waters that had not been covered by treaty. That complication, and the likelihood by 1908 that the railway would soon begin, pushed Ottawa to appoint treaty and scrip commissioners to deal with First Nations and Métis in a series of gatherings in 1908, 1909, and 1910. The federal government, faced with a choice between getting the bands to adhere to Treaty 5 to the south or Treaty 10 to the west, chose the former, apparently because its compensation terms were less generous than those of the later pact. As a result, the Woods Cree and Dene bands that adhered received annuities of five dollars (twelve in Treaty 10), reserves of 160 acres (64.8 hectares) rather than 640, and smaller gratuities to chiefs and councillors. All in all, it was a depressingly familiar Indian Affairs performance. Scrip policy was no more encouraging. In the fifty years between the negotiation of Treaty 1 and the signing of Treaty 11, the government of Canada carried out thirteen scrip commissions that issued 4,078 square miles (10,561.5

sq km) of land scrip and money scrip amounting to $2,888,157.[6]
So far as the Métis as a community were concerned, they had
little to show for the effort.

The final adhesion to the numbered treaties was the adhesion
to Treaty 9 in the far northern portions of Ontario in 1930. In
fact, the 1930 adhesion was not the first major addition to Treaty
9. In 1908, Commissioner Samuel Stewart had gone north again
to incorporate a group of 'Quebec Indians' who initially had
been barred from the treaty because of their location.[7] Requests
to be taken into treaty from the groups north of the Albany River
had begun soon afterwards. By the time of the Great War, bands
in what formerly had been the Northwest Territories, but since
1912 was incorporated into Ontario following the extension of
that province's and Quebec's boundaries northward, were
seeking treaties. They were motivated by a combination of disgruntlement with encroaching fur harvesters, the adverse impact
of poor fur prices, and irritation with Ontario's attempts to apply
provincial fish and game laws. As James Stoney wrote in 1915 on
behalf of the First Nations along the Hudson Bay coast near
Winisk, 'We would like to join in a Treaty as the other Indians at
York Factory on the west of us or Albany, Fort Hope, Osnaburg,
Attawapiskat on the south of us.' They had 'never been asked to
get into any of these Treaties. We are practically surrounded by
these Indians who get help from the Government and our
hunting grounds in this cold northern climate are very poor and
we would be very pleased to be able to join in any of these
Treaties. Now that the Hudson's Bay is being approached by railways and whitemen are coming into this northern country we will
be driven from our land.'[8] A federal-provincial commission flew
into the remote sites of Big Trout Lake, Nikip on the Windigo
River, Fort Severn, and Winisk in the summer of 1930. Aside from
the thoroughly modern way the commissioners travelled, there
was no novelty to these treaty adhesions.

The commissioners followed established practice of presenting
the adhesion to the First Nations as an ultimatum. Those who
joined were paid an initial amount of eight dollars and annuities
of four dollars, just as in the original Treaty 9 of 1905–6. They

were also offered reserves, and promised that they would be able to hunt and fish in future without interference. A careful analysis of the documentary and oral history of the talks at Winisk reveals that the discussions left the First Nations with the impression that they were being promised assistance and non-interference with their traditional ways of maintaining themselves, although the written documents, of course, contain all the usual caveats about future non-Native use that were standard features of treaties. In particular, the commissioners' written report did not reveal the Crown's representatives alluding at all to the Migratory Birds Convention Act, to which Canada became a party in 1918. The Act's wording obviously would have an impact on fowl-hunting, a vitally important subsistence activity in the Hudson Bay Lowlands.[9] As had been the case with Treaty 9 talks earlier, the adhesion meetings also featured a 'feast' provided by the governments to the First Nations. The events in northern Ontario in 1930 suggested that treaty-making and adhesion-signing had settled down into a government-directed routine.

According to Ontario premier Howard Ferguson speaking on the morrow of the Williams Treaties, '... every tribe that could possibly have a claim on the "white man's" government had been taken care of.' The money paid to Ojibwa and Mississauga in 1923 was 'the last payment' Ontario would have to make. For his part, he was 'naturally glad to have seen the last of the problem.'[10] It turned out that Premier Ferguson was something of a prophet, too, for the Williams Treaties would be the last new treaties signed for half a century. A number of factors account for the hiatus. One consideration was that the Dominion had already acquired formal title to a vast patrimony in the West and North that it would take some time to exploit fully. A minor factor was the perception that First Nations were 'a vanishing race,' a view that reinforced Canada's lack of interest in acquiring more land in 'Indian country.' The most serious factor behind the lack of interest in treaty-making after Treaty 11 was that by the 1920s Indian Affairs' attitudes towards First Nations had hardened, and leading bureaucrats were not inclined to respond positively to First Nations' desires. This potent mix of influences against treaty-making would begin to lose strength only towards the middle of the twentieth century, and then owing to a conjunction of changing economic conditions and rising political pressures.

Even for a young state that was becoming an internally colonizing power, Canada after the Great War found itself with a bounty of lands under treaty. The eleven numbered treaties and the three major adhesions (Treaty 5, Treaty 8, and Treaty 9) totalled 1,543,556 square miles (3,997,792 sq km), ranging from 19,390 square miles (50,216 sq km) for Treaty 1 to 374,717 square miles (970,513 sq km) in the case of Treaty 11. The total area represented about 90 per cent of the European Union's 1,669,808 square miles (4,324,782 sq km). Canada's new patrimony included both prime agricultural land in the Prairies and Canadian Shield tracts that were rich in forest products, minerals, and energy in the form of hydroelectric power, oil, and, later, uranium. It simply took Canada and its entrepreneurs willing to invest in the exploitation of these resources a long time to 'digest' what the Dominion had acquired. Moreover, some of the new lands were remote from markets and political decision-makers. One measure of how Ottawa's reach had exceeded its grasp in treaty-making between 1871 and 1921 was the fact that the terms of Treaty 11 remained largely unimplemented. First Nations in this enormous northerly region were still able to maintain themselves mainly by pursuing traditional economic practices, and the federal government was not beating the bushes for more obligations to First Nations in remote regions. Finally, the hectic pace of immigration slowed by the First World War, and while the influx of new arrivals picked up to a degree in the 1920s, it never reached the breakneck rate of the pre-1913 period. Throughout the 1930s, of course, the devastating impact of the Great Depression slowed immigration, deterred direct investment, and strengthened the government's aversion to taking on more liabilities.

Undergirding the government's predisposition not to make treaties was the influence of a widespread belief that First Nations were going to vanish. The idea that indigenous peoples would disappear as a result of contact with European settlers had a lengthy history. Behind Lieutenant-Governor Francis Bond Head's reasons – or perhaps rationalization – for wanting Upper Canadian Indians to surrender their lands to the Crown and relocate to Manitoulin Island had lain his belief that indigenous peoples inevitably suffered from contact with Europeans. 'Whenever and wherever the two races come into contact with each other, it is sure to prove fatal to the red man,' Bond Head had written. Shinguakonse, chief of the Garden River Ojibwa, petitioned Governor General Lord Elgin in 1849, noting that '... we have melted away like snow beneath an April sun; our strength is wasted, our countless warriors dead, our forest laid low ...'[11] A parallel ideology developed in the United States, and became nearly a universal conviction by the late nineteenth century as Washington moved to dispossess Native Americans west of the Mississippi of prime lands coveted by others.[12] While the notion never enjoyed as widespread acceptance in Canada as it did in the republic, in the early twentieth century it acquired the lustre of scientific truth in the Dominion. Anthropologist Diamond Jenness, originally from New Zealand but a long-time researcher and policy advisor in Canada, pronounced the inevitable demise of indigenous peoples in his influential 1931 survey, *The Indians of Canada*: 'Doubtless all the tribes will disappear.'[13] If First Nations were going to disappear, why pay any heed to their requests for new treaties?

From the perspective of the Department of Indian Affairs, the only problem with this scientific nostrum was that their wards were not disappearing fast enough. It was not that the federal government actively sought the physical elimination of Native peoples, although its unresponsive attitude to problems such as widespread disease – especially tuberculosis – in residential schools and on some reserves, certainly did not slow down the rate of population decline. Since the period of treaty implementation following the conclusion of the first seven numbered treaties, hardship, dietary problems, and disease had combined to reduce the western Indian population. While the impact of post-treaty developments was greatest in the Prairies, First Nations throughout the country did not fare well in the late nineteenth century and early years of the next. Canadian census data are notoriously unreliable for First Nations populations in the 1881–1941 period. Often the Dominion Bureau of Statistics lumped 'Indians and Eskimos' together, and in 1901 the census numbers combined First Nations and 'half breeds' into a single category. All the same, what does seem clear is that the First Nations' population, especially in western Canada, declined from 1881 until at least the Great War, with no demonstrable improvement occurring until the 1930s. It was only by the time of the Second World War that the federal government recognized that the long decline in First Nations' population had been reversed. While Ottawa did little until the 1920s to halt the decline, its policies towards First Nations were not designed to extirpate them physically.[14]

Rather, the Department of Indian Affairs (DIA) focused on a systematic effort to eliminate Indians culturally. Enfranchisement, the mechanism by which First Nations males could surrender their distinctive Indian status and become full citizens of the country, had been a centrepiece of Canadian Indian policy since 1857. Not insignificant was the fact that enfranchisement, which would remain a central feature of policy until the late twentieth century, was accompanied by a transfer of the enfranchised male's share of reserve land into a freehold tenure. In other words, as First Nations gave up Indian status through their males, the quantum of reserve land would shrink, too. The fewer the Indians, the smaller the area of reserves until the ultimate was achieved: there would be no more 'Indians' and no more reserves. Indian educational policy – especially the residential schools – was viewed by the DIA as a prime means to the end of enfranchisement. Other policies had their place, too. Government campaigns against cultural practices such as the Potlatch on the North West Coast and summer dance ceremonies on the Plains were part of a general attack on indigenous spirituality. The powers that Parliament began giving the minister of Indian affairs in 1869 to interfere in First Nations governance by deposing chiefs were intended to facilitate removal of leaders who resisted the DIA's campaign. By the early twentieth century, Canada had equipped its Department of Indian Affairs with a panoply of powers to undermine, attack, and eventually eliminate First Nations identity. The cultural elimination of Indians was the unifying feature of Canadian Indian policy for a century after Confederation.

The problem from Indian Affairs' perspective was that this array of policies – which most bureaucrats and many politicians believed were in the best interests of First Nations – did not work. Adult males, even when subjected to residential school education, did not enfranchise in large numbers. That Indian educational policy itself was an abysmal failure that undermined First Nations identity and left its victims demoralized did not seem to lessen enthusiasm for Indian ways. Neither did attacks on spiritual practices, although Christian missionaries, encouraged and financially supported by the federal government, did make many 'converts.' First Nations communities did not accept Ottawa's sporadic, clumsy efforts to interfere with their governance by trying to replace chiefs and councillors who did not cooperate with DIA directives with leaders who would. Indians did not become more like Euro-Canadians. They did not 'join the mainstream' of Canadian society enthusiastically. And, above all, they did not throw off their own ways in favour of the majority's economic pursuits and become self-supporting. The entire DIA campaign, which had always been motivated in part by the desire to change First Nations' identity in order to make them financially independent of government, was a failure. By the Great War, its unsatisfactory results were indisputable.

Unfortunately, Indian Affairs bureaucrats reacted to the policy failure by concluding, not that the policy should be changed, but that more coercion in the application of the policy was the answer. The frustration that underlay Department attitudes came through very clearly in the testimony of its deputy minister, Duncan Campbell Scott, before a parliamentary committee considering enfranchisement in 1920:

I do not want to pass into the citizens' class people who are
paupers. This is not the intention of the Bill. But after one
hundred years, after being in close contact with civilization it is
enervating to the individual or to a band to continue in that state
of tutelage, when he or they are able to take their position as
British citizens or Canadian citizens, to support themselves, and
stand alone. That has been the whole purpose of Indian education
and advancement since the earliest times. One of the very earliest
enactments was to provide for the enfranchisement of the Indian.
So it is written in our law that the Indian was eventually to become
enfranchised ...[15]

The way in which Scott linked education, enfranchisement, and
financial independence was revealing of DIA thinking by 1920.
So, too, was his obvious frustration.

The bill on which Deputy Minister Scott gave evidence, though
extraordinary, was not untypical of Indian Affairs policy in the
1920s. It empowered the minister of Indian affairs to enfranchise
an adult male Indian that the DIA thought was ready for the step
whether or not the man selected wanted to be enfranchised. The
legislation was both an amazing admission of policy failure and
evidence of an aggressive attitude towards First Nations. After
more than six decades of voluntary enfranchisement for males,
the department was in effect admitting that approach did not
work. Moreover, the government was embarking on a much more
coercive path than it ever had contemplated in the past. The
clause providing for involuntary enfranchisement was enacted as
an amendment to the Indian Act in 1920, but it was never used
because a new, Liberal government under William Lyon Mackenzie King had Parliament repeal it in 1922.

The reaction against the coercive measure on enfranchisement was provoked largely because Scott and the government
contemplated using it against the leader of a new First Nations
political organization. Scott's proposed move against Frederick
O. Loft was the first step of what would prove an ongoing,
aggressive campaign against efforts to establish effective political
organizations. Loft was a graduate of the Mohawk Institute, a res-

idential school in Brantford, and had served as an infantry lieutenant with the Canadian forces during the Great War. His background might have made him an ideal candidate for voluntary
enfranchisement. He was anything but. Instead, Loft turned to
organizing the League of Indians of Canada, a nationwide First
Nations political movement, soon after his return to Ontario.
Significantly, one of the prominent concerns that Loft proposed
for the League platform was land rights: 'The first aim of the
League then is to claim and protect the rights of all Indians in
Canada by legitimate and just means; second, absolute control in
retaining possession or dispensation of our lands; that all questions and matters relative to individual and national well-being
of Indians shall rest with the people and their dealing with the
Government shall be by and through their respective band
Councils at all times.'[16] Loft conceived of control of First
Nations lands and respect for First Nations governance as closely
linked. It was revealing that D.C. Scott believed that involuntary
enfranchisement was desirable because it 'would also check the
intrigues of smart Indians on the reserves, who are forming
organizations to foster these aboriginal feelings, and to thwart
the efforts and policy of the Government. Such a man should be
enfranchised.'[17]

Although D.C. Scott's plan to undermine Loft by enfranchising
him against his will was stymied by an outcry from press and
Liberal opposition, the deputy minister persisted with his campaign to control the budding movement among First Nations to
assert themselves through political organization. Loft passed
from the political scene when he relocated to the United States,
but his attempt to form a national movement spun off into the
League of Indians of Western Canada in the 1920s, which proved
a seedbed of later Prairie organizations. The next challenge to
Ottawa's paternalism and control also emanated from the Six
Nations reserve in Ontario. Part of the Six Nations community
pursued a lengthy campaign through the first half of the 1920s to
secure recognition of Six Nations sovereignty. Petitions to Ottawa
and London proving unavailing, the sovereignists took their case
to the young League of Nations in Geneva. When it seemed prob-

able that a coalition that included The Netherlands (early allies
of the Iroquois) and several states that had suffered under imperial rule (Ireland, Estonia, Panama, and Persia [now Iran]) might
succeed at the League, the Canadian government got the British
government to have its diplomats at the League twist arms to stop
the movement. In the course of these disputes, the Department
of Indian Affairs also intervened directly in governance at Six
Nations, deposing a hereditary council in favour of elected
leaders and stationing an RCMP detachment at Oshweken, the
principal town at Six Nations. Like Fred Loft and the League of
Indians of Canada, the Six Nations sovereignists had provoked
Deputy Minister Scott into revealing the lengths to which he
would go to frustrate First Nations' efforts to defend their rights.[18]

A major international event in 1921 might also have been
among the factors that pushed Deputy Minister Scott towards
aggressive action against assertive First Nations. In that year, the
Judicial Committee of the Privy Council (JCPC) handed down its
decision in a case that originated in Africa. In *Amodu Tijani v. Secretary of Southern Nigeria,* the highest court in the empire held that
Chief Docemo had exceeded his authority in 1861 when he
agreed to a treaty that purported to cede all the lands in Lagos to
Queen Victoria. Lord Haldane, speaking for the JCPC, ruled that
Docemo had no feudal authority or seigneurial rights over other
chiefs, much less complete title to the lands in question. Since
Aboriginal title had continued, the complainant, Chief Tijani,
would have to be compensated. The implications of the ruling as
to the existence and robustness of Aboriginal title, as well as the
potential for aggrieved Aboriginal people to litigate to establish
their claims, were enormous. Lord Haldane said that Aboriginal
title was a collective or community right. 'The original native
right was a communal right, and it must be presumed to have
continued to exist unless the contrary is established by the
context or circumstances.' The potential to apply that doctrine to
vast areas of Canada where territorial treaties had never been
negotiated was obvious.[19]

The climactic factor pitting Scott and the DIA against First
Nations featured territorial rights in British Columbia. The chal-

lenge to Indian Affairs that came to a head in 1927 concerned what had become known as the BC land question. The issue here was that colonial British Columbia had stopped making territorial treaties in 1854, and, except in the anomalous case of Treaty 8, no other treaties had been made in British Columbia since. Because the province simply denied the existence of Aboriginal title – or 'Indian title,' as it would have been termed in the nineteenth century – it proved impossible to deal with land issues. Whenever the federal government wished to do something to alleviate the problems of BC First Nations, the province balked. For example, efforts to provide adequate reserves from the 1870s on had broken down over such differences. After the Great War, a federal-provincial inquiry – the McKenna-McBride Commission – had taken another crack at the land question, with bad results for First Nations. The Commission advocated 'cutting off' parts of many existing reserves and substituting larger tracts elsewhere. The problem with that 'solution' was that the new lands were noticeably inferior to the 'cut offs.' A number of BC First Nations and regional organizations had been resisting the Commission's recommendations, all the while becoming more organized and vociferous about their treatment. The latest stage of the BC land question would occur in Ottawa in 1927.

Since the province refused to discuss Aboriginal title issues before a joint parliamentary committee, while BC First Nations were adamant that the title question was critical, conditions did not augur well. The Allied Tribes of British Columbia, a political movement formed to pursue the land question, made their Aboriginal title claim in their submission to the joint parliamentary committee. In response, the Province of British Columbia declined to be represented before the body.[20] The fact that D.C. Scott took a position generally favourable to the province showed clearly that the cards were stacked against the Indians. Scott, not surprisingly, dismissed the Allied Tribes' assertion of Aboriginal title to most of British Columbia, and also made it clear that the land question and political restiveness were closely linked. Speaking to the joint parliamentary committee, he observed, 'From the year 1875 until the present time there has been a definite claim growing in clearness as years went by, gradually developing into an organized plan, to compel the Provincial and Dominion Governments, either or both, to acknowledge an aboriginal title and to give compensation for it.'[21] Thanks in part to Scott's presentation, the joint parliamentary committee rejected the Allied Tribes' position on Aboriginal title. All it would do was recommend that 'in lieu of an annuity your Committee would recommend that a sum of $100,000 should be expended annually for the purposes already recommended, that is, technical education, provision of hospitals and medical attendance, and in the promotion of agriculture, stock-raising and fruit culture, and in the development of irrigation projects.'[22] For the Allied Tribes, it was a crushing defeat.

Worse was still to come, as Indian Affairs followed up on the committee's hearings and recommendations. First, government provided $100,000 'in lieu of treaties,' much as the committee had recommended. Second, Scott took steps to ensure that it would be a long time before any other First Nation was able to mount an Aboriginal title or treaty challenge like BC's. In the spring of 1927, Parliament amended the Indian Act to make pursuing claims so difficult as to be impossible: 'Every person who, without the consent of the Superintendent General expressed in writing, receives, obtains, solicits or requests from any Indian any payment or contribution or promise of any payment or contribution for the purpose of raising a fund or providing money for the prosecution of a claim which the tribe or band of the Indians to which such Indian belongs, or of which he is a member, has or is represented to have for the recovery of any claim or money for the benefit of the said tribe or band, shall be guilty of an offence ...'[23] This remarkable provision – drastic interference in Indians' exercise of political and legal rights – made it impossible to pursue Aboriginal title or other claims by criminalizing fundraising. Needless to say, it had a chilling effect on claims and pro-treaty movements in British Columbia and elsewhere in Canada until its repeal in 1951. In 1933, Parliament brought back involuntary enfranchisement for Indian males, albeit with conditions that made it less threatening. It, too, would remain in the Indian Act until 1951.

The mood and mindset that led Parliament to outlaw peaceful measures in pursuit of claims and a deputy minister to say that he wanted to 'get rid of the Indian problem' did not create an environment in which treaty demands were likely to be addressed. Not only did these attitudes, in combination with the other factors noted, preclude the making of new treaties for half a century, they also explain Canada's refusal to respond to requests from aggrieved groups who earlier had not been included in treaty-making. Indeed, the government of Canada's treatment of the Lubicon Lake Cree, the Teme-Augama Anishnabai, and the Kanesatake Mohawk – like its handling of BC First Nations – revealed the indifference and hostility that underlay federal Indian policy and created a fifty-year hiatus in treaty-making.

A Woods Cree band north of Lesser Slave Lake in Alberta, the Lubicon Lake Cree were 'missed,' or left out, of Treaty 8 negotiations in 1899–1900, principally because of their remote location and the hurried nature of the treaty commissioners' labours. As the follow-up commissioner in 1900, J.A. Macrae, wrote, 'There yet remains a number of persons leading an Indian life in the country north of Lesser Slave Lake, who have not accepted treaty as Indians, or scrip as half-breeds, but this is not so much through indisposition to do so as because they live at points distant from those visited, and are not pressed by want.'[24] Unfortunately for the Lubicon Lake Cree, the happy state of not being 'pressed by want' started to erode as non-Native resource exploration began to probe northern Alberta in the twentieth century. Although Lubicon lands were not suitable for agricultural settlement, they did contain enormous petroleum reserves. Oil exploration prompted the Lubicon Lake Cree both to object to the unauthorized incursions and to seek a treaty that would, they assumed, provide at least some land closed to oil companies. Initially, both federal and provincial governments were disposed to meet the Lubicon's needs. (Alberta had to be involved now, unlike the earlier case of Treaty 8, because in 1930 the three Prairie provinces had gained jurisdiction over Crown lands and natural resources.) However, that positive attitude was soon replaced by a much more antagonistic one.

Not only did the Lubicon not get a treaty and a reserve, but they soon found themselves under attack by Indian Affairs. Perhaps acting in the spirit of D.C. Scott's injunction about ridding Canada of the 'Indian problem,' DIA officials drastically reduced the number of members of the Lubicon community that Ottawa recognized. This action, which was apparently motivated by the per capita formula for creating reserves that meant that the larger a band was the greater the area of its reserve, was totally arbitrary and without justification. As a complex series of events involving both federal and provincial actions that were hostile to the interests of the Lubicon played out, the band did not enter treaty and never got a reserve. In the early twenty-first century, they still are seeking satisfaction for their claim. What should be astonishing – but is not – about the treatment the Lubicon received is that much of it was meted out by the Crown, which was obligated both constitutionally and by the law of trusteeship to act in their best interests. This sorry story does not surprise because, as the history of making territorial treaties clearly shows, the federal government has usually acted in the interests of non-Native economic forces when it came to treaties.

The case of the Teme-Augama Anishnabai (TAN) was as lengthy and at least as complicated as that of the Lubicon. The TAN, whose Ojibwa name translated into English as Deep Water People, were hunter-gatherers in the area around Bear Island, in the Temagami region in northern Ontario.[25] Although an appeal court in Ontario would rule in the 1980s that they were covered by the Robinson Huron Treaty of 1850, they never adhered to and never received benefits under it, which in any event was concluded at sites far south of Temagami. Beginning early in the twentieth century, the Temagami district became a favourite haunt of southern Ontarians and Americans, who began to build cottages and children's camps in the area. A corner of the region the TAN claimed, n'Daki-Menan, was also traversed by the

Temiskaming and Northern Ontario Railway (later named the Ontario Northland Railway) following the onset of construction in 1903. As was not uncommon with railway construction in the Canadian Shield, track builders soon spotted evidence of valuable minerals, particularly cobalt. The development of base mineral mining in the region meant that the lands the Teme-Augama Anishnabai claimed were also used by an influential combination of affluent southern recreational visitors, forestry companies, miners, and a railway. It was hardly surprising that during the first half of the twentieth century, both the Ontario and Canadian governments turned a blind eye to the protests and requests of the TAN. The Temagami dispute would assume major legal and political proportions in the later decades of the twentieth century, but its intractability was largely attributable to the unwillingness of governments in earlier periods to accommodate the Teme-Augama Anishnabai's request for a treaty and protected lands. This disagreement is still unresolved in the early twenty-first century.

The grievances of the Mohawk at Kanesatake, which are also still not settled, are at least as complicated as those of the Lubicon Lake Cree and the Teme-Augama Anishnabai, and have roots that go more than a century deeper into Native-newcomer history.[26] The First Nations settlement at Kanesatake on Lake of Two Mountains, just north of the confluence of the Ottawa and St Lawrence Rivers, began in the early eighteenth century as a mixed population of Algonkin, Nipissing, and Mohawk converts to Christianity who were ministered to by the Sulpicians, an important Roman Catholic missionary organization. The lands they occupied were originally conveyed by the French Crown to the Sulpicians, although there was a provision in the legal conveyance that said the missionaries were to use them to provide religious services to their Native charges. When Britain's defeat of France in the Seven Years' War ended up transferring the former French colony of Canada to Britain, the property and other rights of Catholic groups such as the Sulpicians were thrown into question because the United Kingdom was legally an anti-Catholic state. At several points from the 1770s onward, the First

Nations at Kanesatake petitioned the British authorities for recognition of their claim to ownership of the lands, but the new rulers rejected the requests.

In the nineteenth century, the situation at Lake of Two Mountains was complicated by two new factors. First, the region began to feel the impact of increasing numbers of agricultural settlers after the end of the War of 1812, and the French-Canadian town of Oka began to develop nearby. The demographic change affected all three First Nations at Kanesatake adversely, but it did more damage to the hunter-gatherers – the Nipissing and Algonkin – than it did to the more agriculturally inclined Mohawk. The non-Mohawk responded to the crisis brought on by settlement by shifting to more remote parts of the Upper Ottawa Valley and the Muskoka district of Ontario in search of an environment in which they could maintain themselves in the manner to which they were accustomed. The other factor concerned the Mohawk who stayed behind, with many of them in the 1850s converting to Methodism, at least partially because of friction they were experiencing with their Sulpician landlords. In the 1870s the dispute, which at its heart was over control of forest and other resources, became quite bitter, figuring as one of many irritants between Quebec Catholics and Ontario Protestants. These clashes made post-Confederation federal governments, which depended on votes from both Christian denominations for long-term support, decidedly uneasy.

It should not surprise that neither federal nor provincial government evinced much sympathy for the Mohawk in these troubled years. The Quebec government, of course, was always heavily dependent on Catholic voters and good relations with the Catholic hierarchy. The federal governments of Conservative John A. Macdonald and Liberal Wilfrid Laurier tended to view the First Nation as the source of a difficulty that threatened religious harmony and the unity of their party. Federal governments responded in one of two ways to the Kanesatake problem, neither of which appeared to have the interests of the Mohawk as its inspiration. The Conservatives promoted and subsidized two of the relocations of non-Mohawk, and later contemplated taking action to get the dispute between the Mohawk and Sulpicians over ownership of the lands into court and away from the political realm. As it transpired, it was during Laurier's prime ministry that the judicial ploy finally was put into operation. After many years of research and litigation, the case finally was decided in 1911 by the Judicial Committee of the Privy Council in favour of the Sulpicians. However, the law lords also noted that the tangled legal and legislative history of the question had created a charitable trust, which obligated the Sulpicians to provide religious care and secular education for the Mohawk.

Though the decision appeared a victory for the Sulpicians, the dispute did not go away. For one thing, the Mohawk refused to accept it and continued to agitate for recognition of what they regarded as their rights. For another, the qualification to the Judicial Committee's verdict provided grounds on which the federal government might have sought to lend support. Canadian Methodists certainly thought Ottawa should. The federal government, however, was no more interested in keeping the matter alive by intervening than the provincial government was in helping the Mohawk. Over the next five decades, the Mohawk's position at Kanesatake deteriorated as the Sulpicians transferred parcels of the disputed land to others, and a large number of non-Natives acquired land on which they built houses. The area near Oka that the Mohawk called Kanesatake became a patchwork of lands held by Indians and non-Native properties. The Mohawk protested what they continued to view as a breach of their rights to Parliament, particularly to different joint parliamentary committees in 1946–8 and 1959–61, but there was no response from Ottawa. What appeared to be rock bottom in their fortunes occurred in 1959 when the Quebec legislature authorized the construction of a nine-hole golf course on disputed land. Not only did the creation of the Club de Golfe d'Oka preclude them from using common lands on which they had previously cut wood and grazed cattle, but the golfers built their clubhouse close to the Mohawk graveyard. The Kanesatake Mohawk asked the federal government of John Diefenbaker to disallow the provincial statute establishing the golf club, but, of course, no action was forthcoming.

All three of these cases – Lubicon Lake, Teme-Augama Anishnabai, and Kanesatake – illustrate the dynamics that made treaty-making unlikely after 1923. In each case, the federal government, which legally was the First Nations' trustee, showed enormous deference to provincial sensitivities and the interests of powerful economic and political interests. Whether it was oil companies, forestry firms, or a major religious corporation, the provinces were far more inclined to appease and facilitate the efforts of non-Natives, and the federal government made little effort to prevent the negative effects that ensued. This conjunction of economic and political interests also underlay the long hiatus in treaty-making between the 1920s and 1970s.

When governmental attitudes towards negotiating treaties reversed, they changed because of another conjunction of forces: altered economic circumstances and recently emerged First Nations militancy and organization. Enhanced economic activity from the 1940s onward tended to focus on the location, extraction, and export of natural resources, many of which were found in territories still controlled by First Nations. Coincidentally, Aboriginal communities were becoming better organized politically, better equipped, and more willing to assert themselves politically about the continuing disregard of their rights. These twin forces largely explain the re-emergence of treaty-making in the 1970s.

When the Canadian economy roared back to life during the Second World War, it was fuelled principally by wartime demand for both manufactured, strategic products and raw materials. To take but one example, the enormous number of military vehicles and aircraft that Canada produced created greater demand for energy, minerals, and wood. Also increasingly important was one particular strategic energy source, uranium. While the domestic uses of uranium in areas such as medicine had been known for decades, during the 1940s the strategic possibilities of this awesome source of energy attracted the attention of the major powers. As it happened, Canada held enormous deposits of uranium ore in boreal forest locations such as Athabaska Lake in Saskatchewan. Development of uranium, among many other materials, was greatly accelerated by the war and military consid-erations. Particularly important in relation to the demand for Canadian natural resources was the increasingly closer alignment of Canada with the United States that wartime brought. The two North American democracies concluded bilateral agreements covering defence production and military preparedness. That cooperation was based during the Second World War on Canada's storehouse of strategically important raw materials and its geographical location.

The military and economic continentalism of wartime has never disappeared, thanks initially to the onset of the Cold War by 1947. If anything, military planners' division of the world into two camps – communist and 'freedom-loving' – enhanced Canada's importance to its powerful southern neighbour. Not only was Canada viewed as a secure source of strategically important materials such as base minerals and energy, but its physical location between the U.S.A. and the U.S.S.R. meant its cooperation was essential to the republic that viewed itself as 'the leader of the free world.' During the late 1940s and the 1950s ,the United States and Canada agreed to cooperate in air detection and interception, with the result that U.S. troops were stationed in high Arctic locations and radar sites were built in three transcontinental lines across the continent, the most northerly of which was in the Arctic. As a result, the wartime investment by the United States in resource development con-tinued and expanded, warmly encouraged by a succession of Canadian governments that shared American ideological con-cerns and were eager for economic growth. The mainly resource-based economic boom that had been kicked off by the world war continued with interruptions (e.g., 1957–65 and early 1980s) for decades. Neither military nor economic planners took the trouble to notice that their schemes depended on use of Aboriginal lands, some of which had never been dealt with by treaty.

If governments were oblivious to Native concerns, a newly emerged cadre of Aboriginal leaders was not. From the 1940s onward, political mobilization was a marked feature of life among First Nations and other Aboriginal groups across the country. Of course, there had always been political organization and activity of some sort in Indian communities. After all, that was what Duncan Campbell Scott had complained of when he told the joint parliamentary committee on the BC land question in 1927 that an 'organized plan to compel' governments 'to acknowledge aboriginal title' had been developing since the late nineteenth century. The 1927 amendment to the Indian Act that outlawed soliciting or donating funds for pursuit of an Indian claim was intended to prevent litigation and discourage political agitation. While it had the effect of suspending Nisga'a legal efforts to pursue their Aboriginal title case, it did not completely smother political organization. Particularly in the Prairie provinces, where both Alberta and Saskatchewan produced province-wide First Nations organizations in the 1940s, the progress of Aboriginal political organizations was noticeable. A marked feature of this political organization from the 1940s until the early 1980s was its dominance by former residential school students. In British Columbia, graduates such as Peter Kelly and Andrew Paull were leaders in the process, as was James Gladstone in Alberta and John B. Tootoosis in Saskatchewan. A leader who would emerge in Quebec in the 1970s, the Cree Billy Diamond, was another whose attitudes and skills had been formed in part by residential school experience. These First Nations political leaders appear to have acquired the familiarity and skills to contend with non-Native society, as well as powerful resentment at how they and their peoples had been treated.

The joint parliamentary committee on the Indian Act that heard delegations and accepted written submissions between 1946 and 1948 provided a barometer of how conditions had changed politically in Indian country. The committee's mandate was to review and propose changes to the legislation that almost everyone now recognized was outdated and counterproductive. The recent world war, in which First Nations had voluntarily participated in disproportionately large numbers, had provided lessons that underlined the need to change policy. A war against Germany and Japan, countries in which racism had been institutionalized, served to remind thoughtful Canadians that the basis of their own Indian policy was inherently racist. Moreover, there was a general feeling at war's end that a brave new age was dawning in which human rights would be much more important than they had been earlier.[27] As part of the joint committee's preparations, First Nations were invited to submit briefs for the committee's consideration. Many took up the invitation, and a smaller number also managed to appear before the review body to express their opinions in person. As a result, the joint parliamentary committee heard far more about treaty rights, the deficiencies of Indian Affairs' educational policy, and a host of other issues than Indian Affairs was comfortable with. Although the bureaucrats did succeed in the end, ensuring that the fundamental goals of legislation did not change in the 1951 overhaul of the Act, First Nations managed to register their opinions and succeeded in getting at least some of the most objectionable features of the Indian Act removed. For example, the bans on the Potlatch and on raising funds to pursue claims were removed.

The trend towards more Aboriginal political organization and assertiveness entered a new stage in 1960 with the formation of the National Indian Council (NIC). Composed of representatives of First Nations, non-status Indians, and Métis organizations, the NIC was never an effective advocate in Ottawa. Personality clashes between some of its leaders and the more fundamental issue of competing interests among its three constituent groups were always impediments to uniting behind a single agenda. In 1968 the members of the Council faced up to the limitations of their organizational structure and amicably agreed to subdivide into two successor bodies. Métis and non-status Indians remained linked in a new Canadian Metis Society, while status Indians refashioned their political vehicle as the National Indian Brotherhood (NIB). As it turned out, the NIB emerged on the scene at just the right moment.

The neophyte NIB established itself by spearheading the opposition to the federal government's White Paper on Indian policy that was released in June 1969. The White Paper was simply a policy proposal that the government put forward for discussion prior to revising it for incorporation into legislation. As such, it was only a continuation of the search for a new, viable Indian policy that had also led to the creation of the joint parliamentary committee on the Indian Act after the Second World War. Although the Department of Indian Affairs and Northern Development had carried out a series of what it termed 'consultations' with First Nations representatives prior to release of the White Paper, the real inspiration for the contents of the document was Pierre Elliott Trudeau, the dashing new Liberal prime minister who had surged to political power in 1968. Propelled by Trudeauites in the Prime Minister's Office, the creators of the White Paper proposal ignored the warnings of Indian Affairs personnel and the contents of the consultations, to fashion a document that embodied Trudeau's strong commitment to individualism and antipathy to collective ideologies such as nationalism.[28] The consequence was that the White Paper decried Indian status and attributed all the problems First Nations faced to their being kept apart from other Canadians by such distinctiveness. So far as treaties and treaty claims were concerned, the document denounced 'the anomaly of treaties between groups within society and the government of that society,' promised that they would 'be reviewed to see how they can be equitably ended,' and dismissed 'aboriginal claims to land' as 'so general and undefined that it is not realistic to think of them as specific claims capable of remedy except through a policy and program that will end injustice to Indians as members of the Canadian community.'[29]

How much First Nations political leadership had changed was revealed by the breadth, intensity, and impact of Indian organizations' response to the White Paper. Across the country, and also from the new National Indian Brotherhood as the representative of all status Indians, a chorus of denunciation quickly issued that soon had the federal government backpedalling. Probably the most eloquent statements came from Alberta, where the Indian Association of Alberta's *Red Paper* response and the individual statement of the young Cree leader Harold Cardinal, *The Unjust Society*, won admiration. In a moving section, Cardinal contrasted Trudeau's view ('It is inconceivable that one section of a society should have a treaty with another section of a society') with the First Nations' understanding of treaties:

> To the Indians of Canada, the treaties represent an Indian Magna Carta. The treaties are important to us, because we entered into these negotiations with faith, with hope for a better life with honour. We have survived for over a century on little but that hope. Did the white man enter into them with something less in mind? Or have the heirs of the men who signed in honour somehow disavowed the obligation passed down to them? The Indians entered into the treaty negotiations as honourable men who came to deal as equals with the queen's representatives. Our leaders of that time thought they were dealing with an equally honourable people.[30]

The reaction of Cardinal and other First Nations leaders was so strong and scathing that within a year of the release of the White Paper, the Trudeau government announced that it was not proceeding with its implementation. The entire episode of the abortive White Paper made it clear that the old ways of doing things – in which governments acted at the behest of non-Natives when it suited them in dealing with First Nations – were over.

9

'Growing old at the negotiating table':[1] Treaties and Comprehensive Claims, 1975–2008

Two events in the early 1970s symbolize the complexity of recent treaty-making. In 1972 the James Bay Cree responded to a typical provincial initiative with resistance that led to the negotiation of Canada's first treaty in over fifty years. The following year, the Supreme Court of Canada brought down a ruling in a long-standing British Columbia case that revolutionized Canadians' understanding of Aboriginal title and caused the federal government to establish a process for resolving claims based on assertions of unextinguished indigenous title. These two important developments – the James Bay confrontation and the decision in *Calder* – shared a number of features. Both exemplified the willingness and ability of late-twentieth-century First Nations to combat actions by the majority population that violated their territorial rights. Both proved to be long drawn-out confrontations. The James Bay agreement, which took several years to achieve, proved to have a lengthy history of problematic implementation, a travail that ended only some thirty years after signature of the treaty. And both the James Bay negotiations and the Nisga'a saga brought to the national stage a number of remarkable Aboriginal leaders, most prominently Joseph Gosnell of the Nisga'a and Billy Diamond of the James Bay Cree. The best summary of modern treaty-making since 1972 was provided by Gosnell: protracted treaty negotiations forced Aboriginal leaders to 'grow old at the negotiating table.'

It was not just Joseph Gosnell who turned grey at the table; generations of Nisga'a leaders before him had suffered the same fate with less success. The roots of the Nass River dispute lay in the fact that most land in British Columbia had never been brought under treaty and the equally important reality that BC First Nations refused to accept the consequences of that fact. The non-Native population of BC very quickly concluded that their government had gained title to indigenous lands, though they did not trouble themselves much to grapple with how that had happened. If First Nations had not been conquered militarily and had not entered into treaty with the Crown, how had they lost title? In this mindset, British Columbians were not much different from other Canadians from regions of the country where territorial treaties had not been made, but what made the BC situation unusual was that the provincial government proved remarkably obstinate in rebuffing attempts to regularize the land title issue.

For their part, the Nisga'a were forceful in asserting their belief in their continuing title to lands they had occupied since long before the first fur traders had appeared off British Columbia's coast in the late eighteenth century. In 1887 a Nisga'a delegation paddled the long journey from the Nass to Victoria to ask for 'a treaty' similar to the ones east of the Rockies about which they had heard. Premier William Smithe inquired where they heard of such a thing, to which delegate John Wesley answered, 'It is in the law books.' Replied Smithe, 'There is no such law either English or Dominion that I know of,' and suggested that 'the Indians or their friends have been misled on that point.' Not content to lie, the premier also insulted the delegation: 'When the whites first came among you, you were little better than wild beasts of the field.'[2] The Nisga'a were offended and rebuffed, but not deterred. Ten years later, when a joint federal-provincial reserve commission visited Nisga'a territory, Sub-chief Charles Russ told the surprised officials that 'we want the words and hands of the chiefs on both sides, Indian and Government, to make a promise on paper – a strong promise – that will be not only for us, but for our children and forever.'[3] (See map 10.)

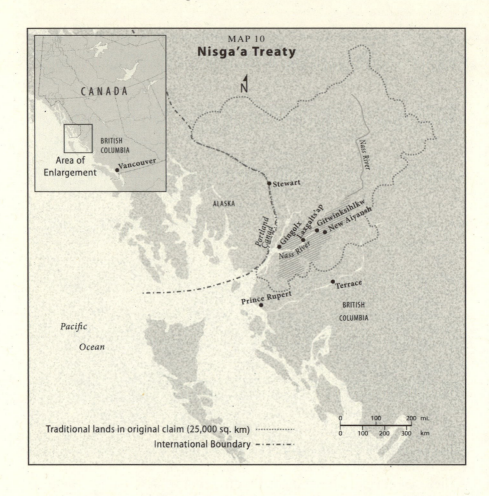

MAP 10
Nisga'a Treaty

Traditional lands in original claim (25,000 sq. km) ┄┄┄┄┄┄
International Boundary ─·─·─·─

The Nisga'a would need the determination they displayed in their early dealings with government because the province proved unyielding in its refusal to recognize unextinguished Aboriginal title and the federal government spineless in discharging its constitutional duty to protect First Nations' rights.[4] As well, the terms of union by which the province entered Confederation specified that 'the charge of the Indians, and the trusteeship and management of the lands reserved for their use and benefit, shall be assumed by the Dominion Government, and a policy as liberal as that hitherto pursued by the British Columbia Government shall be continued by the Dominion Government after the Union.' The deal also specified that to 'carry out such policy, tracts of land of such extent as it has hitherto been the practice of the British Columbia government to appropriate for that purpose, shall from time to time be conveyed by the Local Government to the Dominion Government ...'[5] When Ottawa pressed Victoria to provide for First Nations reserves in the 1870s and 1880s, the province interpreted the agreement narrowly and used every negotiating device at its disposal to ensure that little land would be allocated to First Nations.

A succession of federal-provincial commissions considered the issue on and off for four decades. At every stage the federal government deferred to the province and did not press hard to achieve solutions. The same was true of the last phase in the 1920s, the establishment of the terms of reference by which a joint parliamentary committee considered what was now known as 'the BC land question' in 1927. Ottawa acquiesced to Victoria's refusal to allow the committee to consider claims based on Aboriginal title. And, of course, the result of those deliberations was rejection of such claims and an amendment of the Indian Act designed to thwart future campaigns for recognition of indigenous title.

The extraordinary 1927 amendment only deferred the Nisga'a campaign. Understandably, the legislative ban and the death in 1928 of Arthur O'Meara, a staunch legal ally of the Nisga'a, took the steam out of the Nisga'a effort. However, it was not long after Parliament rescinded the prohibition on funding claims activity in 1951 that the Nisga'a began to reorganize, with Frank Calder, the latest in a succession of able and determined Nisga'a leaders, playing a prominent role. Calder had been active in the Native Brotherhood of British Columbia since the 1930s, and in 1949, the same year the province granted status Indians the right to vote in provincial elections, he was elected to the BC legislature. The Nisga'a re-established the Nisga'a Land Committee, the body that had pursued their land claim earlier, as the Nisga'a Tribal Council (NTC) in 1955. They often referred to the organ-

9.1 Frank Calder (left) with Senator James Gladstone and Premier Tommy Douglas. It was in Frank Calder's name that the Nisga'a Case finally reached the Supreme Court of Canada.

ization as 'a common bowl.'[6] In 1967, by which time it was obvious a negotiated solution of the Nisga'a case was beyond reach, the NTC hired a young lawyer named Thomas Berger to represent them. Litigation that sought a judicial declaration that Nisga'a Aboriginal title had not been extinguished was launched the following year. It was rebuffed by the BC Supreme Court in 1969, and by the Court of Appeal the following year. When the Supreme Court of Canada granted leave to appeal, Berger, Calder, and the Nisga'a Tribal Council prepared themselves for one last, climactic effort.

The Supreme Court of Canada's decision in *Calder* in 1973 was as unusual as it was momentous. For one thing, the Nisga'a actually lost their appeal, the ruling being three justices in favour, three opposed, and one opposed on technical grounds. The jurist who rejected the appeal on technical grounds did so because the Nisga'a Tribal Council had not, as required by provincial law, obtained permission from the BC attorney general before suing the province. Three others ruled that, while the Nisga'a had once held Aboriginal title to the territory they claimed in the Nass Valley, it had been extinguished by both colonial measures prior to union and provincial action after 1871. But three other Supreme Court judges concluded that the Nisga'a had held title to the Nass Valley 'from time immemorial,' and that this Aboriginal title remained unextinguished because the legislature had not taken overt action that explicitly sought to extinguish title. This was, indeed, a landmark decision, for it advanced legal recognition of indigenous land rights far beyond the 'usufructuary and personal right,' a legal *interest* in land that encumbered the Crown's underlying title, that the Judicial Committee of the Privy Council had recognized in *St Catherines Milling* in 1888 or the *Tijani* decision concerning Nigeria in 1921. This ruling said that Aboriginal title was a legal right and was cognizable, or enforceable, at law. The Nisga'a might have lost their appeal, but six of the seven Supreme Court judges agreed that Aboriginal title was a legal reality. The decision would stand until the 1997 *Delgamuukw* verdict expanded the definition.[7]

'Perhaps you had more rights than we thought you had when we did the White Paper.'[8] Prime Minister Pierre Elliott Trudeau's rueful comment in the aftermath of *Calder* indicated that he understood that his position on Aboriginal title claims had been nullified by the Supreme Court. The Liberals' 1969 White Paper had described claims such as the Nisga'a's as 'so general and undefined' as to be irresolvable except through a broad program for ameliorating Native problems.[9] Once the *Calder* decision forced the government to adjust its policy, it announced a new process for the resolution of Native claims. The policy distinguished between specific claims, characterized as being based on a lawful obligation to First Nations that the Crown had failed to discharge, and comprehensive claims, which were claims based on an assertion that a group's Aboriginal title had not been extinguished. The lawful obligation that made a specific claim valid might arise from treaty, legislation such as the Indian Act, or law, such as the law of trusteeship. Aboriginal title claims would be valid if the claimant had not lost its primordial entitlement by conquest, treaty, or other means, usually legislation that nullified legal control. As the government later acknowledged on the Indian Affairs website, comprehensive claims settlements are 'Modern Treaties.'[10]

The following year, the government established the Office of Native Claims (ONC) to deal with both specific and comprehensive claims. The ONC was intended to discharge many functions. A claimant, after doing research on a case, lodged the claim with the ONC, which then adjudicated it according to its own criteria. If the ONC was satisfied that the claim had merit, it recommended its acceptance for negotiation to the government, which, in turn, included ONC personnel in the federal bargaining team that sat down with the claimants. If and when an agreement was reached, the ONC was charged with responsibility for its implementation. And, finally, the ONC was the federal office that considered requests for financial assistance to support research and legal representation from potential claimants, and could award 'contributions' and/or 'loans' to facilitate the work. Such a loan became a first charge on any settlement compensation. Clearly, the claims resolution process that the federal government established was one in which the Crown held all the high cards, a hard reality that was not lost on claimants. In addition, as those who entered the comprehensive claims maze soon learned, the government had dealt itself other advantages. It refused at first to negotiate more than six comprehensive claims at any one time. It declined to consider oral history, the only form of record that many Aboriginal communities had, on the same basis as documentary history in evaluating a claim. And the federal government required what it euphemistically termed 'finality' as part of any comprehensive claims resolution. In practice, this insistence meant that successful claimants had to agree that the settlement extinguished all their Aboriginal rights before the government would sign on.

For First Nations and other Aboriginal people who were not attracted to the ONC to pursue resolution of Aboriginal title claims, the early 1970s had another option, as the James Bay Cree demonstrated. The confrontation that produced Canada's first modern treaty originated in events that First Nations had witnessed dozens of times before. On 30 April 1971 Robert Bourassa, the young Liberal premier of Quebec, announced the 'Project of the Century,' development of the hydroelectric potential of a large part of the James Bay watershed. In a province in which hydroelectricity had been entangled with provincial politics and francophone pride for most of the twentieth century, Bourassa said that the project would cost six billion dollars and create 125,000 jobs. 'James Bay is the key to the economic and social progress of Quebec, ... the key to the political stability of Quebec, the key to the future of Quebec.'[11] What the premier failed to take into account was that his 'future of Quebec' would fundamentally transform the homeland of the James Bay Cree and blight their chance of remaining self-sufficient.[12] (See map 11.)

Bourassa also failed to consider – no doubt because no one had ever heard of him outside his home community of Fort Rupert (Waskaganish) on the east shore of James Bay – a young Cree named Billy Diamond. Diamond was an example of the sort of Aboriginal representative that had been emerging across the country since the middle of the century, leaders who were now making Aboriginal political organizations articulate, determined, and effective. Billy Diamond came from a family that had long provided leadership to its community, and his father, Malcolm, was a man who had no fear of government. From Malcolm Diamond, young Billy learned to refer to the Indian Affairs officials who flew into the Cree villages, for many a source of fear and intimidation, as 'the men who get off the plane, take a piss, and get back on.' In 1968, soon after young Diamond had completed high school, his father and other Elders in his village took him aside and asked him to defer going to university in order to help the community deal with changes they felt were imminent.[13] The

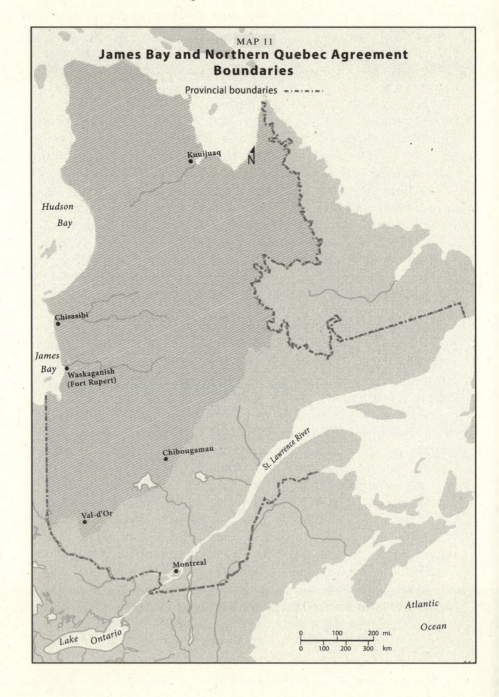

MAP 11
**James Bay and Northern Quebec Agreement
Boundaries**

Provincial boundaries – · – · – · –

Hudson
Bay

Kuuijuaq

Chisasibi

James
Bay

Waskaganish
(Fort Rupert)

Chibougamau

St. Lawrence River

Val-d'Or

Montreal

Atlantic

Ocean

Lake   Ontario

0   100   200 mi.
0   100   200   300 km

younger Diamond had also demonstrated his own toughness in the face of authority in the Anglican residential school he had attended in Moose Factory. On one memorable occasion, nine-year-old Billy had refused to eat his vegetables and, when the supervisors told him he would sit in his place till the vegetables were consumed, had defied them for eight hours, until they finally sent him to bed at two in the morning.[14] The confrontation that Billy Diamond and other Aboriginal leaders would have over the Quebec government's James Bay hydroelectric development plans would test that steely resolve.

The first step of defiance was an unusual one in the troubled history of hydro projects on Native land. The usual pattern had been that provincial governments met little resistance as they announced and proceeded with the construction of dams and head ponds that flooded the hunting and fishing lands that First Nations used and made them useless. In the case of the James Bay project, however, the pattern was broken when leaders of the James Bay Cree and Quebec Inuit, with help from the provincial First Nations organization, the Indians of Quebec Association (IQA), tried to persuade the province to negotiate. When that effort failed, they went to court in November 1972 to stop the project.

Working with a young team that Billy Diamond assembled, the Natives' lawyer, James O'Reilly, put together a formidable case. It was a historically based argument to show that the Crown had recognized indigenous rights in a train of official documents that began with the Royal Proclamation of 1763, and that those rights remained intact. Over the objections of the province, Quebec Superior Court judge Albert Malouf concluded that the Natives had shown that they appeared to have rights in the territory and allowed them to argue their case for an injunction to halt the project. Over the next seven months, Billy Diamond and 166 other witnesses in seventy-eight days of testimony argued that the groups they represented had unextinguished Aboriginal rights in the territory that the James Bay Development Corporation proposed to flood. Finally, in November 1973, a year after the action had been launched, Judge Malouf ruled that 'the evidence also shows that the rights of the Cree Indian and Inuit populations have never been extinguished,' and granted the Natives an injunction ordering all work on the James Bay power project stopped.[15] Not surprisingly, the James Bay Corporation immediately appealed the Malouf decision.

Although the Quebec Court of Appeal fairly quickly suspended the interim injunction, the parties found that there was no alternative but to negotiate a settlement of the dispute that would allow the power project to go ahead without Native opposition. Even if a Quebec Superior Court injunction could be reversed on appeal, the Supreme Court of Canada, based on the decision in *Calder*, would probably prevent the Bourassa Liberals from acting in the high-handed manner in which governments had acted in the past. Legislation passed in 1912, when Ontario and Quebec's boundaries were extended northward, obligated the province to deal with First Nations' claims. If they refused to negotiate a settlement, might the Cree not return to court seeking damages and using the *Calder* precedent and the historical case they had developed when seeking an injunction? Even if the James Bay Corporation prevailed in the end, the protracted litigation would create uncertainty that would be inimical to the economic climate of Quebec and, perhaps, harmful to the political health of the Bourassa government. On the Aboriginal side, although their legal team and a number of sympathetic environmentalists wanted an appeal to be launched, the Cree communities almost unanimously insisted on a more cautious negotiating response. They were fearful that protracted legal battling would allow work on the project to get so advanced that judicial relief could not accomplish much.[16] They also launched a comprehensive claim for the disputed territory.

Over the many months of difficult negotiations, great stresses occurred within the ranks of First Nations in Quebec, not to mention between the James Bay Cree and a variety of political agents. The Cree negotiating team guarded against disruptions in their own camp by regularly consulting their scattered home communities to ensure the rank and file' understood what was transpiring and to maintain their mandate to negotiate.[17] Strains in the relationship between the IQA and leaders of the James Bay Cree had developed while the latter were seeking an injunction, caused in part by the fact that the provincial organization was dominated by southern-based First Nations and its leaders did not always see eye to eye with Billy Diamond and the other northern leaders. Finally, in August 1974 the northern groups formed the Grand Council of the Cree as their own political vehicle.[18] As well, once negotiations began, the James Bay Cree found that the federal government, which hitherto had quietly encouraged and supported their struggle, now began to pressure them to agree to a deal.[19] They feared that Ottawa would cut off their funding if they held out too aggressively. Finally, the Cree found themselves bested in the public relations war. Robert Bourassa and his government succeeded in portraying the Cree campaign, which sought to protect as much of the Cree way of life as possible, as being simply about money. The result was that public opinion tended not to be supportive of the Cree, further weakening their negotiating position.

The 450-page James Bay and Northern Quebec Agreement (JBNQA), while far from being what the James Bay Cree and their Inuit allies had wanted, contained many good features and some important innovations. As far as the press and Quebec public were concerned, the most salient term was the $225 million that the indigenous groups would get, $75 million within ten years and the remainder from royalties derived from the hydroelectric project over a much longer period. The Agreement also contained a total extinguishment clause. However, for the northerners, the most important aspects of the Agreement were the terms that sought to shore up and protect their traditional hunting-gathering economy. In what were termed Category I lands, 2,140 square miles (5,545 sq km) in all, they would enjoy exclusive rights. These lands are divided into IA lands, where the federal government has jurisdiction, and IB lands, where the province has authority. The Category II lands, 27,018 square miles (69,996 sq km) surrounding the settlements in Category I, were also under provincial jurisdiction, but on them the Cree had sole rights to gather. The remaining 320,380 square miles

9.2 Signing the James Bay Agreement, 1975; seated from right, Billy Diamond, Jean Chrétien, John Ciaccia, Robert Bourassa, Charlie Watt, and Judd Buchanan

(830,000 sq km) of lands in Category III were open to everyone, although the Cree were exempt from most provincial regulations and guaranteed harvesting rights for some species. More important in some ways, and certainly most original, was the provision to subsidize the traditional hunting economy through an Income Security Program (ISP). Simply put, the ISP would supplement hunters' income from the JBNQA compensation in a manner not dissimilar to the way in which Canada supported western farmers or, later, East Coast fishers, during times of financial stress. The JBNQA also contained elaborate educational, health policy, and justice articles, as well as environmental protection provisions that were supposed to guarantee the Cree a prime role in managing the territory.[20]

Perhaps most important of all was the fact that the process of battling for an Agreement to protect their interests had forged political unity among the northern Cree bands where none had existed before. As Billy Diamond's biographer put it, the struggle for the JBNQA 'created the Cree Nation.'[21] There would be many more battles, because implementation of the Agreement would prove in many ways even more difficult and frustrating than obtaining it, but the political cohesiveness that Quebec's Cree achieved during 1972–5 would serve them well during the quarrels over implementation and later confrontations over Quebec's attempts to expand the hydroelectric project. A new pact, the Northeastern Quebec Agreement signed in 1978, extended the protected areas to cover some of the territories of the Innu (Naskapi) as well.

Not only First Nations who negotiated directly with government were frustrated; those who tried to secure recognition of their territorial rights through the comprehensive claims resolution process similarly found their road long and rocky. The way the Office of Native Claims process was stacked in favour of the federal government was quickly revealed to the Kanesatake Mohawk and their allies from the other Mohawk reserves of Kahnawake and Akwesasne. The three combined in 1974 to launch a comprehensive claim to a large area of southwestern Quebec, and early in 1975 the Department of Justice advised the ONC to reject it. The legal opinion was that the Mohawk had not been in possession of the territory when Europeans arrived, and, in any event, even if they had had Aboriginal title, it had been extinguished by a succession of government actions during the French colonial period, as well as the decision by the British after 1763 to open the region to non-Native settlement. The same opinion said that its arguments did not apply to 'any specific claims which the Mohawks of Oka [Kanesatake], St. Regis [Akwesasne], and Caughnawaga [Kahnawake] may have with respect to lands contiguous or near their existing reserves.' The government, then, rejected the Mohawk Aboriginal title claim, but took no position on whether or not there was merit to more limited, specific claims by the three bands individually.[22]

The Kanesatake Mohawk filed a specific claim dealing with the immediate area of their settlement on Lake of Two Mountains in June 1977. Then they cooled their heels until October 1986, when the ONC got around to deciding that the claimant 'has not demonstrated any outstanding lawful obligation on the part of the Federal Crown.'[23] They had been turned down flat, and the argument for a specific claim blandly dismissed without explanation after more than nine years. The Oka experience with the Office of Native Claims revealed starkly that the government retained most of the weapons, including delay, in any battle over claims.

The delays and one-sided nature of the claims process go a long way to explain the failure of the Office of Native Claims to deal effectively with Aboriginal title claims. Contributing factors in the woeful story were that the ONC and its procedures had been implemented without consultation with Aboriginal political organizations, often leaving them suspicious of requirements that were laid down unilaterally. Another difficulty was the way in which the ONC approached comprehensive claims. For one thing, the government's refusal to negotiate more than six claims at one time after they had been accepted for negotiation – in other words, once the government was largely satisfied as to their validity – caused a bottleneck to develop. The ONC also required that a comprehensive claim come from an organized group that had occupied the territory it was claiming exclusively and continuously from pre-contact times, thereby barring bands that had migrated following contact with Europeans either in pursuit of economic opportunities or as a result of warfare. Migration, both pre- and post-contact, was a common response to dangers and opportunities. Ottawa was also inclined to be legalistic – being reluctant, for example, to accept oral history as evidence – a disposition that probably was the consequence of handing claims resolutions over principally to lawyers. The result of all these problems was that comprehensive claims did not get resolved and Aboriginal groups became increasingly frustrated.

The raw data of comprehensive claims processing were revealing. A review in 1981 showed that there were no comprehensive claims yet settled via the ONC route, and thirteen others were at various stages of negotiation. By 1985 there was one claim settled, six under negotiation, and another fifteen that had passed preliminary inspection stacked up waiting to begin negotiations. As Murray Coolican, the chair of a committee that reviewed the process, wrote in 1985, '... in spite of more than a decade of negotiating, little progress has been made in the settlement of claims.' Moreover, at 'the current rate of settlement it could be another 100 years before all the claims have been addressed.'[24] Many observers thought Coolican was an optimist.

The federal government tried to improve the process, but the efforts never amounted to more than tinkering with the details. The result of the 1981 review, issued as *In All Fairness: A Native Claims Policy*, was largely a restatement of the original policy.[25] The revision of the Canadian Constitution in 1982, which 'recognized and affirmed' existing Aboriginal and treaty rights, aggravated a problem that many groups had with the process. The government had insisted on extinguishment of Aboriginal rights as one component of a comprehensive claims settlement. In keeping with long-standing practice, indigenous people sought through treaty or comprehensive claims settlement to establish a relationship with the majority population that would be mutually supportive, beneficial, and enduring. Another review of the process in 1985, one that this time involved consultations with Aboriginal people, modified requirements. Now the policy 'allowed for the retention of Aboriginal rights on land which Aboriginal people will hold following the conclusion of a claim settlement, to the extent that such rights are not inconsistent with the settlement agreement.'[26] Government policy still talked about 'granting' rather than 'recognizing' self-government as part of settlement packages, and many Aboriginal groups found that attitude offensive. A split of the Office of Native Claims into a Comprehensive Claims Branch and a Specific Claims Branch did not deal with fundamental issues. Relaxation of the limit of six comprehensive claims under negotiation at one time in 1990 did not alter attitudes much either, as the rejection of a Dene-Métis claim settlement in a plebiscite in the western Arctic in that year suggested.[27]

It is hardly surprising, then, that the number of modern treaties crafted through the comprehensive claims resolution process has been small. (The Indian Affairs Department treats the James Bay and Northern Quebec Agreement [1975] and the associated Northeastern Quebec Agreement [1978] as comprehensive land claims agreements, but in reality they were reached by separate negotiations rather than through the claims resolution mechanism.)[28] During the first decade of the ONC's existence, only one comprehensive claim, that of the Inuvialuit, or western Inuit, was settled in 1984. The 1990s were more fruitful. The Gwichin' Agreement (1992) was followed by the Council of Yukon Indians settlement (1993), the Sahtu Dene and Métis Agreement (1994), the Tlicho Agreement (2005), and the Labrador Inuit Agreement (2005). What is striking about these comprehensive claims agreements is that they all have occurred in the North, most in the territorial North. Even in the case of Labrador, there was only a small number of non-Natives directly affected. The reason for the concentration of agreements in the territories is that there was no provincial government with jurisdiction over lands and resources to complicate matters in Yukon and the territories.

Over time. negotiation of comprehensive claims settlements has become increasingly bound up with constitutional considerations. One such issue, already noted, is the matter of continuing Aboriginal rights in territory that is brought under treaty by such agreements. In recent years, the federal government has shifted from seeking limited extinguishment of Aboriginal rights, specifically Aboriginal title, to focusing on what it terms 'certainty.' The Tlicho Agreement of 2005, for example, 'draws a distinction between land rights and non-land rights. Finality is achieved for land rights while clarity and predictability are achieved for non-land rights. The Tlicho Agreement applies a non-assertion technique, whereby the Tlicho agree not to exercise or assert any rights other than those set out in the Tlicho Agreement.'[29] In other words, while the claimant is not forced to surrender its general Aboriginal rights in the agreement, it concedes that it will not exercise rights not covered in the final terms. Whether or not this formula will prove satisfying and effective remains to be seen.

The other constitutional matter that has emerged is Aboriginal self-government. Retaining the right to control their own affairs has long been a goal of Aboriginal groups. Their ability to press for concessions in this area was enhanced by the federal government's adoption in 1995 of a policy that recognized the inherent right of self-government. Among those who have participated in comprehensive claims resolution processes, the groups who have benefited most from this shift in federal policy have been eleven of the fourteen First Nations covered by the Council of Yukon Indians settlement of 1993. Between 1995 and 2005, these northern First Nations negotiated self-government arrangements that gave them wider jurisdiction than most other groups enjoyed. Among the areas of First Nations jurisdiction are the province-like powers of education and training, health services, the administration of justice, and the maintenance of law and order. They also can legislate on spiritual and cultural beliefs and practices, indigenous language, welfare services, citizenship, solemnization of marriage of their own citizens, and 'resolution of disputes outside the courts.'[30] On the other hand, they have had to accept a trio of limitations: denial of an international role, application of the Charter of Rights and Freedoms, and eventual liability for taxes.[31] Creation of modern treaties by means of the comprehensive claims resolution machinery and provision of indigenous self-government recognition have now become inseparable.

The comprehensive claims route to modern territorial treaties established in 1973–4 has produced limited results. After more than three decades, there are only a handful of settlements, without exception in northern regions where non-Native population is sparse and usually provincial governments are not around to complicate pursuit of an agreement. This process has enjoyed limited support from Aboriginal groups, with good reason. Many of them have chosen to avoid it and pursue their own separately negotiated treaties, as Quebec's Cree and Inuit had pioneered in the 1970s.

To date the treaties that have been negotiated are Nunavut, Nisga'a, and the British Columbia Treaty Commission agreements. Like the travail of the James Bay Cree, Quebec Inuit, and claimants under the comprehensive claims process, the experience of the Inuit, Nisga'a, and BC First Nations with separately negotiated treaties over the past two decades has also been lengthy and oft-times harrowing. Those who have taken the route of separate negotiation have also been 'growing old at the negotiating table.'

Although the government of Canada classifies the Nunavut pact as a comprehensive claims settlement because the Inuit had lodged an Aboriginal title claim with the Office of Native Claims in 1976, the many distinctive features of the case make it a treaty apart. Like the James Bay confrontation, the situation of the Arctic Inuit was complicated by sharp differences between the groups involved. Although all the claimants were Inuit, those in the eastern Arctic had always seen themselves as different from their brethren to the west, and the easterners were generally regarded by outsiders as politically less sophisticated. In part, this was because the eastern Inuit had been in contact with non-Natives for a much briefer period, most only establishing regular dealings with government and police from the 1950s onward. However, what the eastern Inuit had that would give them an advantage in the long run was a high degree of social cohesiveness and a different political strategy. They tended to avoid the more confrontational political style of the westerners, who, for example, joined with the Dene in 1975 in *The Dene Declaration*, which proclaimed they were 'a nation' and evinced a sense of alienation from southern Canada. Instead, in their dealings with government and the media, the eastern Inuit emphasized that they wanted to join Canada through a land settlement and become part of the Canadian social fabric.

A quieter style did not mean a lack of political will. The eastern Inuit also flexed their muscles in the late 1970s and 1980s, effectively overthrowing the business community's dominance of the Northwest Territories (NWT) legislature by electing strongly pro-Aboriginal representatives and enlisting the support of a sympathetic territorial commissioner, the official appointed by Ottawa to act something like a lieutenant-governor. They also began to distance themselves from their colleagues in the western Arctic, calling in the early 1980s for the division of the NWT into eastern and western territories. Prime motivation for this initiative was growing frustration with the political style of the westerners, which the eastern Inuit leaders did not think would be successful in the long run. To the surprise of many people, the easterners engineered a successful plebiscite on the future of the NWT in 1982, in which they achieved a high voter turnout and strong support for division. From that point onward, the project of creating Nunavut – Our Land, in Inuktitut – was their primary objective.

Creating a separate territory through a land claim settlement and related self-government agreement was not a simple task. The Tungavik Federation of Nunavut (TFN), the political agency that carried eastern Inuit hopes, had to bargain long and hard with federal officials, the negotiations often complicated by differences with other Aboriginal groups over the extent of a new territory, the boundary with the west, the powers of a new territorial government, and financial arrangements. Eventually, in 1990, TFN and Canada reached an agreement in principle, legislation was passed in 1993 to provide for implementation, and Nunavut, with its territorial capital at Iqualuit (formerly Frobisher Bay), came into existence on 1 April 1999. The agreement's area covered an astonishing 849,200 square miles (2.2 million sq km) that stretched from James Bay to the North Pole and from a zigzag western boundary roughly north of Saskatchewan and Alberta at various points to Quebec and Labrador on the east. (See map 12.) Some 135,100 square miles (350,000 sq km) are held by the Inuit in fee-simple title.

Not surprisingly, the Nunavut final agreement entailed many complications. One was the continuing opposition of other groups who objected that the new territory's boundary infringed on their customary lands. Dene in northern Manitoba and Saskatchewan complained that Nunavut's southern boundary cut them off from areas they had harvested for millennia, while those

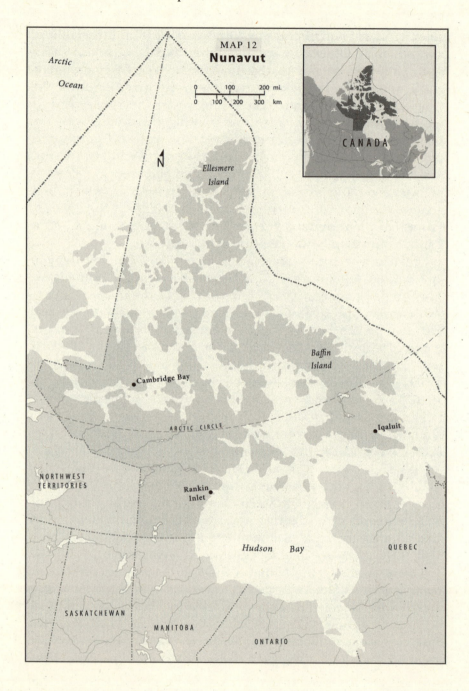

MAP 12
Nunavut

in the west similarly objected that the western limit placed some of their important hunting regions within Nunavut. Such overlapping claims are a common feature of settlement agreements, a phenomenon that, while not simple to resolve, is hardly surprising. Many indigenous groups in the past used the same territory, often at different seasons and frequently after agreements to share were reached following Aboriginal protocol.[32] The formalization of political boundaries as a result of a settlement such as the Nunavut Final Agreement forces the parties to get recognition of their rights if they wish to continue to exercise them unchallenged. The competing claims by these Dene groups in Nunavut remain unresolved.

Another major difficulty facing Nunavut is a social one. The eastern Inuit constitute approximately 80 per cent of the territory's population of about 25,000, but sharply marked characteristics of the indigenous population present challenges. One is its relative youthfulness, a demographic tilt that means that there are huge requirements for education and training, and that staffing positions in a newly expanded bureaucracy with Inuit people has been extremely difficult. Since 1999, Nunavut has been on a crash course to expand schooling to meet the demographic and vocational challenges, a thrust whose apex is a Nunavut-based law school exclusively for Nunavut residents staffed by University of Victoria academics. The young indigenous population also increases pressures on housing, always an issue in Aboriginal communities, as large families require better accommodation. More generally, the nature of the Nunavut population and its relatively low educational levels are a major reason for the territory's widespread poverty. It is not surprising that the need to mount a wide range of social programs rapidly to assist the population has created financial demands that resulted in tensions between the government of Nunavut and the federal government over the level of annual financial support that Ottawa provides.

However, the new territory of Nunavut has also had some distinctive successes. One is the effective way that the negotiators of the Final Agreement found to reconcile the desire of the eastern

Inuit for political control with Canadian constitutional norms. The mechanism adopted was a 'public government,' relying on the population dominance of the Inuit to ensure the protection of Aboriginal culture. A long-standing problem for indigenous peoples in the North has been that large numbers of non-Native transients in pursuit of economic opportunities can overwhelm the local population and threaten maintenance of their culture. Since the northern economy is one heavily dependent on mining, an industry that is notorious for its cyclical nature, Nunavut is vulnerable to such political dangers. In Nunavut, by popular consensus, stiff residency requirements ensure that temporary upsurges in non-Native population will not overthrow accustomed norms before the interlopers move out again. Nunavut has a voter residency requirement of twelve months, rather than the six found in most other jurisdictions. Another unusual aspect of Nunavut's political culture is that it has continued the tradition first established in the Northwest Territories of avoiding partisan politics and party governments in the legislature. In a small population, the divisions created by partisanship can threaten social cohesiveness, and northerners east of Yukon have chosen to avoid them by operating with non-party governments and legislatures.

Nunavut, the new northern territory created by a modern treaty, has shown during its first decade of existence that it is an extraordinary experiment. Its achievement in 1999 is a tribute to the political determination of the eastern Inuit, not to mention their tenacity in negotiations that forced them to contend with both Aboriginal opponents and the federal government. The constitutional structure that was created, a public government, is an ingenious device that might provide a model for other settlements in remote, sparsely populated regions. At the same time, its social and economic characteristics mean that Nunavut faces, no doubt for some time, formidable challenges. The future will reveal if the political skill, determination, and tenacity that produced Nunavut will carry its population over the hurdles they face.

The Nisga'a Tribal Council (NTC) and government of Canada began negotiations in 1976 under highly inauspicious circumstances. While Ottawa had accepted the implications of the *Calder* ruling – it focused politicians' and bureaucrats' minds on Aboriginal issues[33] – the other level of government whose participation was essential to a settlement had not. British Columbia still refused to recognize Aboriginal title. The Pacific province continued to hold out for fourteen years. The federal government and NTC reached agreement on a framework for bilateral negotiations by the two of them in 1989, but BC was still not interested. What finally overcame Victoria's aloofness on Aboriginal title was the decision of the Supreme Court of Canada in *R. v. Sparrow*. The Sparrow case was an Aboriginal rights rather than an Aboriginal title case, the issue being whether or not Ronald Sparrow of the Musqueam band in Vancouver had an Aboriginal right to fish in spite of federal fisheries regulations. In the course of ruling on that question, the high court also laid down criteria to determine if an Aboriginal right, including title, had been extinguished. In essence, it declared that title could be nullified only by legislation that had explicitly declared extinguishment as its purpose, had a legitimate public policy reason for overriding the right, and encroached on the Aboriginal right only so far as was necessary to achieve that policy goal.[34] After *Sparrow* it was clear even to British Columbia that it had never legislated in a manner consistent with the *Sparrow* test and that Aboriginal title in most of the province was still a legal reality. The provincial government responded by agreeing with Ottawa and the province's First Nations Summit to set up the BC Claims Task Force to review Aboriginal claims in general, and it also joined the negotiations with the Nisga'a.

The simple chronology of events in the Nisga'a negotiations hardly does justice to the reality. In 1991 the NTC, BC, and Canada signed a framework agreement setting out the terms for negotiations; in 1996 they struck an Agreement in Principle that was subsequently endorsed by votes of the Nisga'a people, the BC government, and the federal cabinet; and in the summer of 1998, they reached a Final Agreement that was quickly ratified by the Nisga'a. BC passed legislation to ratify the Agreement in 1999; and, finally, Parliament passed legislation to ratify the deal in Ottawa. Each one of those stages was difficult and contested for several reasons. One was that there was hardly unanimity to be found in any of the three parties at the negotiating table. Even within the Nisga'a community there were dissidents who doubted the wisdom of participating in talks with governments that had never done anything but disappoint them. Among the federal delegation there were competing interests at play represented by various departments that made striking a firm federal position on issues in a number of sectors complicated. Ottawa's chief nego-tiator at the Nisga'a talks, Tom Molloy, has explained that the federal bargaining team had frequently to engage in two sets of negotiations simultaneously: with the Nisga'a Tribal Council, of course, but also with a number of federal departments that sought to influence the federal position.[35]

However, the most difficult cross-currents in the talks were those generated by interests in British Columbia. There were strong anti-treaty sentiments in play that were based on history, self-interest, and ignorance. The province's lengthy refusal to recognize Aboriginal title had created a school of thought – led volubly and effectively by former provincial attorney general Mel Smith and open-line radio host Rafe Mair – that there was no reason to accept the validity of Aboriginal title now. Such anti-treaty spokesmen had the vociferous backing of some eco-nomic groups who rightly feared that a settlement with the Nisga'a would have an adverse impact on them. In earlier times, the forestry industry, traditionally the most powerful group in BC, had opposed dealing with Aboriginal title, but by the 1990s the leaders of forestry companies and some mining concerns had changed their minds. They had come to realize that the uncertainty that unresolved Aboriginal title created about all land-holding in the province was a deterrent to investment. However, even after the biggest players, such as forestry companies, came onside, the commercial fishers did not. These were relatively small operators who had already been alienated by the Aboriginal Fishing Strategy (AFS) that Ottawa had implemented to conform with the *Sparrow* decision. The AFS reserved a portion of the annual fishery for First Nations. Finally, there were many municipal leaders and ordinary citizens who were unsure whom to believe in the arguments about the necessity to negotiate and the perils of doing so. And into this unstable mix came the province's opposition Liberals, whose leader, Gordon Campbell, firmly opposed the treaty.

Somehow, in spite of the many forces against the process, the tripartite negotiations produced a Final Agreement in July 1998. As Joseph Gosnell had put it at the Agreement in Principle stage, 'At 8:27 a.m. our canoe arrived. The journey our ancestors began more than a century ago ended.'[36] The terms in the Final Agreement specified that the Nisga'a would retain 769 square miles (1992 sq km), which they would hold in fee-simple title in the Nass Valley, an area that represented approximately 8 per cent of their traditional territory. They would govern themselves by means of a Nisga'a Lissims government, their central government, and four village councils in the Valley. The jurisdiction of their government would include Nisga'a citizenship, language, and culture; Nisga'a property in their lands; public order and safety; employment; transportation; solemnization of marriages; child and family social and health services; child custody, adoption, and education. The Nisga'a Lissims government is obligated by the Agreement to consult with non-Nisga'a who live in the territory and to make provision for them to participate in elected bodies that affect them, although the details of these arrangements are not spelled out. Both federal and provincial law, including the Criminal Code, apply in Nisga'a territory, and its residents and citizens are subject to the Charter of Rights and Freedoms. Nisga'a also become liable for sales tax in eight years and income tax in twelve, and are removed from the Indian Act.

In future, the Nisga'a were guaranteed about one-quarter of the important salmon fishery of the Nass River for commercial and subsistence uses, with the proviso that if the fishery for species of salmon that were part of the Nass fishery was suspended for conservation reasons by the federal government, the Nisga'a commercial fishery would not operate either. Finally, the controversial matter of certainty was handled in a sophisticated manner. The Agreement was said to be a full and final settlement of Nisga'a rights and set out the Nisga'a's continuing section 35 rights. The Nisga'a, in turn, agreed by the treaty that they gave up any Aboriginal rights that were not spelled out in the Agreement or that were different from their section 35 rights set out in the treaty.[37]

Although the Nisga'a and the federal government, in particular, had realized the Nisga'a Treaty would have a rough reception, the ensuing turbulence exceeded everyone's expectations. Commercial fisheries operators predictably argued against the pact, raising the temperature of public debate by denouncing its supposedly 'race-based fishery.' Those who subscribed to a conventional liberal political philosophy also objected to such provisions and the Nisga'a Lissims government on the grounds that they created one legal and constitutional regime for the Nisga'a and another for other British Columbians. Not all such objections were explicitly linked to political philosophy. For example, the Reform Party MP for Skeena, Mike Scott, said of the 1996 Agreement in Principle that it 'ignores the basic principle of equality before the law, entrenching inequality as a major feature. It is the product of a grand vision held by social engineers who want to do good by righting historic wrongs without regard to history's lessons.' He also claimed that the arrangements contained 'the notion that communism can be successfully reinvented.'[38] Many people of this stripe regarded such provisions as violations of the rule that all should be treated equally under the law, apparently not recognizing that the 1982 Constitution's section 35 created special constitutional rights for Aboriginal people. The self-government provisions of the Nisga'a Lissims government under the treaty were an advance on earlier self-government provisions because they were explicitly protected by section 35 of the Constitution.[39]

Opposition to acceptance of the Nisga'a Treaty coalesced around two points: a demand for a referendum on it, open to all voters; and a threat of litigation to block it. Advocates of a general vote argued that all should vote on it because the Nisga'a had got to vote on it, and because the treaty amended the Constitution. The provincial New Democratic Party government of Glen Clark, which had all along been a strong supporter of a Nisga'a treaty and which had organized a massive 'selling' campaign to win support for it,[40] refused to call a referendum. The government and its supporters argued that the Nisga'a Treaty did not amend the Constitution because the 1982 Constitution had provided for such treaty settlements, and that it was inappropriate to subject the rights of a minority to the votes of a different majority. The provincial legislature led by Clark ratified the Nisga'a Treaty in 1999.

Not even ratification stilled the agitation over the treaty. When the provincial general election of 2001 returned a Liberal government under Gordon Campbell with the largest majority in BC history, a new chapter opened. Campbell had already launched litigation in a BC court that argued that the treaty was not constitutional, and had promised that if elected, he would hold a referendum on it. In spite of the fact that all parties had ratified the treaty, Campbell's government proceeded with the referendum, thereby keeping the issue alive a little longer. The BC Supreme Court had ruled in 2000 on *Campbell v. British Columbia (A.G.)*, holding that the treaty and the legislation that implemented it were constitutionally sound. Now Campbell was faced with referendum results that seemed to indicate opposition to the treaty among the populace, although the poor wording of the questions and the low voter turnout rendered the validity of the results questionable. The Nisga'a and other BC First Nations threatened disruptive action if the provincial government acted on the results. Finally, Campbell and his government indicated that they would drop their opposition. In fact, Gordon Campbell soon emerged as an enthusiastic supporter of other efforts in BC to conclude treaties.

The area in which the now pro-treaty Campbell would work for more agreements was the unique process known as the British Columbia Treaty Commission (BCTC). This mechanism was set up in 1992 by agreement among the provincial chiefs' organization, known as the First Nations Summit, Canada. The BCTC itself was not to be the negotiator of the anticipated treaties; its role was to facilitate negotiations. The process consisted of six steps, beginning with the filing of a notice of intent to negotiate and culminating in a final agreement that was implemented after ratification by all the parties. (See box, opposite.)[41] Eventually, fifty-eight British Columbia First Nations participated in these treaty negotiations.[42]

The process established by the BCTC and the parties has been difficult, time-consuming, and expensive. Although many First Nations chose to participate, not all persisted when progress was slow. Part of the problem was the cost in human resources and money of preparing and negotiating a case, a draining experience for many. Compounding that difficulty was a legacy of suspicion and distrust over the province and its motives.

Furthermore, decades of bad experience had made some First Nations negotiators 'gun-shy.' If they got close to a settlement, they pulled back for fear of being criticized for 'selling out' their people by critics in their own community.[43] The problems were not all attitudinal, though, by any means. The fact was that trying to reach agreement in the southerly part of the province, where population densities were often high and economic activities had been established on First Nations land, was difficult. A stark example of these complications was found in the territory of the Tsawwassen First Nation, a Coast Salish people located fifteen miles (24 km) south of Vancouver on the ocean. They were sandwiched among a mammoth BC Ferries terminal, the Roberts Bank superport, which loaded ships with BC coal and other products, and innumerable non-Native homes and businesses.[44] Finding land to compensate the Tsawwassen First Nation in a settlement was akin to unscrambling an omelette.

BC Treaty Commission Process

1. First Nation files statement of intent to negotiate.
2. Commission meets with parties to determine their readiness to negotiate. Approves negotiation.
3. Parties negotiate a framework agreement.
4. Parties negotiate an Agreement in Principle.
5. Parties negotiate a Final Agreement.
6. After ratification, Agreement is implemented.

By the time the BC Treaty Commission had its tenth anniversary in 2002, it was nearing a crisis. As the Commission itself revealed in a hard-hitting re-examination that it published that year, there were no final agreements achieved and the process had cost in excess of one billion dollars. The Commission called on the parties to get realistic about negotiations, and proposed 'time outs' for some First Nation participants who were not doing well in the talks.[45] Another worrisome point was that some claimants who had borrowed large amounts from the Commission to finance their work would soon face the due date on their loans. Negotiations continued in spite of the difficulties, and seemed to have finally achieved some success in the autumn of 2006 when the Lheidli T'enneh First Nation, located near Powell River on the BC coast, signed a Final Agreement. Unfortunately, when the package was put before the community for ratification in March 2007, it was defeated. According to the chief of the Tla'Amin (Sliammon) First Nation, the problem was that the Lheidli T'enneh negotiators 'moved along too quickly.'[46] Once more the usual questions about the Commission's work and costs arose. About the same time, the Carrier Sekani Tribal Council in the interior of the province threatened to withdraw from the process. 'We have a treaty process shaken to its foundation and beginning to collapse inward,' said Chief David Luggi.[47]

The BCTC received a reprieve later in 2007. In July the Tsawwassen First Nation, which had initialled a Final Agreement in December 2006, ratified it by a large margin, giving the Commission its first solid achievement after fifteen years. The Tsawwassen settlement had earlier been attacked by the local Conservative Member of Parliament, who claimed that the true value of the package was closer to $300 million than the official figure of $70 million. He alleged that the First Nation and Commission were 'trying to low-ball' the total cost by assuming a lower valuation for the 1,072 acres (434 hectares) involved than the market justified.[48] Whether or not his figures helped to 'sell' the agreement to band voters is not clear. The Commission got another bit of encouraging news when the first of five First Nations who made up the Maa-nulth First Nations on Vancouver Island ratified their 9 December 2006 Final Agreement by a large margin at the end of July 2007. Parliament ratified the Tsawwassen Treaty on 26 June 2008.[49] The positive developments in 2007–8 suggested that the BC Treaty Commission process would continue. Kim Baird, chief of the Tsawwassen First Nation, explained one reason: 'The treaty represents our final break from the Indian Act – through self-government, not assimilation.'[50] In July 2008 there were two First Nations at stage six, (implementation); eight at stage five (negotiating a final agreement); thirty-nine at stage four (negotiating an agreement in principle); five at stage three (negotiating a framework agreement); and seven at stage two (determining readiness to negotiate).[51]

Modern treaty-making since the *Calder* decision reveals that the game goes, not to the swift, but to the persistent. The Nisga'a battle from the 1870s until the late 1990s is merely an extreme instance of a general problem. The comprehensive claims process, in place since 1974, has produced relatively few settlements, all of them in sparsely populated regions and most in the territorial North. It has taken an especially determined group, such as the Inuit of the eastern Arctic, to stick with their strategy until they succeed. For those who were tempted by the glacial pace of claims resolution to turn to the courts instead, the experience there since the 1970s has been daunting. For a time, after the creation of section 35 of the 1982 Constitution provided additional protection for Aboriginal title, the judicial system appeared sympathetic to indigenous peoples. In spite of major victories such as *Sparrow* and *Delgamuukw*, however, there was a disturbing trend in legal affairs towards increasing complexity, delay, and expense for whose who resorted to the courts to deal with their concerns. In 1969 the trial stage of the *Calder* case took four days to put in evidence, but *Delgamuukw* between 1987 and 1990 required 318 days to deal with evidence and 374 days in all at the trial stage.[52] One effect of the delays has been that First Nations sometimes looked for other ways to deal with their problems, such as those in British Columbia who negotiated deals with resource companies to permit operations on their territory in return for payments and a role in environmental monitoring of the companies' work.[53]

A development in the James Bay region of Quebec, where the most recent phase of treaty-making opened in the 1970s, typified the post-*Calder* problems Aboriginal groups have faced. It was not long after the James Bay and Northern Quebec Agreement was concluded that Cree and Inuit leaders began to complain that the two levels of senior government that had been signatories to it were not fulfilling its terms. Billy Diamond observed that 'implementation was one fight after another,' and the Grand Council of the Cree noted in 1986, 'What the Crees and Inuit have learned over the last 11 years is that negotiation of a claim settlement is only half the battle and implementation is the other half.'[54] Their agitation was ignored until they took more aggressive action. In 1989 the Cree launched litigation in Quebec's Superior Court and the Federal Court demanding compensation for the broken promises. Moreover, they soon began an energetic public campaign against the Great Whale hydroelectric project, another stage beyond the initial development, which Quebec had announced in 1988. Their public relations onslaught was particularly effective in the northeastern United States, where power utility companies were expected to be the major customers for

10

'We are all treaty people':[1]
Conclusion

Treaties were, are, and always will be an important part of Canadian life. Binding agreements between the Crown and Aboriginal peoples have played a central role in Native-newcomer relations since contact, and are still a significant public policy issue now. Non-Native Canadians might not universally recognize their significance, but treaties will continue to play an important role in Canada for the foreseeable future.

Although Aboriginal-Crown treaties are generally viewed as means to dispossess indigenous people of their lands, the treaty story is much more complex than that single dimension. True, treaty-making was the North American manifestation of a nearly worldwide process of dispossessing indigenous people that recently has attracted scholarly attention.[2] Because land-related treaty-making lasted so long – from the 1760s until the present – it overlapped with a lengthy period of oppression of indigenous people by European newcomers. Memory of it has been so searing that it has blotted out other parts of the treaty story. There were other types of pacts that were not concerned principally with land. The agreements over the last four centuries have also taken the less damaging forms of commercial compacts and alliances of peace and friendship. It was only after more than a century and a half of the less malignant forms of treaty-making that the more destructive territorial treaties took over. The longer narrative of treaty-making is useful as a means to understand how the Native-newcomer relationship has changed since the early seventeenth century. It also permits an appreciation of how indigenous populations have responded to the challenges treaty-making created. Moreover, in the early twenty-first century, this shifting, multi-faceted treaty-making process continues. Treaty-making in Canada has a future as well as a past and present.

The initial Aboriginal response to the arrival of Europeans – Dutch, French, and English – who wanted to establish some sort of relationship with them was to integrate the newcomers into their existing systems. Prior to contact, eastern First Nations had well-developed mechanisms for relating to one another as civil societies, for facilitating commercial exchange, and for making peace to end the strife that broke out from time to time. The confederacies that existed among the Five Nations and the Huron or Wendat were a form of internal treaty. They regulated relationships, provided for shared ceremonial observances, promoted commercial exchange between horticulturalists and hunters or between hunters and fishers, and established non-violent ways of resolving conflicts. The key to these mechanisms was kinship. All the northeastern First Nations had kin systems that provided linkages between people from different parts of the political community.

To deal with strangers, First Nations extended, or replicated, kin ties by ascribing to outsiders what anthropologists term fictive kinship. Such links were instituted through formal ceremonies and renewed regularly by more shared observances. The ritual, or protocol, initiating commercial exchange in the fur trade or negotiating treaties of peace and friendship created what a later generation might characterize as 'imagined communities,' virtual collectivities fashioned for shared purposes. Trade and peace – commerce and friendly relations – were closely related in pre-contact First Nations societies because they were twin outgrowths of kinship.

As Europeans saw matters, the earliest phase of entente-making in the northeast produced both commercial compacts and treaties of peace and friendship. For First Nations, what Europeans thought to be two categories of agreements were merely two sides of the same coin. As the Five Nations diplomat said in 1735, First Nations took peace and trade to be one thing. So Mi'kmaq chief Membertou and Jean de Biencourt, sieur de Poutrincourt, became 'kin' at Port Royal in 1606 by exchanging gifts and speeches of friendship. Poutrincourt's countryman, Samuel de Champlain, also entered into kin-like relations with the Huron, and found that his 'relatives' expected his support on a military expedition against the Iroquois. Champlain discovered that the fictive kinship he helped to establish involved the French in both commercial and military networks.

First Nations fitted the Europeans into their existing systems. First and foremost was the matter of language. Neither the Huron nor the Iroquois would lower themselves to use European languages, not even at Albany, the capital of New York. Further evidence of indigenous initiative and immigrant responsiveness in the early relationships was provided by Europeans' adoption of the protocols that First Nations used to establish and renew relations. From the early seventeenth century until at least the late years of the nineteenth century, newcomers adapted to Native ways of making kin by means of shared ceremonies. No matter how elaborate the ceremonialism, Europeans had to participate because they needed the Native peoples much more than the indigenous population needed them. The newcomers were less attached to protocol than the Natives; for the strangers, ceremonies were merely a means to an end.

The complexity of the rituals that European traders and diplomats learned to practise reflected a ceremonial formality characteristic of Aboriginal societies in general. Native parties heading for another village or a European trading post did not just barge into the site of intended commerce. They stopped a short distance away, out of sight of the village or post, to prepare their costume and grooming for the occasion. One such stopping place near the mouth of the Rupert River on the east side of James Bay was known to local Cree as 'Dress-Up Creek' at least until the middle of the twentieth century. Once the travellers were prepared, they approached with their canoes in line, and fired their muskets to announce their arrival. The Europeans discharged a small cannon in reply, and prepared an elaborate welcome.

The ensuing ceremonies included formal welcomes, speeches, gift exchange, and feasting. Great solicitude for the other party was always part of the oratory. It is noteworthy that there were clear similarities between these expressions of concern in fur-trade protocol and the ritualized expressions of sympathy in the Iroquois condoling ceremony. An extremely important part of the ritual to renew the relationship between Native and newcomer, for that is what these shared actions aimed to do, was smoking the pipe together. The calumet to First Nations was a sacred instrument, for it brought the Great Spirit into the gathering and bound all the participants to honest words and honourable acts. The head of a First Nations party that was satisfied with its relationship with the Europeans would leave his pipe at the post, signalling that he and his party would return next season. Taking the pipe away intimated a rupture of the relationship.

In this fashion, Native and newcomer joined to create extraordinary trade networks from the seventeenth century onward. Natives wanted European goods; Europeans sought furs. A fictive kin relationship was required for the exchange to occur, and fur-trade protocols were the mechanism for establishing these links and keeping them strong. By taking up these rituals, newcomers were adjusting to Aboriginal ways and mechanisms. Similarly, the newcomers' governors had to get used to being addressed as 'Onontio' or 'Corlaer,' needing to understand and accept the personalized nature of kin-like relationships in forest diplomacy. If the strangers wanted the Natives to provide most of the labour of fur-gathering and -processing, the Europeans had to adjust to North American methods.

Together in the fur trade, Natives and newcomers fashioned commercial networks that were, in the French case, extremely widespread geographically, and, in the English, marked by extraordinarily sophisticated relationships. The French, both in Acadia and on the St Lawrence, traded with some Iroquoians and many more Algonkian peoples from the Atlantic littoral through northern Quebec and what is now Michigan-Wisconsin, down into the present-day American Midwest. The most adventurous French traders ranged from the Maritimes to Hudson Bay or down the Mississippi. The commercial system that the English inherited from the Dutch came to depend on elements of the Five Nations of the Iroquois and their First Nations partners and dependants in the interior. Out of the latter system, in which the Mohawk were the closest geographically to the English, Iroquois and English fashioned what would become known as the Covenant Chain. The Chain was an elaboration – and extension to incorporate Europeans – of Five Nations practice that included the condolence and requickening ceremonies. Both French and English trading networks, far-flung and intricate as they were, demonstrated how indigenous peoples dominated early commercial compacts.

Out of the commercial compacts, Natives and newcomers developed peace and friendship treaties. French representatives quickly perceived and acted upon the reality that strategic alliances had to be founded on material bases such as ongoing trade and frequent gifts. The English in New York, with spectacularly successful exceptions such as Sir William Johnson, took longer to absorb this information and make it a factor in their policies towards First Nations. In the eighteenth century, both Britain and France put a premium on treaties of peace and friendship and the alliances that were assumed to result from them because both European powers sought allies for an expected showdown for control of eastern North America. European forest diplomats such as Frontenac and Johnson were motivated in part to improve their own economic conditions, but their diplomacy advanced the interests of their home countries as well.

France relied mainly on informal means to establish and maintain its alliance systems, with the result that it made fewer formally recorded treaties. French fur traders, known usually as *coureurs de bois*, had also been ready and able to work closely with Native people in pursuit of pelts, and for France it was a simple matter to capitalize on these commercial relations – suitably renewed and reinforced periodically, of course – to keep their partners friendly. This was especially true in Canada, the St Lawrence colony, in the *pays d'en haut*, and down the Mississippi. In Acadia, the French Atlantic colony, there was an additional link that helped to maintain informal alliances between the people of His Most Catholic Majesty and the various Algonkian nations. Religion had been an important component of French presence in the Maritimes from the conversion of Membertou and his extended family in 1610 to the period of intense rivalry with the British in the eighteenth century. One scholar has suggested perceptively that Membertou viewed Christian baptism as a ritual for 'kin-making,' a protocol in its consequences not unlike what he and Poutrincourt had shared.[3] Missionary priests, French traders, and sometimes intermarriage between Acadians and Mi'kmaq combined to make French policy in the era of treaties of peace and friendship particularly effective.

The English (the British after 1707) depended more on formal treaties to maintain their links, though informal treaty-making was hardly unknown to them. The Covenant Chain that linked British interests with the Mohawk and some of the other nations of the Iroquois League, and through the Five or Six Nations to other Indian groups, was an especially impressive example of informal alliance. The Covenant Chain was founded on mutual trade, annual presents, First Nations protocol, and shared strategic self-interest. English interests were also most effectively advanced when British aims served the purpose of First Nations, as was usually the case with the Mohawk. For the Seneca, however, whose location at 'the western door' of Iroquoia brought them into more direct contact with interior First Nations allies of the French, the appeal of the Covenant Chain and the British was always less. This variation even within the Iroquois League is a reminder of two important realities: First Nations placed a high value on autonomy within their own society; and Natives always pursued their own self-interest in negotiations, rather than acting as the 'dupes' or 'tools' of Europeans. Europeans acted from personal and national self-interest too, of course.

Treaty-making policy in the Maritime region after the 1713 Treaty of Utrecht revealed the limits of British resources and skills. The representatives of His Britannic Majesty did not have the affinities of shared religion or as well-established a claim for Native cooperation in the fur trade as the French. As a consequence, the more settlement-oriented British colonizers in the region had to depend on economic and military strength to encourage First Nations to see things their way. They also relied heavily on formal treaty-making – treaties of peace and friendship that also addressed trade relations – to forge beneficial relations with the indigenous peoples. Britain's need to make treaties repeatedly in Nova Scotia between the Treaty of Utrecht and the Seven Years' War showed that, absent mutual self-interest and cultural ties, informal alliance systems would always trump formal treaties of peace and friendship. As long as the French exploited ties with the Natives effectively, Great Britain was at a severe strategic disadvantage in that region. That reality explains why it was British naval power, rather than land-based forces including Native allies, that brought about the defeat of France and the cession of New France to Britain in 1763.

The Royal Proclamation that Britain issued in October 1763 embodied some indigenous practice while simultaneously attempting to appease Native anger. The Proclamation established institutions of government and justice for Britain's newly acquired North American colonies, including the Province of Quebec. It also sought to make British policy more pleasing to France's former First Nations allies by creating a regime, or protocol, for acquiring Native lands 'reserved for them as their hunting grounds' that it recognized as Aboriginal-controlled territory within a domain supposedly owned outright by the king. Commentators have often noted that the Proclamation embodied and extended policy developments that had been under way for some years.

Certainly the Proclamation's territorial provisions – only the Crown could negotiate for Indian lands, and only at a public meeting called specifically for that purpose – implemented a policy that the skilled forest diplomat Sir William Johnson had long been advocating. The Proclamation attempted to put an end to what it described as 'great frauds and abuses' and scholars later have characterized as 'the deed game.' It forbade freelance land acquisition by speculators and land-hungry interests that could embroil the British authorities in conflicts with Indians outraged by such travesties. The Proclamation's clauses dealing with Indian lands also recognized Aboriginal claims to ownership and control, and implemented procedures they would accept as fair and honourable. The conference at Niagara that William Johnson convened in 1764 seemed to demonstrate that a large number of First Nations accepted the British policy.

The Proclamation ushered in the lengthy third era of treaty-making, the age of territorial treaties. Britain, and later British colonial and Canadian administrators and politicians, created a treaty-making tradition that still dominates efforts to get access to indigenous lands in Canada. Crown representatives frequently did not follow the letter of the Proclamation in negotiations, and certainly governors occasionally had to remind both their underlings and settlers in central British North America of those regulations. Nonetheless, in two phases prior to and after the War of 1812, territorial treaty-making in Upper Canada usually abided by the necessity to have negotiations carried out by representatives of the Crown at talks held openly and conducted to ensure that First Nations communities were aware of what the governor sought from them in terms of their lands. The treaties made pursuant to the Royal Proclamation are the agreements between First Nations and the Crown representing non-Native society that most Canadians equate with treaty-making in general.

Upper Canadian treaty-making prior to the War of 1812 revealed that the Royal Proclamation was a guide to, not an inviolable rule of, procedure. The twelve treaties made in this period that exchanged access to Mississauga-controlled lands for one-time compensation and limited protection for fishing rights certainly initiated Aboriginal dispossession south of the Precambrian Shield, paving the way for establishment of settler society along 'the front' of waterways. But the negotiating process that brought them about also retained customary Aboriginal protocol, including the rhetoric of family and kinship, speeches, and gift-giving. These practices from an earlier era persisted for two reasons. Non-Native officials and settlers badly needed the support of indigenous populations for strategic and economic reasons. In addition, in the period before 1812, the representatives of the Crown who staffed the Indian Department in Upper Canada were all products of the Johnson school of forest diplomacy.

Before the War of 1812 there were harbingers of serious change, no doubt, but the old relationship and style of treaty-making still remained largely intact. Officials from the Johnson tradition remained in charge, Upper Canadian fisheries regulations explicitly noted continuing Aboriginal rights and called for respect for them, and indigenous protocol was the general rule in negotiations. At the same time there were intimations that the standing and influence of indigenous peoples were beginning to slip. That the governor twice found it necessary to reiterate the requirements of the Royal Proclamation to officials indicated that some negotiators ignored the rules. Other evidence included the growing distrust of some First Nations in negotiations during the early nineteenth century. Some complained of settler encroachments and asked for assistance in repelling them. Others asked for explicit reservation of fishing sites or corn fields because they had learned that settlers did not always respect customary rights.

Following the War of 1812, all the indicators turned bad for Upper Canadian First Nations. British immigration and settlement not only swamped them, but British policy began to promote efforts to change them through a 'civilization program.' A shift in treaty compensation from one-time payments to annuities seemed positive on the surface: annual payments resembled the familiar and much valued presents that their 'father the king' provided. The underlying motivation for the change in compensation, however, was to shift the burden of treaty-making from the homeland to the colonies. The old annual presents themselves would be abolished by 1858. The colonial fisheries ordinance of 1827 continued to respect Aboriginal rights, but that recognition would not last. Like the presents from the Crown, that protection of a valuable resource would be ended by the late 1850s. Still more revealing were the changes in personnel in the Indian Department, innovations that signalled the waning of the Johnson school and the triumph of settler society. The old hands retired, died, or, like T.G. Anderson prior to the Robinson Treaties, were pushed aside in favour of younger men from settler society. The appointments of William Robinson as treaty commissioner in 1850 and William McDougall to negotiate the Manitoulin Island Treaty of 1862 symbolized the shift.

Perhaps the most blatant transition was the elevation of Alexander Vidal above the more senior T.G. Anderson to head the 1849 inquiry on Lake Huron and Lake Superior. Vidal was a surveyor, the symbol of the new society that was choking out the indigenous population. Surveyors were an essential part of the process of reducing the natural contours of a resource-generating land to the straight lines and regulation of surveyed agricultural townships. Given what surveyors and surveying represented, it is not at all surprising that Chief Edowishcosh in 1861 rejected a treaty on Manitoulin Island with the words, 'We have the laws God has established. I wish you would take back your proposition and your Surveyor with you.'

The mid-century Upper Canadian agreements exemplified the changing nature of Native-newcomer and treaty relations. Governmental actions prior to both clearly violated the Royal Proclamation. In 1846, Canada provoked leaders such as Chief Shinguakonse of Garden River by handing out mining licences in territory not yet covered by treaty, and prior to 1862 the province issued fishing licences that included rich grounds off Manitoulin Island that the local First Nations considered theirs. These high-handed actions revealed the dominance of the new society, just as the resistance by Shinguakonse and Edowishcosh testified to the enduring attachment of First Nations to their territory and refusal to endure encroachments without protest. There was even a plaintive persistence of the older version of the Crown–First

Nations relationship in Governor General Elgin's critical commentary between 1846 and 1850.

Although the Upper Canadian treaties represented a deterioration of the relationship underlying earlier peace and friendship and commercial agreements, they were an advance over anything else in contemporary British North America. The Maritimes and Quebec did not trouble with land-related treaties at all. When the leading edge of settlement reached the prairies in the second decade of the nineteenth century, the best that the Selkirk Settlement could do was fashion a 'quit rent' agreement in 1817 to conciliate local Saulteaux. In the Hudson's Bay Company lands in the far west, the pre-Confederation era produced only fourteen localized land agreements on Vancouver Island where settlement seemed imminent. For all their shortcomings, the Upper Canadian territorial treaties were more significant than anything available elsewhere at the time.

The Robinson Treaties of 1850 were also exemplars of the new treaty order. With their coverage of large areas, reserves as part of the treaty settlement, and recognition of continuing hunting and gathering rights, they introduced a new package of terms that would be replicated in post-Confederation treaties in the West and North. As the Ontarian who would be a commissioner for four of the seven numbered treaties of the 1870s put it, 'The main features of the Robinson Treaties – viz., annuities, reserves for the Indians, and liberty to fish and hunt on the unconceded domain of the Crown' – all were found 'in these [western] treaties.'[4]

The Upper Canadian influence on post-Confederation treaties was hardly surprising. For one thing, it was Ontario interests, principally agrarian, commercial, and financial, that were the strongest advocates of acquisition of the Hudson's Bay Company lands. During the 1870s, a program of western development that emphasized Prairie settlement and a transcontinental railway made gaining peaceful access to western lands imperative. The political leaders who dominated the first two generations of federal politics were central Canadians whose political education had occurred mainly in the Province of Canada. Post-Confederation civil Indian policy was largely a continuation of policies developed earlier in Canada. Sir John A. Macdonald, for example, introduced the Gradual Civilization Act in the Canadian legislature in 1857. When leaders such as Macdonald and George-Étienne Cartier or Alexander Mackenzie hurriedly formulated instructions for Canada's treaty commissioners in the 1870s, they turned instinctively to methods fashioned earlier in Upper Canada and the Province of Canada. Thus, the Upper Canadian treaty-making model became a rough guide for negotiating treaties in the West.

The primary difference between treaty-making in central Canada and Rupert's Land was the First Nations with whom the Crown negotiated. The woodlands and Plains peoples of the West in 1867 were numerous, strong, and assertive. From the foothills of the Rockies to northwestern Ontario, they made it clear to Ottawa between 1869 and 1875 that, first, they opposed Canada's assertion of control without prior agreement, and, second, they were prepared to discuss treaties. Why were most – not all, but most – western leaders amenable to making treaty? While their societies were strong, they had recently been weakened by epidemic disease and inter-tribal wars. They also felt economic anxieties. The Plains nations were worried about the rapid decline of the bison, while in northwest Ontario the hunting-gathering-fishing Ojibwa and woodland Cree were seeing their economy disrupted by drastic changes in the Hudson's Bay Company (HBC) transportation system that severely reduced seasonal employment. All western nations were being told by both HBC men and missionaries that the arrival of large numbers of agricultural settlers was inevitable, and the First Nations knew all too well what parallel developments in the United States had earlier meant for Native Americans. Western groups, especially the leaders of the Plains nations, tended to see the U.S. government and settlers as a menace, whereas they regarded the British Crown as a positive alternative. If the future was uncertain, drastic change inevitable, and a probably good partner available, why not explore setting the terms on which newcomers would come and obtaining assistance with agriculture through treaties with the Great White Queen Mother?

It is clear that western First Nations and Crown negotiators had different understandings of the negotiating process and the meaning of the treaties. The indigenous leadership believed it was dealing with the Queen through designated representatives. Crown commissioners encouraged them in this belief. To a considerable extent, First Nations' expectations and perceptions were shaped by their lengthy dealings with the Hudson's Bay Company and by their negative image of Americans. The use of fur-trade protocol in most of the negotiating sessions in the 1870s would have encouraged them to perceive the people with whom they were dealing, to some extent, as they had seen Bay people. While treaty commissioners often employed that protocol, there is little evidence that they understood its true significance. A comment by the secretary in Alexander Morris's party indicates as much: he wrote that the pipe ceremony signified friendship. Morris knew that when the Ojibwa denied him a formal welcome and pipe ceremony at Fort Qu'Appelle in 1874, their behaviour conveyed a negative message. Neither his spoken nor written words indicate, however, that he understood the ceremony's full significance. Officials did not realize that the protocol, including the pipe ceremony, converted the product of the talks into a covenant to which the Great Spirit was also a party, that the heart of the treaty was the kin-like relationship it created, and that everything spoken was as much part of the treaty as whatever government scribes recorded. Many of the differences of interpretation that later caused so much difficulty were rooted in that contrast.

With the Métis there was no such ambivalence or imprecision. Canada made it clear in the western treaty talks, as it had in 1850 on Lake Huron, that it would not make treaty with the Métis, however much both they and their Indian kin might desire it. The Dominion's primary concession to the Métis in the 1870s was allowing them to choose to be treated either as treaty or non-treaty people. Canada later made scrip available to the Métis, though the way it was administered largely deprived the policy of long-term value to the community. The government's attitude was that, while they had to deal with First Nations by treaty, they did not, and would not, do anything similar with the Métis. Outside Red River, their cooperation was more expendable than that of First Nations. Therefore, government dealt with them by means of one-time commitments that carried no ongoing financial obligations.

Once treaty-making was concluded in the 1870s, the self-interested and at times insensitive nature of federal treaty-making was revealed. There were numerous problems with treaty implementation because a distant government had little interest in the welfare of the western peoples. Even when the collapse of the bison economy by 1879 created conditions of extreme hardship, Ottawa showed little concern. In fact, that collapse made it easier to ignore First Nations' protests because the dissidents had been weakened militarily. Some later commentators – especially undergraduates, who tend towards cynicism – suggest that this heartlessness 'proves' that Canada never intended to honour its treaty promises. There is no evidence from the treaty negotiations themselves to sustain such an interpretation. Rather, once setbacks in the West weakened the peoples there, it became all too easy in a parliamentary democracy in which votes – something First Nations did not have, of course – were what counted for politicians to drop treaty obligations down the priority list when it came to allocating resources. Federal indifference also manifested itself in the government's refusal to grant the requests of many northern First Nations for adhesions after 1877. Since non-Natives felt no need of new lands in Indian Country, Canada was uninterested.

There was a disturbing parallelism between the northern numbered treaties of 1899–1921 and the earlier ones. Canada initiated treaty talks with the northern peoples from northwestern British Columbia to northern Ontario only when non-Natives voiced an economic interest in the regions and usually after decades of ignoring requests from the region for treaties. Many of the treaty expeditions, especially for Treaty 8, were hurriedly thrown together and recklessly executed, with disastrous results for some First Nations, most notably the Lubicon Lake Cree. The Dominion's deference to the wishes of Ontario in the negotiation of Treaty 9, most egregiously on ruling out potential hydro sites as reserves, is an especially pointed example of governmental self-ishness. So, too, was the alacrity with which Ottawa moved to conclude Treaty 11 one year after oil was discovered at Norman Wells in 1920.

The use of fur-trade protocol continued, though clearly to a reduced degree in the northern treaties. In Treaty 9 the rich fur-trade ritual seemed to survive principally in the feasts that the commissioners sponsored after the conclusion of each session. Nor was there any detectable improvement in the appreciation among government officials of the significance of protocol to First Nations. Specially appointed commissioners offered only scrip to the northern Métis, although by now the flaws in the scrip system were undeniable. If there was a change in scrip policy in the North, it was that federal treaty commissioners were less likely now to agree to the preference of some Métis to enter treaty rather than take scrip. One phenomenon of the northern treaties that was reminiscent of developments in Upper Canada a century earlier was the greatly increased suspicion of First Nations negotiators, and their reluctance to accept bland assurances about gathering rights. In some instances in the North, commissioners were pressed hard to give undertakings about continuing rights, something they did orally but not in writing. The disparity between the oral and written records of treaty-making was probably greater in the northern agreements than it had been in the 1870s in the West.

Given the federal government's attitude towards treaties between 1877 and 1921, the cessation of negotiations after 1923 was hardly surprising. The lack of federal empathy for First Nations, already painfully evident, became much more pronounced as Indian policy became increasingly intrusive and coercive from the end of the Great War to the 1950s. By the early twentieth century, Canada was more interested in changing Indians than in negotiating with them. With little non-Native appetite for acquiring more pieces of Indian Country by treaty, Ottawa, aside from a large adhesion in northern Ontario, wanted no part of more agreements. The way in which the federal government simply ignored its treaty commitments to First Nations in the Natural Resources Transfer Agreements of 1930 was probably the clearest instance of Ottawa's indifference to Aboriginal peoples. When non-Native Canada did begin to awaken to a renewed interest in Native lands during the Second World War and afterwards, the government found it was dealing with very different leadership than it had faced earlier.

The resumption of treaty-making after 1973 in response to renewed non-Native interest in gaining territory revealed a number of novelties. Better organized, more articulate, and considerably more aggressive Native leadership was one factor, as individuals such as Frank Calder, Billy Diamond, and Joseph Gosnell demonstrated. The influence of the decisions of the Supreme Court of Canada in such cases as *Nisga'a* (1973), *Sparrow* (1990), and *Delgamuukw* (1997) was profound. The impact manifested itself in the Trudeau government's concession in creating a process for resolving Aboriginal title claims and the latter-day conversion of the British Columbia government in the early 1990s. Another profound political influence was the overhaul of the Constitution in 1982. Section 35's recognition and affirmation of Aboriginal and treaty rights, which constitutionalizes treaties and provides them with immunity against legislatures, enhanced the ability of Inuit and First Nations to advance their rights prior to treaty and protect their interests afterwards.

The other marked features of the most recent treaties and comprehensive claims settlements have been their complexity and the length of time required to negotiate them. There is a marked legalism to treaty-making now that results in negotiators, in Chief Gosnell's words, growing old at the negotiating table, and gargantuan written agreements full of complex technical language. The Nunavut final agreement has 282 pages, while the Nisga'a pact weighs in at 854 pages. At times, the legalism has run amuck. Tom Molloy, a lawyer himself and head of the federal team of negotiators for Nisga'a, reported that, once the parties had initialled the final agreement, the people 'representing the three parties to the negotiations crazy-glued the expansion posts so they could not hereafter be tampered with. I had not known that this was one of the functions of the Chief Federal Negotiator.'[5] In an atmosphere that produces negotiations and agreements like this, Aboriginal protocol is absent, at least as a shared ceremony.

The history of treaty-making in Canada shows clearly that negotiating binding agreements between the Crown and Aboriginal peoples is a story that has a past, a present, and a future. In the four centuries between the 1606 pact forged at Port Royal to the final agreements secured by the British Columbia Treaty Commission in the early twenty-first century, treaty-making has demonstrably evolved. From simple agreements reached by small groups of Europeans and Native people using Aboriginal rituals to facilitate the exchange of goods, treaties spread out geographically and changed their character. There is not a part of Canada whose early post-contact history was not founded on commercial exchange between indigenous peoples and immigrants, and nowhere did that commerce go on without Aboriginal protocol to create and maintain the kinship that such transactions required in the Native world. Commercial compacts were soon joined by strategically motivated agreements in the northeastern woodlands. They also emerged by the late seventeenth century in the northern Hudson's Bay Company lands. They spread as well to the resource-rich North, where they would have their most enduring life. Commercial compacts emerged outside the fur trade, too, although these agreements were not, strictly speaking, Crown-Aboriginal treaties. The coerced agreements in the Fraser Valley in the 1850s between rampaging miners and Salish people certainly were intended to facilitate trade. So, too, were the agreements between resource companies and First Nations that began to pop up in the 1990s in British Columbia as the BCTC process stalled. Commercial compacts have existed since first contact.

The treaties of peace and friendship that emerged in the eastern woodlands alongside the commercial pacts in the 1600s have had as lengthy a record chronologically, though not as extensive a range geographically. Unlike the northeastern woodlands, no European state rivalries disturbed the other regions – with the brief exception of French-English jockeying on James and Hudson Bays in the late seventeenth century – and made the European newcomers eager for treaties of alliance. Treaties of peace and friendship did not disappear when treaty-making acquired a territorial focus with the end of the Seven Years' War. First Nations, of course, continued to regard all agreements, including territorial treaties, as multi-faceted. And the Crown equally incorporated the peace and friendship element into territorial treaties from the eighteenth to the twentieth centuries. Pledges of mutual friendship and support were a component of the ritual that constituted part of treaty negotiations for most of the Upper Canadian treaties, as they were in the numbered treaties of the late nineteenth and twentieth centuries. Undertakings to maintain friendly relations appear more to be assumed than explicitly affirmed in the much more legalistic comprehensive claims settlement agreements and the treaties of the last three decades.

If the record shows that treaty-making was always diverse, is it as true of the present and the future that treaty-making endures and will persist? The existence of more than fifty sets of negotiations in the BCTC process, ongoing talks to resolve comprehensive claims, and federal government overtures to a variety of Aboriginal groups in Atlantic Canada and the North all demonstrate that treaty-making has a future.[6] It could hardly be otherwise. Since treaties are foundational documents establishing the bases of relations between indigenous and immigrant peoples, they will always be important.

In addition to having a long and diverse history, treaty-making is a projection of underlying Native-newcomer relations throughout our shared history. When the two parties had reasons of mutual interest for interacting, as in the fur trade or in combining to resist others diplomatically and militarily, the relationship was generally positive. While there were problems, such as severe population loss to epidemic disease and the debilitating impact of alcohol, the Native-newcomer relationship during the era of the fur-trade and imperial rivalries was beneficial on the whole. Europeans got skilled labour, knowledge of local conditions, and assistance in accomplishing their ends. Native people got access to European goods as well as diplomatic and military assistance, though the latter was not always reliable. In the early phases, in which commercial compacts and treaties of peace and friendship predominated, the Native-newcomer relationship was generally positive. Both sides benefited from the interaction; neither sought to interfere with the other or change its society fundamentally.

When Native-newcomer interactions shifted to relations organized around the settlement frontier, the quality of the association declined and a new type of treaty came to the fore. After the periods when trade and alliance were the primary European motives for contact, the strangers' desire to make farms and towns – in other words, to create colonies of settlement rather than commerce and diplomacy – took over. Unfortunately for the relationship, Europeans no longer considered Aboriginal peoples vital for the achievement of the newcomers' goals. While trade and Native people were compatible, sedentary agriculture and migratory peoples were not. The result was a dramatic shift in European, that is, British and British-Canadian, policy to measures designed to alter the essentials of Aboriginal societies through so-called 'civilization' policies and to dispossess them through territorial treaties. As the relationship deteriorated, the nature of the treaties was transformed, and the impact of the changes in both civil policy and treaties was devastating to indigenous societies.

Since territorial treaties were artifacts of a deteriorating relationship, it is little wonder that First Nations had problems with them. Because Native peoples were now little valued by newcomers, and declining precipitously in population because of disease and hardship, non-Native governments acted in high-handed and coercive ways towards them. Residential schools were one example. So far as treaties were concerned, the consequence was dilatory and inadequate implementation of the Crown's commitments. Put simply, non-Native governments did not honour their treaty undertakings because they no longer

". . . and the Great White Mother shall honor this treaty for as long as the river runs, the mountain stands, and the buffalo roams . . . or as under subsection Q (para. 2) until a duly elected politician chooses to ram through patriation of the BNA Act, see section H, subsection 16 (paras. 6 through 81)."

10.1 Legalistic government language was not understood in negotiations.

valued the people with whom they had made them, and those populations were now small, weak, and lacking in political tools to resist. From central Canada to the prairie West, First Nations protested quickly and frequently. The Six Nations in southern Ontario, for example, petitioned the governor general, Lord Dufferin, in 1872 emphasizing 'their ancient Wampum Treaty; The Silver Chain which does not tarnish.' The Cree of south-central Saskatchewan complained to Ottawa in 1884 that the government had lured them into treaty with 'sweet promises' in 1876 and then betrayed them.[7] Initially, Native signatories to treaties resorted to petitions because they assumed that the agreements were sacred and binding, and that their non-Native partners were honourable. This pattern of governmental non-compliance followed by First Nations protest would be repeated for the better part of a century.

First Nations' protests and resistance changed slowly. The one form of opposition that remained constant was resort to the Crown to publicize Natives' complaints. Other tactics became more prominent, however, as time went on. One highly symbolic way to protest the onrushing settlement frontier was to resist the surveyor, the quintessential representative of it. Alexander Vidal represented the encroachment of settler society into the mining country of the Shield around Sault Ste Marie in the late 1840s, and Chief Edowishcosh on Manitoulin Island expressed Native opposition to such people. So, too, the Ojibwa in the North West Angle in 1869 recognized and objected to surveyors. In the 1880s in the Nass Valley of British Columbia, Frank Calder's grandfather was one of the Nisga'a chiefs who ejected surveyors: '... every canoe was loaded with Nisga'a braves, every one of them carrying a Hudson's Bay musket. At 8 o'clock those people started to cook; they were just getting ready to go to work. All these braves went up there, confronted them and pointed the gun, and just uttered these words, "Get off my land." Well, God, when you're facing hundreds of Hudson's Bay muskets, what are you going to do. They would have to dismantle the tent and get off.'[8]

In the twentieth century, protests against Crown failures became more activist. For example, in 1937 Dene in the Northwest Territories ostentatiously refused to accept their annuities. As the *New York Times* reported, 'Treaty Indians of the Great Slave Lake area, 600 miles [960 km] north of Edmonton, are on strike against payment arrangements and have refused to accept treaty money from Dr. J.E. Amyot, Indian Agent at Resolution, asserting that he has imposed too severe restrictions upon them ... They wish, they said, to present their complaints to an impartial government official.'[9] First Nations, such as the Kanesatake Mohawk, took the opportunity to protest in official settings that became available to them beginning with the 1946–8 sittings of the Joint Parliamentary Committee on the Indian Act. Complaints about non-compliance with treaties were part of the widespread uproar over the White Paper of 1969. Once the Office of Native Claims

was created in 1974, the disgruntled had an institutionalized
means they could use, although the experience on specific claims
– those that arose from a 'lawful obligation' such as a treaty commitment – was no more impressive than that with comprehensive
claims. Increasingly in the latter part of the twentieth century,
Aboriginal protests about treaty and other matters tended to take
the form of litigation and organized political objections. The use
of the courts by the Quebec Wendat in the *Sioui* case, which recognized the Murray Treaty, was a good example of the judicial
route.

The increasingly assertive protest tactics of First Nations and
Métis in the latter decades of the twentieth century have not
always been well received. A review of treaty history shows that
non-Natives are generally not receptive to treaty-related complaints and protests, even though public opinion polls have
repeatedly shown a general sympathy for Aboriginal people,
especially those in situations of hardship brought on through no
fault of their own. The explanation for the relatively harsh public
attitude on treaties would appear to be that governments and
interest groups have won the public relations battle by portraying
Aboriginal claims as extreme, grasping, and unjustified. The
clearest example of the tactic and its consequences was the way in
which the government of Robert Bourassa depicted the compensation in the James Bay and Northern Quebec Agreement in
1975 as a windfall for the Cree and Inuit. More recent instances,
which are numerous, would include the concerted attack on the
Nisga'a Final Agreement in the late 1990s by opponents who
argued, among other things, that governments were 'giving' too
much to reach a settlement. Decades of such rhetoric appear to
have taken their toll on non-Native support of Aboriginal claims
concerning treaties.
   Although this jaundiced view of treaties is unjustified, it is a
reality that needs to be combated. In the Nisga'a Treaty, the
Crown gave the Nisga'a exactly nothing. The First Nation gave up
some 92 per cent of its traditional lands in return for a settlement
that included compensation. Non-Native opinion-makers need to

explain to the Canadian electorate that lands that have not been dealt with by treaty are still Aboriginal lands. Since section 35 was inserted into the Constitution in 1982 and the Supreme Court of Canada ruled that Aboriginal title was 'a right to the land itself' in *Delgamuukw,* the reality is that lands without treaty are in a special category.

Similarly, objections that recent treaties created 'race-based' rights for particular groups that violate constitutional convention ignore historical reality. Since 1982 the Aboriginal peoples of Canada have joined the ranks of Canadians who receive special recognition before the law. Like the citizens of Quebec, who have special rights when it comes to Supreme Court appointments, or Catholics in Ontario and Protestants in Quebec, who have con-stitutionally protected educational rights, or a number of other Canadians, Aboriginal peoples now *do* have different constitu-tional and legal standing. It would be a sign of political maturity for the rest of the Canadian population to recognize the fact.

It would also be a demonstration of political adulthood if Canada's political leaders recognized and accepted the obliga-tions in the 1982 Constitution. Section 35's statement that 'Abo-riginal and treaty rights are hereby recognized and affirmed' was only a generalization. It required definition and refinement. In four first ministers' meetings between 1983 and 1987, political leaders tried and failed miserably to bring precision to the clause. The consequence of this political disappointment has been that Aboriginal groups have had to resort to the courts to defend their rights. Aboriginal fishing rights began to be delineated in the *Sparrow* decision in 1990, and some Maritime treaty rights gained modern definition in the *Marshall* ruling in 1999. When the Supreme Court has handed down pro-Native decisions in Abo-riginal and treaty rights cases, the reaction from some non-Natives, including some political leaders, has been to complain of 'activist' judges who trample on the role of legislators. The truth, however, is that the courts are most reluctant, as they have said explicitly in cases such as *Delgamuukw,* to move beyond their appropriate role. The failure of politicians to deliver solutions to problems of interpreting Aboriginal constitutional matters has thrust two alternatives on the justices: leave Aboriginal people and their constitutionally recognized rights undefended, or provide rulings that advance definition of section 35. Canadians who object to 'activist judges' should direct their annoyance at non-performing politicians. It is politicians' inaction, not the so-called activism of judges, that is the problem.[10]

The presence of Aboriginal people with constitutional and legal rights is a reality that Canadians need to recognize. As Chief Justice Antonio Lamer said in his decision in *Delgamuukw*, 'Let's face it. We are all here to stay.' First Nations were here first, and they're staying. They have endured in spite of efforts since the 1830s to change them culturally, politically, and economically. All such efforts have failed to achieve their objectives, and have resulted mainly in misery and hardship for their targets. Neither Natives nor non-Natives are leaving any time soon. Politicians need to adjust their rhetoric and policies accordingly. They also would be doing the country an enormous favour by getting behind efforts to educate the non-Native public about treaty rights through public education and curriculum reform. Such initiatives have been undertaken in Saskatchewan within the last decade, and will also be soon in Manitoba. In the medium term such programs, which aim at correcting the historical record on treaties and explaining Aboriginal and treaty rights to non-Native people, could achieve wonderful changes in public opinion.

It is important for the future well-being of Native-newcomer relations, treaty implementation, and the social cohesion of Canada that everyone come to recognize that 'we are all treaty people.' Treaties convey rights and benefits on non-Natives and Natives alike. Properly understood, for example, territorial treaties legitimize the presence on formerly Native lands of non-Natives and establish a relationship between indigenous and immigrant peoples that promotes social harmony. Similarly, where territorial treaties are made, such as in British Columbia, they create better conditions for economic development by ending the uncertainty that deters investment.

Treaties also have the potential to serve as common ground on which Aboriginal and non-Aboriginal people could get together

10.2 If treaties do not endure, then non-Native title is not secure.

10.3 An ironic take on 'We are all treaty people.'

to develop greater social cohesion in Canada. At present, First Nations leaders, especially, often refuse to identify as citizens of Canada. The reason for this stance is historical. For well over a century, citizenship and Indian status were incompatible: a First Nations person could enjoy citizen status only by renouncing Indian status in a process known as enfranchisement. The Canadian state conditioned First Nations to regard themselves and non-Native citizens as fundamentally different. On the other side of the relationship today, many non-Natives find First Nations leaders' well-articulated aversion to the Canadian state and citizenship offensive, something that lessens their sense of common cause with Natives.[11] If non-Natives publicly acknowledge that they are participants in and beneficiaries of treaties, that recognition might provide reassurance to First Nations that their distinctiveness is accepted. Such an acknowledgment could begin the process of softening the hostility to citizenship that now exists. Eventually, First Nations might come to embrace citizenship, thereby encouraging greater empathy between Natives and non-Natives.[12]

An environment in which treaties were properly understood and appreciated would also be one in which the strong social ties that Aboriginal people have always believed were essential to treaty-making would become general. That is a consummation devoutly to be wished and long overdue.

Notes

1: Early Commercial Compacts

1 Toronto Reference Library, Baldwin Room, S13, George Nelson Journals, folder 'Journals 6 July–22 Aug. 1822,' entry of 10 July 1822

2 *The Canadian Oxford Dictionary*, ed. Katherine Barber (Don Mills, ON: Oxford University Press, 1998)

3 R. Cole Harris, ed., *From the Beginning to 1800*, Vol. 1 of *Historical Atlas of Canada*, 3 vols (Toronto: University of Toronto Press, 1987), Plate 14, 'Prehistoric Trade'

4 Joseph-François Lafitau, *Customs of the American Indians Compared with the Customs of Primitive Times*, 2 vols (Toronto: Champlain Society, 1974; first French edn, Paris, 1724), 2: 171

5 James Axtell, *Natives and Newcomers: The Cultural Origins of North America* (New York and Oxford: Oxford University Press, 2001), 201. For an excellent overview of the role of kinship among France's *domiciliés* allies in communities such as Kahnawake, see Jean-Pierre Sawaya, *La Fédération des Sept Feux de la vallée du Saint-Laurent: XVIIe au XIXe siècle* (Sillery, QC: Septentrion, 1998), 78–99.

6 H.P. Biggar, ed. and trans., *The Voyages of Jacques Cartier* (Ottawa: King's Printer, 1924), 49

7 HBC to John Nixon, 29 May 1680, in *Copy-Book of Letters Outward &c: Begins 29th May, 1680 Ends 5 July, 1687*, ed. E.E. Rich (London: Hudson's Bay Record Society, 1948), 9. Like all students of the North American fur trade, I am greatly indebted to Arthur J. Ray, who taught us an enormous amount about Native-European relations in the commerce.

8 HBC to Nixon, 29 May 1680, in ibid., 13

9 HBC to John Bridgar, 15 May 1682, in ibid., 36. Port Nelson was nineteen kilometres west of York Factory, at the mouth of the Nelson River.

10 HBC to Gov. John Nixon, 22 May 1682, in ibid., 46
11 The Royal Charter for incorporating the Hudson's Bay Company, A.D. 1670, http://www.solon.org/constitutions/Canada/English/PreConfederation/ hbc_charter1670.html, accessed 11 May 2006
12 Roy MacGregor, *Chief: The Fearless Vision of Billy Diamond* (Markham, ON: Penguin, 1989), 8
13 Glyndwr Williams, ed., *Andrew Graham's Observations on Hudson's Bay, 1767–91* (London: Hudson's Bay Record Society, 1969), 316
14 Ibid., 316–17
15 Ibid., 317
16 Ibid., 318
17 Ibid., 319
18 Jordan Paper, *Offering Smoke: The Sacred Pipe and Native American Religion* (Edmonton: University of Alberta Press, 1988), 5
19 Daniel K. Richter, *The Ordeal of the Longhouse: The Peoples of the Iroquois League in the Era of European Colonization* ([Williamsburg, VA]: Institute of Early American History and Culture, 1992), 28
20 Christian Le Clerq, *First Establishment of the Faith in New France*, trans. John Gilmary Shea, 2 vols (New York: AMS, 1973; New York: John G. Shea, 1881), 1:126–7
21 Williams, ed., *Andrew Graham's Observations*, 321–2
22 Ibid., 320–1
23 See, for example, E.E. Rich, *The History of the Hudson's Bay Company, 1670–1870, Volume I: 1670–1763* (London: Hudson's Bay Record Society, 1958), 62–3, 139
24 John Oldmixon, *The British Empire in America* (1708), reprinted in J.B. Tyrrell, ed., *Documents Relating to the Early History of Hudson Bay* (Toronto: Champlain Society, 1931), 400–1
25 George Nelson Journals, 1802. Similarly, see entry for 13 July 1803.
26 George Nelson Journals, 1802
27 George Nelson Journals, entries of 23–4 Aug. and 3 Sept. 1803. See also Jennifer S.H. Brown, '"Man in His Natural State": The Indian Worlds of George Nelson,' in *Rendezvous: Selected Papers of the Fourth North American Fur Trade Conference, 1981*, ed. Thomas C. Buckley (St Paul, MN: North American Fur Trade Conference, 1984), 200–1.
28 Robert A. Williams, *Linking Arms Together: American Indian Treaty Visions of Law and Peace, 1600–1800* (New York: Routledge, 1999), 79
29 Bruce M. White, '"Give Us a Little Milk": The Social and Cultural Significance of Gift Giving in the Lake Superior Fur Trade,' in Buckley, ed., *Rendezvous*, 187

30 Ibid., 188
31 Thomas L. McKenney and James Hall, *The Indian Tribes of North America*, 3 vols, new edn, ed. Frederick Webb Hodge (Edinburgh: J. Grant, 1933–4), 1:256. The full greeting is as follows: '*Brother*, when you put that dress on, feel up there – there are five feathers; I have put one in for each scalp I took from your people – remember that!'
32 Onondaga Sachem to Col. Schuyler, 19 July 1712, in Peter Wraxall, *An Abridgment of the Indian Affairs Contained in Four Folio Volumes, Transacted in the Colony of New York, from the Year 1678 to the Year 1751*, ed. Charles Howard McIlwain (1915; New York: Benjamin Blom: 1968), 95
33 Le Clerq, *Establishment of the Faith*, 1:124
34 R.G. Thwaites, ed., *The Jesuit Relations and Allied Documents*, 73 vols (Cleveland: Burrows, 1896–1901), 22:201. Similarly, see Daniel Richter, *Facing East from Indian Country: A Native History of Early America* (Cambridge: Harvard University Press, 2001), 131, concerning presents at a 1679 conference between the Mohawk and representatives of Virginia.
35 Wraxall, *An Abridgment of the Indian Affairs*, 13
36 Ibid., 106
37 Ibid., 119
38 H.P. Biggar, ed., *The Works of Samuel de Champlain*, 6 vols (Toronto: Champlain Society, 1922–6), 1:98–101, 104
39 Marc Lescarbot, *The History of New France*, ed. and trans. W.L. Grant, 3 vols (Toronto: Champlain Society, 1907–14), 2:343–5
40 Richter, *Ordeal of the Longhouse*, 93–5
41 Harris, ed., *Historical Atlas of Canada*, vol. 1, Plate 14, 'Prehistoric Trade'
42 For more detail, see the following individual maps in the plates indicated in Harris, ed., *Historical Atlas of Canada*, vol. 1: Plate 33, 'Trade Patterns and Warfare, ca 1530': 'Trade Patterns and Warfare, ca 1590' and 'Trade Patterns and Warfare, ca 1600'; Plate 35, 'The Great Lakes Basin, 1600–1653': 'Native Trade and Warfare, 1600–1648,' 'Ottawa Valley and Saguenay Trade, 1600–1620,' 'Huron-Nipissing Trade, 1620–1640,' and 'Huron Trade and Iroquois Disruptions, 1640–1648'; Plate 37, 'The Re-Establishment of Trade, 1654–1666': 'Trade Resumes, 1654–1660'; Plate 38, 'Expansion of French Trade, 1667–1696'; and Plate 60, 'Bayside Trade, 1720–1780.'

2: Treaties of Peace, Friendship, and Alliance

1 A Six Nations spokesman to governor of New York, 20 Sept. 1735, in Peter Wraxall, *An Abridgment of the Indian Affairs Contained in Four Folio Volumes,*

Transacted in the Colony of New York, from the Year 1678 to the Year 1751, ed. Charles Howard McIlwain (1915; New York: Benjamin Blom, 1968), 195

2 Bruce G. Trigger, *The Children of Aataentsic: A History of the Huron People to 1660*, reprint edition in one volume (1976; Montreal and Kingston: McGill-Queen's University Press, 1987), 162–3

3 Trigger, *Children of Aataentsic*, 54–7, 59–61, and 748–9; Elizabeth Tooker, *An Ethnography of the Huron Indians, 1615–1649* (Washington, DC: Smithsonian Institution, [1967]), 55, 128

4 Tooker, *Ethnography of the Huron*, 134–40; Trigger, *Children of Aataentsic*, 85–90

5 Daniel K. Richter, *The Ordeal of the Longhouse: The Peoples of the Iroquois League in the Era of European Colonization* ([Williamsburg, VA]: Institute of Early American History and Culture, 1992), 20–1, 42–3

6 See the description and analysis of the 'nine stages' of a council between the Mohawk and representatives of Virginia at Albany in 1679 in Daniel K. Richter, *Facing East from Indian Country: A Native History of Early America* (Cambridge: Harvard University Press, 2001), 30–41. Richter notes, '… in the North American context, "treaty" referred to the entire process of meeting, or "treating," with Indian leaders; "treaty minutes" were the record of that process' (134). See also pp. 135 and 137 for his emphasis on fictive kinship.

7 Allen W. Trelease, *Indian Affairs in Colonial New York: The Seventeenth Century* (Ithaca, NY: Cornell University Press, 1960), 212

8 Eastern woodlands Indians also called all Jesuit superiors 'Achiendassé,' the name they had given Father Jérôme Lalemant (Jean Hamelin, 'Charles Huault de Montmagny,' *Dictionary of Canadian Biography* [*DCB*], vol. 1, online edition, accessed 20 May 2006). Although Samuel de Champlain is often referred to as the first governor, his title actually was 'commandant in New France in the absence of Richelieu.' Huault de Montmagny was the first governor and lieutenant-general of New France. See also Richter, *Ordeal of the Longhouse*, 131–2.

9 Peter Cook, 'Vivre comme frères: Le rôle du registre fraternel dans les premières alliances franco-amérindiennes au Canada (vers 1580–1650),' *Recherches amérindiennes au Québec*, 31, no. 2 (2001): 55–65

10 Richter, *Ordeal of the Longhouse*, 94–5

11 Barbara Graymont, *The Iroquois in the American Revolution* (Syracuse, NY: Syracuse University Press, 1972), 221

12 I am indebted to Dr Marley Waiser, a research scientist with Environment Canada, for this information.

13 Kathryn V. Muller, 'The Two Row Wampum: Historic Fiction, Modern

Reality' (M.A. mémoire, Université Laval, 2004), 2 (I am indebted to Dr Muller for advice on many wampum-related matters); Richter, *Ordeal of the Longhouse*, 47 (quotation)

14 Wraxall, *An Abridgment*, 98–9

15 'Memoir of the Negotiations in Canada with the Iroquois' (1694), in *Documents Relative to the Colonial History of the State of New York*, ed. E.B. O'Callaghan (Albany, NY: Weed, Parsons and Co., 1853), 9:578

16 Wraxall, *An Abridgment*, 150–1

17 Ibid., 210

18 W.J. Eccles, 'Buade de Frontenac et de Palluau, Louis de,' *DCB*, vol. 1, on-line edition, accessed 22 May 2006; W.J. Eccles, *Frontenac: The Courtier Governor* (Toronto: McClelland and Stewart, 1959), 105–7. A useful summary of forest diplomacy is found in Jean-Pierre Sawaya, *La Fédération des Sept-Feux de la vallée du Saint-Laurent: XVIIᵉ au XIXᵉ siècle* (Sillery, QC: Septentrion, 1998), chapter 3, 101–35.

19 Cadwallader Colden, *The History of the Five Nations of Canada*, rev. edn, 2 parts (London: T. Osborne, 1747; 1st edn, 1727), part 2, 163. See also ibid., 164: 'When the Indians came near the Town of Albany, ... Mr Johnson put himself at the head of the Mohawks, dressed and painted after the Manner of an Indian War-Captain ...'

20 De Monts's commission of 8 Nov. 1603, in Marc Lescarbot, *Nova Francia; or, The Description of That Part of New France Which Is One Continent with Virginia*, trans. P. Erondelle (London: Andrew Hebb, [1626]), 3, Early English Books Online, accessed 23 May 2006

21 H.P. Biggar, ed., *The Works of Samuel de Champlain*, 6 vols (Toronto: Champlain Society, 1922–6), 2:92–105

22 James Sullivan, ed., *The Papers of Sir William Johnson*, 14 vols (Albany: University of the State of New York, 1921–65), 13:158

23 Francis Jennings et al., eds, *The History and Culture of Iroquois Diplomacy: An Interdisciplinary Guide to the Treaties of the Six Nations and Their League* (Syracuse, NY: Syracuse University Press, 1985), 127

24 'Relation of 1644 and 1645,' in *Jesuit Relations and Allied Documents*, ed. R.G. Thwaites, vol. 27 (Cleveland: Burrows Brothers, 1898), 147–61

25 *Jesuit Relations*, 27:267

26 Articles between Col. Cartwright and the New York Indians, 24–5 Sept. 1664, in O'Callaghan, ed., *Documents Relative to the Colonial History*, 6:67–8

27 Richter, *Ordeal of the Longhouse*, 111

28 William Fenton, 'Return of Eleven Wampum Belts to the Six Nations Iroquois Confederacy on Grand River, Canada,' *Ethnohistory*, 36, no. 4 (Fall 1989): 396

29　Muller, 'The Two Row Wampum,' *passim*, esp. chapters 2–4. Examples of the Two Row Wampum and the Covenant Chain Wampum can be found in ibid., 1 and 61; and in Fenton, 'Return of Eleven Wampum Belts,' 396. See also Kathryn V. Muller, 'The Two "Mystery" Belts of Grand River,' *American Indian Quarterly*, 31, no. 1 (Winter 2007): 129–64, esp. 131, 139, and 152.

30　Wraxall, *An Abridgment*, 10–12

31　Cadwallader Colden, *The History of the Five Indian Nations Depending on the Province of New-York* (New York, 1727), on-line version, Early Eighteenth Century Collections, Part 1, 87, accessed 13 June 2006. Trelease notes, 'The Iroquois submission to England was in reality no more than a facet of their independent diplomacy. They admitted Corlaer's jurisdiction in order to get his support against the French; but their admissions and promises never prevented them from acting as they later saw fit' (*Indian Affairs in Colonial New York*, 268).

32　This is the dominant view, promulgated by Richter. See especially his 'Ordeals of the Longhouse: The Five Nations in Early American History,' in *Beyond the Covenant Chain: The Iroquois and Their Neighbors in Indian North America, 1600–1800*, ed. Daniel K. Richter and James H. Merrell (Syracuse, NY: Syracuse University Press, 1987), 11–27. In contrast, Allen Trelease sees the Iroquois League as a maker, but not especially effective enforcer, of external policy (*Indian Affairs in Colonial New York*, 21–1, 23).

33　Richter, 'Ordeals of the Longhouse,' 11–27, esp. 21–7

34　W.J. Eccles, 'Teganissorens,' *DCB*, vol. 3, on-line edition, accessed 6 June 2006

35　This account of the Great Peace of Montreal of 1701 is based primarily on Gilles Havard, *The Great Peace of Montreal of 1701: French-Native Diplomacy in the Seventeenth Century*, trans. Phyllis Aronoff and Howard Scott (Montreal and Kingston: McGill-Queen's University Press, 2001; 1st French edn 1992); Alain Beaulieu and Roland Viau, *The Great Peace: Chronicle of a Diplomatic Saga* (Montreal: Editions Libre Expression 2001); William N. Fenton, 'Kondiaronk (Le Rat),' *DCB*, vol. 2, on-line edition, accessed 6 June 2006; José A. Brandão, *Your fyre shall burn no more: Iroquois Policy toward New France and Its Native Allies to 1701* (Lincoln, NE: University of Nebraska Press, 1997), esp. chapter 9; J.A. Brandão and William A. Starna, 'The Treaties of 1701: A Triumph of Iroquois Diplomacy,' *Ethnohistory*, 43, no. 2 (Spring 1996): 209–44; Eccles, 'Teganissorens.'

36　Richter, *Ordeal of the Longhouse*, 210–11

37　Wraxall, *An Abridgment*, 40. The editor adds in a footnote: 'In the contents of this Meeting is minuted the [Title] Deed of Surrender of this Land to the King dated the 19 July 1701, but no such Deed appears recorded.'

38 Richter, *Ordeal of the Longhouse*, 212: 'The purpose seems not to have been literally to transfer ownership of the land or to gain English military protection of Iroquois western hunting rights. The Five Nations had no clear title to the territory – which was crawling with their victorious Indian enemies – and the previous decade of experience had disabused them of any illusions about New York's martial value.' See also ibid., 245, 247.

39 William W. Warren, *History of the Ojibway People*, with an introduction by W. Roger Buffalohead (St Paul, MN: Minnesota Historical Society Press, 1984), 146–7; George Copway, *The Traditional History and Characteristic Sketches of the Ojibway Nation* (London: C. Gilpin, 1850), 87–91; Peter Jones, *History of the Ojebway Indians* (London: Bennett, 1861), 111–13; Peter S. Schmalz, *The Ojibwa of Southern Ontario* (Toronto: University of Toronto Press, 1991), 5, 18–19; and H.H. Tanner et al., eds, *Atlas of Great Lakes Indian History* (Norman and London: University of Oklahoma Press, 1987), 31–4

40 Wraxall, *An Abridgment*, 182–3. See also pp. 188–9. The exception to the Iroquois practice of ignoring Corlaer's claims to protect their lands occurred in 1751, when the French were encroaching on Iroquois territory and building forts. At a council on 1 July 1751 the Iroquois sachems 'beg that the King will inform the King of France of the Proceedings of his Subjects that he may put a Stop to it for that the Land belongs to the King our Father & the Govr of this Province' (ibid., 250–1). Whether this statement was a reference to the 1701 agreement or simply an invocation of the Iroquois right as allies to get the support of the British Crown is not clear.

41 William Johnson to Gen. Thomas Gage, 31 Oct. 1764, in Sullivan, ed., *The Papers of Sir William Johnson*, 11:394–5

42 Melvill Allan Jamieson, *Medals Awarded to North American Chiefs, 1714–1922* (London: Spink & Son Ltd, 1936), 3–4

43 James Youngblood Sákéj Henderson, *The Mikmaq Concordat* (Halifax: Fernwood, 1997). Concerning the wampum, see pp. 85, 87–9.

44 Concerning the status of the Mi'kmaq in the eyes of the seventeenth-century Vatican, I am indebted to private communications by two specialists on Vatican–North American relations, Luca Codignola, University of Genoa (e-mail message of 29 Sept. 1999), and Roberto Perin, York University (e-mail message of 29 June 1999). Concerning the inauthenticity of the wampum, see Supreme Court of Nova Scotia, *Keith Lawrence Julien v. Her Majesty the Queen*, 2002 N.S.S.C. 057, at lines 59–61.

45 David L. Schmidt and B.A. Balcom, 'The Règlements of 1739: A Note on Micmac Law and Literacy,' *Acadiensis*, 23, no. 1 (Autumn 1993): 110

46 Treaty of Boston, 15 Dec. 1725, in W.E. Daugherty, *Maritime Indian Treaties*

in Historical Perspective (Ottawa: Indian and Northern Affairs Canada, 1983), 75–7

47 Treaty of Halifax, 1752, in Daugherty, *Maritime Indian Treaties*, 84–5

48 Treaty made by Mi'kmaq chief Michael Augustine with governor of Nova Scotia, 10 March 1760, in Daugherty, *Maritime Indian Treaties*, 86–7. For similar treaties with Saint John and Passamaquoddy Indians (1760) and Joseph Shabecholouest of Miramichi (1761), see ibid., 88–91.

49 Ironically, the justice who wrote the majority decision in *Marshall* considered himself a historian of sorts, though he argued in the ruling that courts could not wait for academic historians to reach a stable consensus in interpreting disputed historical events. In the majority ruling, Mr Justice Ian Binnie cited at length expert opinion from a Crown witness to uphold the Mi'kmaq's case. The expert in question complained loudly that his interpretation of eighteenth-century Maritime history had been distorted by the Court. See *National Post Online*, 28 Oct. 1999, 'Court accused of "distorting" history: Professor says his testimony used out of context: Supreme Court judge "simply ignored" historical evidence in ruling on native fishing.'

3: The Royal Proclamation and the Upper Canadian Treaties

1 Royal Proclamation of 1763, in *British Royal Proclamations Relating to America, 1603–1783*, ed. Clarence S. Brigham, vol. 12 of *Transactions and Collections of the American Antiquarian Society* (Worcester, MA: American Antiquarian Society, 1911), 215

2 Jack Stagg, *Anglo-Indian Relations in North America to 1763 and an Analysis of the Royal Proclamation of 7 October 1763* (Ottawa: Indian Affairs and Northern Development, 1981), 229–31, 335

3 Royal Proclamation of 1763, 215–18

4 J. Michael Thoms, 'Ojibwa Fishing Grounds: A History of Ontario Fisheries Law, Science, and the Sportsmen's Challenge to Aboriginal Treaty Rights, 1650–1900' (Ph.D. diss, University of British Columbia, 2004), 92. I am indebted to Dianne Newell and Arthur J. Ray, who brought this dissertation to my attention.

5 Johnson to General Thomas Gage, 23 Dec. 1763, in *The Papers of Sir William Johnson*, ed. James Sullivan, 14 vols (Albany: University of the State of New York, 1921–65), 10:973. Johnson distributed the Proclamation widely in a proclamation of his own of 24 Dec. 1763 (ibid., 976–85). Other British officials, such as General Gage, also disseminated news of the 1764 Niagara conference to other First Nations through military officers. See T.

Gage to the Earl of Halifax, 13 April 1764, in *Documents Relative to the Colonial History of the State of New York*, ed. E.B. O'Callaghan, 15 vols (Albany, NY: Weed, Parsons, and Co., 1853–87), 7:517.

6 Paul Williams, 'The Chain' (LL.M. thesis, Osgoode Hall Law School, York University, 1982), 76; John Borrows, 'Wampum at Niagara: The Royal Proclamation, Canadian Legal History, and Self-Government,' in *Aboriginal and Treaty Rights in Canada: Essays on Law, Equality, and Respect for Difference*, ed. Michael Asch (Vancouver: University of British Columbia Press, 1997)

7 W. Johnson to T. Gage, 19 Feb. 1764, in Sullivan, ed., *The Papers of Sir William Johnson*, 4:328–33

8 Ibid., vol. 7:307, 309–10. Comprehensive accounts of the extensive negotiations and agreements at Niagara between 17 July and 4 August, are found in ibid., 11:278–324; and in Johnson to Cadwallader Colden, 23 Aug. 1764, ibid., 4:511–14. Note, though, that none of these sources contains explicit reference to the Royal Proclamation of 1763.

9 D. Peter MacLeod, *The Canadian Iroquois and the Seven Years' War* (Toronto: Dundurn / Canadian War Museum, 1996), 144–6. The agreements made at the end of the Seven Years' War are well covered in Denys Delâge and Jean-Pierre Sawaya, *Les traités des Sept-Feux avec les Britanniques: droits et pièges d'un héritage colonial au Québec* (Sillery, QC: Septentrion, 2001).

10 Murray Treaty, in *Report of the Work of the Archives Branch for the Year 1911* (Ottawa: Government Printing Bureau, 1911), 50–1

11 For example, Denis Vaugeois, *La fin des alliances franco-indiennes: enquête sur un sauf-conduit de 1760 devenu un traité en 1990* (Montreal: Boréal / Septentrion, 1995); and Alain Beaulieu, 'Les Hurons et la Conquête: un nouvel éclairage sur le "traité Murray,"' *Recherches amérindiennes au Québec*, 30, no. 3 (2000): 60–5. The opposite interpretation is given in Delâge and Sawaya, *Les traités des Sept-Feux*, 57–61.

12 T. Gage to the Earl of Halifax 3 April 1763, in O'Callaghan, ed., *Documents Relative to the Colonial History of the State of New York*, 7:620, enclosing 'Articles of Peace concluded with the Seneca Indians,' 621–3

13 Barbara Graymont, *The Iroquois in the American Revolution* (Syracuse, NY: Syracuse University Press, 1972), 260

14 Quoted in Cornelius J. Jaenen, *Friend and Foe: Aspects of French-Amerindian Cultural Contact in the Sixteenth and Seventeenth Centuries* (New York: Columbia University Press, 1976), 7

15 Quoted in D.C. Scott, 'Indian Affairs, 1763–1841,' in *Canada and Its Provinces*, ed. A. Shortt and A.G. Doughty, vol. 4 (Toronto: Glasgow, Brook and Co., 1914), 708

16 Quoted in Robert S. Allen, *His Majesty's Indian Allies: British Indian Policy in*

the Defence of Canada, 1774–1815 (Toronto: Dundurn Press, 1993), 93

17 Robert J. Surtees, 'Indian Land Cessions in Ontario, 1763–1862: The Evolution of a System' (Ph.D. diss., Carleton University, 1982), 57

18 Library and Archives Canada (LAC), MG 21, B 158, Sir Frederick Haldimand Papers, 366, reel 746, Capt. W.R. Crawford to F. Haldimand, 9 Oct. 1783

19 Provincial Archives of Ontario, John Graves Simcoe Papers, MU 2790, envelope 39, Council of the Indians of Oswegathcie to Simcoe, 2 Feb. 1795; in Surtees, 'Indian Land Cessions,' 77

20 Haldimand Papers, Crawford to Haldimand, 9 Oct. 1783

21 Ibid.

22 Melvill Allan Jamieson, *Medals Awarded to North American Indian Chiefs, 1714–1922* (London: Spink & Son, 1936), 9–15

23 Haldimand Papers, Crawford to Haldimand, 9 Oct. 1783

24 P.A. Cumming and N.H. Mickenberg, *Native Rights in Canada*, 2nd edn (Toronto: General Publishing, 1972), 117 and note 67

25 Surtees, 'Land Cessions,' 61

26 Haldimand Papers, Crawford to Haldimand, 9 Oct. 1783

27 Anthony J. Hall, 'The Red Man's Burden: Land, Law, and the Lord in the Indian Affairs of Upper Canada, 1791–1858,' (Ph.D. diss., University of Toronto, 1984), 44–50, 52–4, and 57–9

28 Ibid., 46–7

29 Canada, *Indian Treaties and Surrenders*, 3 vols (Ottawa: Queen's Printer, 1891), 1:32–4

30 Surtees, 'Land Cessions,' 93

31 Lord Dorchester, Additional Instructions, Indian Department, 26 Dec. 1794, in *The Correspondence of John Graves Simcoe*, ed. E.A. Cruikshank, 5 vols (Toronto: Ontario Historical Society, 1923–31), 3:241–2

32 Treaty 11, 30 June 1798, in *Indian Treaties and Surrenders*, 1:27–8; facsimile reproduction kindly supplied by Sally Gibson of Parks Canada, Fort St Joseph's. Two 'Indian witnesses' also attested to the treaty with their totems. I am grateful to Ms Gibson for providing me with the facsimile copy.

33 University of Western Ontario Archives, Alexander Vidal Papers, box 4437, typed copy of Report of Commissioners A. Vidal and T.G. Anderson to His Excellency, the Governor General, in Council, 5 Dec. 1849, Appendix E

34 William Chewett to E.G. Littlehales, in Cruikshank, ed., *Correspondence of Simcoe*, 3:24

35 Proclamation of Peter Russell, President, Administering the government, 14 Dec. 1797, in *The Correspondence of the Honourable Peter Russell with Allied*

Documents Relating to His Administration of the Government of Upper Canada during the Official Terms of Lieut.-Governor J.G. Simcoe While on Leave of Absence, ed. E.A. Cruikshank, 3 vols (Toronto: Champlain Society, 1932–6), 2:41

36 Surtees, 'Land Cessions,' 115–16
37 LAC, RG 10, vol. 1, 294–8, reel C-10,006, Account of meeting with Mississauga at River Credit, 1–2 Aug. 1805; Treaty 14 and Indenture, in *Indian Treaties and Surrenders*, 1:36–40
38 LAC, CO 42, 351, Colonial Office Correspondence, Upper Canada, 1811 Despatches, reel B295, 138–9, Minutes of a meeting with the Mississauga Indians of the River Moira, Smith's Creek, 24 July 1811. In nineteenth-century councils between First Nations and Crown representatives, 'milk' was usually a euphemism for alcohol.
39 Ibid.

4: The Upper Canadian Treaties, 1818–1862

1 Minutes of a Council at Smith's Creek [Port Hope], 5 Nov. 1818, in Ontario Court of Appeal, *The Queen v. Taylor and Williams*, 16 Oct. 1981, *34 Ontario Reports (2d)*, 363. I am indebted to my colleagues law professor Rob Flannigan and librarian Ken Whiteway for providing me with a copy of this *Ontario Reports*. Efforts to locate the original of these minutes in the Claus Family Fonds at Library and Archives Canada (LAC) (William Claus was the Crown negotiator) have proven unavailing. So, too, have efforts to find the minutes in LAC, RG 10, Records of the Department of Indian Affairs, although the actual 'Articles of an Agreement' are found in RG 10, vol. 35, 20605, reel C-11011.
2 Minutes of a Council at Smith's Creek, 5 Nov. 1818, in Ontario Court of Appeal, *The Queen v. Taylor and Williams*, 16 Oct. 1981, *34 Ontario Reports (2d)*, 363
3 Claus Family Fonds, vol. 11, 101–3, reel C-1480, Minutes of an Indian Council, 17 Oct. 1818
4 Claus Family Fonds, vol. 11, 109–12, reel C-1480, Record of a Council at River Credit, 27, 28, and 29 Oct. 1818
5 Minutes of a Council, 5 Nov. 1818, 363
6 Canada, *Indian Treaties and Surrenders*, 3 vols (Saskatoon: Fifth House, 1992; Ottawa: Queen's Printer, 1891), 1:35
7 Treaty 20, in ibid., 1:48, 49
8 Minutes of a Council, 5 Nov. 1818, 363
9 Claus Family Fonds, vol. 11, 94–6, reel C-1480, Minutes of a Council held at Amherstburg, 16 Oct. 1818

10 *Indian Treaties and Surrenders,* 1:65

11 Robert J. Surtees, 'Indian Land Cessions in Ontario, 1763–1862: The Evolution of a System' (Ph.D. diss., Carleton University, 1982), 173–4

12 Record of a Council at River Credit, 27, 28, and 29 Oct. 1818

13 Minutes of a Council, 5 Nov. 1818, 363–4

14 Claus Family Fonds, vol. 11, 101–3, reel C-1480, Minutes of an Indian Council, 17 Oct. 1818

15 *Indian Treaties and Surrenders,* 1:1–42, for pre–War of 1812 treaties; and 1:42–86, for 1815–31 agreements. The ratio of indentures to agreements in the latter group is higher than in the former.

16 Claus Family Fonds, vol. 11, 94–6, reel C-1480, Minutes of a Council at Amherstburg, 16 Oct. 1818. As noted above, Chief Buckquaquet made a similar request a bit later.

17 Archives of Ontario (AO), F 4337-11-0-8, reel M2607, Gun Shot Treaty – various, statements of 'Capt. Paudash, Capt. Nott, Capt Cow, [and] Mr. Crow.'

18 J. Michael Thoms, 'Ojibwa Fishing Grounds: A History of Ontario Fisheries Law, Science, and the Sportsmen's Challenge to Aboriginal Treaty Rights, 1650–1900' (Ph.D. diss., University of British Columbia, 2004) 137, 138, 143, 145. Dr Thoms concludes that Crown negotiators misrepresented what had been agreed to orally.

19 Surtees, 'Land Cessions,' 206

20 See, for example, Treaty 27½, 1825, in *Indian Treaties and Surrenders,* 1:66.

21 Surtees, 'Land Cessions,' 172–3, 178

22 2 Geo. IV, c. 10, s. 8; in Thoms, 'Ojibwa Fishing Grounds,' 150

23 RG 10, vol. 1011, reel T-1456, petition to Lieutenant-Governor Maitland, 11 Nov. 1825; ibid., petition to the House of Assembly, 31 Jan. 1829; *Revised Statutes of Upper Canada, 1792–1840,* 1829, c. 3, in *Pre-1868 Legislation Concerning Indians: A Selected and Indexed Collection,* ed. Thomas Isaac (Saskatoon: Native Law Centre, 1993), 83–4; Donald B. Smith, 'Jones, Peter (Kahkeqaquonaby),' *Dictionary of Canadian Biography (DCB),* vol. 7, on-line edition, accessed 5 Oct. 2007

24 Sir G. Murray to Sir J. Kempt, 25 Jan. 1830, *British Parliamentary Papers* (Irish University Press Series), 'Correspondence and Other Papers Relating to Aboriginal Tribes in British Possessions,' 1834, no. 617, 88

25 Francis Bond Head, *A Narrative,* 2nd edn (London: John Murray, 1839), Appendix A, 'Memorandum on the Aborigines of North America,' to Lord Glenelg, 20 Nov. 1836, 1–2

26 Ibid., 3

27 Bond Head to Lord Glenelg, 20 Aug. 1836, in *British Parliamentary Papers: Correspondence Returns and Other Papers Relating to Canada and to the Indian Problem Therein, 1839, Colonies Canada,* Irish University Press Series, vol. 12 (Shannon: Irish University Press, 1969), 122–3. This version of Head's speech has the signature of chiefs and a wampum attached. The version in *Indian Treaties and Surrenders,* 1:112, has the chiefs' signatures, but no reference to the wampum. Cooperative archivists at the Public Record Office, Kew, undertook an unsuccessful search for the wampum that accompanied Head's dispatch.

28 Head's address, in *Indian Treaties and Surrenders,* 1:113

29 Surtees, 'Land Cessions,' 218–19

30 For an example of Saugeen protest, see University of Western Ontario Archives (UWO), Wawanosh Family Papers, box 4381, file I-3-4, Petition to Governor General Metcalfe, n.d., signed 'by order of the Council' by 'Joseph Sawyer, President; George Copway, Vice President; John Jones Secretary.'

31 RG 10, vol. 612, 115–19, reel C-13,385, 'Petition of Chief Chingwauk,' 10 June 1846

32 Alan Knight and Janet E. Chute, 'A Visionary on the Edge: Allan Macdonell and the Championing of Native Resource Rights,' in *With Good Intentions: Euro-Canadian and Aboriginal Relations in Colonial Canada,* ed. Celia Haig-Brown and David A. Nock (Vancouver: University of British Columbia Press, 2006), 88

33 Arthur J. Ray, Jim Miller, and Frank Tough, *Bounty and Benevolence: A History of Saskatchewan Treaties* (Montreal and Kingston: McGill-Queen's University Press, 2000), 35–6; UWO Archives, Alexander Vidal Papers, box 4437, typed copy of Report of A. Vidal and T.G. Anderson to the Governor General in Council, 5 Dec. 1849, 8–9

34 Knight and Chute, 'Visionary,' 90–4

35 Vidal Papers, box 4437, folder of letters to father 1833, 1849, A. Vidal to My dear Father, 17 Oct. 1849; ibid., Report of Commissioners Vidal and Anderson, 1–2

36 Report of Commissioners Vidal and Anderson, 4

37 Toronto Reference Library, Baldwin Room, S 27 Thomas Gummersall Anderson Papers, folder 7, doc. 40 (draft), Rev. Gustavus Anderson's report to his bishop, n.d.

38 Surtees, 'Land Cessions,' 252, 255n

39 AO, Aemilius Irving Papers, F1027-1-2, item 23/32/9, reel MS 1780, statements made in March 1893 by Alexis Biron and interpreted and recorded

by John Driver, interpreter, of Sault Ste Marie, 27 May 1893; and ibid., statement by Joshua Biron 'last year, 1892,' interpreted and recorded by John Driver, 27 May 1893

40 Elgin to Grey, 23 Nov. 1849, in *The Elgin-Grey Papers, 1846–1852*, 4 vols, ed. A.G. Doughty (Ottawa: King's Printer, 1937), 4:1485–6

41 Julia Jarvis, 'Robinson, William Benjamin,' *DCB*, vol. 10, on-line edition, accessed 7 Nov. 2006

42 Appendix A to Report of Commissioners Vidal and Anderson, Extracts from notes taken at the conference with the Indians at Fort William, Lake Superior, Sep. 25th, and 26th, 1849

43 Aemilius Irving Papers, F1027-1-2, item 27/32/8, typed copy of W.B. Robinson to Col. Bruce, Superintendent General of Indian Affairs, 24 Sept. 1850; AO, F 44, Acc. 30212, W.B. Robinson Diaries, entries of 4–7 Sept. 1850

44 Robinson to Bruce, 24 Sept. 1850; W.B. Robinson Diaries, entries of 9 and 11 Sept. 1850

45 Robinson to Bruce, 24 Sept. 1850

46 Robinson to Bruce, 24 Sept. 1850; Robinson Superior and Robinson Huron Treaties, in Alexander Morris, *The Treaties of Canada with the Indians of Manitoba and the North-West Territories* (1880; reprint, Saskatoon: Fifth House, 1991), 303–6

47 I have benefited greatly from a paper by Janet Chute, 'Moving on Up: The Rationale for, and Consequences of, the Escalation Clause in the Robinson Treaties,' which Dr Chute kindly allowed me to use.

48 Quoted in 'From the Anishinabek, the Ojibway, Ottawa, Potowatomi and Algonquin Nations to the Parliament of the Dominon of Canada,' *Ontario Indian*, 3, no. 12 (1980): 25

49 Ray, Miller, and Tough, *Bounty and Benevolence*, 44

50 Robinson to Bruce, 24 Sept. 1850

51 Manitoulin Island Treaty, in *Indian Treaties and Surrenders*, 1:235

52 Suzanne Zeller, 'McDougall, William,' *DCB*, vol. 13, on-line edition, accessed 10 Nov. 2006

53 Robert J. Surtees, *Treaty Research Report: Manitoulin Island Treaties* (Ottawa: Treaties and Historical Research Centre, Indian and Northern Affairs Canada, 1986), on-line version, unpaginated, accessed 10 Nov. 2006

54 Proceedings of a Council at Manitowaning, Manitoulin Island, 5 Oct. 1861, in Province of Canada, *Sessional Papers* (63), 1863, unpaginated

55 Ibid.

56 Douglas Leighton, 'Assiginack, Jean Baptiste,' *DCB*, vol. 9, on-line edition, accessed 15 Nov. 2006

57 William McDougall to cabinet, 3 Nov. 1862, in Morris, *Treaties,* 23
58 *Indian Treaties and Surrenders* 1:235–6
59 W.B. Robinson Diaries, entries of 1 May ('Immediately after issue of the presents ...'), 4 Sept. ('Cpt. [*sic*] Ironsides came with the Indians in the Gore & brot. [sic] the presents for Peau de Chat & those who were with him ...'), and 5 Sept. ('Agreed to this [delay in negotiations] & after giving orders to Capt. Ironsides respecting provisions, went to my lodgings'); Robert J. Surtees, *Treaty Research Report: The Robinson Treaties (1850)* (Ottawa: Treaties and Historical Research Centre, Indian and Northern Affairs Canada, 1986), on-line version, unpaginated, accessed 17 Nov. 2006
60 Thoms, 'Ojibwa Fishing Grounds,' 222–4

5: Prelude to the Western Treaties

1 Library and Archives Canada (LAC), RG 10, Records of the Department of Indian Affairs, vol. 448, reel C-9644, 184324-30, Head Chief of Fort Frances Indians at a Council, 20 June 1870, quoted in Wemyss S. Simpson to Joseph Howe, 19 Aug. 1870
2 This account of the politics of the Union is based on: J.-C. Bonenfant, 'Cartier, Sir George-Etienne,' *Dictionary of Canadian Biography* (*DCB*), vol. 10, on-line edition, accessed 28 Nov. 2006; J.M.S. Careless, *The Union of the Canadas: The Growth of Canadian Institutions, 1841–1857* (Toronto: McClelland and Stewart, 1967); Careless, *Brown of the Globe,* 2 vols (Toronto: Macmillan, 1959, 1963); D.G. Creighton, *John A. Macdonald: The Young Politician* (Toronto: Macmillan, 1952); Creighton, *The Road to Confederation: The Emergence of Modern Canada, 1863–1867* (Toronto: Macmillan, 1964); Jacques Monet, *The Last Cannon Shot: A Study of French-Canadian Nationalism, 1837–1850* (Toronto: University of Toronto Press, 1969); W.L. Morton, *The Critical Years: The Union of British North America, 1857–1873* (Toronto: McClelland and Stewart, 1964); Brian J. Young, *George-Etienne Cartier: Montreal Bourgeois* (Montreal: McGill-Queen's University Press, 1981); Suzanne Zeller, 'McDougall, William,' *DCB,* vol. 13, on-line edition, accessed 10 Nov. 2006
3 Goldwin Smith, *Canada and the Canadian Question* (Toronto: Hunter, Rose & Co., 1891), 143
4 The precise terms on which the Reform-Conservative coalition was formed were that the cabinet would seek a solution for Canada's constitutional impasse in either a general union of BNA or a federal union of the existing Province of Canada. By the summer of 1864, it was clear that a general

BNA union was possible, and the alternative of federating the existing Province was set aside.

5 British North America Act, in *Documenting Canada: A History of Modern Canada in Documents*, ed. Dave De Brou and Bill Waiser (Saskatoon: Fifth House, 1992), 11, 17

6 A.I. Silver, *The French-Canadian Idea of Confederation, 1864–1900* (Toronto: University of Toronto Press, 1982), 67–76, 138

7 Archives of Ontario, F4337-11-0-9, reel m 2607, Grandes Oreilles's speech, 1814 (transcript)

8 The Selkirk Treaty, in Alexander Morris, *The Treaties of Canada with the Indians of Manitoba and the North-West Territories* (1880; reprint, Saskatoon: Fifth House, 1991), 13–15, 299–301

9 Frank Tough, *'As Their Natural Resources Fail': Native Peoples and the Economic History of Northern Manitoba, 1870–1930* (Vancouver: University of British Columbia Press, 1996), 44–58

10 E.E. Rich, *The History of the Hudson's Bay Company, 1670–1870*, 2 vols (London: Hudson's Bay Record Society, 1958–9), 2:841, 847. See also Arthur J. Ray, *The Canadian Fur Trade in the Industrial Age* (Toronto: University of Toronto Press, 1990), 9–10.

11 Rich, *Hudson's Bay Company*, 2:848

12 Arthur J. Ray and Donald B. Freeman, eds, *'Give Us Good Measure': An Economic Analysis of Relations between the Indians and the Hudson's Bay Company before 1763* (Toronto: University of Toronto Press, 1978), 22

13 Edward Ahenakew, *Voices of the Plains Cree*, ed. Ruth M. Buck (Toronto: McClelland and Stewart, 1973), 72–3

14 LAC, MG 17, B 2, Church Missionary Society Records, reel A-86, Cowley's entry of 4 May 1852. I became aware of this source from reading Winona L. Stevenson, 'The Church Missionary Society's Red River Mission and the Emergence of a Native Ministry, 1820–1860, with a Case Study of Charles Pratt of Touchwood Hills' (M.A. thesis, University of British Columbia, 1988), Appendix 1, 189.

15 Henry John Moberly, *When Fur Was King* (Toronto: J.M. Dent, 1929), 72, 74. More generally, see Hugh A. Dempsey, 'Western Plains Trade Ceremonies,' *Western Canadian Journal of Anthropology*, 3, no. 1 (1972): 29–33, esp. 31–2.

16 Gerald Friesen, *The Canadian Prairies: A History* (Toronto: University of Toronto Press, 1984), 97–9

17 Sylvia Van Kirk, *'Many Tender Ties': Women in Fur-Trade Society in Western Canada, 1670–1870* (Winnipeg: Watson & Dwyer, [1980]), chapters 7 and 8

18 Frits Pannekoek, *A Snug Little Flock: The Social Origins of the Riel Resistance of 1869–70* (Winnipeg: Watson & Dwyer, 1991), 77, chapter 7, and 159–62; Friesen, *Canadian Prairies*, 94–7

19 John S. Milloy, *The Plains Cree: Trade, Diplomacy and War, 1790 to 1870* (Winnipeg: University of Manitoba Press, 1988), esp. chapters 6–9

20 Janet E. Chute and Alan Knight, 'Taking Up the Torch: Simon J. Dawson and the Upper Great Lakes Native Resource Campaign of the 1860s and 1870s,' in *With Good Intentions: Euro-Canadian and Aboriginal Relations in Colonial Canada*, ed. Celia Haig-Brown and Davd A. Nock (Vancouver: University of British Columbia Press, 2006), 109–10

21 Lewis H. Thomas, "Riel, Louis," *DCB*, vol. 11, on-line edition, accessed 6 Dec. 2006. Riel's mother's surname is sometimes rendered Lagimonière.

22 An Act for the Temporary Government of Rupert's Land and the North-Western Territory When United with Canada, in De Brou and Waiser, eds, *Documenting Canada*, 25

23 W.L. Morton, Introduction, *Alexander Begg's Red River Journal*, ed.W.L. Morton (1956; reprint, New York: Greenwood Press, 1969), 62–3, 69–70, and 72

24 George T. Denison, *The Struggle for Imperial Unity: Recollections and Experiences* (Toronto: Macmillan, 1909), chapters 3–4; Norman Shrive, *Charles Mair: Literary Nationalist* (Toronto: University of Toronto Press, 1965), 109–11, 119; Carl Berger, *The Sense of Power: Studies in the Ideas of Canadian Imperialism, 1867–1914* (Toronto: University of Toronto Press, 1970), 57–9

25 De Brou and Waiser, eds, *Documenting Canada*, 33

26 Canada, Parliament, *Debates of the House of Commons*, 4 May 1870, 1353

27 Imperial Order in Council, 23 June 1870, in De Brou and Waiser, eds, *Documenting Canada*, 41

28 Simpson's report of a Council, 20 June 1870, near Fort Frances, in Simpson to Howe, 19 Aug. 1870

29 Paul Tennant, *Aboriginal People and Politics: The Indian Land Question in British Columbia, 1849–1989* (Vancouver: University of British Columbia Press, 1991), 18–25

30 For the Fraser gold rush and agreements, see Daniel Patrick Marshall, 'Claiming the Land: Indians, Goldseekers, and the Rush to British Columbia' (Ph.D. diss., University of British Columbia, 2000), chapter 6. I am grateful to my colleague Keith Carlson, who acquainted me with this source. For an example of making an agreement under duress, see H.M. Snyder, Captain of the Pike Guards, to Governor James Douglas, 28 Aug. 1858, in *Native Studies Review*, 11, no. 1 (1997): 140–5. See also Donald Hauka, *McGowan's War* (Vancouver: New Star Books, 2003), 84–93, 97–9.

31 Terms of Union, articles 13 (Indian affairs) and 11 (railway), in De Brou and Waiser, eds, *Documenting Canada*, 55, 54

6: The Southern Numbered Treaties, 1871–1877

1 Cree chief Ahtahkakoop in chiefs' caucus, Fort Carlton, August 1876, in Peter Erasmus, *Buffalo Days and Nights*, ed. Irene Spry (1976; reprint, Calgary: Glenbow Alberta Institute / Fifth House, 1999), 250

2 John Hines, *The Red Indians of the Plains: Thirty Years' Missionary Experience in the Saskatchewan* (Toronto: McClelland & Stewart, 1916), 79; Deanna Christenson, *Ahtahkakoop: The Epic Account of a Plains Cree Head Chief, His People, and Their Struggle for Survival, 1816–1896* (Shell Lake, SK: Ahtahkakoop Publishing, 2000), 159–70

3 Hines, *Red Indians of the Plains*, 80–2

4 *The Manitoban*, 1 July 1871; Department of Indian Affairs, *Annual Report for 1871*, 8, 10–11

5 Provincial Archives of Manitoba (PAM), MG 12, B 1, Alexander Morris Papers, box 6, file 1265, petition of Blackfoot chiefs to Lieutenant-Governor Morris, n.d. The Blackfoot Council took place in the autumn of 1875, but the written petition did not reach Red River until the summer of 1876.

6 Sweet Grass, Kihewin, The Little Hunter, and Kiskion (Short Tail) to Lieutenant-Governor Adams Archibald, April 1871, in Alexander Morris, *The Treaties of Canada with the Indians of Manitoba and the North-West Territories* (1880; reprint, Saskatoon: Fifth House, 1991), 170–1. The Little Hunter asked Archibald to 'treat me as a brother, that is, as a Great Chief,' and Kiskion said, 'I want you to pity me, and I want help to cultivate the ground for myself and descendants.' The petition was composed for the chiefs and transmitted to Red River by W.J. Christie, the HBC's chief factor for the Saskatchewan District.

7 D.G. Creighton, *Sir John A. Macdonald: The Old Chieftain* (Toronto: Macmillan, 1955), 254. Macdonald was quoting the Austrian chancellor, Metternich, who in 1814 dismissed Italy as a mere 'geographical expression' because it was divided politically into many states.

8 Morris, *Treaties*, 316–17. More generally concerning the role of the Crown in western treaty negotiations, see J.R. Miller, '"I will accept the Queen's hand": First Nations Leaders and the Image of the Crown in the Prairie Treaties,' in J.R. Miller, *Reflections on Native-Newcomer Relations: Selected Essays* (Toronto: University of Toronto Press, 2004), 242–66; and Sarah Carter, '"Your Great Mother across the Salt Sea": Prairie First Nations, the British

Monarchy and the Vice-Regal Connection to 1900,' *Manitoba History*, no. 48 (Autumn–Winter 2004–5): 38–9.

9　Library and Archives Canada (LAC), MG 26A, Sir John A. Macdonald Papers, vol. 252, 113998-4003, A. Morris to J.A. Macdonald, 16 Jan. 1873

10　Morris, *Treaties*, 67

11　Ibid., 359, 372; Glenbow Museum artwork 74.7.76, R.B. Nevitt, 'NWMP Camp at Treaty 7'

12　Morris Papers, box 5, item 1136, George McDougall to Alexander Morris, 23 Oct. 1875

13　Morris, *Treaties*, 316–60; Arthur J. Ray, Jim Miller, and Frank Tough, *Bounty and Benevolence: A History of Saskatchewan Treaties* (Montreal and Kingston: McGill-Queen's University Press, 2000), Tables A2–A8, 218–36

14　Morris, *Treaties*, 209, for Morris's words and McKay's services. For other references to the Great Spirit, see ibid., 90, 102, 221, 225; and ibid., 86, for Christie's comment at Fort Qu'Appelle in 1874. See also Harold Johnson, *Two Families: Treaties and Government* (Saskatoon: Purich Publishing, 2007). I have also benefited from reading a manuscript version of an article by Brendan Kelly, 'Three Uses of Christian Culture in the Numbered Treaties,' *Prairie Forum* (forthcoming). I am grateful to Brendan Kelly for providing me with a copy of his article.

15　Wemyss Simpson to Secretary of State for the Provinces [i.e., minister of Indian affairs], 3 Nov. 1871, in Morris, *Treaties*, 43

16　This remarkable group and their contributions have been surveyed in Allyson Stevenson, 'The Metis Cultural Brokers and the Western Numbered Treaties, 1869–1877' (M.A. thesis, University of Saskatchewan, 2004).

17　Stevenson, 'Metis Cultural Brokers,' 149. James McKay's elevated status (see Alan R. Turner, 'McKay, James,' *Dictionary of Canadian Biography* [*DCB*], vol. 10, on-line edition, accessed 13 Dec. 2006) is consistent with this interpretation, although the marginal status of Potts and Bird is not. Peter Erasmus was more petit bourgeois than successful merchant. If class-motivated, the behaviour of this group appears to reflect that of the successful Métis farmers and business people who had stayed aloof from the Red River Resistance in the late autumn of 1869.

18　This account is based on the following sources: dispatches of A. Archibald and Wemyss Simpson in Morris, *Treaties*, 31–9; *The Manitoban*, 1 and 29 July, 5 and 12 Aug. 1871, and 18 Oct. 1873; and Ray, Miller, and Tough, *Bounty and Benevolence*, chapter 5.

19　Simpson's dispatch, 3 Nov. 1871, in Morris, *Treaties*, 39–40

20　The government text of Treaty 1 is found in Morris, *Treaties*, 313–16; the verbal promises concerning agricultural assistance in Simpson's dispatch of 3 Nov. 1871, ibid., 39–40; and Archibald's reassurance about continuing hunting rights, ibid., 29.

21 Morris Papers, box 6, item 1299, Wemyss Simpson to E.A. Meredith, 2 Aug. 1876

22 Morris Papers, box 5, item 1033, David Laird to A. Morris, 7 July 1875, enclosing Order in Council of 30 April 1875. Although the government pretended to be acting unilaterally out of goodwill, the minister of the interior instructed Morris to obtain approval from the chiefs: 'It is left entirely to your discretion to determine as to the best mode of securing the formal acceptance by the Chiefs of the terms offered by the Order in Council, but, assuming that you will think it desirable to obtain such acceptance over their own signatures, a copy of the Order is sent herewith specially intended to be signed by them' (ibid., 4). Concerning medals distributed during 1870s treaty negotiations, see Melvill Allan Jamieson, *Medals Awarded to North American Chiefs, 1714–1922* (London: Spink & Son Ltd, 1936), 47–55.

23 Morris, *Treaties*, 59, 62

24 Jean Friesen, 'Morris, Alexander,' *DCB*, vol. 11, on-line version, accessed 19 Dec. 2006. Morris was, of course, the author of *Treaties*. The quotation is from Morris's 1858 lecture 'Nova Britannia,' reprinted in *Nova Britannia; or Our New Canadian Dominion Foreshadowed* (Toronto: Hunter, Rose, 1884), 32.

25 Morris, *Treaties*, 74 (owe much to the Métis), 69 (request to include Métis)

26 Ibid., 61–5. Frank Tough provides the explanation for the northerly groups' concern in *Bounty and Benevolence*, 73. Professor Tough drafted the chapter on Treaties 1, 2, and 3.

27 Morris, *Treaties*, 322–5; Ray, Miller, and Tough, *Bounty and Benevolence*, Table A23, 220–2

28 *The Manitoban*, 29 July and 12 Aug. 1871

29 Morris, *Treaties*, 74: 'I will now show you a medal that was given to those who made a treaty at Red River by the Commissioner. *He* said it was silver, but *I* do not think it is. I should be ashamed to carry it on my breast over my heart. I think it would disgrace the Queen, my mother, to wear her image on so base a metal as this. [Here the Chief held up the medal and struck it with the back of his knife. The result was anything but the "true ring," and made every man ashamed of the petty meanness that had been practised.] Let the medals you give us be of silver – medals that shall be worthy of the position our Mother the Queen occupies.'

30 Morris, *Treaties*, 75

31 Ibid., 101–2 (The Gambler), 106 (Pasqua)

32 Ibid., 92–3

33 Ibid., 93

34 Ibid., 321–2, 333; and James Morrison, 'Treaty One of 1871: Background, Context and Understanding of the Parties,' Opinion Report for Public Interest Law Centre, Winnipeg (unpublished report, 2003), 82, 120–1. I am most grateful to Jim Morrison for providing me with a copy of this excellent study.

35 Treaty 4, in Morris, *Treaties*, 332

36 Ray, Miller, and Tough, *Bounty and Benevolence*, 129. Tough drafted the chapter on Treaty 5.

37 Morris Papers, box 4, item 783, Petition of 'the Christian Indians of Rossville and Nelson River,' 25 June 1874

38 PAM, MG 12, E 1, John C. Schultz Papers, box 19, Letterbook (Keewatin), 25 Oct. 1888 to 26 Nov. 1890, 366–73, 'Notes of Indian Council at Treaty Rock Beren's River,' 12 July 1890; Morris, *Treaties*, 148, 149 (severing reserve issue), 147, 148, and 150 (firing salutes), and 346 (hunting and fishing). Treaty 5 also contained (ibid., 345–6) the familiar clause by which 'Her Majesty agrees to maintain schools for instruction in such reserves hereby made as to her Government of the Dominion of Canada may seem advisable, whenever the Indians of the reserve shall desire it.'

39 Morris, *Treaties*, 162; Frank Tough, 'Economic Aspects of Aboriginal Title in Northern Manitoba: Treaty 5 Adhesions and Metis Scrip,' *Manitoba History*, no. 15 (1988): 3–16.

40 Erasmus, *Buffalo Days and Nights*, 235–6 (invitation) and 246–50 (caucus)

41 Morris, *Treaties*, 197–8

42 Ibid., 177, 185 (food relief), 178 (Morris's view), and 355 (medicine chest clause)

43 Ibid., 231 ('cunning' and hunting and fishing), 236–7 ('loud ejaculations'), 239 ('medals, flags and uniforms')

44 Ibid., 242 ('do not sign') and 240 ('rope about my neck')

45 Treaty 7 Elders and Tribal Council with Walter Hildebrandt, Dorothy First Rider, and Sarah Carter, *The True Spirit and Original Intent of Treaty 7* (Montreal and Kingston: McGill-Queen's University Press, 1996), *passim*; Morris, *Treaties*, 368–74

46 Morris, *Treaties*, 258. I would like to thank Dr Barry Cottam for pointing this out.

47 Ibid., 272

48 Ibid., 371 (cattle) and 258 (hunting bison)

49 Ibid., 370 ('medal and flag'), 371 ('teachers'), 361–2 (Bob Tail)

50 Johnson, *Two Families*, 13. See also ibid., 27–33.

7: The Northern Numbered Treaties, 1899–1921

1 Charles Mair, *Through the Mackenzie Basin: An Account of the Signing of Treaty No. 8 and the Scrip Commission* (1908; reprint, Edmonton: University of Alberta Press and Edmonton & District Historical Society, 1999), 67

2 J.R. Miller, *Lethal Legacy: Current Native Controversies in Canada* (Toronto: McClelland and Stewart, 2004), 128 (Northwest Angle); A. Morris, *The Treaties of Canada with the Indians of Manitoba and the North-West Territories* (1880; reprint, Saskatoon: Fifth House, 1991), 353 (Treaty 6 text); Deanna Christenson, *Ahtahkakoop:The Epic Account of a Plains Cree Head Chief, His People, and Their Struggle for Survival,1816–1896* (Shell Lake, SK: Ahtahkakoop Publishing, 2000), 353–7; Charles Aeneas Shaw, *Tales of a Pioneer Surveyor*, ed. Raymond Hull (Toronto: Longman, 1970), 105 (surveyor's experience)

3 Glenbow Archives, Edgar Dewdney Fonds, Series 13, Journal, entry of 17 July 1879, on-line, accessed 12 Jan. 2007

4 Maureen Lux, *Medicine That Walks: Disease, Medicine, and Canadian Plains Native People, 1880–1940* (Toronto: University of Toronto Press, 2001), chapter 4

5 John L. Tobias, 'Canada's Subjugation of the Plains Cree, 1879–1885,' in *Sweet Promises: A Reader on Indian-White Relations in Canada*, ed. J.R. Miller (Toronto: University of Toronto Press, 1991), 212–40, esp. 216–25

6 R.C. Macleod, *The North West Mounted Police and Law Enforcement, 1873–1905* (Toronto: University of Toronto Press, 1976), 8; R.C. Macleod and Heather Rollason [Driscoll], '"Restrain the Lawless Savages': Native Defendants in the Criminal Courts of the North-West Territories, 1878–1885,' *Journal of Historical Sociology*, 10, no. 2 (1997): 157–83

7 Library and Archives Canada (LAC), RG 10, Records of the Department of Indian Affairs, vol. 3768, file 33,642, reel C-10122, Notes of Councils at Fort Qu'Appelle and Battleford, 1881

8 RG 10, vol. 3697, file 15,423, reel C-10122, J.A. Macrae to Edgar Dewdney, 25 Aug. 1884

9 Tobias, 'Subjugation of the Plains Cree'; Blair Stonechild and Bill Waiser, *Loyal till Death: Indians and the North-West Rebellion* (Calgary: Fifth House, 1997)

10 My understanding of scrip has benefited from reading Camilla Augustus, 'The Scrip Solution: The North West Metis Scrip Policy, 1885–1887' (M.A. thesis, University of Calgary, 2005); and Nicole O'Byrne, 'Legislative History of Scrip' (unpublished paper, n.d.). I am grateful to Ms Augustus and Ms O'Byrne, who generously provided me with copies of their works.

11 RG 10, vol. 3708, file 19,502, reel C-10124, Dieudonne Desjarlais to Edgar Dewdney, 4 Feb. 1890

12 RG 10, vol. 3033, file 235,225-1, reel C-11314, J.A. Macrae to Clifford Sifton, 3 June 1901. Sifton was minister of the interior and superintendent general of Indian affairs.

13 RG 10, vol. 4009, file 241,209-1, reel C-10171, L. Vankoughnet to John A. Macdonald, 5 Nov. 1883

14 Canada, *Sessional Papers (No. 28) 1910*, 182–3, patrol report of Sgt Richard Field, Jan. 1909. At Resolution, Field noted: 'Great scarcity of fur reported by the traders, though moose and caribou are very numerous, the Indians being well supplied with meat.' On the trail between Fort Providence and Fort Simpson, however, Field encountered a number of groups 'in a shocking state of destitution; they were subsisting totally on fish and very few of these ...' An old couple 'had eaten nothing then for five days, and were in such a weak condition that they could not move; they simply looked like skeletons.' 'We ... found the same state of starvation everywhere.'

15 RG 10, vol. 4009, file 241,209-1, D. Laird to J.D. McLean, 29 April 1904

16 This terminology derives from Thomas Flanagan, 'Adhesion to Canadian Indian Treaties and the Lubicon Lake Dispute,' *Canadian Journal of Law and Society*, 7, no. 2 (Fall 1992): 190–3. (Frank Tough, in conversation, suggested another set of appropriate terms: 'band adhesion' corresponding to 'internal adhesions,' and 'territorial adhesions' corresponding to 'external adhesions.') I am grateful to Dr Flanagan for providing me with a copy of his article.

17 RG 10, vol. 3787, file 42,239, reel C-10138, John Sinclair to D.W. Macdowall, 9 Aug. 1887; 'Department of Indian Affairs Annual Report 1889,' in Canada, *Sessional Papers (No 12) 1890*, xiii

18 This account depends on reports and correspondence by Commissioner A.G. Irvine, Rev. J. Mackay, and Indian Affairs employee A.N. McNeill in Canada, *Sessional Papers (No. 12) 1890*, xlii–xlix; 'Aski-Puko: The Land Alone. A Report of the Expected Effects of the Proposed Hydroelectric Installation at Wintego Rapids' (mimeograph, 1976); and Peter Goode, Joan Champ, and Leslie Amundson, *The Montreal Lake Region: Its History and Geography* (Saskatoon: Sentar Consultants, 1996), 22–4. I have also benefited from the insights of Christine Charmbury, 'The Treaty Six Adhesion at Montreal Lake: Negotiating for a Guaranteed Lifestyle,' research paper, HIST 859.3, 2005, University of Saskatchewan.

19 RG 10, vol. 3848, file 75,236-1, reel C-10149, L. Vankoughnet to cabinet, 7 Jan. 1891; and report of Privy Council, 26 Jan. 1891

20 RG 10, vol. 3848, file 75,236-1, J. Walker to C. Sifton, 30 Nov. 1897; ibid., F. White, 'Extract from a Report of the N.W.M. Police Stationed at Fort Smith,' 31 Oct. 1898. For the unrest that formed the background to Treaty 8, see Arthur J. Ray, Jim Miller, and Frank Tough, *Bounty and Benevolence: A History of Saskatchewan Treaties* (Monteal and Kingston: McGill-Queen's University Press, 2000), 156–8; Arthur J. Ray, 'Treaty 8: A British Columbia Anomaly,' *BC Studies*, no. 123 (Autumn 1999): 24–8.

21 RG 10, vol. 3848, file 75,236–1, Clerk of the Privy Council to the Lieutenant-Governor of British Columbia, 6 Dec. 1898. In 'Treaty 8,' Professor Ray reports (36–8) that there is no evidence in provincial records that the BC cabinet took any action on the communication. He infers that Victoria chose to maintain a diplomatic silence, neither becoming involved directly in treaty negotiations nor opposing the federal government's plans.

22 Treaty Elders of Saskatchewan, with Harold Cardinal and Walter Hildebrant, *Our Dream Is That Our Peoples Will One Day Be Clearly Recognized as Nations* (Calgary: University of Calgary Press, 2000), 64

23 Canada, *Treaty No. 8 Made June 21 1899 and Adhesions, Reports, Etc.*, Report of Commissioners for Treaty 8 (Ottawa: Queen's Printer, 1899), 5–6. The First Nations also asked for medical assistance.

24 Christine Mary Smillie, 'The People Left Out of Treaty 8' (M.A. thesis, University of Saskatchewan, 2005); John Goddard, *Last Stand of the Lubicon Cree* (Vancouver/Toronto: Douglas & McIntyre, 1991), esp. chapter 2

25 O.C. Edwards, *On the North Trail: The Treaty 8 Diary of O.C. Edwards*, ed. D. Leonard and B. Whalen (Calgary: Alberta Records Publication Board, 1998), 52

26 As the research of Frank Tough and his team at the University of Alberta has shown, scrip sellers and buyers also colluded to alienate scrip issued in the name of children, even though such a transfer was theoretically illegal. See Linda Goyette, 'The X Files,' *Canadian Geographic*, March/April 2003, 70–80.

27 RG 10, vol. 2289, file 57,641, reel C-11196, Louis Espagnol to 'Mon cher Monsieur,' 15 Dec. 1884; my translation of : 'toutes mes vieux sauvages qui était dans l'habitude de chasser ici près sont dans un grand besoins. Les trappeurs nous ont tous voler nos Castors, ils chassent et ne prennent rien, et sont trop vieux pour allez au loin ... ils se joignent tous à moi pour vous prier de nous assister.'

28 Charles Camsell, *Son of the North* (Toronto: Ryerson Press, 1954), 172–3

29 J.A. Macrae, memo for Superintendent General of Indian Affairs, 3 June 1901

30 D.C. Scott, S. Stewart, and D.G. MacMartin to the Superintendent General

of Indian Affairs, 6 Nov. 1905, in *The James Bay Treaty: Treaty No. 9*, INAC on-line version, accessed 17 Jan. 2007, 1, quoting *Statutes of Canada* 54–55 Vic., chap. V, s. 6

31 RG 10, vol. 3033, file 235-225(1), reel C-11314, F. Pedley to J.J. Foy, 8 May 1905, and draft federal Order-in-Council

32 *The James Bay Treaty*, INAC on-line version, accessed 19 Jan. 2007, 3. The government text version: 'And His Majesty the King hereby agrees with the said Indians that they shall have the right to pursue their usual vocations of hunting, trapping and fishing throughout the tract surrendered as heretofore described, subject to such regulations as may from time to time be made by the government of the country, acting under the authority of His Majesty, and saving and excepting such tracts as may be required or taken up from time to time for settlement, mining, lumbering, trading or other purposes' (INAC on-line version, accessed 20 Jan. 2007). John S. Long, 'How the Commissioners Explained Treaty Number Nine to the Ojibway and Cree in 1905,' *Ontario History*, 98, no. 2 (Spring 2006), esp. 15–21, 25–9, provides a careful analysis of the written commissioners' report and their diary accounts, concluding that far more was promised orally than the written record suggests. Samuel Stewart's journal, 21 August 1905: 'As usual, the point on which the Indians desired full information was as to the effect the treaty would have on their hunting and fishing rights. When assured that these would not be taken from them, they expressed much pleasure and then willingness to sign the treaty, which was accordingly done, and the signatures duly witnessed' (RG 10, vol. 11, 399, reel T-6924, 126). See also Queen's University Archives, D.G. MacMartin diary, 25 July and 21 Aug. 1905.

33 MacMartin diary, 1905, entry of 19 July 1905

34 See MacMartin diary, *passim*

35 *The James Bay Treaty*, 4–5; RG 10, vol. 1028, reel T-1460, D.C. Scott's diary, 39, 12 July 1905; Stewart diary, 39–40, 12 July 1905. See also MacMartin diary, entry of 12 July 1905 *re* Missabay's speech: 'the plot of his speech' at the feast was 'that the white men were their friends, were good, had assisted them giving money and lands for their benefit ...'

36 Anthony Gulig, 'In Whose Interest? Government-Indian Relations in Northern Saskatchewan and Wisconsin, 1900–1940' (Ph.D. diss., University of Saskatchewan, 1997), 45–8

37 LAC, RG 18, Records of the Mounted Police, vol. 128, file 37-97, S/Sgt. S. Hetherington to Officer Commanding Fort Saskatchewan, 11 July 1897. The policeman believed the attitude was attributable in part 'to the fear of the Fishery and Game Laws being fully enforced, and also the bad influ-

ence of a number of tough half-breeds, some of whom have been in the hands of the Police.' See also ibid., S/Sgt. S. Hetherington to Officer Commanding Fort Saskatchewan, 14 Sept. 1897.

38 Ray, Miller, and Tough, *Bounty and Benevolence*, 171

39 Chief William Apesis, Peter Dodson, and the Elders of Birch Narrows, Buffalo River, Canoe Lake, and English River, *In Their Own Land: Treaty Ten and the Canoe Lake, Clear Lake, and English River Bands* (Saskatoon: Office of the Treaty Commissioner, 2007), 14n

40 Chief Apesis, in Dodson et al., *In Their Own Land*, 21

41 Report of Commissioner McKenna, 18 Jan. 1907, INAC on-line version, accessed 23 Jan. 2007

42 Dodson et al., *In Their Own Land*, 28

43 Report of Commissioner McKenna, 18 Jan. 1907

44 Dodson et al., *In Their Own Land*, 30

45 *Treaty No. 11 (June 27, 1921) and Adhesion (July 17, 1922) with Reports, etc.* (1927; reprint, Ottawa: Queen's Printer, 1956), 3–5, INAC on-line version, accessed 23 Jan. 2007

46 Ibid., 3. Treaty 11 promised 'each band shall receive once and for all equipment for hunting, fishing and trapping to the value of fifty dollars for each family of such band, and that there shall be distributed annually among the Indians equipment, such as twine for nets, ammunition and trapping to the value of three dollars per head for each Indian who continues to follow the vocation of hunting, fishing and trapping' (ibid., 7).

47 René Fumoleau, *As Long As This Land Shall Last: A History of Treaty 8 and Treaty 11, 1870–1939*, 2nd edn (Calgary: University of Calgary Press, 2004), 218–19. Victor Lafferty served as interpreter in 1921 (ibid., 217n). Father Fumoleau explains (xxi) when the interviews were conducted; his own research began in 1971 (R. Fumoleau to J.R. Miller, 13 Feb. 1978, in author's possession). The account continued:
    John Farcy: The Commissioner said, 'This land shall be as it is, you shall keep on living on it as before ...'
    Michel Landry: The commissioner went on to say: 'As long as the earth is still here there shall be no more restrictions placed on the Indians in regard to hunting, fishing, etc.' The chief said: 'You people say things like that but you lie, so you better put it down on paper.' The commissioner returned to mention the sun and the river and said the government will not run back on their word. The Treaty was interpreted again and it was at the time satisfactory to the chief so he accepted the treaty.

8: The Hiatus in Treaty-Making, 1923–1975

1　D.C. Scott, evidence before special parliamentary committee on compulsory enfranchisement amendment to Indian Act, 1920, Library and Archives Canada (LAC), RG 10, Records of the Department of Indian Affairs, vol. 6810, file 470-2-3, pt. 7, reel C-8533

2　E.A. Cruikshank and A.F. Hunter, eds, *The Correspondence of the Honourable Peter Russell*, 3 vols (Toronto: Ontario Historical Society, 1935), 2:161. Yellowhead had opened the council by presenting two strings of white wampum and saying: 'Father, These strings which I hold in my hand are your words which we have received and have come down to know what it is you would have to say to us.' Russell reciprocated with tobacco and 'Seven Strings Black and White Wampum.'

3　'Report of R.V. Sinclair re The Chippewa Claim,' Appendix A of Robert J. Surtees, 'Treaty Research Report: The Williams Treaties (1923)' (1986), 21, Indian and Northern Affairs Canada on-line, accessed 20 June 2007. The Canada-Ontario agreement of April 1923 that authorized the inquiry and later treaty talks is found appended to *Copy of the Treaty Made October 31, 1923 between His Majesty the King and The Chippewa Indians of Christian Island, Georgina Island and Rama* (Indian Claims Commission website), 7–8, accessed 20 June 2007.

4　'Report of R.V. Sinclair,' 26–7

5　See, for example, RG 10, vol. 3722, file 24,161, reel C-10126, J. Semmens's report of request of Jeremiah Chubb, Chief of Oxford House, and John Wood, Chief of Island Lake, 26 Sept. 1901; ibid., file 249,462, part 5, reel C-10171, 1, Semmens's report of 17 Oct. 1907. Semmens was a former Methodist missionary.

6　Ken Hatt, 'The Northwest Scrip Commissions as Federal Policy – Some Initial Findings,' *Canadian Journal of Native Studies*, 3, no. 1 (1983): 119

7　RG 10, vol. 11,399, 131–97, reel T-6942, Samuel Stewart's journal of 1908 trip

8　Letter of 29 July 1915, in James Morrison, 'Treaty Research Report, Treaty No. 9,' Indian and Northern Affairs Canada, 1986, unpaginated, fourth section ('The Adhesion Period, 1907–1930'), at note 27

9　John S. Long, 'Treaty Making, 1930: Who Got What at Winisk?' *The Beaver*, 75, no. 1 (Feb./March 1995): 23–31

10　Quoted in ibid., 23

11　Francis Bond Head, *A Narrative*, 2nd edn (London: John Murray, 1839), Appendix A, 'Memorandum on the Aborigines of North America' to Lord Glenelg, 20 Nov. 1836, 3; Shinguakonse: 'From the Anishinabek, the

Ojibwa, Ottawa, Potowatomi and Algonquin Nations to the Parliament of the Dominion of Canada,' *Ontario Indian*, 3, no. 12 (1980): 25

12 See the superb analysis in Brian W. Dippie, *The Vanishing American: White Attitudes and U.S. Indian Policy* (Middleton, CT: Wesleyan University Press, 1982).

13 Diamond Jenness, *The Indians of Canada*, 7th edn (Toronto: University of Toronto Press, 1977; 1st edn, National Museum of Man, 1932), 264. Jenness continued: 'Some will endure only a few years longer, others, like the Eskimo, may last centuries.'

14 *The Canada Year Book 1911*, 2nd series (Ottawa: King's Printer, 1912), Table VII, 'Sex, Conjugal State, Birthplace, Race and Religion'; *The Canada Year Book 1914* (Ottawa: King's Printer, 1915), Table 15, 'Origins of the People in 1901 and 1911'; *The Canada Year Book 1922–23* (Ottawa: King's Printer, 1924), Table 21, 'Racial Origin of the Population by Provinces and Territories, 1921'; *The Canada Year Book 1933* (Ottawa: King's Printer, 1933), Table 19, 'Racial Origins of the Population'; *The Canada Year Book 1943–44* (Ottawa: King's Printer, 1944), Table 10, 'Racial Origins of the Population, 1871–1941.' *The Canada Year Book* used decennial census data. The inconsistency and unreliability of these data are explored in Gustave J. Goldmann, 'The Aboriginal Population and the Census: 120 Years of Information, 1871–1991,' paper presented at the International Union of Scientific Studies in Population Conference, Ottawa, 1993; and Gustave Goldmann and Andrew Siggner, 'Statistical Concepts of Aboriginal People and Factors Affecting the Counts in the Census and the Aboriginal Peoples Survey,' paper presented to the 1995 Symposium of the Federation of Canadian Demographers, Ottawa, 1995. I am enormously grateful to my colleagues Librarian David Smith and Canada Research Chair Evelyn J. Peters, who kindly supplied data and papers in an effort to reduce my innumeracy.

15 Scott, evidence before special parliamentary committee on compulsory enfranchisement, 1920

16 RG 10, vol. 3212, file 527, 787-4, reel C-11341, F.O. Loft, 26 Nov. 1919

17 RG 10, vol. 6810, file 470-2-3, reel C-8533, Scott's notes on 'Enfranchisement'

18 A fine summary of the issues and events is E. Brian Titley, *A Narrow Vision: Duncan Campbell Scott and the Administration of Indian Affairs in Canada* (Vancouver: University of British Columbia Press, 1986), chapter 7.

19 *Amodu Tijani v. The Secretary, Southern Provinces [Nigeria]*, 11 July 1921, http.//www.Nigeria-law.org/Amodu%20Tijani%20%20V%20The %20Secretary,%20Southern%20Provinces.htm, accessed 8 July 2007. I am

indebted to University of Saskatchewan Law Librarian Ken Whiteway and Law Reference Librarian Gregory Wurzel for providing me with the link to this decision. I first became aware of the case and its significance from an unpublished paper by Dr Bonny Ibhawoh of McMaster University, 'Negotiating Domination and Resistance: Indigenous People and Colonial Treaty Making in British West Africa and Upper Canada' (Canadian Historical Association Annual Meeting, 2007), 1–3. Whether or not the Department of Indian Affairs was aware of the decision and took it into account in setting policy is unclear. Brian Titley's public biography of D.C. Scott, *A Narrow Vision*, does not mention the case. Aboriginal law specialist Hamar Foster of the University of Victoria, who has done considerable research on the 1920s, does not think this case influenced the emergence of the 1927 amendment to the Indian Act that prohibited soliciting or donating money for pursuit of a claim (personal communication, 6 June 2007).

20 *Special Joint Committee of the Senate and House of Commons Appointed to Inquire into the Claims of the Allied Indian Tribes of British Columbia, as Set Forth in Their Petition Submitted to Parliament in June 1926: Report and Evidence*, Appendix to the *Journals of the Senate of Canada*, First Session of the Sixteenth Parliament, 1926–27 (Ottawa: King's Printer, 1927), viii–xxii (petition and memorial of Allied Tribes), and 3 (Charles Stewart, Superintendent General of Indian Affairs, to Premier John Oliver, 18 March 1927)

21 Ibid., 3

22 'Committee Report,' ibid., xvi–xvii. On Aboriginal title: '... it is the unanimous opinion of the members thereof [the Committee] that the petitioners have not established any claim to the lands of British Columbia based on aboriginal or other title ...'

23 *S.C. 1926–27*, c. 32 (17 Geo. V.) In the large overhaul of the Indian Act in 1927, this prohibition was repeated (*RSC* 1927, c. 98, sec. 141). It continued in the *Act* until the major revision of 1951.

24 *Report of the Commissioner for Treaty No. 8* (Ottawa: King's Printer, 1900), 21, INAC on-line version, accessed 6 July 2007. On the background of the Lubicon case, see also Christine Mary Smillie, 'The People Left Out of Treaty 8' (M.A. thesis, University of Saskatchewan, 2005); and John Goddard, *The Last Stand of the Lubicon Cree* (Vancouver: Douglas & McIntyre, 1991).

25 See Bruce W. Hodgins and Jamie Benedickson, *The Temagami Experience: Recreation, Resources, and Aboriginal Rights in the Northern Ontario Wilderness* (Toronto: University of Toronto Press, 1989).

26 For the background, see J.R. Miller, 'Great White Father Knows Best: Oka and the Land Claims Process,' *Native Studies Review*, 7, no. 1 (1991): 23–51.

27 R. Scott Sheffield, *The Red Man's on the Warpath: The Image of the 'Indian' and the Second World War* (Vancouver: University of British Columbia Press, 2004), especially chapters 6 and 7; J.R. Miller, *Skyscrapers Hide the Heavens: A History of Indian-White Relations in Canada*, 3rd edn (Toronto: University of Toronto Press, 2000; 1st edn, 1989), 324–6

28 Sally M. Weaver, *Making Canadian Indian Policy: The Hidden Agenda, 1968–1970* (Toronto: University of Toronto Press, 1981) provides an excellent analysis of the process.

29 Canada, Department of Indian Affairs and Northern Development, *Statement of the Government of Canada on Indian Policy* (Ottawa: Indian Affairs, 1969), 11, www.ainc-inac.gc.ca/pr/lib/phi/hist/ws/c1969_e.html, accessed 10 July 2007

30 Harold Cardinal, *The Unjust Society: The Tragedy of Canada's Indians* (Edmonton: Hurtig, 1969), 28

9: Treaties and Comprehensive Claims, 1975–2008

1 Joseph Gosnell, quoted in joint press release of Nisga'a Tribal Council, Province of British Columbia, and Canada, 15 Feb. 1996, nativenet.edu/archive/nl/9602/0088.html, accessed 27 July 2007. The full quotation by the president of the Nisga'a Tribal Council was: 'This represents a hard-fought compromise that has seen a generation of Nisga'a growing old at the negotiating table but we are making that compromise in order to become full and active participants in the social, political and economic life of this country.'

2 British Columbia, 'Report of Conferences between the Provincial Government and Indian Delegates from Fort Simpson and Naas River, 3rd and 8th Feb. 1887,' *Sessional Papers*, 1887, 254–6, 264. Premier Smithe's depiction of First Nations' condition at contact was couched in developmental terms: the Tsimshian had been like 'the wild beasts of the fields' (264), had advanced considerably by February 1887, though were still childlike and not qualified for the vote (256), and, he expected, with education, 'will be so far advanced as to be the same as a white man in every respect (257).

3 *Papers Relating to the Commission Appointed to Enquire into the State and Condition of the Indians of the North-West Coast of British Columbia* (BC *Sessional Papers*, 1888; reprint, Toronto: Canadiana House, 1979), 18. Other comments by Russ made it clear that he meant a treaty: 'But we want a solemn promise – a treaty' (ibid.).

4 A valuable chronology of the complicated campaign is found in Hamar Foster, Heather Raven, and Jeremy Webber, eds, *Let Right Be Done: Aborigi-*

nal Title, the Calder Case, and the Future of Indigenous Rights (Vancouver: University of British Columbia Press, 2007), 231–40.

5 Imperial Order in Council, 16 May 1871, *in* Dave De Brou and Bill Waiser, eds, *Documenting Canada: A History of Modern Canada in Documents* (Saskatoon: Fifth House, 1992), 55

6 Interview with Tom Molloy, Saskatoon, 12 October 2007. Mr Molloy was chief federal negotiator with the Nisga'a in the 1990s.

7 *Delgamuukw v. British Columbia*, [1997] 3 SCR 1010, www.scc.lexum .umontreal.ca/en/1997/1997rcs3-1010, accessed 15 Aug. 2007

8 P.E. Trudeau, quoted by Flora MacDonald, MP, House of Commons, *Debates*, 11 April 1973, 3207. Arthur Kroeger (interview, Ottawa, 25 Sept. 2007) thought that federal officials became flexible and innovative post-*Calder*, thanks in no small part to the attitude of Prime Minister Trudeau.

9 Canada, Department of Indian Affairs and Northern Development, *Statement of the Government of Canada on Indian Policy* (Ottawa: Indians Affairs, 1969), 11, www.ainc-inac.gc.ca/pr/lib/phi/hist/ws/c1969_3.html, accessed 10 July 2007

10 www.ainc-inac.gc.ca/ps/clm/gbn/index1_e.html#1-1, accessed 27 July 2007

11 Quoted in Roy MacGregor, *Chief: The Fearless Vision of Billy Diamond* (Markham, ON: Penguin, 1989), 54

12 Billy Diamond, 'Aboriginal Rights: The James Bay Experience,' in *The Quest for Justice: Aboriginal Peoples and Aboriginal Rights*, ed. Menno Boldt, J. Anthony Long, and Leroy Little Bear (Toronto: University of Toronto Press, 1985), 266. I am grateful to James O'Reilly, who provided me with a copy of this article.

13 Interview with Billy Diamond, Gatineau, QC, 7 Dec. 2007

14 MacGregor, *Chief*, 14 and 25–6

15 Diamond interview; MacGregor, *Chief*, 78–86, 103–4; interview with James O'Reilly, Montreal, 23 Oct. 2007

16 Diamond interview; O'Reilly interview; John S. Murdoch, 'Challenging the Credibility of the Crown's Expert Witnesses in Aboriginal Title or Rights Court Cases,' unpublished paper presented to the 36th Algonquian Conference, Madison, WI, 2004, 5. Dr Murdoch is the brother-in-law of Billy Diamond.

17 Diamond interview

18 MacGregor, *Chief*, 125. For background, see also ibid., 103, 111, 120, 123; and Boyce Richardson, *Strangers Devour the Land: A Chronicle of the Assault upon the Last Coherent Hunting Culture in North America, the Cree Indians of*

Northern Quebec, and Their Vast Primeval Homelands (New York: Alfred A. Knopf, 1976), 121, 305.

19 Diamond, 'The James Bay Experience,' 279

20 Evelyn J. Peters, 'Protecting the Land under Modern Land Claims Agreements: The Effectiveness of the Environmental Regime Negotiated by the James Bay Cree and Northern Quebec Agreement,' *Applied Geography*, 12, no. 2 (April 1992): 135–6; Wendy Moss, 'The Implementation of the James Bay and Northern Quebec Agreement,' in *Aboriginal Peoples and the Law: Indian, Metis and Inuit Rights in Canada*, ed. Bradford W. Morse (Ottawa: Carleton University Press, 1985), 684–7

21 MacGregor, *Chief*, 134

22 Opinion of Paul Ollivier, Associate Deputy Minister, Department of Justice, to P.F. Girard, Office of Claims Negotiations, INAC, 26 Feb. 1975. A copy of this document was obtained in 1991 through an application under the Access to Information Act and is in the author's possession.

23 'An Overview of the Oka Issue,' INAC press release, July 1990, 3; Bill McKnight to Grand Chief Hugh Nicholas, 14 Oct. 1986; and R.M. Connelly, Specific Claims Branch, to Chief Nicholas, 10 May 1984. Copies of the McKnight and Connelly letters were obtained under the Access to Information Act and are in the author's possession.

24 Canada, *Living Treaties: Lasting Agreements*, Report of the Task Force to Review Comprehensive Claims Policy (Ottawa: INAC, 1985), 13

25 (Ottawa: INAC, 1981). The INAC website acknowledges that 'the Comprehensive Claims Policy was reaffirmed in 1981...' (INAC, 'General Briefing Note on the Comprehensive Land Claims Policy of Canada and the Status of Claims,' http://www.ainc-inac.gc.ca/ps/clm/gbn/index_e.html, accessed 27 July 2007).

26 'General Briefing Note on the Comprehensive Land Claims Policy'

27 Ted Moses (quoted in Peters, 'Protecting the Land,' 143) had warned his colleagues in the NWT in 1988: '... we trusted the Federal Government to respect the spirit and intent of the ... Agreement; and because of that we have had to fight for the very things that were recognized in the Agreement ... So one thing should be clearly understood: you are not dealing with a government that is acting in good faith ... It is a long standing *policy* of the Federal government to break treaties. It is a technique of negotiation.' Peters cites Moses' remarks as part of an unpublished address, 13 June 1988, Yellowknife.

28 'General Briefing Note'

29 Ibid. Tom Molloy (interview) describes this approach as current federal policy.

30 These specific powers are from *The Tr'ondëk Hwëch'in Self-Government Agreement* (Ottawa: Public Works and Government Services, 1998), esp. 3, 7, and 15–18. See also Yukon Umbrella Final Agreement, chapter 24, 'Yukon Indian Self-Government, www.ainc-inac.gc.ca, accessed 15 May 2001.

31 Molloy interview

32 See, for example, the case of two peoples who disputed ownership of fishing sites in the Nass River Valley, in *Papers Relating to the Commission Appointed to Enquire into the State and Condition of the Indians of the North-West Coast of British Columbia*, 8, 17–18; and E. Palmer Patterson, 'A Decade of Change: Origins of the Nishga and Tsimshian Land Protests in the 1880s,' *Journal of Canadian Studies*, 18, no. 3 (Autumn 1983): 41, 47–9.

33 Interview with Barry Strayer, Ottawa, 12 June 2007; Kroeger interview. Dr Strayer had been director of constitutional law in the Department of Justice in 1974. Mr Kroeger was deputy minister of Indian affairs and northern development, 1975–9.

34 *R. v. Sparrow*, [1990] SCR 1075, scc.lexum.umontreal.ca/en/1990 /1990res1-1075, accessed 10 Aug. 2007

35 Tom Molloy, *The World Is Our Witness: The Historic Journey of the Nisga'a into Canada* (Calgary: Fifth House, 2000), 34–5, 47–52; Molloy interview

36 *Globe and Mail*, 13 Feb. 1996

37 This account is based on the summary of the complex Final Agreement in Molloy, *The World Is Our Witness*, 220–31; Molloy interview

38 Quoted in Charles R. Menzies, 'The Challenge of First Nations History in a Colonial World,' *Canadian Issues* [Association of Canadian Studies], Fall 2006, 45

39 Greg Poelzer and Ken Coates, 'Aboriginal Peoples and the Crown in Canada: Completing the Canadian Experiment,' in *Continuity and Change in Canadian Politics: Essays in Honour of David E. Smith*, ed. Hans Michelmann and Cristine De Clercy (Toronto: University of Toronto Press, 2006), 152–3. Poelzer and Coates are right to stress the importance of the explicit reference in the Nisga'a Treaty to section 35, but miss the point that the self-government arrangements under the Yukon Final Agreement are probably covered by section 35 as well, even though there is no explicit reference to the constitutional provision in those pacts.

40 See J. Rick Ponting, *The Nisga'a Treaty: Polling Dynamics and Political Communication in Comparative Context* (Peterborough, ON: Broadview Press, 2006) for an analysis of the pro-treaty campaign.

41 www.bctreaty.net, accessed 8 Aug. 2007

42 BC Treaty Commission [BCTC], *Treaty Commission Update*, September 2007, 8

43 Molloy interview

44 See the map in the *Globe and Mail*, 26 July 2007.

45 BCTC, *Looking Back / Looking Forward: A Review of the BC Treaty Process*
(N.p.: [BC Treaty Commission, 2001]), 16. On the BCTC in general, see
Richard T. Price, 'The British Columbia Treaty Process: An Evolving Insti-
tution' (unpublished paper).

46 *The Powell River Peak*, 24 April 2007. The item from the *Peak* was kindly provided by the communications office of the Manitoba Treaty Relations
Commission. The Lheidli T'enneh Final Agreement, which would have
provided 10,564 acres (4,275 hectares) of land, $50 million, fishing rights,
and self-government, received only 47 per cent of the vote. BCTC regulations require 70 per cent approval.

47 *Globe and Mail*, 31 March 2007

48 *Vancouver Sun*, 8 Feb. 2007; *Globe and Mail*, 26 July 2007

49 Press release of Huu-ay-aht, 29 July 2007, and BC Treaty Commission
release, available at www. bctreaty.net, accessed 14 Aug. 2007 and 29 July
2008; *Globe and Mail*, 30 July 2007

50 Press release of Tsawwassen First Nation, 25 July 2007, www.bctreaty.net,
accessed 9 Aug. 2007

51 www.bctreaty.net, accessed 29 July 2008; *Update*, Sept. 2007, 8. The
numbers do not add up to fifty-eight because some negotiating 'tables'
had more than one First Nation.

52 P. Usher, F. Tough, and R. Galois, 'Reclaiming the Land: Aboriginal Title,
Treaty Rights and Land Claims in Canada,' *Applied Geography*, 12, no. 2
(April 1992): 129

53 For example, the agreement between Tahltan Central Council in northern
BC and Nova Gold Resources, Inc. (*Globe and Mail*, 14 Feb. 2006). See also
Tony Penikett, *Reconciliaion: First Nations Treaty Making in British Columbia*
(Vancouver: Douglas & McIntyre, 2006). I am grateful to my colleague
Keith Carlson, who alerted me to these negotiations.

54 Billy Diamond interview; Grand Council of the Crees (of Quebec), the
Cree Regional Authority, and the Cree Bands of Quebec, quoted in Peters,
'Protecting the Land,' 142. For Grand Council testimony before the parliamentary committee, see Canada, House of Commons, Standing Committee on Aboriginal Affairs and Northern Development, Minutes of Proceedings and Evidence, 13 May 1986, esp. 17:11 and 17:13; and Library and
Archives Canada, RG 14, Parliamentary committee documents, accession
1996–97/193, box 49, Brief of The Grand Council of the Crees (of
Quebec), the Cree Regional Authority, [and] the Cree Bands of Quebec
presented to the Standing Committee of the House of Commons on Abo-

riginal Affairs and Northern Development Respecting Bill C-93, The Sechelt Indian Self-Government Act, 13 May 1976.

55 *Globe and Mail,* 17 July 2007. In 2002 the Cree had also signed a so-called Paix des Braves (Peace of the Braves), by which the Quebec government promised to pay $3.5 billion over fifty years in return for dropping a $8 billion suit for violations of the JBNQA and agreement to allow hydroelectric development on the Rupert and Eastmain Rivers. For background on the dispute, see Peters, 'Protecting the Land,' 133–45; and Moss, 'The Implementation of the James Bay and Northern Quebec Agreement,' 684–94. In August 2007, Canada, Quebec, and the Inuit of Quebec reached an Agreement in Principle on the creation of an Inuit government, to be known as the Regional Government of Nunavik, for 10,000 Inuit north of the fifty-fifth parallel (*Globe and Mail,* 13 Aug. 2007).

10: Conclusion

In this chapter, only events and quotations that have not been cited or quoted, and documented, previously are documented in the following notes.

1 Adrienne Clarkson, 'The Society of Difference,' LaFontaine-Baldwin Lecture 2007, www.lafontaine-baldwin.com/speeches, accessed 17 Aug. 2007. Ms. Clarkson said, 'In fact, we are all treaty people because it takes two sides to make a treaty, and that's what we agreed to do.' The phrase was frequently used prior to 2007 by Hon. David Arnot, Treaty Commissioner for Saskatchewan, 1997–2007.

2 John C. Weaver, *The Great Land Rush and the Making of the Modern World, 1650–1900* (Montreal and Kingston: McGill-Queen's University Press, 2003), esp. 133–74, 402–17

3 John Mack Farragher, *A Great and Noble Scheme: The Tragic Story of the Expulsion of the French Acadians from Their American Homeland* (New York: W.W. Norton, 2005), 22. Increasing the likelihood that Membertou interpreted the baptism ceremony as creating kinship is the fact that he chose 'Henri,' the given name of the French king, as his baptismal name, while his wife chose 'Marie,' the queen's name. Membertou on other occasions made it clear to Frenchmen that he regarded himself as occupying the same social and political status as the king. I am grateful to a colleague and friend, John Borrows, who recommended this work.

4 Alexander Morris, *The Treaties of Canada with the Indians of Manitoba and the North-West Territories* (1880; reprint, Saskatoon: Fifth House, 1991), 16

5 Tungavik and Indian and Northern Affairs Canada, *Agreement between the*

Inuit of the Nunavut Settlement Area and Her Majesty the Queen in Right of Canada (Ottawa: INAC, 1993); Tom Molloy, *The World Is Our Witness: The Historic Journey of the Nisga'a into Canada* (Calgary: Fifth House, 2000), 164–5

6 Tom Molloy interview

7 Library and Archives Canada (LAC), Dufferin Papers, Canadian Addresses, 1978–049, box 1, petitions of Six Nations, 21 Aug. 1872. I am indebted to my colleague Keith Carlson, who drew this and other petitions to Dufferin to my attention. See also LAC, RG 10, vol. 1011, reel T-1456, petition of Credit River Mississauga to Lieutenant-Governor Peregrine Maitland, 11 Nov. 1825; ibid., petition of Credit River Mississauga to the Legislature, 31 Jan. 1829. It is revealing that, when the chiefs were petitioning the legislators, rather than the Crown's representative, they dropped the totems from their names. See also RG 10, vol. 3697, file 15,423, reel C-1-122, J.A. MacRae to E. Dewdney, 25 Aug. 1884.

8 'Frank Calder and Thomas Berger: A Conversation,' in *Let Right Be Done: Aboriginal Title, the Calder Case, and the Future of Indigenous Rights,* ed. Hamar Foster, Heather Raven, and Jeremy Webber (Vancouver: University of British Columbia Press, 2007), 40

9 *New York Times* on-line, 27 June 1937, accessed 27 Aug. 2007

10 On this point, I part company with my highly respected colleague and good friend Alan Cairns, who calls on judges to be more liberal in interpreting section 35 in *First Nations and the Canadian State: In Search of Coexistence* (Kingston, ON: Institute of Intergovernmental Relations, Queen's University, 2005), 57.

11 For this analysis, I am indebted to several works by Alan Cairns, in particular, his 'Citizenship and Indian Peoples: The Ambiguous Legacy of Internal Colonialism,' in *Handbook of Citizenship Studies*, ed. Engin F. Isin and Bryan S. Turner (Thousand Oaks, CA: Sage Publications, 2002), 209–30, esp. 224–7.

12 Alan Cairns, 'Afterword: International Dimensions of the Citizen Issue for Indigenous Peoples/Nations,' *Citizenship Studies*, 7, no. 4 (2003): 497–517. I am grateful to Professor Cairns for providing me with a copy of this article.

Bibliography

Reference

The Canadian Oxford Dictionary Ed. Katherine Barber. Don Mills, ON: Oxford
   University Press, 1998
Harris, R. Cole, ed. *From the Beginning to 1800.* Vol. 1 of *Historical Atlas of
   Canada.* 3 vols. Toronto: University of Toronto Press, 1987

Primary Sources

Archival Collections

Glenbow Museum
   74.7.76, R.B. Nevitt, 'NWMP Camp at Treaty 7'
Library and Archives Canada
   Claus Family Fonds, microfilm, reel C-1480
   Dufferin Papers, Canadian Addresses, 1978–049, box 1
   CO 42 Colonial Office Correspondence, Upper Canada, 1811 Despatches,
      reel B295
   MG 17, B 2, Church Missionary Society Records, reel A-86
   MG 21, B 158, Sir Frederick Haldimand Papers, reel 746
   MG 26, A, Sir John A. Macdonald Papers
   RG 10, Records of the Department of Indian Affairs, microfilm, various
      reels
   RG 14, Parliamentary committee documents, accession 1996–97/193
   RG 18, Records of the Mounted Police
Provincial Archives of Manitoba
   The Manitoban, microfilm

MG 12, B 1, Alexander Morris Papers
MG 12, E 1, John C. Schultz Papers
Provincial Archives of Ontario
    F4337-11-0-8, reel M2607, Gun Shot Treaty
    F4337-11-0-9, reel M2607, Grandes Oreilles's speech, 1814
    F1027-1-2, Aemelius Irving Papers
    F44, Acc. 30212, W.B. Robinson Diaries
Queen's University Archives
    D.G. MacMartin Diary
Toronto Reference Library, Baldwin Room
    S13 George Nelson Journals
    S 27 Thomas Gummersall Anderson Papers
University of Western Ontario Archives
    Wawanosh Family Papers, box 4381
    Alexander Vidal Papers

Published Primary Sources

Ahenakew, Edward. *Voices of the Plains Cree.* Ed. Ruth M. Buck. Toronto: McClelland and Stewart, 1973
Apesis, Chief William, Peter Dodson, and the Elders of Birch Narrows, Buffalo River, Canoe Lake, and English River. *In Their Own Land: Treaty Ten and the Canoe Lake, Clear Lake, and English River Bands.* Saskatoon: Office of the Treaty Commissioner, 2007
BC Treaty Commission. *Looking Back / Looking Forward: A Review of the BC Treaty Process.* N.p.: [BC Treaty Commission, 2001]
Biggar, H.P., ed. and trans. *The Voyages of Jacques Cartier.* Ottawa: King's Printer, 1924
– *The Works of Samuel de Champlain.* 6 vols. Toronto: Champlain Society, 1922–6
Brigham, Clarence S., ed. *British Royal Proclamations Relating to America, 1603–1783.* Vol. 12 of *Transactions and Collections of the American Antiquarian Society.* Worcester, MA: American Antiquarian Society, 1911
British Columbia. 'Papers Relating to the Commission Appointed to Enquire into the State and Condition of the Indians of the North-West Coast of British Columbia.' *Sessional Papers,* 1888
– 'Report of Conferences between the Provincial Government and Indian Delegates from Fort Simpson and Naas River, 3rd and 8th Feb. 1887.' *Sessional Papers,* 1887
British Parliamentary Papers: Correspondence Returns and Other Papers Relating to

Canada and to the Indian Problem Therein, 1839. Irish University Press Series. Shannon: Irish University Press, 1969

Camsell, Charles. *Son of the North*. Toronto: Ryerson Press, 1954

Canada. *The Canada Year Book 1911, ...1914, ...1922–23, ...1933, ...1943–44*. Ottawa: King's Printer, 1912, 1915, 1924, 1933, 1944

– *Debates of the House of Commons*

– *Indian Treaties and Surrenders*. 3 vols. Ottawa: Queen's Printer, 1891

– *Living Treaties: Lasting Agreements*. Report of the Task Force to Review Comprehensive Claims Policy. Ottawa: Indian and Northern Affairs Canada, 1985

– *Sessional Papers (No. 28) 1910*. North West Mounted Police Annual Report

– *Sessional Papers*, various numbers and reports. Annual Report of the Department of Indian Affairs

– *Special Joint Committee of the Senate and House of Commons Appointed to Inquire into the Claims of the Allied Indian Tribes of British Columbia, as Set Forth in Their Petition Submitted to Parliament in June 1926: Report and Evidence*. In *Journals of the Senate of Canada*, 1926–27. Ottawa: King's Printer, 1927

– *Statutes of Canada*. various years

– *Treaty No. 8 Made June 21 1899 and Adhesions, Reports, Etc*. Ottawa: Queen's Printer, 1899

– *The Tr'ondëk Hwëch'in Self-Government Agreement*. Ottawa: Public Works and Government Services, 1998

Cardinal, Harold. *The Unjust Society: The Tragedy of Canada's Indians*. Edmonton: Hurtig, 1969

Colden, Cadwallader. *The History of the Five Nations of Canada*. Rev. edn. 2 parts. London: T. Osborne, 1747; 1st edn, 1727

Copway, George. *The Traditional History and Characteristic Sketches of the Ojibway Nation*. London: C. Gilpin, 1850

Cruikshank, E.A., ed. *The Correspondence of the Honourable Peter Russell with Allied Documents Relating to His Administration of the Government of Upper Canada during the Official Terms of Lieut.-Governor J.G. Simcoe While on Leave of Absence*. 3 vols. Toronto: Champlain Society, 1932–6

– *The Correspondence of John Graves Simcoe*. 5 vols. Toronto: Ontario Historical Society, 1923–31

De Brou, Dave, and Bill Waiser, eds. *Documenting Canada: A History of Modern Canada in Documents*. Saskatoon: Fifth House, 1992

Denison, George T. *The Struggle for Imperial Unity: Recollections and Experiences*. Toronto: Macmillan, 1909

Doughty, A.G., ed. *The Elgin-Grey Papers, 1846–1852*. 4 vols. Ottawa: King's Printer, 1937

Edwards, O.C. *On the North Trail: The Treaty 8 Diary of O.C. Edwards.* Ed. D.
Leonard and B. Whalen. Calgary: Alberta Records Publication Board, 1998

Erasmus, Peter. *Buffalo Days and Nights.* Ed. Irene Spry. 1976; reprint, Calgary:
Glenbow Alberta Institute/Fifth House, 1999

'From the Anishinabek, the Ojibway, Ottawa, Potowatomi and Algonquin
Nations to the Parliament of the Dominion of Canada.' *Ontario Indian,* 3,
no. 12 (1980)

Graham, Andrew. *Andrew Graham's Observations on Hudson's Bay, 1767–91.* Ed.
Glyndwr Williams. London: Hudson's Bay Record Society, 1969

Head, Francis Bond. *A Narrative.* 2nd edn. London: John Murray, 1839

Hines, John. *The Red Indians of the Plains: Thirty Years' Missionary Experience in
the Saskatchewan.* Toronto: McClelland and Stewart, 1916

Isaac, Thomas, ed. *Pre-1868 Legislation Concerning Indians: A Selected and Indexed
Collection.* Saskatoon: Native Law Centre, 1993

Jones, Peter. *History of the Ojebway Indians, with Especial Reference to Their Conversion to Christianity.* London: Bennett, 1861

Lafitau, Joseph-François. *Customs of the American Indians Compared with the
Customs of Primitive Times.* 2 vols. Toronto: Champlain Society, 1974; 1st
French edn, Paris, 1724

Le Clerq, Christian. *First Establishment of the Faith in New France.* Trans. John
Gilmary Shea. 2 vols. New York: AMS, 1973; 1st edn, New York, 1881

Library and Archives Canada. *Report of the Work of the Archives Branch for the Year
1911.* Ottawa: Government Printing Bureau, 1911

Mair, Charles. *Through the Mackenzie Basin: An Account of the Signing of Treaty No.
8 and the Scrip Commission.* 1908; reprint, Edmonton: University of Alberta
Press and Edmonton & District Historical Society, 1999

Moberly, Henry John. *When Fur Was King.* Toronto: J.M. Dent, 1929

Molloy, Tom. *The World Is Our Witness: The Historic Journey of the Nisga'a into
Canada.* Calgary: Fifth House, 2000

Morris, Alexander. *Nova Britannia; or, Our New Canadian Dominion Foreshadowed.*
Toronto: Hunter, Rose, 1884

– *The Treaties of Canada with the Indians of Manitoba and the North-West Territories.*
1880; reprint, Saskatoon: Fifth House, 1991

Morton, W.L., ed. *Alexander Begg's Red River Journal.* 1956; reprint, New York:
Greenwood Press, 1969

O'Callaghan, E.B., ed. *Documents Relative to the Colonial History of the State of New
York.* 15 vols. Albany, NY: Weed, Parsons and Co., 1853-87

Oldmixon, John, *The British Empire in America* (1708). Reprinted in *Documents
Relating to the Early History of Hudson Bay.* Ed. J.B. Tyrrell. Toronto: Champlain Society, 1931

Rich, E.E., ed. *Copy-Book of Letters Outward &c.: Begins 29ᵗʰ May, 1680 Ends 5 July, 1687*. London: Hudson's Bay Record Society, 1948

Shaw, Charles Aeneas. *Tales of a Pioneer Surveyor*. Ed. Raymond Hull. Toronto: Longman, 1970

Smith, Goldwin. *Canada and the Canadian Question*. Toronto: Hunter, Rose & Co., 1891

Sullivan, James, ed. *The Papers of Sir William Johnson*. 14 vols. Albany: University of the State of New York, 1921–65

Thwaites, R.G., ed. *The Jesuit Relations and Allied Documents*. 73 vols. Cleveland: Burrows, 1896–1901

Treaty Elders of Saskatchewan, with Harold Cardinal and Walter Hildebrandt. *Our Dream Is That Our Peoples Will One Day Be Clearly Recognized as Nations*. Calgary: University of Calgary Press, 2000

Tungavik and Indian and Northern Affairs Canada. *An Agreement between the Inuit of the Nunavut Settlement Area and Her Majesty the Queen in Right of Canada*. Ottawa: Indian and Northern Affairs Canada, 1993

Warren, William W. *History of the Ojibway People*. With an introduction by W. Roger Buffalohead. St Paul, MN: Minnesota Historical Society Press, 1984

Wraxall, Peter. *An Abridgment of the Indian Affairs Contained in Four Folio Volumes, Transacted in the Colony of New York, from the Year 1678 to the Year 1751*. Ed. Charles Howard McIlwain. 1915. New York: Benjamin Blom, 1968

Judicial Decisions

Keith Lawrence Julien v. Her Majesty the Queen, 2002, Nova Scotia Supreme Court

The Queen v. Taylor and Williams, 16 Oct. 1981, *34 Ontario Reports (2d)*

R. v. Donald Marshall, Jr. Supreme Court of Canada, 1999

Websites and Electronic Sources

British Columbia Treaty Commission. www.bctreaty.net

Canada. Department of Indian Affairs and Northern Development. *Statement of the Government of Canada on Indian Policy*. Ottawa: Indian Affairs, 1969. www.ainc-inac.gc.ca/pr/lib/phi/hist/ws/c1969_e.html

Clarkson, Adrienne. 'The Society of Difference.' LaFontaine-Baldwin Lecture 2007. www.lafontaine-baldwin.com/speeches

Delgamuukw v. British Columbia, 1997, 3 SCR 1010. www.scc.lexum.umontreal.ca/en/1997/1997rcs3-1010

Dictionary of Canadian Biography. On-line edn. www.biographi.ca

Edgar Dewdney Fonds, Series 13, Journal, entry of 17 July 1879. www.glenbow. org/archives

Hudson's Bay Company Charter, 1670. www.solon.org/constitutions/Canada /English/PreConfederation/hbc_charter1670. html

Indian Claims Commission. www.indianclaims.ca

Lescarbot, Marc. *Nova Francia; or, The Description of That Part of New France Which Is One Continent with Virginia*. Trans. P. Erondelle. London: Andrew Hebb, [1626]. Early English Books Online

National Post on-line. www.canadacom/nationalpost

New York Times on-line. www.nytimes.com

Indian and Northern Affairs Canada (INAC). Treaty Research Reports. inac-ainc.gc.ca

Interviews

Diamond, Billy. Gatineau, QC, 7 Dec. 2007
Kroeger, Arthur. Ottawa, 25 Sept. 2007
Molloy, Tom. Saskatoon, 12 Oct. 2007
O'Reilly, James. Montreal, 23 Oct. 2007
Strayer, Dr. Barry. Ottawa, 12 June 2007

Secondary Sources

Books

Allen, Robert S. *His Majesty's Indian Allies: British Indian Policy in the Defence of Canada, 1774–1815*. Toronto: Dundurn Press, 1993

Asch, Michael, ed. *Aboriginal and Treaty Rights in Canada: Essays on Law, Equality, and Respect for Difference*. Vancouver: University of British Columbia, 1997

Axtell, James. *Natives and Newcomers: The Cultural Origins of North America*. New York and Oxford: Oxford University Press, 2001

Beaulieu, Alain, and Roland Viau. *The Great Peace: Chronicle of a Diplomatic Saga*. Montreal: Editions Libre Expression, 2001

Berger, Carl. *The Sense of Power: Studies in the Ideas of Canadian Imperialism, 1867–1914*. Toronto: University of Toronto Press, 1970

Brandão, José A. *Your fyre shall burn no more: Iroquois Policy toward New France and Its Native Allies to 1701*. Lincoln: University of Nebraska Press, 1997

Cairns, Alan C. *First Nations and the Canadian State: In Search of Coexistence*. Kingston, ON: Institute of Intergovernmental Relations, Queen's University, 2005

Careless, J.M.S. *Brown of the Globe.* 2 vols. Toronto: Macmillan, 1959
– *The Union of the Canadas: The Growth of Canadian Institutions, 1841–1857.*
Toronto: McClelland and Stewart, 1967
Christenson, Deanna. *Ahtahkakoop: The Epic Account of a Plains Cree Head Chief,*
His People, and Their Struggle for Survival, 1816–1896. Shell Lake, SK:
Ahtahkakoop Publishing, 2000
Creighton, D.G. *The Road to Confederation: The Emergence of Modern Canada,*
1863–1867. Toronto: Macmillan, 1964
– *Sir John A. Macdonald.* 2 vols. Toronto: Macmillan, 1952–5
Cumming, P.A., and N.H. Mickenberg. *Native Rights in Canada.* 2nd edn.
Toronto: General Publishing, 1972
Daugherty, W.E. *Maritime Indian Treaties in Historical Perspective.* Ottawa: Indian
and Northern Affairs Canada, 1983
Delâge, Denys, and Jean-Pierre Sawaya. *Les traités des Sept-Feux avec les Britan-*
niques: droits et pièges d'un héritage colonial au Québec. Sillery, QC: Septentrion,
2001
Dippie, Brian W. *The Vanishing American: White Attitudes and U.S. Indian Policy.*
Middleton, CT: Wesleyan University Press, 1982
Eccles, W.J. *Frontenac: The Courtier Governor.* Toronto: McClelland and Stewart,
1959
Farragher, John Mack. *A Great and Noble Scheme: The Tragic Story of the Expulsion*
of the French Acadians from Their American Homeland. New York: W.W. Norton
& Co., 2005
Foster, Hamar, Heather Raven, and Jeremy Webber, eds. *Let Right Be Done: Abo-*
riginal Title, the Calder Case, and the Future of Indigenous Rights. Vancouver:
University of British Columbia Press, 2007
Friesen, Gerald. *The Canadian Prairies: A History.* Toronto: University of
Toronto Press, 1984
Fumoleau, René. *As Long as This Land Shall Last: A History of Treaty 8 and Treaty*
11, 1870–1939. 2nd edn. Calgary: University of Calgary Press, 2004
Goddard, John. *The Last Stand of the Lubicon Cree.* Vancouver/Toronto: Douglas
& McIntyre, 1991
Goode, Peter, Joan Champ, and Leslie Amundson. *The Montreal Lake Region: Its*
History and Geography. Saskatoon: Sentar Consultants, 1996
Graymont, Barbara. *The Iroquois in the American Revolution.* Syracuse, NY: Syra-
cuse University Press, 1972
Haig-Brown, Celia, and David A. Nock, eds. *With Good Intentions: Euro-Canadian*
and Aboriginal Relations in Colonial Canada. Vancouver: University of British
Columbia Press, 2006
Hauka, Donald. *McGowan's War.* Vancouver: New Star Books, 2003
Havard, Gilles. *The Great Peace of Montreal of 1701: French-Native Diplomacy in the*

Seventeenth Century. Trans. Phyllis Aronoff and Howard Scott. Montreal and Kingston: McGill-Queen's University Press, 2001; 1st French edn, 1992

Henderson, James Youngblood Sákéj. *The Mikmaq Concordat.* Halifax: Fernwood, 1997

Hodgins, Bruce W., and Jamie Benedickson. *The Temagami Experience: Recreation, Resources, and Aboriginal Rights in the Northern Ontario Wilderness.* Toronto: University of Toronto Press, 1989

Jaenen, Cornelius J. *Friend and Foe: Aspects of French-Amerindian Cultural Contact in the Sixteenth and Seventeenth Centuries.* New York: Columbia University Press, 1976

Jamieson, Melvill Allan. *Medals Awarded to North American Chiefs, 1714–1922.* London: Spink & Son Ltd, 1936

Jenness, Diamond. *The Indians of Canada.* 7th edn. Toronto: University of Toronto Press, 1977. (1st edn, National Museum of Man, 1932)

Jennings, Francis, et al., eds. *The History and Culture of Iroquois Diplomacy: An Interdisciplinary Guide to the Treaties of the Six Nations and Their League.* Syracuse, NY: Syracuse University Press, 1985

Johnson, Harold. *Two Families: Treaties and Government.* Saskatoon: Purich Publishing, 2007

Lerat, Harold, with Linda Ungar. *Treaty Promises, Indian Reality: Life on a Reserve.* Saskatoon: Purich Publishing, 2005

Lux, Maureen. *Medicine That Walks: Disease, Medicine, and Canadian Plains Native People, 1880–1940.* Toronto: University of Toronto Press, 2001

MacGregor, Roy. *Chief: The Fearless Vision of Billy Diamond.* Markham, ON: Penguin, 1989

McKenney, Thomas L., and James Hall. *The Indian Tribes of North America.* 3 vols. New edn. Ed. Frederick Webb Hodge. Edinburgh: J. Grant, 1933–4

MacLeod, D. Peter. *The Canadian Iroquois and the Seven Years' War.* Toronto: Dundurn / Canadian War Museum, 1996

Macleod, R.C. *The North West Mounted Police and Law Enforcement, 1873–1905.* Toronto: University of Toronto Press, 1976

Miller, J.R. *Lethal Legacy: Current Native Controversies in Canada.* Toronto: McClelland and Stewart, 2004

– *Reflections on Native-Newcomer Relations: Selected Essays.* Toronto: University of Toronto Press, 2004

– *Skyscrapers Hide the Heavens: A History of Indian-White Relations in Canada.* 3rd edn. Toronto: University of Toronto Press, 2000

– *Sweet Promises: A Reader on Indian-White Relations.* Toronto: University of Toronto Press, 1991

Milloy, John S. *The Plains Cree: Trade, Diplomacy and War, 1790 to 1870*. Winnipeg: University of Manitoba Press, 1988

Monet, Jacques. *The Last Cannon Shot: A Study of French-Canadian Nationalism, 1837–1850*. Toronto: University of Toronto Press, 1969

Morton, W.L. *The Critical Years: The Union of British North America, 1857–1873*. Toronto: McClelland and Stewart, 1964

Pannekoek, Frits. *A Snug Little Flock: The Social Origins of the Riel Resistance of 1869–70*. Winnipeg: Watson & Dwyer, 1991

Paper, Jordan. *Offering Smoke: The Sacred Pipe and Native American Religion*. Edmonton: University of Alberta Press, 1988

Penikett, Tony. *Reconciliation: First Nations Treaty Making in British Columbia*. Vancouver: Douglas & McIntyre, 2006

Ponting, J. Rick. *The Nisga'a Treaty: Polling Dynamics and Political Communication in Comparative Context*. Peterborough, ON: Broadview Press, 2006

Ray, Arthur J. *The Canadian Fur Trade in the Industrial Age*. Toronto: University of Toronto Press, 1990

– *Indians in the Fur Trade: Their Role as Trappers, Hunters, and Middlemen in the Lands Southwest of Hudson Bay, 1660–1870*. Toronto: University of Toronto Press, 1974

Ray, Arthur J., and Donald B. Freeman, eds. *'Give Us Good Measure': An Economic Analysis of Relations between the Indians and the Hudson's Bay Company before 1763*. Toronto: University of Toronto Press, 1978

Ray, Arthur J., Jim Miller, and Frank Tough. *Bounty and Benevolence: A History of Saskatchewan Treaties*. Montreal and Kingston: McGill-Queen's University Press, 2000

Rich, E.E. *The History of the Hudson's Bay Company, 1670–1870*. 2 vols. London: Hudson's Bay Record Society, 1958–9

Richardson, Boyce. *Strangers Devour the Land: A Chronicle of the Assault upon the Last Coherent Hunting Culture in North America, the Cree Indians of Northern Quebec, and Their Vast Primeval Homelands*. New York: Alfred A. Knopf, 1976

Richter, Daniel K. *Facing East from Indian Country: A Native History of Early America*. Cambridge: Harvard University Press, 2001

– *The Ordeal of the Longhouse: The Peoples of the Iroquois League in the Era of European Colonization*. [Williamsburg, VA]: Institute of Early American History and Culture, 1992

Richter, Daniel K. and James H. Merrell, eds. *Beyond the Covenant Chain: The Iroquois and Their Neighbors in Indian North America, 1600–1800*. Syracuse, NY: Syracuse University Press, 1987

St Germain, Jill. *Indian Treaty-Making Policy in the United States and Canada, 1867–1877*. Toronto: University of Toronto Press, 2001

Sawaya, Jean-Pierre. *La Fédération des Sept Feux de la vallée du Saint-Laurent: XVIIe au XIXe siècle*. Sillery, QC: Septentrion, 1998

Schmalz, Peter S. *The Ojibway of Southern Ontario*. Toronto: University of Toronto Press, 1991

Sheffield, R. Scott. *The Red Man's on the Warpath: The Image of the 'Indian' and the Second World War*. Vancouver: University of British Columbia Press, 2004

Shrive, Norman. *Charles Mair: Literary Nationalist*. Toronto: University of Toronto Press, 1965

Silver, A.I. *The French-Canadian Idea of Confederation, 1864–1900*. Toronto: University of Toronto Press, 1982

Stagg, Jack. *Anglo-Indian Relations in North America to 1763 and an Analysis of the Royal Proclamation of 7 October 1763*. Ottawa: Indian Affairs and Northern Development, 1981

Stonechild, Blair, and Bill Waiser. *Loyal till Death: Indians and the North-West Rebellion*. Calgary: Fifth House, 1997

Tanner, Helen Hornbeck, et al., eds. *Atlas of Great Lakes Indian History*. Norman and Lincoln: University of Oklahoma Press, 1987

Tennant, Paul. *Aboriginal People and Politics: The Indian Land Question in British Columbia, 1849–1989*. Vancouver: University of British Columbia, 1991

Titley, E. Brian. *A Narrow Vision: Duncan Campbell Scott and the Administration of Indian Affairs in Canada*. Vancouver: University of British Columbia Press, 1986

Tooker, Elizabeth. *An Ethnography of the Huron Indians, 1615–1649*. Washington, DC: The Smithsonian Institution, [1967]

Tough, Frank. *'As Their Natural Resources Fail': Native Peoples and the Economic History of Northern Manitoba, 1870–1930*. Vancouver: University of British Columbia Press, 1996

Treaty 7 Elders and Tribal Council with Walter Hildebrandt, Dorothy First Rider, and Sarah Carter. *The True Spirit and Original Intent of Treaty 7*. Montreal and Kingston: McGill-Queen's University Press, 1996

Trelease, Allen W. *Indian Affairs in Colonial New York: The Seventeenth Century*. Ithaca, NY: Cornell University Press, 1960

Trigger, Bruce G. *The Children of Aataentsic: A History of the Huron People to 1600*. Reprint edition in one volume. 1976; Montreal and Kingston: McGill-Queen's University Press, 1987

Van Kirk, Sylvia. *'Many Tender Ties': Women in Fur-Trade Society in Western Canada, 1670–1870*. Winnipeg: Watson & Dwyer, [1980]

Vaugeois, Denis. *La fin des alliances franco-indiennes: enquête sur un sauf-conduit de 1760 devenu un traité en 1990*. Montreal: Boréal / Septentrion, 1995

Weaver, John C. *The Great Land Rush and the Making of the Modern World, 1650–1900*. Montreal and Kingston: McGill-Queen's University Press, 2003

Weaver, Sally M. *Making Canadian Indian Policy: The Hidden Agenda, 1968–1970*. Toronto: University of Toronto Press, 1981

Wicken, William C. *Mi'kmaq Treaties on Trial: History, Land, and Donald Marshall Junior.* Toronto: University of Toronto Press, 2002

Williams, Robert A. *Linking Arms Together: American Indian Treaty Visions of Law and Peace, 1600–1800*. New York: Routledge, 1999

Young, Brian J. *George-Etienne Cartier: Montreal Bourgeois*. Montreal: McGill-Queen's University Press, 1981

Articles and Book Chapters

Beaulieu, Alain. 'Les Hurons et la Conquête: un nouvel éclairage sur le "traité Murray."' *Recherches amérindiennes au Québec*, 30, no. 3 (2000)

Brandão, José, and William A. Starna. 'The Treaties of 1701: A Triumph of Iroquois Diplomacy.' *Ethnohistory*, 43, no. 2 (Spring 1996)

Brown, Jennifer S.H. '"Man in His Natural State": The Indian Worlds of George Nelson.' In *Rendezvous: Selected papers of the Fourth North American Fur Trade Conference, 1981*. Ed. Thomas C. Buckley. St Paul, MN: North American Fur Trade Conference, 1984

Cairns, Alan C. 'Afterword: International Dimensions of the Citizen Issue for Indigenous Peoples/Nations.' *Citizenship Studies*, 7, no. 4 (2003)

– 'Citizenship and Indian Peoples: The Ambiguous Legacy of Internal Colonialism.' In *Handbook of Citizenship Studies*. Ed. Engin F. Isin and Bryan S. Turner. Thousand Oaks, CA: Sage Publications, 2002

Cook, Peter. 'Vivre comme frères: le rôle du registre fraternal dans les premières alliances franco-amérindiennes au Canada (vers 1580–1650).' *Recherches amérindiennes au Québec*, 31, no. 2 (2001)

Dempsey, Hugh A. 'Western Plains Trade Ceremonies.' *Western Canadian Journal of Anthropology*, 3, no. 1 (1972)

Diamond, Billy. 'Aboriginal Rights: The James Bay Experience,' In *The Quest for Justice: Aboriginal Peoples and Aboriginal Rights*. Ed. Menno Boldt, J. Anthony Long, and Leroy Little Bear. Toronto: University of Toronto Press, 1985

Fenton, William. 'Return of Eleven Wampum Belts to the Six Nations Iroquois Confederacy on Grand River, Canada.' *Ethnohistory*, 36, no. 4 (Fall 1989)

Flanagan, Thomas. 'Adhesion to Canadian Indian Treaties and the Lubicon Lake Dispute.' *Canadian Journal of Law and Society*, 7, no. 2 (Fall 1992)

Foster, Hamar. '"Honouring the Queen's Flag": A Legal and Historical
   Perspective on the Nisga'a Treaty.' *BC Studies*, no. 120 (Winter 1998–9)
Goyette, Linda. 'The X Files.' *Canadian Geographic*, March/April 2003
Hatt, Ken. 'The Northwest Scrip Commissions as Federal Policy – Some Initial
   Findings.' *Canadian Journal of Native Studies*, 3, no. 1 (1983)
Long, John S. 'How the Commissioners Explained Treaty Number Nine to the
   Ojibway and Cree in 1905.' *Ontario History*, 98, no. 2 (Spring 2006)
– 'Treaty Making, 1930: Who Got What at Winisk?' *The Beaver*, 75, no. 1
   (Feb./March 1995)
Macleod, R.C., and Heather Rollason [Driscoll]. '"Restrain the Lawless
   Savages": Native Defendants in the Criminal Courts of the North-West Terri-
   tories, 1878–1885.' *Journal of Historical Sociology*, 10, no. 2 (1997)
Menzies, Charles R. 'The Challenge of First Nations History in a Colonial
   World.' *Canadian Issues* [Association of Canadian Studies], Fall 2006
Miller, J.R. 'Great White Father Knows Best: Oka and the Land Claims
   Process.' *Native Studies Review*, 7, no. 1 (1991)
Moss, Wendy. 'The Implementation of the James Bay and Northern Quebec
   Agreement.' In *Aboriginal Peoples and the Law: Indian, Metis and Inuit Rights in
   Canada*. Ed. Bradford W. Morse. Ottawa: Carleton University Press, 1985
Muller, Kathryn V. 'The Two "Mystery" Belts of Grand River.' *American Indian
   Quarterly*, 31, no. 1 (Winter 2007)
Patterson, Stephen F. 'Indian-White Relations in Nova Scotia, 1749–61: A
   Study in Political Interaction.' *Acadiensis*, 23, no. 1 (Autumn 1993)
Peters, Evelyn J. 'Protecting the Land under Modern Land Claims Agree-
   ments: The Effectiveness of the Environmental Regime Negotiated by the
   James Bay Cree and Northern Quebec Agreement.' *Applied Geography*, 12,
   no. 2 (April 1992)
Poelzer, Greg, and Ken Coates. 'Aboriginal Peoples and the Crown in Canada:
   Completing the Canadian Experiment,' In *Continuity and Change in Cana-
   dian Politics: Essays in Honour of David E. Smith*. Ed. Hans Michelmann and
   Cristine De Clercy. Toronto: University of Toronto Press, 2006
Powers, Natasha. 'Beyond Cultural Differences: Interpreting a Treaty between
   the Mi'kmaq and the British at Belcher's Farm, 1761.' *Atlantis*, 29, no. 2
   (Spring 2005)
Ray, Arthur J. 'Treaty 8: A British Columbia Anomaly.' *BC Studies*, no. 123
   (Autumn 1999)
Schmidt, David L., and B.A. Balcom. 'The Règlement of 1739: A Note on
   Micmac Law and Literacy.' *Acadiensis*, 23, no. 1 (Autumn 1993)
Scott, Duncan Campbell. 'Indian Affairs, 1763–1841.' In *Canada and Its*

Provinces. Ed. A. Shortt and A.G. Doughty. Vol. 4. Toronto: Glasgow, Brook and Co., 1914

Tough, Frank. 'Economic Aspects of Aboriginal Title in Northern Manitoba: Treaty 5 Adhesions and Metis Scrip.' *Manitoba History,* no. 15 (1988): 3–16

Usher, Peter, Frank Tough, and R. Galois, 'Reclaiming the Land: Aboriginal Title, Treaty Rights and Land Claims in Canada.' *Applied Geography,* 12, no. 2 (April 1992)

White, Bruce M. '"Give Us a Little Milk": The Social and Cultural Significance of Gift Giving in the Lake Superior Fur Trade.' In *Rendezvous: Selected Papers of the Fourth North American Fur Trade Conference, 1981.* Ed. Thomas C. Buckley. St Paul, MN: North American Fur Trade Conference, 1984

Theses, Dissertations, and Unpublished Reports

'Aski-Puko: The Land Alone. A Report of the Expected Effects of the Proposed Hydroelectric Installation at Wintego Rapids.' 1976

Augustus, Camilla. 'The Scrip Solution: The North West Metis Scrip Policy, 1885–1887.' M.A. thesis, University of Calgary, 2005

Charmbury, Christine. 'The Treaty Six Adhesion at Montreal Lake: Negotiating for a Guaranteed Lifestyle.' Research paper, HIST 859.3, University of Saskatchewan, 2005

Goldmann, Gustave J. 'The Aboriginal Population and the Census: 120 Years of Information, 1871–1991.' Paper presented at International Union of Scientific Studies in Population Conference, Ottawa, 1993

Goldmann, Gustave J., and Andrew Siggner. 'Statistical Concepts of Aboriginal People and Factors Affecting the Counts in the Census and the Aboriginal Peoples Survey.' Paper presented to the 1995 Symposium of the Federation of Canadian Demographers, Ottawa, 1995

Gulig, Anthony. 'In Whose Interest? Government-Indian Relations in Northern Saskatchewan and Wisconsin, 1900–1940.' Ph.D. diss., University of Saskatchewan, 1997

Hall, Anthony J. 'The Red Man's Burden: Land, Law, and the Lord in the Indian Affairs of Upper Canada, 1791–1858.' Ph.D. diss., University of Toronto, 1984

Marshall, Daniel Patrick. 'Claiming the Land: Indians, Goldseekers, and the Rush to British Columbia.' Ph.D. diss., University of British Columbia, 2000

Morrison, James. 'Treaty One of 1871: Background, Context and Understanding of the Parties.' Opinion Report for Public Interest Law Centre, Winnipeg, 2003

Muller, Kathryn V. 'The Two Row Wampum: Historic Fiction, Modern Reality.' M.A. mémoire, Université Laval, 2004

Murdoch, John S. 'Challenging the Credibility of the Crown's Expert Witnesses in Aboriginal Title or Rights Court Cases.' Paper presented to the 36th Algonquian Conference, Madison, WI, 2004

O'Byrne, Nicole. 'Legislative History of Scrip.' n.d.

Reid, John. '*Pax Britannica* or *Pax Indigena*? Planter Nova Scotia (1760–1782) and Competing Strategies of Pacification.' *Canadian Historical Review*, 85, no. 4 (Dec. 2004)

Smillie, Christine. 'The People Left Out of Treaty 8.' M.A. thesis, University of Saskatchewan, 2005

Stevenson, Allyson. 'The Metis Cultural Brokers and the Western Numbered Treaties, 1869–1877.' M.A. thesis, University of Saskatchewan, 2004

Stevenson, Winona L. 'The Church Missionary Society's Red River Mission and the Emergence of a Native Ministry, 1820–1860, with a Case Study of Charles Pratt of Touchwood Hills.' M.A. thesis, University of British Columbia, 1988

Surtees, Robert J. 'Indian Land Cessions in Ontario, 1763–1862: The Evolution of a System.' Ph.D. diss., Carleton University, 1982

Thoms, J. Michael. 'Ojibwa Fishing Grounds: A History of Ontario Fisheries Law, Science, and the Sportsmen's Challenge to Aboriginal Treaty Rights, 1650–1900.' Ph.D. diss., University of British Columbia, 2004

Williams, Paul. 'The Chain.' LL.M. thesis, Osgoode Hall Law School, York University, 1982

Illustration Credits

Index

Bold numbers indicate illustrations.

227–8; total lands under treaty,
230; Treaty 1, 162–5; Treaty 3,
167–70; Treaty 4, 170–3; Treaty 5,
173–5; Treaty 6, 175–81; Treaty 7,
181–3; Treaty 11, 218–21, 336n47;
White Paper, 248–9. *See also*
Canada, Province of; Department
of Indian Affairs (DIA); Indian
Act; Laurier government; Trudeau
government
Canada, Province of: Manitoulin
Island Treaty, 118–21; mining
claims, 110–14, 292; origins of,
125–6; and political deadlock,
126–8; Robinson Huron and
Superior Treaties, 114–18
Canadian Metis Society, 247
Canadian Pacific Railway, 148–9,
156
Canadian party, 130–1, 141, 143
Cardinal, Harold, 249
Cartier, Jacques, 11
Catholic Church, 60, 125, 130, 216,
219, 241, 242–3
ceremonies: in earliest trade agreements, 12, 13; in fur trade, 14–21,
137–9; Huron Feast of the Dead,
36–7; Iroquois, 20, 39, 41–2, 44;
for making kin of strangers, 8–10,
285–6; and Mississauga treaty,
95–7; in northern numbered
treaties, 221, 297; in numbered
treaties, 184, 295; in territorial
treaties, 82, 291; in Treaty 3,
169–70; in Treaty 5, 175; in Treaty
6, 177–9, 200; in Treaty 9, 210,
211, 212, 229. *See also* gift giving;
kinship; pipe smoking; wampum
Champlain, Samuel de, 25–6, 27, 44,
285

Charter of Rights and Freedoms,
267, 275
Chaurette, 22
Chipewyan, 206
Chrétien, Jean, **262**
Christian Indians of Rossville and
Norway House, 173
Christianity, 52, 60, 185
Christie, William, 161
Church Missionary Society, 152, 160,
185
Ciaccia, John, **262**
citizenship, 309
Claasse, Laurence, 42
clans, 38
Clark government (BC), 277
Claus, Daniel, 104
Claus, William, 95–7, 99
Clear Grits, 123, 125
Colbert, Jean-Baptiste, 47
Colden, Cadwallader, 42–3
Coldwater-Narrows, 105–6
Collins, John, 84, 224
commercial compacts: early exam-
ples of, 12, 13, 14; and fur trade
networks, 30–1, 286–7; geographi-
cal imperative of, 27–30; historical
view of, 299; importance of ritual
to, 21; overview, 4; political consequences of, 31, 32. *See also* trade
agreements
comprehensive claims process,
263–8, 280, 298–9
condolence-requickening ritual, 37,
38, 41, 47
Confederation of Canada, 129,
325n4
Conroy, H.A., 218, 219–20, 336n47
Conservative Party, 126–8
Constitution, Canadian: and extin-